From the Dark Tower

From the # Dark Tower

Afro-American Writers

1900 to 1960

by

Arthur P. Davis

Howard University Press
Washington, D.C.
1974

Printed in the United States of America.

Library of Congress Cataloging in Publication Data

Davis, Arthur Paul, 1904–
  From the dark tower.

  Bibliography: p.
  1. American literature—Negro authors—History and criticism. 2. American literature—20th century—History and criticism. I. Title.
PS153.N5D33   810′.9′896073   73-88969
ISBN 0-88258-004-3

Acknowledgments are gratefully extended to the following:

Arno Press—from *A Long Way From Home* by Claude McKay, reprinted by Arno Press, Inc., 1969.

Beacon Press—from *Black Thunder* by Arna Bontemps, published by Beacon Press, 1968; from *Notes of a Native Son* by James Baldwin, published by Beacon Press, 1955.

Albert Boni—from *The New Negro* by Alain Locke, published by Albert & Charles Boni, 1925.

Books for Libraries—from *I Am The American Negro* by Frank Marshall Davis, published from the Books for Libraries reprint edition, 1971.

Broadside Press—for "The Third Sermon on the Warpland" from *Riot* by Gwendolyn Brooks, published by Broadside Press, 1969.

CLA Journal—for "The Harlem Renaissance in Literary History" by Abraham Chapman from the *CLA Journal*, XI, no. 1, September 1967.

The Crisis—for "Tree" by Arna Bontemps from *The Crisis*, XXXIV, April, 1927; for "Ann Petry Talks About First Novel" by James W. Ivy from *The Crisis*, LIII, February, 1946.

Thomas Y. Crowell—from *Harriet Tubman, Conductor on the Underground Railroad* by Ann Petry, published by Thomas Y. Crowell Co., 1955.

The Dial Press—from *The Fire Next Time* by James Baldwin. Copyright © 1962, 1963 by James Baldwin. Reprinted by arrangement with The Dial Press; from *Nobody Knows My Name* by James Baldwin. Copyright © 1954, 1956, 1958, 1959, 1960, 1961 by James Baldwin. Used with permission of The Dial Press; from *No Name in the Street* by James Baldwin.

Copyright © 1972 by James Baldwin. Reprinted by permission of The Dial Press.

Doubleday & Co.—from *If He Hollers Let Him Go* by Chester Himes, published by Doubleday & Co., 1945.

Mrs. Shirley Du Bois—from *Dusk of Dawn* by W. E. B. Du Bois.

Fawcett World Library—from *Souls of Black Folk* by W. E. B. Du Bois.

Harcourt, Brace, Jovanovich, Inc.—from *Many Thousand Gone* by Ronald Fair.

Harper & Row—from *The Bean Eaters* by Gwendolyn Brooks, published by Harper & Row, Publishers, Inc., 1960; from *Annie Allen* by Gwendolyn Brooks, published by Harper & Row, Publishers, Inc., 1949; from *A Street in Bronzeville* by Gwendolyn Brooks, published by Harper & Row, Publishers, Inc., 1945; from *In the Mecca* by Gwendolyn Brooks, published by Harper & Row, Publishers, Inc., 1968; from *Color* by Countee Cullen: "Yet Do I Marvel," "Incident," Epitaphs "For a Lady I Know." Copyright © 1925 by Harper & Row, Publishers, Inc.; renewed, 1953 by Ida M. Cullen (The latter three poems are also included in *On These I Stand* by Countee Cullen 1947.); for "A Wish" from *The Black Christ* by Countee Cullen. Copyright © 1935 by Harper & Row, Publishers, Inc.; renewed, 1963 by Ida M. Cullen; for "Self Criticism," "To Certain Critics," "Song in Spite of Myself," and "Counter Mood" from *The Black Christ and Other Poems* by Countee Cullen, published by Harper & Row, Publishers, Inc., 1927; for "The Litany of the Dark People" and "From the Dark Tower" from *Copper Sun* by Countee Cullen, published by Harper & Row, Publishers, Inc., 1927; for "Harsh World That Lasheth Me," "The Shroud of Color," and "Heritage" from *Color* by Countee Cullen, published by Harper & Row, Publishers, Inc., 1925; from *Caroling Dusk* by Countee Cullen, published by Harper & Row, Publishers, Inc., 1927; for "Scottsboro, Too, Is Worth Its Song" from *The Medea* by Countee Cullen, published by Harper & Row, Publishers, Inc., 1935; for "A Poet's Odyssey" by Melvin B. Tolson from *Anger and Beyond* edited by Herbert Hill, published by Harper & Row, Publishers, Inc., 1966; from *Black Boy* by Richard Wright, published by Harper & Row, Publishers, Inc., 1966; for "How Bigger Was Born" from *Native Son* by Richard Wright, published by Harper & Row, Publishers, Inc., 1969; from *Uncle Tom's Children* by Richard Wright, published by Harper & Row, Publishers, Inc., 1938.

Joel Hurston and John C. Hurston—from *Tell My Horse* by Zora Neale Hurston. Copyright © 1938 by Zora Neale Hurston. Copyright © renewed 1966 by Joel Hurston and John C. Hurston.

Bernard Jaffe—from *Darkwater* by W. E. B. Du Bois, with permission from Bernard Jaffe.

The Journal of Negro Education—for "Negro Characters as Seen by White Authors" by Sterling A. Brown from the *Journal of Negro Education*, vol. II, no. 2, April 1933.

Alfred A. Knopf, Inc.—for "Impasse" from *The Panther and the Lash; Poems of Our Times* by Langston Hughes, published by Alfred A. Knopf, Inc., 1967; from *Not Without Laughter*, published by Alfred A. Knopf, Inc., 1930.

J. B. Lippincott Company—from *Moses, Man of the Mountain* by Zora Neale Hurston, published by J. B. Lippincott Company. Copyright 1939 by Zora Neale Hurston. Copyright © renewed 1967 by John C. Hurston and Joel Hurston.

Liveright—from *Cane* by Jean Toomer. Copyright © 1951 by Jean Toomer. Reprinted by permission of Liveright Publishers, New York; from *There Is Confusion* by Jessie Fauset. Copyright renewed 1952 by Jessie Redmon Fauset. Reprinted by permission of Liveright Publishers, New York.

Harold Ober Associates, Inc.—from *The Weary Blues* and *Montage of a Dream Deferred* by Langston Hughes, reprinted by permission of Harold Ober Associates, Incorporated, copyright © 1926 by Alfred A. Knopf, Inc. Copyright renewed.

Random House—from *Shadow and Act* by Ralph Ellison, published by Random House, Inc., 1964; from *The Sign in Sidney Brustein's Window* by Lorraine Hansberry, published by Random House, Inc., 1965.

Twayne Publishers, Inc.—from *Libretto for the Republic of Liberia* by Melvin B. Tolson, published by Twayne Publishers, Inc., 1953; from *Selected Poems of Claude McKay* copyright 1953 by Bookman Associates, Inc., reprinted with the permission of Twayne Publishers, Inc.

The University of Chicago Press—for "The Critical Imperatives of Alienation; The Theological Perspectives of Nathan Scott's Literary Criticism" from *The Journal of Religion,* XLVIII, No. 1, January 1968, published by The University of Chicago Press.

The Viking Press, Inc.—from *God's Trombones* by James Weldon Johnson. Copyright © 1927 by The Viking Press, Inc.; Copyright © renewed 1955 by Grace Nail Johnson. Reprinted by permission of The Viking Press, Inc.

Yale University Press—for "Sorrow Home," "Delta," "Southern Song," "For My People," "We Mave Been Believers," "The Struggle Staggers Us," "Our Need," "Bad-Man Stagolee," and "Molly Means" from *For My People* by Margaret Walker, published by Yale University Press, 1942.

Thanks are due Carl Cowl for the Estate of Claude McKay for excerpts from *Home to Harlem* by Claude McKay.

Thanks are also due Sterling A. Brown for "Old Man Buzzard," "Foreclosure," "Step-Children of the Mississippi," "Southern Road," "Memphis Blues," "Strong Men," "Odyssey of Big Boy," "Slim in Atlanta," and "Sister Lou" from *Southern Road.*

To Audrey Paulette Davis

Preface

In 1931 Vernon Loggins published *The Negro Author,* a study which covered the development of Afro-American writing from 1760 to 1900. This volume will take up where Loggins stopped and trace the development to 1960. This book, however, will not be like the above in either format or extent of coverage. Because there were so few Negro writers in the years up to 1900, Loggins was able to include in this 300-page volume practically all of the then known authors, both major and minor. This study, on the other hand, covers the 1925 New Negro Renaissance, with its creative upsurge, and the increase in black writing since that period. As a consequence, the present volume has to survey a far greater number of writers than Loggins had to consider. For this reason, *From the Dark Tower* limits its scope to the *major* writers from 1900 to 1960.

This work is divided into two long sections or chapters: *The New Negro Renaissance (1900–1940)* and *In the Mainstream (1940–1960).* Social and literary backgrounds will be given in the introductions to each section. The authors within each chapter are arranged, not wholly, but roughly, in chronological order. The varied productions of each author, whether poetry, fiction, drama, or nonfiction, are treated in order of importance, starting, of course, with the author's major field of interest. Although biographical material is not stressed in this work, an attempt has been made to give those facts concerning a writer's life which enhance one's appreciation of his works. A selective bibliography for each major author is found at the end of the volume. This volume has been designed to serve as a supplementary text or reference book for courses in Negro American literature or black studies. It will be found, I hope, particularly helpful as a central text for classes using a list of selected authors in paperback.

In the preparation of this study I have made some use of most of the critical works now in print which cover the years from 1900 to 1960, and I acknowledge my *general* indebtedness to all of them. I am more specifically indebted, however, to the graduate students at Howard University who during the last seven years took English 248–249, my course in Negro American literature. Many of the ideas and interpretations found here have come from the discussions and the term papers of the members of this seminar. I am grateful to them. I am also deeply grateful to Miss Beverly Jean Lanier, a graduate student at Howard, who is responsible for most of the biographical and bibliographical material found in this volume. As everyone knows who has attempted a work of this type, the finding, checking, and rechecking of biographical and bibliographical data is an endless, thankless, and frustrating assignment. My debt to Beverly Lanier is indeed great.

Arthur P. Davis

Table of Contents

Introduction

The new interest in Negro American literature has brought forth an amazing number of original works, anthologies, reprints, and critical commentaries. Several studies of the Afro-American novel, several volumes on drama, an ever-increasing number of critical studies of individual authors, and several recent studies of the New Negro Renaissance have appeared. With these many publications available, one might ask why another book on the years from 1900 to 1960.

The answer, of course, is simple. None of these works is designed to do what is attempted in this book. This volume is geared primarily to the classroom needs of Negro literature or black studies courses; indeed, it has grown out of the teaching of such courses. Arranged in chronological (not thematic) order, giving *adequate* biographical details, and possessing helpful and relatively ample selected bibliographies of primary and secondary material for each author, this text, I hope, will give to a student the kind of assistance not to be found in any other work at the present time.

Because we are living in the midst of a literary revolution and because names during such periods take on explosive qualities, I have had some difficulty with the problem of racial tags: shall I use *Negro, black,* or *Afro-American?* In the subtitle to this work, I use the phrase *Afro-American* although I am aware of the current prejudice against hyphenated ethnic designations. I use it here as a compromise between *Negro* and *black,* both of which arouse far more opposition from differing camps than *Afro-American.* For general use I prefer the word *Negro* rather than *black,* and I do so for two reasons. First, "Afro-American" writers up to about 1960 called themselves *Negroes* and their productions *Negro literature.* Since we deal here with that literature, *Negro* is more appropriate than *black.* Second, because of its traditional neutral use, *Negro* lends itself better than *black* to the description of the varying color shades within the group. Black as a skin color conflicts with *black* as a group name. In this work, however, I shall use *black* as most Negro writers used it prior to about 1960, and that is as a synonym to give diversity to a sentence or paragraph containing a monotonous repetition of the word *Negro*.

As this text is limited to major Negro authors, it is perhaps necessary to define the term *major*. On what grounds have certain writers been chosen and others omitted? For example, why has an extremely popular and prolific Negro best seller like Frank Yerby been left out and a one-book author like Jean Toomer been included? The answer amounts to a definition of the word *major,* as used in this work. Yerby's novels, except for the most recent, do not use Negro themes or principal characters; they give little or no interpretation of black life in America; and they add very little to the development of that dual-rooted segment of national writing which we call Negro. (Willard Motley, the author of *Knock on Any Door,* 1947; *We Fished All Night,* 1951; *Let No Man Write My Epitaph,* 1958; and *Let Noon Be Fair,* 1966, has been left out for the same reason.) Toomer's *Cane,* on the other hand, aside from dealing wholly with Negro material, inaugurated a new approach in black writing and influenced in several respects the New Negro Movement. In addition, *Cane* is artistically a brilliant work measured by any standards. On the basis of this comparison, we define a major Negro writer as one whose work deals largely with black experience, measures up to appropriate aesthetic standards, and influences to some extent his contemporaries and/or those who come after him.

In the background introductions I discuss a considerable number of minor writers, using them not only for comparison with major writers but also to illustrate certain trends in the period with which I am concerned. The line between minor and major in Negro writing is often tenuous, and I shall probably make mistakes in classifying a few of them, but that is to be expected. Time will eventually rectify such errors.

One final thought: practically all Negro writers prior to about 1960 took for granted that Negro literature, although it dealt with a unique experience in American life and although it was largely excluded from white anthologies and critical commentaries, was *American* literature and as such would become one with the main body of our national writing. Since 1960, however, many black authors have come to believe that black literature *cannot* and should not become a part of mainstream American writing. These authors strongly contend that black writing should break completely with the Western tradition and produce a literature by blacks for blacks, with its own mythology and aesthetic. Whether the thrust of "Afro-American" writing will lead toward integration or black nationalism, again, only time can give the answer.

From the Dark Tower

part ONE

The New Negro Renaissance (1900-1940)

Introduction

During the mid-twenties there occurred an unprecedented creative up-surge among Negro writers and artists which is commonly called the New Negro Renaissance. Since this burgeoning was largely centered in Harlem, it is sometimes called the Harlem Renaissance. Like all similar movements, the Renaissance had its roots in the past, in this case primarily in the social and literary conditions that obtained in the first twenty-five years of the present century.

In this introduction we shall discuss the social and historical forces that helped to bring the New Negro Renaissance into being; the literary influences at work during the 1900–1925 period, with a comment on certain minor authors; the social and literary background for the 1925–1940 period, with comments on minor writers and on the Little Theatre movements, the Renaissance had its roots in the past, in this case pri-ences of the Renaissance itself.

The years between 1900 and 1925 were harsh years for the American Negro. They saw the culmination of hostile forces that had been set in motion in 1876–1877 when, through the Hayes-Tilden Compromise, Federal troops were withdrawn from the South, and the Negro, just eleven years out of slavery, was returned, in effect, to the control of his former masters. By 1902, as is well known, segregation had become the law in all of the Southern states (and the custom for most of the North). The vast majority of blacks were kept from the polls in the South either by legalistic tricks like the grandfather clause or by outright violence or the threat of violence. Adding insult to injury, the Negro was caricatured in the American press during these years, even in the best periodicals. He was attacked and demeaned almost daily by Southern Congressmen

1

and Senators, many of them expert in the art of caricature and vilification. There arose in the South a school of apologists for the "good old days," headed by such writers as Thomas Nelson Page, Joel Chandler Harris, and Thomas Dixon. Very popular, these apologists, using the Northern press, convinced most of the nation that the Negro was either a child or a brute, and whatever else he was, he was certainly the white man's natural inferior.

In 1901 Theodore Roosevelt became President, and the Negroes experienced a momentary feeling of hope. As a symbol of his concern with their problems, Roosevelt invited Booker T. Washington to dine with him at the White House, arousing thereby the fury of millions of Southern whites. He also made at least two important black appointments in the customs service. During his second term, however, in an effort to gain Republican votes in the South, Roosevelt turned on the Negro. This effort failed, and it left the black man bitter and politically friendless.

William Howard Taft was no improvement on Roosevelt as far as Negroes were concerned, and many in desperation broke with tradition and voted for Woodrow Wilson, a Southern-born Democrat. This, too, they were soon to regret. Wilson not only appointed a number of Southerners to his Cabinet (too many in the eyes of black citizens), he also brought segregated facilities to the Federal buildings in the capital, an act that embittered Negroes. For these and other anti-Negro policies, black citizens came to dislike Woodrow Wilson more than they had disliked any other President.

In the early decades of the twentieth century a wave of violence aimed at Negroes swept the nation. Lynchings became almost daily occurrences, and riots took place not only in Southern cities like Atlanta and Houston but also in Omaha, Chicago, and the nation's capital. During 1915, two years after the fiftieth anniversary of the signing of the Emancipation Proclamation, 69 Negroes were lynched, the Ku Klux Klan was revived, and the film *The Birth of a Nation,* based on Thomas Dixon's viciously racist novel, *The Clansman,* came to American theatres, spreading venom from coast to coast. Even after World War I—a war supposedly fought to protect democracy throughout the world—conditions seemed to worsen. The "Red Summer of 1919" (a name given it by James Weldon Johnson) was particularly bad. Between June and December 31, 1919, there were 25 major race riots, the one in Chicago being the worst. It left 38 persons dead, 537 injured, and over 1,000 families, most of them black, homeless. Eighty-three Negroes were lynched that year, 10 of them in the uniform of their country.

During the bleak years from 1900 to 1925 most Negroes had been patient and nonmilitant, believing in the intrinsic, if delayed, justice of

American democracy and trusting to the biblically stated promise of Christianity to succor the heavy laden. The chief spokesman for this silent majority was Booker T. Washington, the eminent founder and principal of Tuskegee Institute. A very able man, Washington counseled racial good will, patience, and industrial education; he urged Negroes to soft-pedal political demands and demands for social equality; he recommended rapport with the Southern whites. Because of his accommodating attitude, Washington was liked by both North and South. Yankee industrialists-philanthropists channeled their contributions to Negro education through Mr. Washington, using their money to help the black man in ways quite different from those their abolitionist fathers had used. They were glad to work through a no-nonsense Negro like Booker T. Washington. The government, likewise, looked to Mr. Washington for approval of their few black appointees, knowing that they would get "safe" men. The South liked his anti social-equality doctrine and found his good-will policies agreeable. In short, Booker T. Washington became the most powerful Negro of his age. Scholars are still divided on whether he harmed the black man's cause more than he advanced it.

Before Mr. Washington's death in 1915, there had appeared on the scene a new and different kind of black leader in W. E. B. Du Bois. Trained at Harvard and Berlin, Germany, Du Bois was historian, pioneer sociologist, and creative artist, a gadfly that aroused and spurred Negroes as much as he disturbed the whites of the South. In 1903 he published *The Souls of Black Folk,* a group of brilliant essays concerning primarily America's treatment of its darker citizens. Among other things, the work pointed out the shortcomings of Booker T. Washington's approach to race relations. It also protested the monopoly on Negro affairs held by Washington. A scholarly but militant (for that day) work, *The Souls of Black Folk* set the scene for a new kind of informed and uncompromising leadership that was to come even before Booker T. Washington's death in 1915.

By 1910 Du Bois, along with a small band of whites and Negroes who had gathered around him, established the National Association for the Advancement of Colored People (NAACP) and its powerful official organ, *The Crisis.* Although young black militants consider the present-day NAACP a conservative organization, up until 1960 it was the most effective weapon against racial injustice that the nation had. They also forget that the NAACP and *The Crisis* helped make possible the unprecedented freedom of expression and action that young blacks enjoy today. The NAACP, of course, did not accomplish miracles overnight, but it did bring a new hope to the American Negro, particularly the middle-class Negro, and it definitely helped prepare the ground for that general social and literary upsurge we call the New Negro Movement.

The NAACP's effort, whatever its intentions, turned out to be largely a middle-class effort. For the Negro lowest down, the Garvey movement was the seeming answer to his frustrations. The first proletarian effort among Negroes was led by Marcus Garvey, a British West Indian from Jamaica. Garvey started his work in his homeland and by 1917 had opened a branch of his organization, the Universal Negro Improvement Association (UNIA), in New York City. Between 1917 and 1927 (when Garvey was deported for using the mails to defraud,) he had built up a following of possibly 500,000 Negroes. Emphasizing blackness, offering the promise of an imminent return to the African motherland, Garvey's Back-to-Africa Movement gave new hope to the blacks who needed it most. It also fostered pride in race and self-respect, which were qualities sorely needed in a people who had been beaten down and ridiculed for almost three hundred years. Although Garvey's plan was ill-advised and visionary, it showed, above all else, the disillusionment of the masses of Negroes with American democracy and their loss of faith in the system. The pride in blackness, the new interest in Africa and its nation-alist-separatist tendencies, not only influenced the New Negro writers but also presaged the present-day concern with such matters.

There were, of course, other factors besides the NAACP and the Garvey movement that brought about changes during the 1900–1925 period. The principal one was the first World War. With European immigration cut off by the conflict, the industrial North turned to the South for its labor force. Beginning around 1915, thousands of Southern Negroes migrated to the industrial centers of the North, finding there no paradise but still a much better "climate" than they had experienced in their home states. When America joined the war, over 367,000 Negro soldiers, including some 1,400 black officers, were involved. Many Negroes discovered new and enlarging experiences being recent migrants to the North as well as by becoming soldiers—particularly those of the latter who went abroad. They learned in France that blacks and whites could mingle as social equals; they found that in the North Negroes could vote without risking their lives and could enjoy an un-segregated public-school and transportation system. They also learned that working-class people, if they belonged to unions, had not only rights but potential power. These lessons and others of a like nature helped build the social climate from which the New Negro Renaissance was to spring.

Of course, one must not forget that Harlem itself played an important part in preparing the climate of the Renaissance. Although most of the best-known writers of the period were born elsewhere, they were *drawn* to Harlem, the New Negro mecca. There they found an exciting black city, a city of their own in a limited sense; there they found other

Negroes in numbers—from the West Indies, from Africa, from South America. One of the sayings of the period was, "The Jews own New York, the Irish control it, and the Negroes enjoy it." There was some truth in the saying because the Harlemites of the twenties admired their city, romanticized it, and, above all else, had a good time in it. Though highly oversimplified, these are the social conditions from which the Renaissance sprang.

The literary forces, along with the social climate, that produced this artistic upsurge are of two kinds: those influences from outside the Negro group—trends that motivated all American writers—and those from within the group, generated largely by a small band of black writers and critics.

Among the outside forces the most important was probably the New Poetry Movement, spearheaded by Harriet Monroe. The date for this poetic renaissance is usually given as 1912, the year that *Poetry: A Magazine of Verse* was founded. After 1912 several significant poets, novelists, and dramatists brought out works which were to change the course of American letters. Such writers as Edgar Lee Masters, Carl Sandburg, Ezra Pound, and T. S. Eliot came into prominence during this period.

Also among the new writers were a considerable number who used Negro themes: Vachel Lindsay, Eugene O'Neill, Sherwood Anderson, DuBose Heyward, Julia Peterkin, Paul Green, Ridgely Torrence, Carl Van Vechten, and others. These writers, although they were inclined to emphasize the sensational in their treatment of the Negro character, nevertheless showed a greater understanding of the Negro, especially the folk Negro, than had most American authors before them. The black writer in a few cases was influenced by these authors and by the New Poetry Movement. From this movement he acquired, along with his white brother, the anti-Victorianism, the antididacticism, the antisentimentalism that characterized the New Poetry. He also learned to experiment with free verse and other innovations. In a few cases a black writer would show the direct influence of a white author. For example, it is alleged that Van Vechten's *Nigger Heaven* motivated the writing of Claude McKay's *Home to Harlem;* but in most instances both groups were touched by the same influences, by the same germinating forces, and reacted in the same way.

The New Negro Renaissance, however, was specifically influenced by the writers whom we have called the Planters: Du Bois, James Weldon Johnson, Claude McKay, Jean Toomer, and Alain LeRoy Locke. These motivators, of course, will be discussed at length later, and we need not touch them here. It is necessary, however, to say a word about some of the *minor* Planters of the Renaissance seed, those authors who influenced the movement in limited and oblique ways. Not necessarily second-rate men, these writers are simply *minor* in their influence on the New Negro Renaissance.

Before considering, however, these minor authors, we must glance at two very successful and distinguished authors who were ending their writing careers at the turn of the century: Paul Laurence Dunbar and Charles W. Chesnutt. Though both belong largely to the nineteenth century and have been treated in other critical works, we must point out briefly several things about them. First, both appeared in America's best periodicals of the age, and both had their works produced by the finest publishing houses. Their success in this respect served as a spur for all Negro writers. In addition, both Dunbar and Chesnutt made use of folk material, thereby establishing for Renaissance writers a precedent. Chesnutt, moreover, wrote a considerable number of passing-for-white stories and other stories of the color line, a vein that would be exploited by several of the most important New Negro authors. Chesnutt also wrote strong protest novels, setting again the stage for the proliferation of such novels in the new age. The two men (Dunbar largely an accommodationist and Chesnutt largely a militant) symbolized by their positions the two routes the Renaissance writer had open to him. From the peak which they represented at the end of the century, we descend into a valley of pedestrian writing before ascending a second elevation in 1925.

The first quarter of the twentieth century saw the rise of a considerable number of minor writers[1] who by their publications kept alive the tradition of Negro writing, even though, for the most part, on a lowly level. They formed a bridge between Dunbar and Chesnutt and the New Negro authors.

The minor poets of the era tended to be divided into two main groups: those who followed Dunbar and wrote dialect poetry and those who, rebelling against the dialect school, wrote verse in standard English. (Several, of couse, lived in both camps.) In the dialect group we find *inter alia* the following poets: Joseph Seamon Cotter, the author of *A Rhyming* (1895) and *Collected Poems* (1938), whose verses in the dialect vein were far more critical of racial conditions than those of Dunbar; James Edwin Campbell, author of *Echoes from the Cabin and Elsewhere* (1905), who was one of the first Negroes to write in dialect and whose verses in that tradition tend to be more realistic than those of Dunbar; Daniel Webster Davis, author of *'Weh Down Souf* (1897),

1. For a fuller discussion of these writers see Sterling A. Brown's *Negro Poetry and Drama,* Washington, D.C.: Associates in Negro Folk Education, 1937; and *The Negro in American Fiction,* Washington, D.C.: Associates in Negro Folk Education, 1937.

next to Dunbar perhaps the most popular writer of the dialect school; J. Mord Allen, author of *Rhymes, Tales and Rhymed Tales* (1906); and John Wesley Holloway, author of *From the Desert* (1919). The dialect poems of these authors, for the most part, have only the two stops: pathos and humor. Rarely do they protest racial conditions, and even then not strongly.

Among the minor poets who wrote mainly in standard English are the following: James D. Corrothers, who published in *The Century* and whose poem entitled "At the Closed Gate of Justice" characterized the thinking of those who held the accommodationist viewpoint as McKay's "If We Must Die," was later to characterize the militant; William H. A. Moore, the author of *Dusk Songs;* George Marion McClellan, author of *The Path of Dreams;* George Reginald Margetson, author of *Songs of Life* and *The Fledgling Bard and the Poetry Society,* the latter work a satire done in the language of the street; Joseph S. Cotter, author of *The Band of Gideon,* a promising young writer whose career was cut short by tuberculosis; and Fenton Johnson, the most prolific of these minor poets and the one whose poetry pointed directly toward the Renaissance. The author of *A Little Dreaming* (1913), *Visions of the Dusk* (1915), and *Songs of the Soil* (1916), Fenton Johnson, who in all of the above-named works was a conventional writer of bland late-Victorian and weak dialect-school verse, finally discovered the New Poetry of Masters and Sandburg, and began to write pieces like "Tired" and "The Scarlet Woman"—pieces whose poetical form and whose tone of social criticism were new to Negro poetry.

Among the writers of standard English verse during this period were several well-known female poets: Alice Dunbar-Nelson, the wife of Paul Laurence Dunbar, who was both poet and short-story writer; Angelina Grimké, poet and the author of *Rachel,* a problem drama produced in 1916 and published in 1920; Georgia Douglas Johnson, author of *The Heart of a Woman* (1918), *Bronze* (1922), and *An Autumn Love Cycle* (1928); and the most talented of this group, Anne Spencer, who is still living and whose sophisticated and insightful verses have appeared in nearly all Negro anthologies to date, but, unfortunately, have never been collected.

Of the minor novelists and Planters during the 1900–1925 period, Sutton Elbert Griggs is perhaps the most important. Relatively unknown for a long while, Griggs in recent years has begun to receive the attention that he deserves. Griggs was the author of more than 33 works, five of them novels: *Imperium in Imperio* (1899), *Overshadowed* (1901), *Unfettered* (1902), *The Hindered Hand* (1905), and *Pointing the Way* (1908). A Baptist minister and an official in his church organization, Griggs printed many of his works in his own publishing concern and sold them personally as he traveled from church to church on organizational business.

The novels of Sutton Griggs are faulty in the extreme; they are as much racial propaganda pamphleteering as they are fiction, but one or two are intriguing. *Imperium in Imperio* is perhaps the first political novel to be written by a Negro. It is also an early militant and black nationalist novel. One of its characters advocates an uprising among American blacks and the seizure of two states, Texas and Louisiana. Negroes would make the first their home and use the second for bargaining with foreign powers. Griggs's *The Hindered Hand* is also a strong protest against Thomas Dixon's vicious attacks on the Negro. On occasion he also opposed the accommodationist philosophy of Booker T. Washington, as in *Overshadowed*. Griggs, however, as critic Robert Bone points out, vacillated between the poles of militancy and accommodationism. He was not alone in his ambivalence. Griggs's novels serve as an excellent index to the thinking of Negroes in the years just prior to the New Negro Renaissance.

Three significant minor Planters should be considered here. The first of them, Charles Spurgeon Johnson, was an eminent sociologist, and a prolific writer in that field. He was also the editor of *Opportunity,* the official organ of the Urban League, which, even before Du Bois with *The Crisis,* inaugurated yearly contests for Negro writers of poetry, short fiction, essays, and one-act plays. Several of the most successful New Negro writers started as *Opportunity* contest writers. Johnson also edited in 1927 *Ebony and Topaz,* an anthology similar to Locke's *New Negro.* Though not as impressive as the latter work, it, too, showed America the creative potential of the Negro. Charles Johnson was an important motivator of young New Negro authors. One of them, Zora Neale Hurston, warmly insists in her autobiography that Charles S. Johnson was really the Father of the New Negro Renaissance.

The next two minor Planters may be introduced jointly. Both were prolific nationally known writers; both influenced the New Negro Movement to some extent; but each of these authors in his own way disapproved of those elements in the Renaissance that were its most original contributions.

Scholar, critic, great teacher, prolific writer of textbooks, biographies, and anthologies, Benjamin Griffith Brawley was an early minor Planter. Two of his works, *A Short History of the American Negro* (1913) and *The Negro in Literature and Art* (1918), were pioneering efforts to encourage the young writer and to show America the Negro's historical and cultural contributions. Because of his many publications, because of his tendency to make all knowledge his province, and because of his insistence on standards, Brawley served as an inspiration to young

Negro writers. But he was too much of a classicist and a puritan to appreciate certain important aspects of the movement: its emphasis on folk materials, such as the work songs and the blues, its emphasis on the seamier side of the life as found in the novels of McKay, and its emphasis on unconventional forms and rhythms as found in the poetry of Hughes and others. To Brawley, literature tended to mean the works of Tennyson, Browning, Shakespeare, and Arnold. Although he made significant contributions to Negro literature in several respectable works during the twenties and thirties, he did not really relate to the movement in the way that Locke, another professor, did. He did not become a part of the new ferment.

In some respects William Stanley Braithwaite suffered from the same limitations as did Brawley. A self-educated man, Braithwaite became a nationally known anthologist and critic. For many years he issued annually the *Anthology of Magazine Verse*. He also published collections of Elizabethan, Georgian, and Restoration verse. Though he contributed an article, "The Negro in American Literature," to *The New Negro* and was a friend of Du Bois, Locke, and other leaders in the movement, and though he praised extravagantly Jessie Fauset's novels, he seemed to stand outside the New Negro Movement. One reason was that his poetry, although excellent of its kind, never used Negro themes. He also advised Claude McKay not to use Negro themes in *his* verses. Braithwaite's literary antecedents were the pre-Raphaelites, and he could not seemingly bring his interest and talents to focus on Harlem and its lively inhabitants. It was an inspiration to young black writers to know that a Negro could be on the editorial staff of the *Boston Transcript* and could become a nationally accepted critic, one whose influence touched such men as Frost, Masters, Pound, and others; it was inspiring to know that he could enter so completely into the mainstream, but there the inspiration ended. The present generation would have called Braithwaite an Oreo Negro, like the cookie, black on the outside but all-white inside, all-white in his attitudes.

The period of First Fruits (1925–1940) started off with the highest of high hopes. Young artists from all over the nation were attracted to the Harlem Mecca by the new so-called Renaissance. Literary groups were formed, and almost every young Negro in the streets of Harlem had a manuscript or plans for a masterpiece. All of them felt that a new day had come and that there was a New Negro to seize it.

Downtown New York came uptown to see the newly discovered black brother and, of course, found him exotic and primitive—really more a figment of *their* expectations than of reality. But as time moved on, the carnival spirit of the early Renaissance years began to give way to sober reality. Writers began to look at Harlem steadily and see it whole.

Eventually, the Depression came and delivered a death blow to many high hopes, hitting the Negro hardest, historically the last to be hired and the first to be fired. Also added to that was a sense of disillusionment which the aftermath to World War I had brought. Southern Negroes who had moved North during the Great Migration found that Northern ghettos could be just as tough as Southern sharecropping communities. The Negro lowest down, who had been encouraged by the visionary Back-to-Africa Movement of Garvey, saw his hope shattered when Garvey was jailed in 1927 and eventually deported.

The Scottsboro Trial of 1933 deepened the disillusionment of the Negro, showing that justice for a black man was not possible in Southern courts and was not found too often in Northern ones. During these years, not a large, but an appreciable, number of black intellectuals turned to Communism, and the effect of this shift is found in the works of writers like Frank Marshall Davis, Langston Hughes, and, of course, Richard Wright. In 1935 came the event that climaxed the end of the New Negro honeymoon: Harlem, "Nigger Heaven," that joyous city of jazz and night life, experienced a devastating riot. As a result, its inhabitants came to realize that it, too, was just another festering black ghetto, which all of the frustrations which poverty and or the lack of employment opportunity foster.

The minor writers of the First Fruits Period were fascinating and legion. Any anthology of the period will show how many there were and how many wrote at least one "catchy" or even good poem, or one-act play, or short story; but few endured. Some improved on the first fine frenzy which the Renaissance nourished. Of the minor poets who endured and who are still producing, three should be mentioned. May Miller, the daughter of the legendary Dean Kelly Miller, has appeared over the years in many anthologies and many periodicals, including *The Antioch Review, The Crisis, Common Ground,* the *Nation,* and several others. May Miller has also published several volumes of skillful and sophisticated verse—verse that has not clung to the New Negro past but which reflects the age in which it was written. Her published volumes are *Into the Clearing* (1959), *Poems* (1962), and in collaboration with two other poets, *Lyrics of Three Women* (1964).

One of the better known poems of the early Renaissance was Frank Horne's ironic "Nigger." Though his pieces have appeared in many periodicals and anthologies over the years, he did not collect them until 1963, when they came out under the title, *Haverstraw.*

Waring Cuney, like Frank Horne, did not collect his poems until late. In 1960 he published *Puzzles,* and showed himself to be the poet of the small but revealing moment in the lives of little people. He is also highly adept in the use of the blues, and most of his poems are in this form. In all likelihood Cuney has used the blues form for poetry more consistently and variedly than any other poet. His short piece "No Images," like Horne's "Nigger," was a minor classic of the New Negro Movement.

A significant minor novelist, Walter White, concerns us here. The distinguished executive secretary of the NAACP (he followed James Weldon Johnson in this position), White probably knew more about lynching than any other person at the time. A "voluntary Negro," he was light enough to pass and could therefore investigate lynchings and the KKK from "inside." His book *Rope and Faggot: A Biography of Lynching* (1929) was the first important study of this heinous American custom. Walter White was also the author of two novels. The first, *The Fire in the Flint* (1924), concerns the tragic experiences of a young Negro physician in a small Southern town. The climax of the novel is a lynching, and the work is probably a better antilynching polemic than it is a novel. The second work, *Flight* (1926), deals with a subject that White also knew first-hand and that Negro novelists had used from the beginning: the theme of passing. The novels of White belong to what has been called the lynching-passing school of Negro fiction. They are novels written from a middle-class, best-foot-forward position, using either a lynching or a passing experience or both to heighten the drama of the lives delineated in the story line.

An aspect of the New Negro literary burgeoning that is often overlooked is drama. Because the Negro was not a part of the American theatrical tradition, except for minstrel and coon shows, he had very little opportunity to serve that apprenticeship in the theatre which most playwrights enjoyed. Moreover, most Negroes lived in the South, where there were very few theatres, even for the whites. It was really not until about 1960 that the Negro began to make his mark on Broadway. It took him a long time to get there.

The first play published by a Negro was *The Escape, or a Leap for Freedom,* by William Wells Brown. Published in 1858, it was not a very good play and was used primarily as an abolitionist vehicle, never being intended for the real stage. The second play by a Negro was the senior Joseph S. Cotter's *Caleb the Degenerate* (1903), again another very bad closet drama on the theme of industrial versus liberal education. The third published drama and first to have professional production was Angelina Grimké's *Rachel,* written in 1916 and published in 1920.

In 1917 a white playwright, Ridgley Torrence, published *Three Plays for the Negro Theatre.* These one-act plays revitalized the field of

Negro drama, showing to the would-be playwrights of the period the dramatic potential in folk material. Torrance's work suggested that Negro peasant life could be exploited in the same way that John Synge and Lady Gregory used Irish peasant life.

The Negro Little Theatre Movement came into being during the 1925–1940 period. Negro colleges fostered the movement, and the contests in *The Crisis* and *Opportunity* spurred it further. Willis Richardson, May Miller, John F. Matheus, Georgia Douglas Johnson, Eulalie Spence, and others were the movement's mainstays.

One of the enduring playwrights from this era is Randolph Edmonds. His *Six Plays For a Negro Theatre* (1934) was the first book of folk plays published by a Negro. He has also published *Shades and Shadows* (1930), *Land of Cotton and Other Plays* (1942), and *Earth and Stars* (1961).

It is now time to talk about the New Negro Renaissance itself, to ask a few questions about it. What, for example, are its dates? What were its objectives and were they realized? What influence did it have on subsequent black artists? These questions, of course, are continually raised and have never been answered satisfactorily. The chances are that they will not be answered satisfactorily here. The attempt, however, must be made in the hope that at least some small new bit of understanding may come from the effort.

Concerning the terminal dates, here is a matter on which there is very little agreement among scholars. For many, the Renaissance extends from 1925, the year of the publication of Alain Locke's *The New Negro,* to 1935, the year of the Harlem Riot; for others, it begins in 1920 (to give it a running start before 1925) and ends in 1929, the year of the Wall Street Crash; for still others, it runs from 1925 to 1960, when the Black Renaissance begins. The advocates of this extended span insist that the attitudes and themes that were popular in 1925 did not change radically until 1960.

In this work the Renaissance is broken down into two phases: the first from 1900 to 1925 (the year of Locke's *New Negro*) and the second from 1925 to 1940 (the year of Wright's *Native Son*). The first phase includes the Planters, those authors whose seminal ideas sparked the Renaissance; the second, the startling and promising First Fruits of the movement. The year 1900 was taken as a starting point because it goes back far enough to include Du Bois's earliest literary efforts. The year of Richard Wright's masterpiece, 1940, was chosen because *Native Son,* by establishing a new school of naturalistic writing, changed the course of Negro literature.

The New Negro Renaissance represented a new alertness, a new confidence, and a new viewpoint for the black writers of those years. It showed the Negro writer that his dual experience as Negro and as American had much to give to American letters; it gave the Negro protest writer a new irony, a new kind of satiric approach in the fight for equality; it gave him a new appreciation for all kinds of folk material, not just that used by the dialect school; it stirred up at least a conventional interest in Africa as the homeland, thereby enhancing to some extent pride in race; it broadened the artistic vision of the Negro writer to include the seamier side of black life; it gave him a quality that Negro writers (except for those in the dialect school) had lacked, a sense of fun and gaiety and whimsy; and above all else, it gave the New Negro writer an attitude that all new movements need: a spirit of cockiness, a spirit best expressed by Langston Hughes in the *Nation* (June 23, 1926):

> We young Negro artists who create now intend to express our individual dark-skinned selves without fear or shame. If white people are pleased we are glad. If they are not, it doesn't matter. We know we are beautiful. And ugly too. The tom-tom cries and the tom-tom laughs. If colored people are pleased we are glad. If they are not, their displeasure doesn't matter either. We build our temples for tomorrow, strong as we know how, and we stand on top of the mountains, free within ourselves.

The New Negro Renaissance was not a closely knit, monolithic movement. There was no one type of black writer. The "lynching-passing-race-praising" novels of Jessie Fauset, Nella Larsen, and Walter White were as unlike the primitive-oriented fiction of McKay, as if they came from two different eras. We tend now to play up the primitive and folk elements of the movement, but the literary and social middle-class values were far more popular than the former elements. The classic sonnets and rhyme royal of Cullen's verse were alien to the folk forms and rhythms of Hughes's poetry, though both, were popular. If the 1925 writers had any one thing in common, it was an awareness that they lived in a new day for Negro writers.

Sterling A. Brown, one of our ablest critics, expressed a few doubts about the Renaissance that should be considered. For one thing, he hesitates to use the term *Negro Renaissance* because he feels the five or eight years generally allotted are too short for the life span of any "renaissance." Brown further states: "The New Negro is not to me a group of writers centered in Harlem during the second half of the twenties." He adds that most of the writers were not born in Harlem and much of the best writing "was not about Harlem, which was the show window, the cashier's till, but no more Negro America than New York is America. The New Negro Movement had temporal roots in the past and spatial roots elsewhere in America, and the term has validity . . . only when considered to be a continuing tradition."

What influence did the Renaissance have on subsequent Afro-American literature? Sterling Brown spoke of the movement in terms of a "continuing tradition." Abraham Chapman, another able critic of the Renaissance, comments on the same theme:

> Looking back at the twenties nearly half a century later, it is clear that the Negro literary movement that welled up then was no flash in the pan, no literary dud. From the writers of the 20's and 30's to Wright, Ellison, Baldwin, and the younger Negro writers who are now coming up, we can appreciate the literary validity and continuing historical significance of the Renaissance.[2]

Chapman also points out another phase of this continuing tradition: "its international context and influence." Leopold Sédar Senghor of Senegal and Aimé Cesaire of Martinique, the Fathers of Negritude, read the New Negro poets when they were students at the Sorbonne in Paris. Peter Abrahams, the well-known South African writer, discovered the Harlem poets in Johannesburg during the twenties. And, according to Chapman, this influence, repeatedly acknowledged by these writers, extended to "black poets from the Portuese colonies in Africa."

A few critics, Ellison[3] among them, believe that the New Negro Renaissance in spite of its hopes, aspirations, claims, and high-sounding rhetoric was a failure. It is true that there were too many one-good-volume authors in the period, that only a very small number of writers continued to produce and mature; that there was more lip service than actual devotion given to the African themes and to blackness; and that too many writers failed to understand the real nature of their dual experience in America and, therefore, put too much emphasis on best-foot-foremost writing. And there were probably other shortcomings. No movement, however, that embraced Du Bois, Johnson, Toomer, McKay, Cullen, and Hughes can be called a complete failure.

2. "The Harlem Renaissance in Literary History." *CLA Journal,* XI (September, 1967), p. 49.
3. See an interview published in *Harper's* (March, 1967).

The Planters (1900-1925)

W. E. B. Du Bois

Among the scholars and creative artists who prepared the ground and planted the seeds of the New Negro Renaissance William Edward Burghardt Du Bois is by far the most influential, and his shadow falls across Negro life and literature for practically the whole period which this work covers. Possessing a keen mind and the best education that America and Europe could render at that time, Du Bois both represented and made articulate the Negro middle class at a crucial moment in its development. With his vision, his sense of commitment to his people, and a self-assurance that he wore protectively, and sometimes arrogantly, Du Bois motivated and molded several generations of middle-class Negroes. He was not always right, but he grew and changed with the years. Beginning as the exponent of what now seems to us a narrow, undemocratic theory of racial adjustment, the doctrine of the "Talented Tenth," he later became a pioneer Pan-Africanist, and finally ended his days as a Communist and as a citizen of Ghana.

W. E. B. Du Bois was born in Great Barrington, Massachusetts, on February 23, 1868. The maternal branch of his family can be traced back to an African who settled in Massachusetts before the Revolutionary War. His father was of French Huguenot and Haitian (African) descent.

Du Bois graduated from Great Barrington's high school as valedictorian of his class in 1884. After receiving a B.A. degree from Fisk University in 1888, Du Bois entered Harvard University as a junior and earned a B.A. degree cum laude in 1890 and his M.A. in 1892. With the aid of a Slater Fund Fellowship he studied history and economics at the University of Berlin from 1892 to 1894. In 1896 he earned his Ph.D. from Harvard University, publishing his dissertation, *The Suppression of the African Slave Trade to the United States of America, 1638–1870,* as the first book of the Harvard Historical Series.

Having difficulty finding a job on his return from Europe, Du Bois finally accepted a position as professor of Greek and Latin at the A. M. E. Church operated Wilberforce University in Ohio. Two years later, in 1896, he was hired as an assistant instructor in sociology at the University of Pennsylvania, an expedient which allowed him to perform the research necessary for *The Philadelphia Negro* but which denied him contact with the students. In 1897 he became a professor of economics and history at Atlanta University, where he had instituted the Atlanta University Studies of the Negro Problem, whose annual publications reflected Du Bois's insistence on utilizing a scientific investigation of social subjects. Du Bois supervised eighteen of these publications, from *Mortality Among Negroes in Cities* (1896) to *Morals and Manners Among Negro Americans* (1914).

Du Bois received national recognition in the Negro civil rights movement when he organized the Niagara Movement in 1905, an organization which merged with the National Association for the Advancement of Colored People (NAACP), founded in 1909. Both organizations espoused a militant drive for equal rights and complete integration. He served as the director of publicity and research and was a member of the board of directors of the NAACP.

Du Bois left Atlanta University in 1910 mainly because his opposition to Booker T. Washington's accommodationist program resulted in a loss of funds for the university. He founded and edited *The Crisis* (1910–1934), led a campaign against lynching and Jim Crow, which included the Silent Protest Parade (1917) in New York, and investigated and exposed the treatment of Afro-American troops in Europe during World War I and the American intervention in Haiti in 1920. Du Bois resigned his position with the NAACP in 1934 mainly because his stated belief that black people should develop their own institutions, preserve their own culture, and embrace Pan-Africanism conflicted with the policy of the NAACP. In 1934 he returned to Atlanta University as chairman of the department of sociology, founding in 1940 *Phylon* magazine, a quarterly dedicated to the scholarly study of race and culture, and editing it until his retirement in 1944. He returned to work with the NAACP from 1944 to 1948 as director of special research.

As a journalist and editor Du Bois founded and edited not only *The Crisis* and *Phylon,* but also *The Moon* in Tennessee (1906), *The Horizon* in Washington, D.C. (1907–1910), *The Brownies' Book,* a children's magazine (1920–1921). He also served on the editorial board of *The New Review,* a radical New York magazine (1913).

Du Bois, once an adherent of the Talented Tenth policy, subsequently adopted a socialistic viewpoint, joining the Socialist Party in 1910 and

W. E. B. Du Bois

N. Nkitsia VI, Chairman of Faculty Council of Ghana, reads citation conferring degree of Doctor of Letters on W. E. B. DuBois, Feb. 23, 1963. This is his 95th birthday.

Courtesy of Moorland-Spingarn Research Center, Howard University.

resigning in 1912. He retained a belief in socialism and became active in the world peace movement, attending conferences in New York, Paris, and Moscow. In 1950–1951, as chairman of the Peace Information Center, he was arrested, indicted, and finally acquitted of the charge of failing to register as a foreign agent. He did not join the Communist Party until 1961.

In that year President Nkrumah of Ghana invited Du Bois to live in that country, where he served as director of the *Encyclopaedia Africana,* a project he had conceived of in 1909 and initiated in 1945 with the publication of the *Encyclopedia of the Negro,* a Preparatory Volume, by Du Bois and Guy B. Johnson. Du Bois became a citizen of Ghana in 1963, the year he died.

Although he will be treated here only as a literary writer, we must remember that he was a distinguished historian, an educator, and a pioneer American sociologist; we must also remember that he was a prolific producer in all of these fields. As a great editor of *The Crisis,* one of the most influential periodicals that Negroes have yet published, Dr. Du Bois became the literary gadfly for the black middle class and, of course, the chief Planter of the New Negro Renaissance.

Du Bois's life and creative works exemplify that dualism which affects all Afro-Americans, a dualism that he has lucidly explained in *The Souls of Black Folk:*

> It is a peculiar sensation, this double-consciousness, this sense of always looking at one's self through the eyes of others, of measuring one's soul by the tape of a world that looks on in amused contempt and pity. One ever feels his twoness,—an American, a Negro; two souls, two thoughts, two unreconciled strivings; two warring ideals in one dark body. . . .
>
> The history of the American Negro is the history of this strife,—this longing to attain self-conscious manhood, to merge his double self into a better and truer self. In this merging, he wishes neither of the older selves to be lost. He would not Africanize America, for America has too much to teach the world and Africa. He would not bleach his Negro soul in a flood of white Americanism, for he knows that Negro blood has a message for the world. He simply wishes to make it possible for a man to be both a Negro and an American . . .[1]

The Negro's attempt to "merge his double self into a better and truer self" has caused and still causes many of the black writer's hang-ups. Should he go all the way toward the left and complete separatism, as many of the contemporary black artists and critics advise, or should he go all the way right to the mainstream? Du Bois and his generation actually sought a place in between. They knew that the "Negro blood has a message for the world," and they fought against bleaching the

1. *The Souls of Black Folk.* New York: The Blue Heron Press, 1953, pp. 3–4.

"Negro soul in a flood of white Americanism," but they did not always succeed. Too often they measured themselves "by the tape of a world that looks on in amused contempt and pity." This was one of the weaknesses of the Renaissance.

Du Bois anticipated the Renaissance long before 1925. As early as 1915 in the April issue of *The Crisis* he stated what would be two of the most significant themes of the movement:

> In art and literature we should try to loose the tremendous emotional wealth of the Negro and the dramatic strength of his problems through writing . . . and other forms of art. We should resurrect forgotten ancient Negro art and history, and we should set the black man before the world as both a creative artist and a strong subject for artistic treatment.

As early as 1903 he was putting into practice the doctrine stated above, for in that year he published *The Souls of Black Folk,* perhaps his most successful literary work. The volume is a miscellany consisting of fourteen essays and sketches describing the position of the Negro in America at the time. The best-known essays in the work are "Of the Sorrow Songs," a pioneer study and appraisal of Negro spirituals, and "Of Mr. Booker T. Washington and Others," a calm but penetrating attack on the accommodationist racial attitude Booker T. Washington represented. One of the sketches, "Of the Passing of the First Born," is a poignant account of the loss of Du Bois's first child. The rest of the work deals for the most part with the social and economic problems of the South, and measured by today's standards, it is a highly reasonable work. One is surprised to find the following admission by Du Bois in "Of the Sons of Master and Man":

> I should be the last to deny the patent weaknesses and short-comings of the Negro people; I should be the last to withhold sympathy from the white South in its efforts to solve its intricate social problems. I freely acknowledge that it is possible, and sometimes best, that a practically undeveloped people should be ruled by the best of their stronger and better neighbors for their own good, until such times as they can start and fight the world's battles alone.[2]

In spite of its reasonableness, however, *The Souls of Black Folk* was anathematized by the Southern press. The work was branded as incendiary and its author labeled a dangerous radical. It is hard now to conceive of racial conditions so tense as to find danger in a work of this sensible nature.

One discovers from this volume that Du Bois has two distinct prose styles. The first, a style that is smooth flowing, heightened yet con-

2. *The Souls of Black Folk.* Chicago: A. A. McClurg and Co., 1907, p. 176.

trolled, lucid, highly readable, and definitely modern in its rhythms and sentence structure. This is the style he uses when presenting scholarly or social or historical facts. Like all good prose, it is a combination of important content and artistry in the presentation of that content. The second style, however, the one that has been admired by many, many Negro readers, is inclined to be flowery, emotional, poetic, and essentially Victorian in the unpopular sense of the term. This second style makes too much use of allegorical and mythological terms, has too many apostrophes and invocations, too many "thee's" and "thou's" in it. Perhaps the worst example of this style is found in "Of the Passing of the First Born." Whatever the faults of this second style (and these faults appear again and again in later works) they are not serious enough to be ludicrous; and they are offset by the clarity of Du Bois's scholarly prose style, the one in which he wrote most of his essays and large portions of his novels and autobiographies.

Darkwater (1920), the second book of essays, is more of a potpourri than *The Souls of Black Folk* and not so well written as the earlier work. In it one finds most of Du Bois's poetry, several short stories and sketches, a considerable amount of autobiography, and at its beginning Du Bois's "Credo," in which he spells out articles of belief, including the following:

> Especially do I believe in the Negro Race: in the beauty of its genius, the sweetness of its soul, and its strength in that meekness which shall yet inherit this turbulent earth.[3]

One smiles at the characteristics "sweetness" and "meekness" when he thinks of the present-day Panthers.

There are six poems and two prose poems in *Darkwater*. The best and the best known of these is the powerful "A Litany at Atlanta," written after the brutal 1906 Atlanta Riot. Although dated in its language, this work possesses an Old Testament power. Passionate and bitter, it echoes the hopelessness of thousands of Negroes in America who daily suffered the cruelty and the shame of lynchings, riots, segregation, and discrimination:

> Sit no longer blind, Lord God, deaf to our prayer and dumb to our dumb suffering. Surely, Thou, too, art not white, O Lord, a pale, bloodless, heartless thing![4]

Although the religious background which the poem postulates is lost on many young black readers of today, the work still moves them.

Because Dr. Du Bois was often far ahead of his contemporaries in social vision, *Darkwater* contains surprises. His attitude toward the

---

3. *Darkwater*. New York: Harcourt, Brace, and Howe, 1920, p. 3.
4. Ibid., p. 27.

liberation of women was unusually advanced. It is intriguing to note that in 1920 in an essay called "The Damnation of Women" Du Bois takes the following position on sexual freedom:

> All womanhood is hampered today because the world on which it is emerging is a world that tries to worship both virgins and mothers and in the end despises Motherhood and despoils virgins. The future woman must have a life work and economic independence. She must have knowledge. She must have the right of motherhood *at her own discretion*. The present mincing horror at free womanhood must pass if we are ever to be rid of the bestialities of free manhood. . . . The world must choose the free woman or the white wraith of the prostitute. Today it wavers between the prostitute and the nun.

Two of the sketches in *Darkwater*, "The Second Coming" and "Jesus Christ in Texas," concern the theme of the black Christ. In the first Du Bois retells the Christmas story in modern terms, placing a black Christ child in Valdosta, Georgia. In the second he rewrites the crucifixion story in Southern lynching terms, anticipating Countee Cullen's *The Black Christ* (1929). In all of this concern with blackness, we note that Du Bois even before the Garvey movement had made use of black madonnas and a black Holy Infant in *The Brownies' Book, A Monthly Magazine for Children of the Sun*, which he brought out in 1920. Abraham Chapman also feels that Du Bois as early as 1899 in *The Horizon* anticipated "a central theme" of the New Negro Renaissance, the emphasis on atavistic blackness, expressed in a poem called "The Song of the Smoke."[5]

In *Dusk of Dawn* (1940) Dr. Du Bois wrote an apology in which he tells us that he thought of that work, *The Souls of Black Folk*, and *Darkwater* as "three sets of thought centering around the hurts and hesitancies that hem the black man in America." The *Souls of Black Folk* he felt "was a cry at midnight thick within the veil, when none rightly knew the coming day." *Darkwater* he considered "an exposition and militant challenge, defiant with dogged hope." When he came to write the third "set of thoughts," *Dusk of Dawn*, he found that it threatened to become "mere autobiography," and that is what he did not want. Instead, he wrote, as the book's subtitle tells us: *An Essay Toward an Autobiography of a Race Concept*. To express it in his words:

> But in my own experience, autobiographies have had little lure. . . . My life had its significance and its only significance because it was part of a Problem; but that problem was, as I continue to think, the central problem of the greatest of the world's democracies and the Problem of the

5. Abraham Chapman, *Black Voices*. New York: New American Library, 1968, pp. 45–46.

future world. [Describing the "concept of race" as one of today's "most unyielding and threatening" problems, Du Bois continues] . . . I seem to see a way of elucidating the inner meaning and significance of that race problem by explaining it in terms of the one human life I know best.

I have written then what is meant to be not so much my autobiography as the autobiography of a concept of race, elucidated, magnified and doubtless distorted in the thoughts and deeds which were mine.

The attitude toward autobiography expressed here throws light on what he had to say about the Black Flame Trilogy to be discussed later.

Of the nine essays in *Dusk of Dawn* perhaps the best is "A New England Boy and Reconstruction," in which the author discusses his family background, his life in a small New England town, and his first exposure to "so many people of my own color" whom he found at Fisk University in 1885—and, most important, the first time he saw "beautiful girls." "The Colored World Within" is a fascinating and penetrating discussion of conditions within the Negro group in 1940, of the several theoretical survival techniques advanced by black thinkers. One of these "ways out" is self-segregation on the part of the Negro; not, however, with separatism as its ultimate goal, but rather the "admission of the colored group to cooperation, and incorporation into the white group on the best possible terms."[6]

We note from *Dusk of Dawn* that Du Bois was also aware and proud of his role as an encourager of young writers toward this end:

> More especially I tried to encourage other Negro writers through the columns of the *Crisis*. By 1920, we could point out that most young writers among American Negroes had made first publication in the columns of the *Crisis*. In the next few years we published works from Claude McKay, Langston Hughes, Jean Toomer, Countee Cullen, Anne Spencer, Abram Harris, and Jessie Fauset.

During his lifetime Dr. Du Bois published five full-length novels, the last three a trilogy started and finished *after* his eighty-ninth birthday. In all of these he made his muse the handmaiden of racial protest, and too often the propagandist crowds out the artist. But for Du Bois, as for most Negro writers of his generation, it was assumed that a black artist would use his creations in the liberation struggle. (When present-day Black Aesthetic writers insist that all art must be political, they are actually imitating, *not the theory,* but the practice of their elders.) Moreover, Du Bois was by nature a purposeful man; one must not forget he was a late-Victorian and a New Englander, and he could no more conceive of writing an art-for-the-sake-of-art work than he could of composing coon songs. Speaking of his first novel, Du Bois, writing in 1940, said: "In 1911, I tried my hand at fiction and published *The*

6. *Dusk of Dawn,* p. 200.

Quest of the Silver Fleece which was really an economic study of some merit." Note the emphasis, the unconscious emphasis, not on "fiction" but on the phrase "an economic study of some merit."[7]

One must also remember that Du Bois at this time, like all of his contemporaries, was always aware of the "amused contempt and pity" of the whites. He and they were determined to put their best foot foremost, and that is why they often went out of their way to be "cultured." For example, Du Bois has characters under improbable circumstances discussing Italian art and Wagnerian music. Showing off? No. Du Bois wanted his white *and* his black readers to know that there were Negroes who could talk about such things and talk about them in good English. These edifying excursions into culture did not always help the novel qua novel, but that was the price the Negro author in 1911 felt his dual heritage demanded.

The Quest of the Silver Fleece deals with the alliance between the industrial North and the cotton South and the resultant involvement of the Negro peasant in the rural Deep South. The main story concerns two young blacks, Bles and Zora, both associated with the missionary school run by a Yankee "schoolmarm"—one of that noble breed who came South after the Civil War and who did a superb job of educating a forgotten and oppressed group. The novel presents realistic pictures of the rural South and its sexual folkways, New York City, and Washington, D.C.—the mecca of middle-class Negroes of that generation. The work is a strange mixture of naturalism and romanticism. When the author describes intricately the effect of Northern money on the Bourbon South, he writes in the tradition of Emile Zola and of Frank Norris (*The Pit*), and he writes convincingly because of his scholarly grasp of economics. Other aspects of the novel are purely romantic, such as those segments in which he seems to allegorize the Swamp, Elspeth, the old Negro "witch" who lives there; and the silver fleece—that superb cotton raised by Bles and Zora with seeds given them by Elspeth that had come from Africa. The silver fleece seems to represent for Du Bois the union of nature and disciplined industry, the kind of union that the American Negro needed. Nature (his African primitivism) added to industry and art (knowledge) could produce a new and valuable American.[8] Primitivism untouched by civilizing influences had no appeal for Du Bois.

In *The Quest* Dr. Du Bois gives us a new type of Negro heroine, a dark-skinned girl. Few female principal characters in Negro fiction from William Wells Brown on down had ever been anything but near white,

7. *Dusk of Dawn*, p. 269.
8. I am indebted in part to one of my students for this interpretation, Dr. Gregory Rigsby.

usually light enough to pass. Zora is also a new type of heroine in another way. In many respects she is a modern woman and, more important for Du Bois, a woman willing to become a helpmate to her husband if he, too, is concerned with the progress of the race. Du Bois tends to have two kinds of women in his novels, the Zora type and the Carolyn Wyn type, both represented in *The Quest of the Silver Fleece.* The latter, though a strong woman, fights only for personal advancement and is willing to play the cheapest of cheap political games to achieve her ambitions.

The second novel, *The Dark Princess* (1928), and Du Bois's favorite, repeats the pattern of the first. The main character, Matthew Towns, like Bles Alwyn in *The Quest,* is desired by two women: one the hard, sophisticated city-type victim of America's crooked political system, Sara Andrews; the other the idealistic type that Du Bois liked, in this case an Indian princess. Both women are intelligent and ambitious, but the heroine is H. R. H. the Princess Kautilya of Bowdpur, India, a socially conscious ruler who seeks to help the darker peoples of the world. It was typical of Du Bois to have his main female character an Indian and his hero a Virginia (the aristocrat of Southern states) Negro. With a cloak-and-dagger plot covering Europe and America and involving Asia, the author becomes realistic enough to give a first-hand and actually prophetic delineation of the events and forces that would elect Chicago's first black Congressman. The problem of the twentieth century, Du Bois wrote in 1903, is the "problem of the color line." In this novel, with its romantic alliance of two colored peoples cemented with the birth of a new Indian prince, he dramatizes the kind of union of darker races that he felt the century would see.

Between *The Dark Princess* (1928) and the publication of the first of the Black Flame Trilogy, *The Ordeal of Mansart* (1957), there is a twenty-nine year span. In the meantime, Du Bois has approached his ninetieth year and has gone all the way to the left politically. The postscript which the author attached to the work explains his purpose in writing *The Ordeal of Mansart:*

> In the great tragedy of Negro slavery in the United States and its aftermath, much of documented history is lacking because of the deep feeling involved and the fierce desire of men to defend their fathers and themselves. This I have sought to correct in my study of the slave trade and of Reconstruction. If I had time and money, I would have continued this pure historical research. But this opportunity failed and time is running out. Yet I would rescue from my long experience something of what I have learned and conjectured and thus I am trying by the method of historical fiction to complete the cycle of history which has for a half century engaged my thought, research and action.[9]

9. *The Ordeal of Mansart.* New York: Mainstream, 1957.

It is unfortunate that Du Bois chose historical fiction as his medium. As the commentary of a good historian and a race leader who helped to make the history about which he writes, the work is illuminating and significant; but it is definitely not a good historical novel. The writer of a historical novel has a twofold responsibility: he must not only know his period thoroughly, he must also convince his readers that the fictional creations are, if not actually real, a necessary part of the historical background in question. *The Ordeal* fails in this latter respect, and the same is true of the other two novels of the trilogy. Even the title characters are not believable individuals but rather personifications who could easily be designated by their stereotype names: Poor White (Scroggs), Southern Aristocrat (Breckenridge), Exotic Primitive (Aunt Betsy), and Yankee Magnate (Pierce).

The Ordeal of Mansart covers the years from 1870 to 1916. On the night that Mansart was born his father was lynched. From then on, using historical names such as Tom Watson, Henry Grady, Booker T. Washington, and James Burghardt (the author himself), Du Bois traces the education of Mansart in Atlanta, his marriage, and his life as a Negro teacher—often humiliated, always underpaid. Mansart lives through the terrible Atlanta Riot, and at the end of the work we find him ready to become the *Negro* superintendent of schools in that city.

In *Mansart Builds a School* (1959), the years from 1916 to 1936 are covered, and we get a realistic and convincing portrayal of the working of the Atlanta school system, of the migration of Negroes to the North during World War I, of the rise into power (money) of the J. C. Walker Hair Company, and of the coming of World War II. Part of the novel concerns the fortunes of the Mansart boys in this war and their subsequent settling in the North. Another section of the work introduces us to a typical Du Bois female character, in this case an efficient and loyal near-white named Jean du Bignon. At the end of the novel Mansart had become president of a state college for Negroes in Georgia.

The last work in the trilogy, *Worlds of Color* (1961), deals with a period from 1936 to 1956. In it we find Mansart, now sixty, facing a new world, a world in which even Negro college presidents could make certain demands. Moreover, college administrators had become more sophisticated. Mansart, for example, travels and broadens his social vision. He finds great help in the efficient Jean du Bignon, whom he makes a dean in spite of her sex. By this time the Mansart children and grandchildren have spread over a large part of the nation and are in all of the major professions. Throughout this last novel, as well as throughout the series, we find Mansart moving steadily toward the political left. At the end he marries Jean du Bignon in spite of age differences. Both are convinced that the future is to be a Communist world.

What is Du Bois telling us in this rambling complex trilogy of three historical novels? For one thing, he is giving an excellent and authoritative account of the educational, political, and socioeconomic position of the Negro during the years in question. On another level, he is painting a picture of the involvement in American life of a typical Negro middle-class family, the kind of Negro that constitutes the backbone and the underpinning of the race. He is showing how typically American such families can be, and how on occasion through passing—conscious and unconscious—they fuse with the white element. On still another level, the trilogy is an allegorical apologia for Du Bois's own life—his early interest in education, his late second marriage, his late conversion to Marxism.

One wishes he had used memoirs or autobiography to cover the same ground. Du Bois is not a good historical novelist. But whatever the artistic merit of these three works, they are a valuable look by a great and wise old warrior at the battlefield on which he fought gallantly.

James Weldon Johnson

Educator, song writer, man of letters, diplomatist, and distinguished secretary of the NAACP, James Weldon Johnson was a many-sided and talented figure. A rare combination of creative artist and man of affairs, he had the ambition, the competency, and the pragmatic outlook of the successful middle-class American, and the sensitiveness of the artist. Johnson also had some of the instincts of a successful journalist.

Impressed with the immense Negro musical and literary potential he found about him, he decided to make America aware of this overlooked treasure. He published a pioneer anthology of Negro literature, with a preface that tells the nation about its black cultural reserves. Sensing the new importance and popularity of Harlem, he wrote a history of that city within a city. Reading in the press about Negro Gold-Star mothers (mothers whose sons were killed in the war) sent to Europe under Jim Crow conditions, he wrote his best satirical poem, "St. Peter Relates an

Incident of the Resurrection Day." There is a down-to-earth awareness in Johnson's work not always found in that of, let us say, Du Bois. Du Bois was a prophet, a seer; Johnson was a pragmatist. He was never a five-talent man, but he used to the fullest the two or three that he possessed. Johnson was a Planter in every sense of the word, and the New Negro Renaissance owes much to him.

Born James William Johnson of middle-class, Afro-American and West Indian parentage in Jacksonville, Florida, in 1871, James Weldon Johnson cultivated a love of letters and music at an early age. He attended the Atlanta University Preparatory School and College, graduating in 1894. After that he became principal of the Negro public school in Jacksonville, founded and published a paper, *The Daily American,* in 1895 (it lasted eight months), studied law, and passed the Florida bar in 1897.

In the summers from 1899 to 1901 James Weldon Johnson went to New York to collaborate with his brother, Rosamond, in the writing of light opera and musical comedy, producing such songs as "Under the Bamboo Tree," "Congo Love Song," "O Didn't He Ramble," and "Lift Every Voice and Sing," commonly known as the Negro national anthem. In 1900 the brothers formed a partnership with Bob Cole, Rosamond's partner in a highly successful vaudeville act. In 1901 Johnson moved to New York to dedicate his time to show business and the study of literature at Columbia University. In 1904 he earned an M. A. degree from Atlanta University.

His interest in politics and knowledge of Spanish won Johnson the position of United States consul at Puerto Cabello, Venezuela, from 1906 to 1907 and at Corinta, Nicaragua, from 1909 to 1912. During his diplomatic career he wrote and published anonymously *The Autobiography of an Ex-Coloured Man* (1912). In 1913 he resigned from the consular service and returned to New York, where he served for ten years as contributing editor for the *New York Age,* at the time one of the oldest Negro papers in New York. In 1915 he wrote the libretto for the Spanish opera *Goyescas,* produced at the Metropolitan Opera House in 1915.

From 1916 to 1931 Johnson worked first as field secretary and then executive secretary of the National Association for the Advancement of Colored People. He led an extensive lobbying campaign for the Dyer Anti-Lynching Bill, subsequently defeated in the Senate. He also investigated the United States' intervention in Haiti. During his stay with the NAACP Johnson published most of his books and essays, receiving a Rosenwald Foundation grant for creative writing in the 1920's. Upon his resignation from the NAACP Johnson served as the Adam K. Spence

Professor of Creative Literature at Fisk University, taking time after 1934 to give an annual series of lectures at New York University, until his death in an automobile accident in Massachusetts in 1938.

The poetry of Johnson is found in three publications: *Fifty Years and Other Poems* (1917), *God's Trombones* (1927), *St. Peter Relates an Incident of the Resurrection Day* (1935). These volumes prove one thing clearly: Johnson showed remarkable growth as a poet. Beginning as a writer of dialect poetry, of coon songs, of sentimental verse, and of didactic and heavy-footed protest poetry, he soon became an innovative handler of folk material and a writer of sophisticated, ironic verse. His poetical works are a good index to changes in themes, techniques, and tone which the New Negro Renaissance brought about.

The first volume, *Fifty Years and Other Poems,* evidences most of the faults found in Negro writing of the pre-Renaissance era. The title poem, written to commemorate the fiftieth anniversary of the Emancipation Proclamation, is virtually a catalogue of cliché themes found in Negro poetry since the Civil War: the black man is an American ("This land is ours by right of birth,/ This land is ours by right of toil . . ."); we were the first to die for America's freedom (Attucks); the Negro has never been a traitor ("And never yet . . . / Has one black, treason-guided hand/ Ever against that flag been raised"); the Negro is a part of a "God-known destiny," a part of some great plan in which he must have faith in spite of oppression. Such themes were expected and usually found in commemorative Negro poems; they were also found in the oratory of the day. Johnson did not disappoint his readers.

Black and white readers of the pre-Renaissance era also expected a Negro poet to write humorous poems in dialect. Paul Laurence Dunbar had conditioned America in this respect. In a section of this first work entitled "Jingles and Croons" Johnson tried his hand at dialect poetry ("July in Georgy," "The Rivals," and others), which left something to be desired; he lacked Dunbar's magic touch in this form. He could write songs better ("Sence You Went Away" became a national favorite), but the dialect verse was not impressive, and he had the good taste to stop writing it not too long after the publication of *Fifty Years.*

Of the protest pieces in the work, the most ambitious is "Brothers," a lynching poem in blank verse with a loaded punchline aimed at the conscience of white America: "Brothers in spirit, brothers indeed are we," the black rapist and the white lyncher. There is also the usual poem about Negro heroes ("The Color Sergeant") and the just as usual ode to Lincoln ("Father, Father Abraham"). In addition, there are the miscellaneous and sentimental poems endemic to the age. The quality of the latter type may be judged from "The Reward":

No greater earthly boon than this I crave,
That those who some day gather round my grave,
In place of tears, may whisper of me then,
"He sang a song that reached the hearts of men."

Johnson was not really a member of the imitative or "mocking-bird school" of black poets, but one finds in his works echoes of Keats, Poe, Longfellow, and of his friend Paul Laurence Dunbar.

The second volume, *God's Trombones,* though appearing only ten years after the first, shows far more than ten years of poetic growth and understanding on the part of Johnson. An index to this maturing is found in the preface to *The Book of American Negro Poetry,* an anthology published in 1922. In this lengthy preface Johnson voiced his dissatisfaction with the limitations of dialect writing and his interest in a new vehicle for Negro expression:

> What the colored poet in the United States needs to do is something like what Synge did for the Irish; he needs to find a form that will express the racial spirit by symbols from within rather than by symbols from without, such as the mere mutilation of English spelling and pronunciation. He needs a form that is freer and larger than dialect, but which will still hold the racial flavor; a form expressing the imagery, the idioms, the peculiar turns of thought, and the distinctive humor and pathos, too, of the Negro, but which will also be capable of voicing the deepest and highest emotions and aspirations, and allow of the widest range of subject and the widest scope of treatment.

In *God's Trombones,* using the old-time Negro folk sermon as his vehicle, Johnson successfully puts his theories into practice. In these eight free-verse poems, without the distortion and limitation of dialect, he captures the rhythm, intonation (as far as one can write it down), sentence structure, breaks, and repetitions of the illiterate black folk preacher. Johnson has shown great skill in transforming folk material into sophisticated art. Note, for example, how he renders the characteristic intoning of the folk sermon; note the interrupted flow of the phrases, the dramatic breaks:

Jesus, my sorrowing Jesus,
The sweat like drops of blood upon his brow,
Talking with his Father,
While the three disciples slept,
Saying: Father,
Oh, Father,
Not as I will
Not as I will,
But let thy will be done.

James Weldon Johnson

Photo by R. McDougall, James Weldon Johnson Memorial Collection of Negro Arts and Letters, Beinecke Rare Book and Manuscript Library, Yale University.

The spiritual as well as the sermon influence is found in these free-verse poems. Johnson's success with these folk forms had considerable effect on later Renaissance writers. It gave impetus to the folk emphasis which characterized much Renaissance verse. Johnson used the spiritual and the sermon and, of course, certain forms common to dialect poetry. Langston Hughes, Sterling Brown, Waring Cuney, and others added ballad and blues forms and otherwise widened the range of folk expression. Johnson, however, was a pioneer influence. He saw the possibilities of folk influence as early as 1922. Because of its folk undergirding, *God's Trombones,* in all probability, will outlast the rest of Johnson's poetry.

St. Peter Relates an Incident of the Resurrection Day (1935) consists of thirty-eight poems, most of them having appeared in *Fifty Years and Other Poems.* Of the nine new pieces, the best known is "Lift Every Voice and Sing." Set to music by J. Rosamond Johnson, the poet's brother, this poem was used for many years as the Negro national anthem. It is now called the black national anthem, and whenever young blacks gather at games and other public affairs, they sing the first verse of the poem.

The title poem, "St. Peter Relates an Incident of the Resurrection Day," had the following origin. In the summer of 1930, while Johnson was working on a project, he read in his morning paper that the United States government was sending Gold-Star mothers to visit the graves of their sons buried in France. The pilgrimage, like the World War I armed forces, was to be strictly Jim Crow. White mothers would go first class on a first-class boat; black mothers would go on a second-class "tub." When he finished reading the news article, Johnson immediately stopped all work on the manuscript before him and did not return to it until he had completed "St. Peter. . . ." The work was originally published in 1930 in an edition of two hundred copies for private distribution. It was republished in 1935.

The title poem is Johnson at his ironic best. In order to relieve boredom in Heaven, Saint Peter one day tells what happened on Judgment Day when the Tomb of the Unknown Soldier was opened. All of the "Trustees of the Patriotism of the Nation," including the Grand Army of the Republic, the Daughters of the American Revolution, the Legion, and others, were on hand to witness the event. When the Unknown Soldier turned out to be a black man, pandemonium reigned in Heaven. The Klan wanted to rebury him, and there were other suggestions; but ignoring the disturbance, the black soldier marched up to Heaven singing:

> Deep river, my home is over Jordan,
> Deep river, I want to cross over into camp-ground.

ᵕich prompted the writing of this poem, the ironic
ut effective mixture of bitterness diluted with
ᵣistic of Renaissance protest poetry. What a far cry
y-handed solemnity of the earlier "Brothers"!

ᵣ's one novel, *The Autobiography of an Ex-Coloured Man*
ᵤz, 1927, 1960), has stood the test of time better than his poetry;
ᵢn fact, it is probably more popular now in its reprints than it was in
1912. Long thought to be a real autobiography, the work is now known
for what it is, a loosely structured novel on the theme of passing. As
such it belongs in that category of race novels which came to be called
lynching-passing fiction. After Johnson, Walter White, Jessie Fauset,
Nella Larsen, and other Negro novelists used the theme, and they owe
much to the *Autobiography*. Johnson, however, did not begin the tradition. It has been a part of black fiction from its very beginning.
William Wells Brown's *Clotel* (1853), Frank J. Webb's *The Garies
and Their Friends* (1857), and Charles W. Chesnutt's *The House
Behind the Cedars* (1900), to give the best works in this vein, all exploit the passing theme. Passing-for-white has always intrigued the
American reader, black and white. The latter group has often been
terrified as well as fascinated by the possibilities of Negro blood crop-
ping up in their families or, to put it more precisely, the *knowledge* of
the presence of black blood (for example, Sinclair Lewis's *Kingsblood
Royal,* and Robert Penn Warren's *Band of Angels*). The Negro, on the
other hand, has liked the theme, primarily because it shows the
absurdity of putting such great importance on race in America when
actually one cannot tell a Negro from a white. These considerations
added to the interest in Johnson's novel.

The main story line of the work delineates the progress from childhood to maturity and marriage of the offspring of a Southern gentleman
and his light-skinned mistress. In this progress Johnson gives us realistic
pictures of Negro life seldom, perhaps never, treated in fiction up to
that time: the activities of Pullman porters on the job and off; the life
in a Key West cigar factory; a good old-fashioned camp meeting; and,
most important, the bohemian night life of black New York before it
moved to Harlem. In his night-life sketches Johnson was a precursor
of much Renaissance literature of the next two decades. Johnson, again,
was not the first to write about this life. In Dunbar's one Negro
novel, *The Sport of the Gods,* he touches on the theme. But Johnson,
as a part of the theatrical world of the era, had a much better knowledge of Black Bohemia than any other writer. (Incidentally, he antici-
pates a theme which has an important place in present-day black novels.
Among his minor characters, Johnson has a white-woman-black-man
situation which looks ahead to Rufus and Leona in Baldwin's *Another*

Country. Johnson handled it ever so lightly, but he did not ig\
This, one must remember, was 1912!)

The Autobiography of an Ex-Coloured Man is different from e\
black fiction in other ways. First of all, his protagonist is almos\ an
anti-hero. A decent person in every respect, he is also a weak and
vacillating human. Facing a series of important choices in his life, he
takes the easier way every time. Starting out to become a distinguished
part of the Negro world, he ends up as an ordinary middle-class white
citizen. First, his "averageness" and his humanness suggest that the
protagonist's individual characteristics, and not race, shaped his career.
And second, Johnson does not belabor the race issue as practically every
other black novelist before him had done. He has to talk about segregation and discrimination, but he does not lose his perspective. He has
to discuss the black-white sexual liaison that produced the protagonist,
but he does not become bitter over the plight of black womanhood.
There is no moral condemnation here, no lecturing. This race mingling
is described as a fact of Southern life.

There are two touching dramatic scenes in the work. The first, the
episode in which the protagonist in grammar school discovers in the
presence of his schoolmates that he is a Negro. The second, the scene
at the opera when the protagonist sits next to his father and presumably
his half-sister and cannot make himself known. Such dramatic but restrained episodes point up far more strongly the tragedy of the American
race situation than sensational and brutal scenes of violence.

Johnson's full-length autobiography, *Along This Way* (1933), adopts
the pattern of Negro autobiography of the age: a combination of
middle-class success story, racial vindication, and social commentary,
rather than "pure" delineation of personality. The work, however, is
valuable because Johnson had such a varied and outstanding career and
knew so many prominent persons, white and black, of his age. The
most fascinating parts are not the ones connected with the Dyer Anti-
Lynching Bill and other important political matters, but rather those
dealing with the vignettes that crop up: Paul Laurence Dunbar's reaction to the poetry of Walt Whitman, midnight parties with black
celebrities at the old Marshall Hotel, contacts with Broadway characters
such as Flo Ziegfeld and Anna Held, and, above all, Black Bohemia in
the 53rd Street area. One enjoys reading *Along This Way*, yet leaves it
with a feeling that this success story is too successful, too upward looking; it is all peaks with few or no pits of failure and ugliness. The
reason, perhaps, is the best-foot-foremost philosophy that motivated
Johnson's generation. Determined to prove to white America that they
could make the grade, these writers became automatic salesmen, selling
the Talented Tenth to the nation, although by 1935 they would not

have used the phrase. What *Along This Way* really says is this: See what I have done in spite of the pressures you put on me. I am like you—the best of you, of course; so count me in.

Black Manhattan (1930) has a twofold purpose: it gives the history of the Negro in New York, emphasizing his presence in Harlem; it also gives a very useful account of the Negro in the theatre from 1821, the time of the African Company, to 1930, the year in which *Green Pastures* played on Broadway. *Black Manhattan* is a very useful source book for those who write on the black theatre. It has sketches of many famous performers of yesteryear, accounts of the first attempts of Negroes to form theatre companies; a record of failures and achievements in the theatre—all written by a man who was himself part of that theatre world, part of that Black Bohemia about which he writes. Needless to say, some of the material in *Black Manhattan* is also found in Johnson's novel and autobiography. Coming out in 1930 in the dead center of the Harlem Renaissance, the work was timely. In the recent upsurge of interest in black life, the work is once more in demand. It has stood the test of time well.

In 1922 Johnson published the first significant anthology of black poetry, *The Book of American Negro Poetry*. In the preface to the revised edition (1931) of this work, he tells us of the need for such a volume: "When this book was compiled . . . the conception of the Negro as creator of art was so new, indeed so unformed, that I felt it was necessary to make a rather extended introduction in presenting to the public an anthology of poetry by Negro writers." Johnson was right. *If* America knew Negro poets at all, it knew only Dunbar. Phillis Wheatley was known as a name to give colored YWCA's, nothing more. *The Book of American Negro Poetry* did yeoman service in reminding the country that it had a backlog of overlooked talent, not in literature only but also in music and the dance.

Johnson's place in Negro American literature is secure. He did many things and did them well. He was an excellent Planter of Renaissance seed because he had an intelligent awareness of the movements going on around him. A pioneer anthologist, an early exploiter of folk material, author of an objective novel, and writer of a fascinating account of Harlem and the black stage, he was a transitional figure who inspired changes in the development of Negro literature both by precept and example.

Claude McKay

"Claude McKay was one of the great forces in bringing about what is now called the 'Negro literary renaissance.' Those who know him and his powers feel that his comparative silence for the past four or five years has meant a great loss to the movement. He is a poet and writer of genius. It is fortunate for Negro and American literature that he is writing again."

This comment, written by James Weldon Johnson for the September, 1928, *Readers' Guide,* shows that at this early date McKay's contemporaries appreciated his great talent and recognized him as a Planter of the Harlem Renaissance. This is unusual. In most cases the perspective of time is required to give a writer this kind of acceptance.

McKay *was* "one of the great forces" helping to shape the New Negro Movement; he was this in spite of several things that would have kept the ordinary writer from this honor. First of all, he was not born in America and did not become a citizen until 1940. Second, from 1922 to 1934, during the most crucial years of the Renaissance, he was abroad. Third, he had during his early days pro-leftist leanings and was at one time associate editor of *The Liberator*. Although they were not hysterically anti-Communist, most of the *early* New Negro writers tended to be somewhat shy of the left. And, fourth, McKay was seemingly contemptuous of the New Negro literary leaders. In his autobiography he was not kind to most of them, including Du Bois. And yet McKay did influence the movement in several ways: his militant sonnets inaugurated a new era in black protest writing; his poetry presented for the first time several themes which were to be used by later New Negro poets; and his novels emphasized for the first time in Negro fiction the themes of primitivism and the seamier side of Negro urban life.

Born in 1889 in the Clarendon Hills of Jamaica, British West Indies, Claude McKay was initially educated by his older brother, a schoolteacher whose interest in free thought and philosophy in general affected the younger Claude. As an adolescent McKay met Edward Jekyll, an English scholar of Jamaican folklore, whose library and active instruction aided McKay in the writing of his early dialect poetry.

Before he came to America, McKay was a well-known poet in his native Jamaica. In 1912 he published *Songs from Jamaica,* a volume written largely in the dialect of the island's peasants, a volume giving a realistic picture of the lives of these people. His second work, *Constab*

Ballads, describes the author's personal experience as an island constable; it plays up the conflict between McKay's sense of duty as an officer and his sympathy for the people. These are small volumes, and because of the local dialect in which many of the poems are written, are not easy reading for an outsider.

In 1912 McKay came to the United States, enrolling for three months in an agriculture course at Tuskegee Institute. Disliking Tuskegee's penchant for regimentation, McKay transferred to Kansas State College for two years (1912–1914). Anxious to pursue an artistic life, he went to Harlem, supporting himself as a waiter, porter, and restaurant proprietor, among other occupations, and contracting an unfortunate marriage to a Jamaican girl, who returned to her home after six months.

In 1917, under the pseudonym of Eli Edwards, McKay entered the American literary scene with the publication of two poems, "Harlem Dancer" and "Invocation," in *The Seven Arts* magazine. He later contributed regularly to *Pearson's Magazine* and Max Eastman's *The Liberator.* From late 1919 to 1921 McKay lived in England, where he wrote for a Communist weekly, *The Worker's Dreadnaught.* McKay traveled to Russia in 1922 for the fourth congress of the Communist International. Although his interest in radicalism never led him to join the Communist Party, McKay was treated as a high-level visitor, touring military installations and evoking spontaneous displays of admiration from the Russian people. After leaving Russia, he stayed abroad until 1934, living in Germany, France, Spain, and North Africa. McKay became an American citizen in 1940, and, after a lifetime of agnosticism and radicalism, joined the Catholic church, in his words, the "authentic church of Christ" whose early history reflected "no race or color prejudice." He died in 1948.

McKay's first book of verse to appear after he left Jamaica was *Spring in New Hampshire and Other Poems,* published in London in 1920. The work has a curious preface by I. A. Richards in which he makes the following statement:

> Claude McKay is a pure blooded Negro, and though we have recently been made aware of some of the more remarkable achievements of African art typified by the sculpture from Benin, and by the spirituals, this is the first instance of success in poetry with which we in Europe at any rate have been brought into contact. The reasons for this late development are not far to seek, and the difficulties presented by modern literary English as an acquired medium would be sufficient to account for the lacuna; but the poems here selected may, in the opinion of not a few who have seen them in periodical form, claim a place beside the best work that the present generation is producing in this country.

Although he probably did not mean to be, there is implied a peculiar kind of condescension on Richards' part. There is also a peculiar kind of ignorance. In spite of Richards' belief in McKay's undiluted ancestry, one wonders why a West Indian, with over three hundred years of English tradition behind him, would have difficulty with "modern literary English" and also why it would be an "acquired medium." As we shall see later, distinguished white critics often go off on unnecessary and sometimes inexplicable tangents when they write about Negroes.

McKay's first American publication, *Harlem Shadows,* came out in 1922 and has become something of a landmark in Negro literature. Since most of the poems (all of the best known) from *Spring in New Hampshire* appear again in *Harlem Shadows,* and since there is no radical change in tone or theme or structure found in the latter volume, both will be treated together here simply as McKay's poetry. *Harlem Shadows,* however, does have an introduction by Max Eastman which is as intriguing as the preface written by I. A. Richards. One notes that like the latter, Eastman begins with that "pure blooded" gambit:

> These poems have a special interest for all the races of man because they are sung by a pure blooded Negro. They are the first significant expression of that race in poetry. We tried faithfully to give a position in our literature to Paul Laurence Dunbar. We have excessively welcomed other black poets of minor talent, seeking in their music some distinctive quality other than the fact that they wrote it. But here for the first time we find our literature vividly enriched by a voice from this most alien race among us.

When Eastman speaks of the "first significant expression of that race in poetry," one asks for an explanation of the word *significant.* Phillis Wheatley was certainly not a great poet (neither was McKay), but she was definitely significant and certainly more "pure blooded" than McKay. And although Mr. Eastman did not think so, Dunbar is as good a poet as McKay, perhaps better. One also wonders what Eastman means by "our" literature. If he has in mind the Anglo-Saxon tradition, he should remember that McKay's roots were probably deeper in this tradition than those of Max Eastman, even though McKay came "from this most alien race among us."

In 1953 *The Selected Poems of Claude McKay* (with an introduction by John Dewey and a biographical note by Max Eastman) was published by the Bookman Associates. Although McKay died in 1948, there is evidence that he made this selection before he died. Dewey's introduction is written as though McKay were still alive, and Eastman's biographical note makes no mention of McKay's death. Most of the poems in this work are old pieces from earlier publications. Somebody (if not McKay) grouped the poems under five heads: "Songs for Jamaica," "Baptism," "Americana," "Different Places," and "Amoroso." McKay was never a prolific poet, but it is obvious that after *Harlem*

Shadows he wrote poetry at a drastically reduced rate, evidently spending most of his time on prose. There are very few new poems in this selection. Those that are of special interest will be discussed along with the ones from earlier publications. In fact, all of McKay's poems will be treated as a unit without too much attention to the volume from which they came, unless the source has particular significance.

Certain themes run throughout McKay's poetry, themes to which he returns again and again. Interestingly, the most popular theme (based on the number of poems devoted to it) is not racial, as one would expect. It is nostalgia, the poet's longing for his tropical homeland, the poet comparing the cold north to his southern island. This theme is found in "North and South," "Wild May," "I Shall Return," "Tropics in New York," and others; but perhaps the finest expression is in "Flame Heart":

> So much have I forgotten in ten years,
>   So much in ten brief years! I have forgot
> What time the purple apple comes to juice,
>   And what month brings the shy forget-me-not.
> I have forgot the special, startling season
>   Of the pimento's flowering and fruiting;
> What time of year the ground doves brown the fields
>   And fill the noonday with their curious fluting.
> I have forgotten much, but still remember
> The poinsettia's red, blood red in warm December.

A second popular theme in McKay is that of the city. He seems to be fascinated with the bustling life of a metropolis like New York, but his attitude is a love-hate affair. For example, in "The City's Love" he tells us that "For one brief golden moment rare like wine,/ The gracious city swept across the line;/ Oblivious of the color of my skin,/ Forgetting that I was an alien guest,/ She bent to me, my hostile heart to win. . . ." But in "The White City" the "hostile heart" is very much in evidence. "I will not toy with it nor bend an inch./ Deep in the secret chambers of my heart/ I muse my life-long hate. . . ." One notes that this hatred of the city is not always racial. It has Wordsworthian overtones on occasion, the disgust of a lover of nature having to return to the ugliness of city living. Witness these verses from "Winter in the Country": "But oh! to leave this paradise/ For the city's dirty basement room. . . ."

McKay also shows his "hostile heart" in a group of very effective poems dealing with the challenge of America to an alien—to a Negro. Two of the best and best known of this group are "America" and "Baptism." In both poems he makes of American animosity an incentive, not to fight back with hate for hate, but as a trial to bring forth the best in him. In "Baptism" McKay uses a crucible image: "Into the furnace let me go along;/ . . . I will come out, back to your world of tears,/ A stronger soul within a finer frame." This poem has always been construed as a racial poem, but there is no mention of race in it; the same is true of "America," which has the same theme:

> Although she feeds me bread of bitterness,
> And sinks into my throat her tiger's tooth,
> Stealing my breath of life, I will confess
> I love this cultured hell that tests my youth!
> Her vigor flows like tides into my blood,
> Giving me strength erect against her hate.
> Her bigness sweeps my being like a flood.

We must remember that McKay was repelled almost as much by America's mechanized civilization as he was by its prejudice. He was essentially a late Rousseauist—anti-city, anti-Western industrial and commericial living. And yet again, his was an ambivalent attitude, a hatred mingled with respect and with love, as he admits in his autobiography:

> For I was in love with the large rough classical rhythms of American life. If I were sometimes awed by its brutal bigness, I was nevertheless fascinated by its titanic strength. I rejoiced in the lavishness of the engineering exploits and the architectural splendors of New York.[10]

As we have seen in the poem "Flame Heart," quoted earlier, McKay had a deep and abiding interest in nature and, like the nineteenth-century romanticists, was a keen observer of it. In many of his poems— "North and South," "After the Winter," "Spring in New Hampshire," to mention a few—he describes nature with his eye on the subject. This is particularly true of the nostalgic poems in which he recalls childhood memories of the fields and streams and flowers of his homeland.

There are several minor themes in McKay's poetry which became of major importance during the Renaissance. His treatment of Harlem ("Harlem Shadows" and "The Harlem Dancer") set a pattern that would be repeated many times by later poets, especially Hughes. In the second of these Harlem poems, he adumbrates the alien-and-exile theme, which was to be carried to its highest artistic expression in Cullen's "Heritage." His treatment of Africa is ambivalent. In the poem called "Africa" he speaks of the glory and power that belonged to the Black Continent, but he then concludes: "They went. The darkness swallowed thee again./ Thou art the harlot, now thy time is done,/ Of all the mighty nations of the sun." In the poem "Enslaved" McKay speaks

10. *A Long Way from Home*. New York: Lee Furman, 1937, p. 244.

bitterly of "my long-suffering race," "denied a human place" in "the Christian West." When he broods on these things his "heart goes sick with hate," "for this my race that has no home on earth." One last poem, "Exhortation: Summer 1919," is a fervent appeal to "Africa! long ages sleeping" to awake and face the new day in the East. This point of view is certainly far harsher and far more realistic than the many poems to come later in the Renaissance, poems playing up Africa as the beautiful homeland. McKay's picture is also quite different from that of his fellow Jamaican, Marcus Garvey, the father and leader of the Back-to-Africa Movement.

The poems for which Claude McKay is best known may be subsumed under the rubic *race*. Among these are "The White House" (which does not appear in either of the two works discussed here), "The Lynching," and "If We Must Die." In the first piece (often entitled "White Houses"),[11] the poet writes with restrained fury against American race hatred (again never using racial terms):

> Your door is shut against my tightened face,
> And I am sharp as steel with discontent . . .
> A chafing savage, down the decent street . . .
> Oh, I must search for wisdom every hour,
> Deep in my wrathful bosom sore and raw,
> And find in it the superhuman power
> To hold me to the letter of your law!
> Oh, I must keep my heart inviolate
> Against the potent poison of your hate.

There is a whiplash in the final couplet. Note also the restraint of the "chafing savage" clinging to a civilized law and order in spite of the "potent poison" of American race hatred. "The Lynching," with its subtle and designedly ambiguous suggestion of Christ's crucifixion, ends with four powerful lines, lines that concisely detail the horror of lynching far better than whole chapters written on the subject:

> The women thronged to look, but never a one
> Showed sorrow in her eyes of steely blue;
> And little lads, lynchers that were to be,
> Danced round the dreadful thing in fiendish glee.

"If We Must Die" is the best known of McKay's poems. During the Renaissance it became a kind of rallying cry for young Negro writers, who felt it expressed their new spirit of defiance. White America con-

11. The poem was sent in manuscript to Alain Locke, who changed the title from "The White House" to "White Houses." McKay never forgave Locke this bit of editing.

sidered the poem radical and incendiary, and Henry Cabot Lodge had it entered in the Congressional Record (1919) because of its bitterness. But, again, there are no references to race in the piece, and, as is generally known, Winston Churchill used it in 1939 to bolster British morale during the worst period of World War II.

In the *Selected Poems* there are several race poems not found in the first two works. Among them are "The Negro's Tragedy," "The Negro's Friend," "Look Within," and "Tiger." McKay has lost some of his subtlety; he tends to state more and suggest less. The poems show an aging on his part rather than a maturing. They are run-of-the-mill protest verse, lacking the magic of his earlier race poems.

Two or three pieces in *Selected Poems* have autobiographical significance. Reared as a freethinker and contemptuous most of his life of organized religion, McKay in his late years became a Roman Catholic. These poems, "Truth" and "The Pagan Isms," show McKay, after "years of Unbelief," humbly asking help from the "Holy Church." The "damned white education" that he complains about in his autobiography seems to have won out over his earlier pagan convictions.

The poetry of Claude McKay is classic expression—clear, sculptured, restrained. Much of his early and best work is written in sonnet form. He seems to like the limitation which the sonnet placed on him, and he used those limitations superbly. Very few writers surpass him in economy of phrasing. It should be noted that his restraint in the use of racial tags and terms makes his poems more than Negro affirmations of defiance and protest. His poems—that is, his best poems—are, as Max Eastman has said, "characteristic of what is deep and universal in mankind."

Although he was much more prolific as a fiction writer than as a poet, McKay in all probability will be remembered for his verse far longer than for his prose. He seems to be a curiously ambivalent figure: though rigidly classic in his poetry, he was convinced that the primitive side of Negro life was more honest and more significant than the sophisticated side, the side that had adopted Western culture. In his autobiography, *A Long Way from Home* (page 229), he wrote this concerning himself: "My damned white education has robbed me of much of the primitive vitality, the pure stamina, the simple unswaggering strength . . . of the Negro race." This conflict between his "white education" and belief in the rightness of the primitive approach is evidenced in most of his fiction,[12] and probably colored his later life.

McKay's most popular novel, possibly his most popular work, *Home to Harlem,* was published in 1928. Van Vechten's *Nigger Heaven* had

12. In this discussion of McKay's fiction I have used suggestions from Mr. John Wroblewski and Mrs. Emma W. Thomas, graduate students.

come out in 1925, and though McKay claimed that he was not influenced by Van Vechten's novel, several critics find similarities in the two works. *Home to Harlem* tells episodically the adventures of Jake, a likable, down-to-earth black "noble savage" who is a deserter from the United States Army. Jake joined the army to fight, and the government made him a laborer (stevedore), as it did most Negroes; he deserted in France. Returning to Harlem, Jake during his first night on the town picks up a lovely brown-skinned girl, Felice, who takes him to her room. When he leaves the next morning, he finds out that she had slipped into his pocket the money he had given her. Because he has fallen in love with her, Jake wants to see her again, but, unfortunately, he has forgotten the address. The rest of the novel takes Jake to many joints, dives, brothels, rent parties, and cabarets in his search for her. The persons with whom Jake works (he is a dining-car waiter), and the many characters, male and female, with whom he plays are the Harlem lower-class workers and hustlers who have nothing to do with the staid middle-class Negroes.

In this work, as in all of his fiction, McKay overplays his emphasis on the exotic and the primitive. As a kind of counter-balance, he creates as a foil for the primitive Jake, the character Ray, an educated foreign Negro who cannot fully understand Jake's attitude toward life. Ray could be McKay himself; or he could be one side of McKay's character, that side influenced by his "damned white education." Jake, of course, is the other half.

One of the first impressions that the reader of *Home to Harlem* receives is that the author is highly color conscious in several ways. As a matter of record he admits this in his autobiography: "What then was my main psychological problem? It was the problem of color. Color-consciousness was the fundamental of my restlessness."[13] In this particular quote he has whites in mind, but it applies equally well to Negroes. McKay seems to revel in the different shades of Negro coloration: "chocolate, chestnut, coffee, ebony, cream, yellow." One of his minor characters, Yaller Prince, is kept by three women: "one chocolate-to-the-bone, one teasing brown, and one yellow." On one occasion he speaks of the "keen ecstatic joy a man feels in the romance of being black."[14] He was convinced that not even New York, that "great metropolitan mill," could grind out of Negroes "their native color and laughter." McKay, however, had a decided bias against light-colored Negroes, and he tended to make them the sorriest of the many sorry characters he created. He spells out in great detail the Negro's self-hatred, the lower-class black's distrust of "dicties," the black man's tendency to

13. *A Long Way from Home*. New York: Lee Furman, 1937, p. 245.
14. *Home to Harlem*. New York: Harper Bros., 1928, p. 154.

desire light-skinned women and his dislike of the light-complexioned male.

Because he dealt exclusively with the seamier side of Harlem Negro life, McKay brought down upon himself the wrath of several important Negro critics, Du Bois among them. Du Bois felt that the book was not "wholly bad." "McKay is too great a poet to make any complete failure in writing." But Du Bois definitely detested the subject matter of the novel: "It nauseates me, and after the dirtier parts of its filth I feel distinctly like taking a bath. . . . It looks as though McKay has set out to cater to that prurient demand on the part of white folk for a portrayal in Negroes of that utter licentiousness which civilization holds white folk back from enjoying—if enjoyment it can be called." There is a real confrontation here. McKay's implied thesis in *Home to Harlem* is that the lower-class Negro, denied the civilizing opportunities of the white man, is the better off because of it. He is more natural and is not distressed as the whites are by the frustrations of an artificial, sterile way of life which is the modern way. On the other hand, Du Bois, who is alleged to have referred to McKay's characters as "the debauched Tenth," insists that Negroes should learn everything about Western civilization that anybody else learns; and when Negroes write about themselves, they should put their best foot foremost (as Jessie Fauset did in her pale novels). McKay let the race down, Du Bois implies.

The contentions of recent critics are perhaps more valid than those of Du Bois. Gloster[15] felt that *Home to Harlem* was too one-sided; it did not give a full picture of the black metropolis. Bone[16] insists that McKay failed to convince the reader that the way of primitivism was superior to the decorous way of the middle-class Negro. And Sterling Brown felt that McKay, who knew the inner life of Harlem so well, failed to produce the kind of full and authentic picture that he was capable of painting.

Banjo: A Story Without a Plot (1929) is essentially *Home to Harlem* moved to the Ditch in Marseilles, the section of that polyglot city in which the working class, the bums, the prostitutes, and other underground people live. The primitive "hero" here is Banjo, an American Negro musician who has what one would now call a combo. He lives with Latnah, an Arabian woman, and his friend is Ray (of *Home to Harlem*). Banjo's way of life is simple. After he has organized his musical group, he goes from dive to dive playing jazz, not really for money but for the love of it. Ray the intellectual, who could not accept

15. Hugh M. Gloster, *Negro Voices in American Fiction*. Chapel Hill: University of North Carolina Press, 1948.
16. Robert A. Bone, *The Negro Novel in America*. Rev. ed. New Haven, Connecticut: Yale University Press, 1965.

Jake's way of life and therefore leaves at the end of the first novel, seems to capitulate in *Banjo*. The fight against white civilization, with all of its smugness and sterility, is even more intense here than in *Home to Harlem;* but, again, McKay is not equal to the task of convincing the reader that Banjo's life style is a desirable one. Frankly, it seems remarkably dull and monotonous. The work, of course, contains all of McKay's pet themes: the hypocrisy of the Negro middle class, color prejudice among Negroes themselves, the superiority of African primitives to American and West Indian blacks. It is also highly antireligious. As a substitute for the existing survival movements among Negroes, he seems to be urging them to study the Irish revolution, the Russian revolution, and the Indian people's movement under Ghandi. There is a certain falseness about *Banjo,* which suggests to the reader that McKay, above all else, was simply capitalizing on the formula which had proved so successful in his first novel.

The last novel, *Banana Bottom* (1933), though belaboring the same primitive thesis found in the first two, is artistically a better work than either *Home to Harlem* or *Banjo*—it has a better plot, better developed characters, and certainly a far fresher scene. The story is placed in Jamaica, McKay's homeland, and he is portraying major and minor characters whose prototypes he probably knew as a boy and youth. The central figure is Bita, a handsome black peasant girl, in some ways a female counterpart of Jake. She is raped when only twelve by Crazy Bow, a town "character." The English missionaries Malcolm and Priscilla Craig (symbols seemingly of all that McKay found hypocritical and unnatural in Anglican puritanism) adopt Bita and are determined through their Christian effort to erase from Bita's memory the degrading experience. They educate her in the island and in England, and when they are certain they have created a vessel worthy to carry on their work, Bita becomes friendly with Squire Gensir, an enlightened Englishman, a nonbeliever, and an advocate of the primitive way of life and thought for the blacks. (Gensir is probably based on Edward Jekyll, the Englishman who influenced McKay's early years.) Bita begins to make her own decisions and, repudiating the way of the Craigs, she follows her own natural inclinations, marries Jubban, her father's drayman, after he has made her pregnant. Although there are some good whites in this work, McKay still rides the same hobbyhorse, the superiority of the simple native naturalness towards sex and life as contrasted with the sterility and hypocrisy of white religion. He is also repeating his anti-mulatto tirades and parading his anti-light-skinned Negro bias.

Color consciousness plays a very important part in the short stories of McKay found in *Gingertown* (1932). The work's name refers to a fictitious Jamaican town, but six of its twelve stories deal with Harlem

Claude McKay

Photo by Carl Van Vechten, Collection of American Literature, Beinecke Rare Book and Manuscript Library, Yale University.

life. The color-caste problem runs through all of the six stories—the conflict between light-colored and dark-skinned Negroes, the conflict between black and white, and the conflict between lower- and middle-class Negroes. For the most part the same kinds of characters found in *Home to Harlem* are paraded here. One poignant story, "Brownskin Blues," concerns Bess, a pretty cabaret singer who loses her dark "sweetman" to a yellow girl. In order to get him back she tries to bleach her skin, but ends in marring it and ruining her good looks *and* her career, because no cabaret owner will now hire her as an entertainer. Of all the Negro writers, McKay was perhaps the one most obsessed with the color differences within the race. Needless to say, he distorts them flagrantly.

McKay's *A Long Way from Home* (1937)[17] is not a wholly honest autobiography. It tells us a lot about those experiences of McKay which he wants us to know, and it slurs over or ignores certain significant episodes in his life: his marriage, for instance, and his brief stay in a Negro school—episodes that the reader would find most interesting. All too often McKay uses a very small and vague bit of autobiographical data to launch into a critical essay. His comments on H. G. Wells are a case in point (pages 122 ff.). Indirectly, however, the work does tell us many things about the character and personality of the author—some of them not pleasant. First of all, he emerges from these pages as a chronic and highly skillful "moocher." He was supported, given trips, and subsidized by many of his friends and patrons, white and black. And we get the impression that he took such help for granted. We also find that in spite of all his breast-beating about being black, he was essentially a "white-folks-nigger." His revolutionary pose is never quite convincing. His concern for the proletariat, despite his Russian idolization, never comes through; in fact, he says very little about the waiters and other lower-class persons with whom he worked. On the contrary, he tends to be a name-dropper. Frank Harris, Max Eastman, Mrs. Pankhurst, Nancy Cunard, and many other white celebrities cross the pages, but very few Negro names are dropped.

One gets the impression that McKay remained all of his life fanatically color conscious. He sees and reacts to the man's color long before he knows the person. Note his treatment of a member of the official American Communist delegation to Russia (pages 159 ff.). He is also anti-Negro middle class, whom he calls the elite (pages 130 and 155). Note also his contemptuous reference to NAACP officials as the "more conservative Negro leaders" (pages 109–110). McKay impresses us as being actually anti-American Negro, and when he writes about Ameri-

17. The original edition of this work (New York: Lee Furman, Inc., 1937) is used here. All page references in the text are from this edition.

can blacks, he tends to assume that irritating *distant* attitude which whites assume when *they* write about the darker brother.

A Long Way from Home, in spite of these obvious shortcomings, is a fascinating work. The author lived a full life in many parts of the world; he knew many of the era's intellectual leaders; and he knew how to make his blackness pay off in a period when interest in the Negro was beginning to burgeon. Moreover, his style is clear and nervous and readable. Reading the work is like talking to an intelligent, sensitive (in both senses of the word), and resentful man of letters—one who has positive dislikes and who is willing to write about them without hesitancy.

Seen in perspective, McKay is not as impressive as he looked in the twenties and thirties. In all probability, very little of his fiction will survive, with the possible exception of *Banana Bottom;* it is too loosely constructed and too topical. His major thesis, the superiority of the primitive black to the middle-class Negro and to the white, was not tenable when he wrote it, and in spite of many foolish things now being said in the name of *blackness,* is not tenable now. The works of McKay which seem most likely to survive are those few poems of the "Flame-Heart" type and that group of racial sonnets of the "If We Must Die" attitude. McKay never bettered these early sonnets and lyrics. Excellent poetry in any language, they will survive their century.

Jean Toomer

After labeling Jean Toomer a Planter or "Father" of the New Negro Movement, one immediately thinks of the differences between Toomer and the other Planters. Toomer published only one significant volume, *Cane* (1923), and not too long thereafter he simply left the race. (Toomer was a "volunteer Negro," that is, he was light enough in color to pass for white.) On the surface this may seem to put in question his status as a Planter, but actually it does not. In this one work, which some critics feel is the most important product of the Renaissance, Toomer made an impressive and lasting contribution to Negro literature.

The grandson of P. B. S. Pinchback, the Reconstruction lieutenant governor and acting governor of Louisiana, Jean Toomer was born in

Washington, D.C., in 1894. His family lived first in a well-to-do white neighborhood in Washington, moving after Pinchback's decline in fortune to a black neighborhood.

A rather undedicated student at Dunbar High School, Toomer studied agriculture for a semester at the University of Wisconsin, attended the Massachusetts College for Agriculture for a week, and then enrolled in a physical training college in Chicago. Rejected by the draft in World War I, he took odd jobs—selling cars in Chicago, teaching physical education in Milwaukee, working as a ship fitter in New Jersey. In 1921 he served as a temporary superintendent of a small Negro industrial school in rural Georgia, an experience that inspired much of *Cane*.

Beginning in 1924 Toomer spent several summers at the Gurdjieff Institute, Fontainebleau, France. In the fall he would organize psychological experiments in the United States, an activity that earned a rather amused and scornful comment from Langston Hughes in his autobiography, *The Big Sea*.[18] After 1926 Toomer underwent a psychological experience which he termed his second conception. His previous lack of purpose and direction gave way to a strong attachment to his new philosophy, which was a mixture of psychology and mysticism.

Among the many works that Toomer wrote, most of them unpublished, were a number of plays. The drama *Natalie Mann* appeared in revised form as "Kabnis" in *Cane. Balo,* the only Toomer play ever produced on stage, appeared in *Plays of Negro Life* (1927), edited by Alain Locke and Montgomery Gregory. Several plays followed: *The Sacred Factory* (1927), *The Gallonwerps* (1928), originally a satirical novel transformed into a play for gigantic marionettes; *A Drama of the Southwest* (1935); some Socratic dialogues for *New Mexico Literary Sentinel* (1937, 1941); and an unpublished satirical drama in 1947.

Appearing in 1923, *Cane* exemplified an objectivity, an artistry, and a stylistic approach entirely new to Negro writing. It made a cleaner break with Negro literary tradition than any other work published before 1923, and for a long time thereafter.

Cane had two printings, the second in 1927 (there is now a 1967 reprint).[19] Sections of the book had appeared in *Broom, The Crisis,*

18. In *The Big Sea* (pp. 241–43) Langston Hughes remarks caustically on Toomer's attempt to bring the "gospel" of Gurdjieff to Harlem. Since Harlemites had to work, Hughes said, and therefore had neither time for contemplation nor the money to pay Toomer for lessons, Toomer gave up Harlem, went downtown, and became a great success. He subsequently married a rich white woman and left the race. When James Weldon Johnson asked Toomer for permission to use Toomer's poems in the *Book of American Negro Poetry,* he was refused. Toomer did not want his verse published in a book of *Negro* writings.
19. All page references here are to that edition, published by the University Place Press (New York, 1967).

Double Dealer, Liberator, Little Review, Modern Review, Nomad, Prairie Schooner, and *S4N.* It was praised by distinguished critics and writers such as Gorham Munson, Sherwood Anderson, and Waldo Frank; but it sold only five hundred copies the first year.[20]

The work is classed as a novel, but in reality it is a mélange of poems, prose sketches, short stories, and drama. Although seemingly a potpourri, *Cane* has a tonal unity—a unity achieved through the contrapuntal contrast of Negro life in rural Georgia with that in Washington, D.C. More like a musical composition than a literary production, *Cane*'s recurring themes and images (to be discussed later) remind one of leitmotifs in music. Appearing throughout the work, they emphasize the tonal oneness of the book, connecting prose, poetry, and drama to build up as it were *Cane*'s overriding theme: the importance of the soil to the Negro.

In *The New Negro* (1925), Toomer has the following revealing statement:

> Georgia opened me. And it may well be said that I received my initial impulse to an individual art from my experience there. For no other section of the country has so stirred me. There one finds soil, soil in the sense the Russians know it,—the soil every art and literature that is to live must be imbedded in.

It is difficult to overemphasize the influence of the soil in *Cane.* Pervading the work is a brooding sense of the "pain and beauty" the Negro finds in the soil of the rural South, as contrasted with the rootlessness and sterility he finds in city living.

Cane is divided into three sections or movements (following our musical comparison). The first, consisting of sixteen prose and poetical parts, concerns the South. The theme poem for this movement seems to be "Georgia Dusk," for in it are adumbrated practically all of the themes developed in the first movement: the suggestiveness of the African background ("Race Memories of king and caravan"); the ever-present awareness of the soil ("plowed lands fulfill/ Their early promise of a bumper crop"); the recurring symbols of cane and pine ("the chorus of the cane,"; "the sacred whisper of the pines"); the lust of the South ("Give virgin lips to cornfield concubines"); the importance of religion to the Negro ("Bring dreams of Christ to dusky cane-lipped throngs"); the beauty of the land ("The setting sun . . ./ a lengthened tournament for flashing gold"); the music of the soil ("O singers, resinous and soft your songs"); the ability of the Negro to transform his pain into artistic acceptance ("Surprised in making folk-songs from soul sounds").

20. Robert A. Bone, *The Negro Novel in America,* rev. ed. New Haven, Connecticut: Yale University Press, 1965.

This first movement has an effeminate quality—not necessarily a softness, but the brooding effeminacy of the Sphinx. One notes immediately that five of the sixteen parts have female name titles, and these sections deal with a group of women never portrayed before in Negro literature: Karintha is a beautiful woman whom men seek, but they will never find out that "the soul of her was a growing thing ripened too soon"; Becky is a white woman who gives birth to two Negro sons; Carma is as "strong as any man," but her actions land her husband on the chain gang; the part-Jewish Fern whose eyes "desired nothing that you could give her" and yet men feel compelled to do things for her; the light-skinned, chaste, middle-class Esther, who tries to give herself to a muscular black Negro preacher but is repulsed. "Blood Burning Moon" does not have a female title, but its central character, Louisa, causes the death of two men, one black, the other white. Three poems in the movement have female personae: "Face," "Evening Song," and "Portrait in Georgia." All of these women are strange; there is an unfathomable depth in them which springs from the soil of their homeland. Each is an individual, but each tells us a lot about her Southern sisters.

The second movement of *Cane* deals with Washington, the mecca of middle-class Negroes during the early decades of the present century. The second division has twelve poetical and prose sections. The tone here is harsher and more strident than that of the first movement. Here is the Negro removed from the soil. His roots cannot penetrate the cement and asphalt of the city; he therefore lives for the most part in a surface world, the kind of world described in the thematic entry "Seventh Street." Seventh Street is a "bastard of Prohibition and the War." (The use of the word *bastard* is significant.) It is "a crude-boned, soft-skinned wedge of nigger life breathing its loafer air; jazz songs and love, thrusting unconscious rhythms, black reddish blood into the whitewashed wood of Washington. Stale soggy wood of Washington."

The mood of the second movement is set by this short sketch, even though the meaning may baffle the reader. It suggests that the Negro who made "soul sounds" in Georgia here makes jazz songs. The war money and the Prohibition money, in spite of "silken shirts" and "zooming cadillacs," has corrupted the Negro and made him "crude-boned" and "soft-skinned." His background is not the soil, but the "Stale soggy wood of Washington. Wedges (nigger life) rust in soggy wood." And, by contrast, Toomer suggests that in spite of the lust and pain found in the South, there is a beauty, a depth to life, and a kind of mystery not felt on the shabby, commercial Seventh streets of the city.

There is no joy, no fulfillment on Seventh Street. "Rhobert," note the affected spelling, wears a "house" (middle-class striving for possessions?) on his head like a "monstrous diving helmet." Naturally, it weighs him down, down. "Avery," another of Toomer's hard-to-understand but intriguing female characters, is an "orphan woman," one who seeks but cannot find a *home* in the decent, patterned, and dull life prescribed for her kind of *nice* girl in Washington. "Theater" points out dramatically the distance between the comfortable better-class Negroes and the *other* Negroes in a place like Washington. "Box Seat," itself an image of pretentiousness, implies the sterility and stuffiness of a life dominated by a puritan landlady. The grotesque symbolism of the fighting dwarfs (little people knocking themselves out) suggests the smallness, the nothingness of it all. "Bona and Paul" is a very subtle "inside" study of the nuances of understanding between a light-colored Negro college boy who has a white date and the black doorman at the Crimson Gardens, where they have danced. "Bona and Paul" is the only story or sketch whose scene is set outside Washington.

The third movement of *Cane* is perhaps the most intriguing and challenging of the three. We are returned to the Georgia scene and given a cast of characters representing several important ways Negroes have adapted to survive in the South—a region to which most have a sort of love-hate relationship. Fred Halsey is the independent Negro artisan who is not too beholden to white folks, whom he understands well and can therefore fool when necessary. He has a great love of the soil from which he sprang. Happy nowhere else, he finds satisfaction so long as he can work with his hands, creating and repairing things. Hanby is almost a stereotype—the pompous, tyrannical, and prudish principal of a Negro school. Lewis reminds one of a present-day union leader. A "trouble-maker," he disturbs the Negroes more than he does the whites. Layman is a traveling teacher-preacher who knows much but has learned the survival wisdom of keeping his mouth shut. Stella, Halsey's sometime mistress, is a tragic victim of a white man's lust for her mother.

The titular character, Kabnis, is a complex and mixed-up soul. A Northern, educated, light-skinned Negro who has returned to the land of his ancestors (blue-blooded and black) to teach in Hanby's school, he is a coward, a drunkard, a sexual neuter, and a misguided dreamer and idealist who fancies himself an artist with words. He boasts that he comes from a family of "orators," not preachers: "Been shaping words t fit my soul" (page 223). Toomer describes Kabnis as "a promise of a soil-soaked beauty; uprooted, thinning out. Suspended a few feet above the soil whose touch would resurrect him" (page 191). Kabnis in his mixed-up soul is attracted and repelled by "nigger religion." Although he curses both God and Father John, he is moved by the singing in a nearby church and is greatly disturbed by Father John's mumbling about "Sin and Death" (page 231). If there is any progression in the drama, it concerns the journey of Kabnis through the dark night of his soul to find some sort of solace from Carrie K., Halsey's virgin and innocent sister. Kabnis calls her a child ("a little child shall lead them") and kneels before her. She in turn kneels before Father John and murmurs, "Jesus, come."

"Kabnis" is a storehouse of allusion and symbolism. There is, of course, a great temptation to read into it many things not there. Underneath all of these elusive meanings, however, one finds a profound knowledge of the Southern scene—its "pain and beauty." There is no overt protest here, but Toomer was always aware of the South's cruelty. Note, for example, his handling of a particularly gruesome lynching scene (pages 178–179). The reader receives a double shock from the description: first, from the horror of the deed itself; second, from the almost casual way in which it is related. And then, before the horror can sink in, a piercing scream comes from a nearby church as a sister "comes through" to Jesus. The scream serves as a sort of Greek-chorus reaction to the lynching, but it also stops the mind from dwelling on the act. A lesser artist would have drawn out every bitter detail of the crime. Toomer prefers to have it stored in the reader's mind along with other impressions of the South, that region of "pain and beauty."

The poems in *Cane* echo, foreshadow, and intensify the themes found in the prose works. As stated earlier, Toomer makes constant use in both prose and poetry of a set of image-symbols, among them cane, pine, the sawdust pile (smoldering or burning), African vestiges, growth and ripeness, dusk, and singing. The two most popular are cane and pine, and they are often combined with the others mentioned to construct a multiple image.

Toomer's two most popular image-symbols are used as though they were abstract concepts rather than physical objects. Nowhere does he describe a cane field or talk about the shape and tallness of some one tree or pine trees in general. Even his piles of pine sawdust tend to be abstractions. Toomer, of course, *can* write with his eye on the subject. His descriptions of certain theatres and places in Washington are very precise. In his Georgia scenes, however, he uses cane and pine trees as one would a recurring musical theme. Whenever the reader comes across either, and this is quite often, he is probably expected to set his mind for a certain mood, seldom, if ever, happy or joyous, usually sad or bitter. In "Nullo," for example, a falling spray of pine needles, though "Dipped in western horizon gold," seems to express a sense of futility. In "Carma" the wind makes the cane leaves "rusty with talk,/ Scratching choruses above the guinea's squawk." In "Georgia Dusk" the author writes of "blood-shot eyes and cane lipped scented mouth."

In the same poem the smoke from the "pyramidal sawdust pile" suggests the devastation of the soil by lumbering activities—a devastation that leaves only "chips and stumps" as evidence of "former domicile." For Toomer, the pine trees are guitars; they accompany, however, not a joyous or gay song, but rather "the chorus of the cane/ . . . caroling a vesper to the stars." The "velvet pine-smoke air of night" theme or image is used often because dusk is the favorite time of day in *Cane.* Toomer's concern with dusk, evening, and night reminds one of the eighteenth-century poets William Collins and Thomas Gray. On occasion he uses an African image ("High-priests, an ostrich, and a jujuman") to suggest the sadness of a departed glory. In practically all these recurring image-symbols there is a brooding, autumnal tone which illuminates the "beauty and pain" of a dying land and a vanishing people; the images also speak of cruelty, lust, death, and the music of "a songlit race of slaves" on whom the sun is setting.

The style of *Cane* is difficult to characterize. It has, of course, certain surface mannerisms: peculiar spellings ("an" for "and"; "godam" for "goddamn"); interesting dialect abbreviations ("t" for "to"; "y" for "you"); the omission of punctuation for contractions ("cant" for "can't"); and a frequent and effective use of repetition, not only of the recurring image-symbols mentioned but also of any line the author feels significant. Again, music comes to mind, because Toomer uses these lines as one would a refrain. His prose as well as his poetry is lyrical and word-happy. The speech is folk speech, and it often has the lilting rhythm of spirituals. Perhaps his outstanding stylistic effect is the indirect way in which he suggests strong feeling without belaboring the attempt. "Portrait in Georgia" is a good case in point:

> Hair—braided chestnut,
>   coiled like a lynchers rope,
> Eyes—fagots
> Lips—old scars, or the first red blisters,
> Breath—the last sweet scent of cane,
> And her slim body, white as the ash
>   of black flesh after flame.

The poem is as scathing a denunciation of lynching as McKay's better known and more obvious treatment. But it is also more than that; there are other subtle overtones of meaning. Is he writing about a girl, a white girl like the one in *Dutchman,* who could bring death or disease or both to a would-be black lover? Is he characterizing the Southland? The decision he leaves to the reader. The end of "Kabnis" is another example of subtle suggestion. When Father John does talk, he manages to articulate the following sentence: "Th sin whats fixed . . . upon the white folks

Jean Toomer

JEAN TOOMER
AUTHOR OF
CANE
PUBLISHED BY BONI & LIVERIGHT $2.00

Courtesy of Moorland-Spingarn Research Center, Howard University.

—f telling Jesus—lies. O th sin th white folks 'mitted when they made th Bible lie." Does the meaning of the drama depend upon understanding this cryptic sentence? Again, the reader must find his own answer.

"Song of the Son" is obviously one of the key poems in *Cane*. In it the speaker describes himself as a son, returning late but yet in time to catch the plaintive soul of his native "soil," the "plaintive soul soon gone" of a "passing generation." The son-speaker brings to his observations a "blood" sympathy but also an outsider's objectivity. No white man could have written this work. Perhaps no Negro who had to spend all of his life in Georgia could have written it. Because of his dual background (North and South) and his status as a "volunteer Negro," Toomer could walk and *feel* on both sides of the racial street. It is this combination that accounts in part for *Cane*'s excellence.

Alain LeRoy Locke

Of the five major Planters, Alain LeRoy Locke is the only one to qualify on the basis of his work as an editor and critic. Among Negro writers, literary criticism has been one of the weaker disciplines. Until quite recently, there has been no large body of criticism coming from black scholars. The first critics of consequence wrote during the New Negro Renaissance, and Alain Locke was of that group.

Dr. Locke really played a triple role in the Renaissance. First, he crystallized and dramatized the movement through his editing of the "Harlem Issue" of the *Survey Graphic,* which enlarged became *The New Negro* (1925), a landmark in black literature. Second, he articulated the critical tenets of the period, adding, of course, his own interpretations and justifications. And, third, he made it his business to know and encourage and advise younger writers, editing and placing their manuscripts.

All the Planters, obviously, had a hand in shaping the Harlem Renaissance, but Locke was more of a direct catalyst than any of the others. A Locke scholar, Eugene C. Holmes, believes: "As critic, philosopher, and teacher, [Locke] did more to shape the attitude and the thinking of a generation of Negro youth than any other educator of his time."[21]

21. "Alain LeRoy Locke: A Sketch." *Phylon* (First Quarter, Spring, 1959), p. 82.

Alain Locke was born in September, 1866, in Philadelphia, Pennsylvania. Educated at Harvard (Phi Beta Kappa, 1907; Ph.D., 1918), Oxford (as the first Negro Rhodes Scholar, 1907–1910), Berlin, and the College of France, Alain Locke studied under Münstenberg, Peirce, Kittredge, Royce, Santayana, and Bergson, receiving the finest education that the Western world could give at the time. He, therefore, brought to the criticism of the New Negro literature a knowledge and a cosmopolitan insight and experience rare among Americans of his day, black or white. Though trained in philosophy, Locke considered himself "more of a philosophical mid-wife to a generation of younger Negro poets, writers, and artists than a professional philosopher." And he was certainly that. His interests were broader than those of the other Planters—he knew art and music as well as literature—and, as a college professor, he was more at home with the young than Du Bois or James Weldon Johnson. He, therefore, became a kind of oracle/gadfly for most of the young writers of the Renaissance, including McKay, Toomer, Cullen, and Hughes.

A many-sided man, Locke published works on Negro art, Negro music, and African art. (He was an early collector in this field, and his very valuable collection is now housed at Howard University.) He helped to motivate the least developed of all Negro disciplines: drama. With Montgomery Gregory, then a professor at Howard University, he established the Howard Players, one of the earliest Little Theatre Groups among Negroes. Also with Gregory he edited the first Negro drama anthology, *Plays of Negro Life* (1927). During the thirties he was editor in chief of the Bronze Booklet Series, a publishing venture designed to "bring within the reach of the average reader basic facts and progressive views about Negro life." The booklets presented the "Negro's own views of his history, problems, and cultural contributions with competent Negro scholars as spokesmen." He contributed to the *Encyclopaedia Britannica* on Negro culture and Harlem from 1940 to 1945, and he wrote regular reviews of contemporary literature for *Opportunity* (1929–1940) and *Phylon* (1947–1953). In 1951–1952 he was granted a leave of absence from Howard to produce a book, *The Negro in American Culture,* but he never finished the task. The book was completed by Margaret Just Butcher in 1956 after Locke's death in 1954.

Locke undoubtedly possessed a brilliant and well-furnished mind, but his writings are not always as clear as they should be. On occasion he seemed to be hiding behind words, and his meaning, as a consequence, eludes the reader. Moreover, he tended to speak and write in generalities, using abstract statements rather than specific and concrete facts and illustrations. Like Samuel Johnson, he was addicted to "tryptology," often saying the same thing two or three times in a slightly altered form. In fairness, however, it must be said that in practically every article or essay he wrote there are occasional scintillating and memorable phrases, sentences, and even paragraphs. Unfortunately, these are the exceptions rather than the rule. Because of this tendency to vagueness in Dr. Locke's critical writings, it is often hard to state his position with definiteness; and this is perhaps as it should be. Dr. Locke was a cultural pluralist and did not believe in absolutes of any kind. During the years he changed his attitude in small ways, but he never seemed to lose faith, as we shall see, in two positions he espoused during the New Negro years: the all-importance of the Negro's folk contribution and the significance of the African heritage. On these two themes his critical comments are fairly consistent.

For *The New Negro* Alain Locke wrote five essays: the "Foreword," "The New Negro," "Negro Youth Speaks," "The Negro Spirituals," and "The Legacy of the Ancestral Arts." In the "Foreword" the author tells America that "there is ample evidence of a New Negro in the latest phases of social change and progress, but still more in the internal world of the Negro mind." Heretofore, he continues, most American writing concerning the Negro has been *about* him, not *of* him. One must now learn *of* the Negro through the kind of self-portraiture found in this volume (*The New Negro*). We are witnessing, Locke contended, the kind of "resurgence of a people" found in Ireland, Russia, and other places; and because of it Negro life is "finding a new soul," its "heralding sign" has been "an unusual outburst of creative expression."

The titular essay, "The New Negro," spells out largely in social terms the message of the "Foreword." The two together constitute a kind of manifesto of the Renaissance—a manifesto serving notice to the nation that a transformation has taken place in the black minority. The Negro, it states emphatically, is no longer merely a formula—something to be argued about, kept down, kept in his place, defended; he is no longer a "social bogey or a social burden." The New Negro had shed the "old chrysalis of the Negro problem," and was now "achieving something like a spiritual emancipation." In short, the day of Uncle Toms and mammys was gone, and there is a new spirit of independence and a new outlook among Negroes of all classes.

For Locke, Harlem was the symbol of the new era and the new awareness because it brought together and fused so many diverse elements, sentiments, and experiences. Harlem, in short, became a laboratory for "race welding"; it promised to be a "race capital" that would play the role that Dublin played for the Irish. Given the new transforming forces at work and Harlem as the symbol, "The American mind must reckon with a fundamentally changed Negro"—a Negro inclined to be radical in tone but not in purpose; a Negro who was still an American, not a separatist, but one who would make the choice between frustrated American institutions on the one hand and progressively fulfilled American ideals on the other.

Locke felt that Negroes of the Harlem Renaissance era had a "consciousness of acting as the advance-guard of the African peoples in their contact with Twentieth Century civilization"; they had a "sense of a mission of rehabilitating the race in world esteem," which it had lost because of slavery. Persecution had made the Negro international; it tended to bring all the darker peoples together in a sort of black Zionism.

The titular article is social; it is an attempt to give the new attitude of the Negro as Locke saw it in 1925. The second article, "Negro Youth Speaks," is really an *artistic* manifesto of the New Negro Movement. Locke said here what he was to say and imply in several succeeding articles for collections and periodicals. His position is roughly this: the younger generation of Negroes, the "talented few" of that generation, were expressing the inarticulate stirrings among the masses. These young artists speak out of a "unique experience" and with a "special representativeness" because they have been welded emotionally through their common experience of suffering. "Their material handicap is their spiritual advantage."

Whereas Negro literature had formerly been "stiltedly self-conscious and racially rhetorical rather than racially expressive," the young poets had stopped speaking "for the Negro" and were then speaking "as Negroes." Whereas the Negro writer formerly spoke to others and tried to interpret, the younger writers spoke to their own and tried to express. They had been released from the self-consciousness, the rhetoric, the bombast, the "cautious moralisms," and the tendency always to be representative, to put the best foot foremost—all of these but "pathetic compensations of a group inferiority complex which our social dilemmas inflicted upon several unhappy generations." Released from this burden, the younger writers expressed themselves; "through acquiring ease and simplicity in serious expression" they "have carried the folk-gift to the attitudes of art." The young writers, he repeats again and again, "dig into the racy peasant undersoil of the race life," and they will derive from it something that is technically distinctive—new accents and rhythms—that will contribute to the "general resources of art."

He points out, however, that "not all of the new art is in the field of pure art values." There is, in addition, a "poetry of sturdy social protest," "fiction of calm, dispassionate social analysis," and forceful satire. The new writers, he found, possessed an instinctive love and pride of race and, compensating for present deficiencies in American living, an "ardent respect and love for Africa, the motherland." The wounds of the social persecution they suffered had wrought in them a "spiritual immunity," and they could, therefore, "offer through art an emancipating vision to America." (This sounds like Wright's "The Negro is America's metaphor.")

Alain Locke would probably have not been pleased to know it, but several of his stands look forward to the positions of the present-day black nationalists: the African emphasis, the importance of the folk contribution, the attempt of young writers to express themselves, and the black vision that had to become the "emancipating vision" of the Western world. Locke would have understood most of the aims of to-day's black nationalists, but their harshness and their insistence on separatism would have appalled him.

The third essay, "The Negro Spirituals," is the second extended treatment by a Negro critic of this great body of folk music and poetry. The first was Du Bois's "Of the Sorrow Songs" in *The Souls of Black Folk* (1903). Between Du Bois and Locke, Henry E. Krehbiel, a well-known American music critic, had written *Afro-American Folk Songs* (1915). Although Krehbiel published his work in 1915, he was actually defending the spirituals from an attack made on them in 1893 by Richard Wallaschek, a German musicologist, who said, in effect, that the spirituals were highly overrated imitations of European songs. The controversy over the origins of spirituals has not been settled yet. Locke certainly did not throw much light on the issue in this essay, which is more of an appreciation of these great folk works than a scholarly analysis.

"The Spirituals," Locke writes, "are the most characteristic product of the race genius as yet in America. But the very elements which make them uniquely expressive of the Negro make them at the same time deeply representative of the soil that produced them. Thus, as unique spiritual products of American life, they become nationally as well as racially characteristic." Locke believed the spirituals would eventually become America's folk songs because as "classic folk expression" they would be "fundamentally and everlastingly human." Locke, as a cultural pluralist, believed firmly in this kind of Negro American dualism.

Locke gives high praise to the spirituals and predicts that "an inevitable art development awaits them, as in the past it has awaited all other great folk music." In his appraisal of these songs Dr. Locke brings to bear a broad cultural background. His references range from Bernard of Clairvaux through John Bunyan, John Wesley, down to Du Bois and Krehbiel. At the time he was writing, several great interpreters of the spirituals were on the concert stage, among them Roland Hayes and Paul Robeson. Living also were the best-known and best Negro composers that the race had produced up to that time: Harry Burleigh, Carl Diton, and R. Nathaniel Dett. They, of course, arranged spirituals; they also created new compositions influenced by the spirituals. He mentions these men and their several styles of singing and arranging this great folk music.

For the spirituals, Locke made his usual plea: that they be studied more, that they not be bastardized, that they be, not merely preserved, but developed. He wanted them to be "the source, not the issue, of our musical tradition." Although he brought much to his discussion of the spirituals, Locke did not add anything significant to their study. He, of course, did not have the knowledge of folk literature that present-day scholars have.

In his discussion of the spirituals Locke commented not too enthusiastically on the division of these songs into two elements or sources: the melodic (European) and the rhythmic (African). As a matter of record, musicologists then did not know enough about the origins of the spirituals to make this type of division, and Locke was aware of that. He, therefore, warned against such an analysis. He stressed the *fusion* of three elements: the harmonic, the melodic, and the rhythmic.

When Professor Locke discussed "The Legacy of the Ancestral Arts," he was perhaps on firmer ground than he was when treating the origins of the spiritual. In this article he points out that the predominant arts of the American Negro have been music, poetry, and, to a lesser extent, dance, whereas the predominant arts of Africa have been plastic and craft arts. He concludes:

> Except then in his remarkable carry-over of the rhythmic gift, there is little evidence of any direct connection of the American Negro with his ancestral arts. But even with the rude transplanting of slavery, that uprooted the technical elements of his former culture, the American Negro brought over as an emotional inheritance a deep-seated aesthetic endowment. And with a versatility of a very high order, this offshoot of the African spirit blended itself in with entirely different elements and blossomed in strange new forms.

Although willing to give up the theory of African survivals as it applied to art, Locke, it seems to us, rather pathetically clings to a version of it here when he claims "an emotional inheritance."

Characteristic African art expressions, Locke points out, are "rigid, controlled, disciplined, abstract, heavily conventionalized," whereas those of the American Negro are "free, exuberant, emotional, sentimental and human." The two are almost exactly opposite in spirit. The outstanding qualities of the primitive Afro-American—"his naïveté, his sentimentalism, his exuberance, and his improvising spontaneity"—cannot be accepted as ancestral heritage; they are the result of his peculiar experience in America.

The American Negro should try to learn from African art the lessons

Alain LeRoy Locke

Photo by Carl Van Vechten, Collection of American Literature, Beinecke Rare
Book and Manuscript Library, Yale University.

of discipline, of style, of technical control, "but he must approach African art as would any other European. His only advantage would be the pride in knowing that his ancestors were capable of producing such art." The American Negro has had outstanding artists such as Henry O. Tanner, but he has had no "school of Negro art." Tanner, for example, as a mature artist, never "touched the portrayal of the Negro subject." The younger artist, Locke advises, should seek a "new style, a distinctive fresh technique, and some sort of characteristic idiom." The younger Negro should not let pass the present interest in African art, should not allow the objets d'art now popular to become once more "mere items of exotic curiosity." In short, Locke pleads for a Negro art inspired and perhaps influenced both by the Negro's peculiar position in America and by the legacy of his ancestral arts.

This whole matter of ancestral legacy was very much in the air at the time Locke wrote *The New Negro,* and Locke himself, as we have seen, was very much concerned with it. In 1928 Locke wrote an article for *The Annals (American Negro Issue)* in which he takes an opportunity to state clearly his position on the subject:

> There are two distinctive elements in the cultural background of the American Negro: one, his primitive tropical heritage, however vague and clouded over that may be, and second, the specific character of the Negro group experience in America both with respect to group history and with regard to unique environing social conditions. As an easily discernible minority, these conditions are almost inescapable for all sections of the Negro population, and function, therefore, to intensify emotionally and intellectually group feelings, group reactions, group traditions. Such an accumulating body of collective experience inevitably finds some channels of unique expression, and this has been and will be the basis of the Negro's characteristic expression of himself in American life. In fact, as it matures to conscious control and intelligent use, what has been the Negro's social handicap and class liability will very likely become his positive group capital and cultural asset. Certainly whatever the Negro has produced thus far of distinctive worth and originality has been derived in the main from this source, with the equipment from the general stock of American culture acting at times merely as the precipitating agent; at others, as the working tools of this creative expression.[22]

As previously stated, Locke, in collaboration with Montgomery Gregory, published *Plays of Negro Life: A Source-Book of Native American Drama* in 1927. This pioneer work consists of twenty one-act plays and dramatic sketches by ten white and ten Negro dramatists. Among the whites there are such well-known names as Eugene O'Neill, Paul Green, and Ridgley Torrence. With the possible exception of Jean

22. "The Negro's Contribution to American Art and Literature." *The Annals (The American Negro),* CXXXX (November, 1928), p. 234.

Toomer, none of the Negro playwrights had won recognition. Four of the plays presented came from the prize winners of *Opportunity* contests of 1925, 1926, and 1927.

There is a certain boldness in this kind of professional-amateur mixing in an anthology, but at the time this was the best that Locke could do if he wanted the contributors to be half black and half white. The field of drama in 1927 was perhaps the weakest of all the disciplines in Negro writing, weaker even than criticism. The first successful stage drama to be written by a Negro was Angelina Grimké's *Rachel,* which was produced by the NAACP's drama committee at the Neighborhood Theatre in New York in 1920. (Two plays published earlier were not intended for the stage.) Locke's anthology showed that real and startling progress in drama had been made during the New Negro Renaissance.

The introduction to this work takes the position that Negro drama flourished because American drama was going through a process of evolution. Although the change was national rather than racial, it heralded "the awakening of the dormant dramatic gifts of the Negro folk temperament." Several white dramatists recognized the undeveloped dramatic potentialities of Negro life and folkways, and saw in them source materials with which to rejuvenate the American drama.

This anthology, Locke points out, represents "a new province in our national literature" because it shows a collaboration of effort on the part of black and white playwrights—the latter seeking materials for a "deeper, firmer grip on the actualities of American life," the former seeking to advance their drama and to find suitable vehicles for Negro actors. The white dramatists had already "raised the general level of this subject matter from vaudeville and farce to significant folk comedy and tragedy," and there is every reason to believe that there will be a greater use of Negro themes in the future, and both the national and the Negro theatre will profit from the trend. This is true because "the Negro experience has been inherently dramatic: surely the substance of great drama is there." No other group experience presents as many or more of the social conflicts with which modern drama deals.

Locke believed that the Negro would vitalize American drama. In spite of generations of enforced buffoonery, "the dramatic endowment of the race has not been completely stifled"; the Negro temperament "still moves natively and spontaneously in the world of make-believe with the primitive power of imaginative abandon and emotional conviction." Given this new concern and awareness, there would come, Locke believed, a national Negro theatre where the black dramatist and actor will interpret "the soul of their people" to win the admiration of the world. (Except for the word *national* in the title, the present-day Black Arts group would agree with Locke's position. They are trying to do in the seventies what Locke optimistically hoped would come sooner.)

When Dr. Locke used the word *national,* he was emphasizing the position he never lost: there would be no racial monopoly in the writing about and the acting out of Negro themes. They must be done by white and black actors and playwrights. The drama of Negro life, he felt, was not yet free. The whites tended to overemphasize sordid realism in their depictions of Negro life, and the blacks had too much propaganda and sentimentalism in their works. In both cases the problem play tended to dominate the Negro theatre, whereas Locke felt that "the folk play . . . is really the more promising path for the sound development of Negro drama."

Locke never emphasized the kind of "exotic primitivism" that Waldo Frank, Eugene O'Neill, Sherwood Anderson, Carl Van Vechten, and others found in the Negro character, but he seemed to agree with them that Negro drama will be an antidote to the smug, commerical puritanism which these writers believed characterized the America of the twenties:

> The drama that will refine and entertain, that may even captivate us before long, is likely to be the uncurdled, almost naive reflection of the poetry and folk feeling of a people who have after all a different soul and temperament from that of the smug, unimaginative industrialist and the self-righteous and inhibited Puritan.

Dr. Locke's critical position during the New Negro period assumed the postulates that the American Negro had experienced a social and spiritual transformation, that as a literary artist he was then in his adolescence but fast approaching maturity, that the Afro-American writer possessed "a primitive tropical heritage," a sense of "remembered beauty" which he needed to exploit, that he should make full use of his vast and valuable storehouse of folk material to find inspiration and fresh techniques in his self-expression, that the black writer through artistic use of his folk material had the means at his disposal to rejuvenate American literature, and that the Negro writer must keep in step with the best of Western literature; he must be separate only in the delineation of his peculiar situation and in the sophisticated use of his folk treasury.

There is little here that is new except the emphasis. Du Bois and Johnson had said practically the same things, but the difference was in the stress. Locke belabors the folk issue more, and he seems to be more concerned with the African survival theme than the other two. Incidentally, he is vague on the issue, never quite definitely spelling out just what he means by such recurring phrases as "primitive tropical heritage," and "an emotional inheritance."[23] Locke, however, had *The New Negro* as a vehicle to put over his ideas and the excitement of the Renaissance itself to make them popular. Whatever their depth and worth, these themes and stands were given their most effective and dramatic presentation by the critical commentaries of Alain Locke.

23. For a gentle satire on Dr. Locke (as Dr. Parkes) and on this African survival theme see Wallace Thurman's *Infants of the Spring.* New York: Macaulay, 1932.

First Fruits (1925-1940)

Langston Hughes

Poet, fiction writer, dramatist, newspaper columnist, writer of auto-biography, anthologist, compiler of children's works, and translator, Langston Hughes was by far the most experimental and versatile author of the Renaissance—and time may find him the greatest.

A man of good will who believed that all races and groups are essentially the same in things that really count, Hughes fought the black-man's fight for dignity and equality with rare insight, great tolerance, and a vast amount of humor. Always a protester, he was seldom if ever bitter; always a race author, he was never a racist. Keenly aware of the Negro's position in America, he never espoused separatism or black nationalism. "I too sing America" was not merely a verse of poetry to him, it was part of his credo.

Negro writing owes much to Hughes: he showed by example and experiment the importance of the folk contribution to black writing through his use of the blues, spirituals, ballads, jazz, and folk speech; he gave Negro drama a shot in the arm when it needed it most; he exemplified the kind of freedom, the breaking away from stereotypes which many New Negro authors preached but did not always practice; and he preserved, in the face of an increasing seriousness on the part of militant young black writers, a much-needed sense of tolerance and old-fashioned humor.

James Mercer Langston Hughes was born in Joplin, Missouri, on February 1, 1902. Between 1902 and 1914 Hughes lived in seven cities: Buffalo, Cleveland, Lawrence (Kansas), Mexico City, Topeka (Kansas), Colorado Springs, and Kansas City. By 1914 Hughes's parents had separated, and in that year he joined his mother and stepfather in Lincoln, Illinois, where he finished grammar school in 1916 and was elected class poet, reading his first poem at the graduation exercises. Moving to Cleveland the same year, he entered Central High School, where as a senior he was elected editor of the class yearbook.

The year 1921 was crucial for Langston Hughes. While with his father in Mexico he taught English to the "best" families in two Mexican schools, and published his first prose piece, "Mexican Games," in *The Brownies' Book,* the children's work published by Du Bois, and his now classic "The Negro Speaks of Rivers" in *The Crisis.* In that year he also entered Columbia University, but remained there only a year.

After a year abroad by way of a tramp steamer, Hughes joined his mother in Washington, D.C., in 1924 and in the following year allowed himself to be discovered by Vachel Lindsay as a "bus boy poet." Also in 1925 he won first prize for poetry in the *Opportunity* contest, second prize for poetry, and third prize for the essay in *The Crisis* contest. He entered Lincoln University in 1926, and he published his first volume of poems, *The Weary Blues,* the same year.

In 1931–1932 Hughes, "encouraged" by Mary McLeod Bethune, took a poetry-reading tour through the South and West. During the same period he made a trip to Haiti and subsequently went to the Soviet Union with a movie-making group. In 1937 he went to Spain as a correspondent for the Baltimore *Afro-American,* reporting for that journal the civil war then in progress. In the period from 1938 to 1940 Hughes, now returned from Spain, became interested in the Negro theatre and founded three important theatre groups, in Harlem, Los Angeles, and Chicago.

During the forties Langston Hughes had a brief and unpleasant, but harmless encounter with Senator Joseph McCarthy's witch hunt over certain of his leftist activities and writings. In 1943 he began his column in *The Chicago Defender* (in which the life and thoughts of Simple, his most famous character, were first presented). During 1947–1948 he was visiting professor of creative writing at Atlanta University, and during 1949–1950 he was poet in residence at the Laboratory School, University of Chicago.

Hughes received many national honors during his lifetime, among them the Anis-Wolfe Award in 1953 for the year's best book on race relations; the Spingarn Medal in 1960; and election to the National Institute of Arts and Letters in 1961.

During the fifties and sixties Langston Hughes traveled less and published far more than he had done in previous decades, turning out a tremendous volume of work of all genres. In 1965 he lectured in Europe for the United States Information Agency. In 1966 he attended the Dakar Arts Festival. He died in 1967.

The bulk of Hughes's poetry is found in ten major publications (see bibliography), ranging from 1926 to 1967, the year of his death. During this span of over forty years he touched on many subjects and experimented with various techniques, but he never quite gave up any of the old approaches he used in the earliest works. One notes that in his last volume of poems, *The Panther and the Lash,* he has examples of works from all the previous volumes. With regard to subject matter, he was equally consistent. As a matter of fact, he really had but one theme during his entire poetic career, and that was to delineate the wrongs, the sorrows, the humor, and the enduring quality of the Negro. There are, of course, brief excursions into nonracial themes, but these are very rare.

His works may be divided into the following major categories: poems of protest and social commentary; Harlem poems; poems influenced by folk material; poems on African and negritude themes; and miscellaneous poems. (Because of space the last-named group will not be considered here. It includes *inter alia* Hughes's relatively small number of nonracial poems.) Naturally, there is some overlapping among these categories, but in the main they are valid. If there is one quality which characterized all Hughes's poetry—in fact all his works—it is simplicity: the plain acts of everyday people written in the uncomplicated language of their speech.

The protest-and-social-commentary theme runs through the whole body of Hughes's poetry. He freely acknowledged that he was a propagandist. One notes, however, that in his first two works, *The Weary Blues* and *Fine Clothes to the Jew,* there are very few protest poems. By the time of *One Way Ticket* (1949) the stream is flowing freely, and from this work on down to his last, social protest and commentary become increasingly important. Like other New Negro poets, Hughes used lynching as the supreme symbol of American injustice, and in *One Way Ticket* devotes a whole section of the work ("Silhouette") to lynch poems. His protest-and-social-commentary poems are usually topical, and if a reader were to put them all together, he would have a dramatic and revealing account of the many glaring instances of injustice perpetrated by America on the black citizen—an account that would include the Harlem Riot of 1935 and the trials and tribulations of Stokely Carmichael and other recent Black Power leaders; an account which would perhaps give as much insight, if not more, than a library of sociological works.

Langston Hughes, like other young Negroes of the thirties and forties, saw hope for the oppressed in the Marxist position. Although he never became a Communist, many of his social poems during this period show leftist influence. But nothing could disturb for long Hughes's innate "coolness," his ability to see both sides of an issue. Characteristic of him is a late poem called "Impasse" in which he cleverly gets at the heart of the racial dilemma in America:

> I could tell you,
> If I wanted to,
> What makes me
> What I am.

> But I don't
> Really want to,
> And you don't
> Give a damn.

It is revealing to contrast Hughes's attitude toward racial protest poetry with that of Countee Cullen. During most of his career Cullen used to complain about being a *Negro poet*. "To make a poet black and bid him sing" was considered a peculiar kind of malevolence on the part of God. Hughes, on the other hand, seemed to glory in his mission as a black propagandist, looking upon his protest poems as a weapon in the arsenal of democracy.

Called the poet laureate of Harlem, Hughes retained all his life a deep love for that colorful city within a city, and he never tired of delineating the changing moods of that ghetto. Except for one, there are specific poems on Harlem in every major poetical work. To Hughes, Harlem was place, symbol, and on occasion protagonist. It is a city of rapid transformation: the Harlem of the first two works is a gay, joyous city of cabaret life, the Harlem that jaded downtown whites seeking the exotic and the primitive flocked uptown to see. This Harlem of "Jazzonia" was never the *real* Harlem; that begins to appear in *One Way Ticket* (1949) after a riot and a depression have made the ghetto into an "edge of hell" for its discouraged and frustrated inhabitants, though still a refuge from the white man's world.

The fullest and best treatment of Harlem (and Hughes's best volume of poetry) is found in *Montage of a Dream Deferred* (1951). Actually one long poem of 75 pages, it employs a "jam-session technique" to give every possible shade and nuance of Harlem life. Very few cities have received such a swinging and comprehensive poetic coverage. The key poem of the work is prophetic in its implications:

> What happens to a dream deferred?
> Does it dry up
> like a raisin in the sun?
> Or fester like a sore—
> And then run?
> Does it stink like a rotten meat?

Or crust and sugar over—
like a syrupy sweet?
Maybe it just sags
like a heavy load.
Or *does it explode?*

Although Dunbar and Chesnutt had trapped the reservoir of Negro folk material during the late nineteenth century, the New Negro writers were the first to make broad use of this important body of songs and literature. No longer interested in the dialect tradition, they fashioned new forms of expression based on the spirituals, the blues, the ballads, the work and dance songs, and the folk sermon. The most important and the most dedicated experimenter with these forms was Langston Hughes.

In his first works he emphasized the blues form, a form for which he had a special fondness probably because it was congenial to his style and to his temperament. The title poem of his first volume has a blues-type form; seventeen of the poems in his second work are blues; and his first novel, *Not Without Laughter* and two of his best-known plays, "Don't You Want to Be Free?" and *Tambourines to Glory,* lean heavily on folk influence and folk blues and spirituals for artistic support. Hughes also employed ballad forms and on occasion dance rhythms, as in:

Me and ma baby's
Got two mo' ways,
Two mo' ways to do de Charleston!
    Da,Da,
    Da,Da,Da!
Two mo' ways to do de Charleston!

The experimentation with folk forms and rhythms reached brilliant heights in two later works: *Montage of a Dream Deferred* and *Ask Your Mama: 12 Moods for Jazz.* In the first work Langston Hughes seeks to capture "the conflicting changes, sudden nuances, sharp and impudent interjections, broken rhythms, and passages some times in the manner of the jam session. . . ." In short, he blends light and shadow, serious and comic, harmony and dissonance after the manner of jazz music to give the reader a unified picture of many-faceted Harlem. *Ask Your Mama* is a different type of jazz experiment, and though not quite as impressive as *Montage,* it is still a successful work. For this volume the poet uses the traditional folk melody of "The Hesitation Blues" as a leitmotif. "In and around it," he tells us, "along with the other recognizable melodies employed, there is room for spontaneous jazz improvisation. . . ." Printed in the margins beside each of the poems one finds elaborate directions for the musical accompaniment to the verse. It should be noted that Hughes, if not the first, as some critics claim, was among the pioneers of the poetry-read-to-jazz movement.

Langston Hughes's treatment of the African-negritude theme changed and deepened over the years. Like other New Negro poets, he featured in his earlier poems the alien-and-exile theme. In "Lament for Dark Peoples" the persona protests losing his "jungles" and "silver moons" and being "caged in the circus of civilization." In "Afraid" the speaker moans: "We cry among the skyscrapers/ As our ancestors/ Cried among the palms in Africa/ It is night,/ And we're afraid." This early treatment of Africa was little more than a literary pose, a kind of literary Garveyism, and neither the New Negro poets nor their readers took it seriously. Hughes's later African poems, however, are not conventional when he writes of a real and embittered Africa battling its way into freedom:

> Lumumba was black
> And he didn't trust
> The whores all powdered
> With uranium dust. . . .
>
> Lumumba was black.
> His blood was red—
> And for being a man
> They killed him dead. . . .

This concern with Africa brings to mind Langston Hughes's role in the negritude movement. Space will not permit a discussion of this question, but it should be noted that the poetry of Langston Hughes greatly influenced West African and West Indian negritude. He is counted among the fathers of that movement.[1] Hughes was always deeply interested in Africa, but he never considered changing his name or metaphorically donning a dashiki. He never renounced his American citizenship—literary or otherwise.

From his earliest years Langston Hughes was interested in drama. One of his first publications was a little dramatic sketch, "The Gold Piece," which appeared in *The Brownies' Book* (July, 1921). Hughes, according to Professor Smalley,[2] deserves great credit for his contribution to the Negro theatre. Writing at a time when such a theatre hardly

1. See an interview with Leopold Senghor in *Negro Digest* (May, 1967); see also an article by Langston Hughes, "The Twenties: Harlem and Its Negritude." *African Forum* (Spring, 1966).
2. *Five Plays by Langston Hughes.* Edited with an introduction by Webster Smalley (Bloomington: University of Indiana Press, 1963), p. ix.

Langston Hughes

Photo by Carl Van Vechten, Collection of American Literature, Beinecke Rare Book and Manuscript Library, Yale University.

existed, Hughes, in order to insure an opportunity for the black drama-tist, founded two groups during the thirties: the Suitcase Theatre in Harlem and the Negro Art Theatre in Los Angeles. In 1940 he started a third group, the Skyloft Players in Chicago.

The plays of Langston Hughes are like his poetry—simple, decep-tively so, in structure and plot. They are written in the language of the "little" Negro of the urban North, the people he knew, loved, and under-stood best. They are also written *for* these folk, presenting ideas, themes, and situations which they understood. Given his objective, to write for a people's theatre, too much subtlety would be out of place. What he lacks in subtlety, however, he makes up in the understanding of these people and the tolerance and compassion he has for them. Perhaps his greatest gift is the gift of laughter—laughter *with,* not *at* his characters. Deep down, Langston Hughes has a great faith in the essential worth and the indomitable spirit of the black man in the street, and this faith comes through in his dramatic works.

The best-known plays of Hughes are: "Don't You Want to Be Free?", a fairly long one-act play which he wrote for the Suitcase Theatre; *Mulatto,* a full-length tragedy; "Soul Gone Home," also a one-act drama; *Little Ham,* a comedy in two acts; *Simply Heavenly* and *Tambourines to Glory,* both long, semimusical plays.[3]

The dramatist describes "Don't You Want to Be Free?" as "(a Poetry Play)/ From Slavery/ Through the Blues/ To Now—and then some! With Singing, Music, and Dancing." The work is a kind of "progress" piece which shows the development of Negro oppression from slavery down to Harlem, a play in which city merchants and landlords do the same things to blacks that the slavery overseers and owners had done. The work, however, ends on the high note, one very much in favor in the 1930's: the organization of black and white workers to overcome the system of oppression. "Don't You Want to Be Free?" is actually more of a pageant than a play, but it pleased Harlem audiences. It ran there for 135 performances and for 30 more in Los Angeles. Hughes himself directed this stirring race drama. The author knew how to ring the changes on the protest theme.

In this work Hughes made excellent use of folk material: the spirituals and the blues. The section dealing with the latter is peculiarly effective because Hughes tells the audience a great deal about the several kinds of blues and their use by Negroes. The play has skillfully interwoven a considerable number of the poet's own verses from his first two volumes. All of these things add up to, not a great play, but a rousing race play that appealed to black audiences in the thirties.

3. "Don't You Want to Be Free?" is printed in *One Act Play Magazine* (October, 1938), the rest in Smalley's *Five Plays.*

Langston Hughes's most successful drama, and the first to be professionally produced, was *Mulatto*. Starting in 1935, it ran a year on Broadway, and then toured the provinces for eight months. The text of the work, first printed in Smalley's *Five Plays,* is different from the stage version, which was "sexed up" by the producer. *Mulatto* is a fascinating example of Hughes's interest in the theme of rejection by one's father. It struck home to him because he felt that he had been rejected by his own father, whom he thoroughly disliked. Hughes joined the rejection theme to that of the tragic mulatto, which in American literature has been presented as a twofold rejection, by parent *and* society.

The origins of *Mulatto* tell us much about Hughes's technique of using and reusing certain basic themes. In *The Weary Blues* (1926), his first book-length publication, the author has a twelve-line poem called "Cross" which deals with the rejection of a Negro son by a white father. In *Fine Clothes to the Jew* (1927) he included a longer and much more sensational poem on the same subject which he called "Mulatto." The full-length play with the same name was produced in 1935. After the play Hughes wrote a short story on the issue which he called "Father and Son." In 1949 he reworked the drama into an opera called *The Barrier,* with music by Jan Meyerowitz; it was first produced at Columbia University in 1950. And, finally, Hughes wrote another short story on the theme, "African Morning," which appeared in *Laughing to Keep from Crying* (1952). In short, over a period of twenty-five or more years, he presented the mulatto-rejection theme in four different genres and in treatments ranging from a twelve-line poem to a full-length Broadway play.[4]

Mulatto is a typical problem play of the thirties, and as such is racial protest at its sensational and melodramatic extreme. Its symbolism is obvious—America's rejection of the black minority—but the viewer or reader forgets the symbolism when he hears or reads the tragic and pathetic interplay of love-hate scenes, ending in the murder of the father by the son and the latter's suicide. The fury and the violence remind one of an Elizabethan play; for example, *The Duchess of Malfi.* Perhaps the best-drawn character in the work is Cora, the mother of Bert and the mistress of Colonel Norwood. She loved both victims of the racial entanglement, and is herself the most tragic victim in the play. Langston Hughes treats her with great understanding and tolerance.

Little Ham is probably Hughes's best comedy. Completed in 1935, it reflects faithfully the life of Harlem's ordinary citizens—their financial insecurity, their amorality, and, above all else, their courage, their high spirits, and their indomitable will to survive. Based on the numbers

4. There are at least two more variants of this theme in Hughes's works, but the six given here are the most pertinent.

racket, the play unfolds on the background of a shoe-shine parlor and a beauty shop (Harlem's most popular social centers). The finale comes at a Charleston contest in the famed Savoy. The characters are surface characters, but at least they are believable and certainly hilarious. The piece is good theatre in the folk manner.

In *Tambourines to Glory* the dramatist makes superb use of gospel hymns and spirituals. Written on the Faustian theme, the ever-recurring contest between God and the Devil, the play develops on a background of the store-front church (in this case finally enlarged into a folk cathedral). In the author's note Hughes tells us: "*Tambourines to Glory* is a fable, a folk ballad in stage form, told in broad and very simple terms—if you will, a comic strip, a cartoon—about problems which can only convincingly be reduced to a comic strip if presented very cleanly, sharply, precisely, and with humor." The play comes very near to being folk opera, and even the reader can feel the impact of the spirituals and gospel hymns which are the basic materials of the drama's structure.

In *Simply Heavenly* Hughes also relies on poetry and music to present his message, but he is not as successful here as in the former work. One reason probably is that the play, based as it is on a series of newspaper columns, lacks the unity of *Tambourines to Glory*.

The one play of Hughes that strikes the reader as being slightly out of character is "Soul Gone Home." Dealing with the hatred of a *dead* son and his *live* mother for each other, the work has the kind of surrealistic social comment seldom found in Hughes's work. It is macabre and bitter; it is also effective drama.

The fiction of Langston Hughes is found in twelve volumes (see bibliography). Of these publications, two are full-length novels, one a very short novella, three are collections of short stories, and the remaining six are works that give the life *and* the philosophy of that great character Mr. Jesse B. Semple, better known as Simple. Most critics feel that the Simple series is Hughes's best work in fiction and that Simple is his greatest single creation. For that reason the Simple volumes will be treated first, although one novel and one book of short stories appeared earlier than *Simple Speaks His Mind* (1950), the first of the series.

Simple was conceived in 1943 and appeared originally in a series of weekly columns written by Hughes for the Chicago *Defender*. The author tells us he got the idea for Simple from a chance encounter:

Before beginning this series, in the early days of the war, I met a fellow in a bar who worked in a war plant. I asked him what he was making.

He said, "Cranks." I said, "What do they crank?" He said, "I don't know. I don't crank with them cranks. I just make 'em. *They don't tell colored folks what cranks crank.*"

Thinking of the fellow's working status, his literal mindedness, and his deep consciousness of race, Hughes created Simple. He used this new character as the voice of folk humor and wisdom and as the representative of the black working class. He then made himself (if one accepts an author as persona) a needling, middle-class, educated "straight man." With Paddy's Bar as a fitting scene for the dialogues and little dramas, Simple came into being during World War II and was still holding forth in 1965, the year of the last publication of the series.

Although suggested by a chance encounter, Simple is no superficial character. Into his creation Hughes put the great wealth of knowledge of Harlem that he amassed over many years. Langston Hughes called him Simple; he made him, however, a complex personality: a Harlem working man, uneducated but intelligent, militant and race conscious but not a fanatic, blessed with a sense of humor but no blackface comedian. In short, Hughes took great pains to make Simple a simple, ordinary Harlem man in the street, with all of the sharpness and prejudices and hang-ups of the breed.

The success of the series depended in large measure on the contrast between the directness and single-minded attitude on race, women, and things in general of Simple and the sophisticated attitude of the liberal and educated "straight man" Hughes. The clash and interplay of the two viewpoints furnish much of the humor in the works, but they have a deeper purpose. They point up and accentuate the dual-level type of thinking which segregation produces among Negroes. As we read these dialogues we find ourselves giving lip service to the liberal side of the debate while our hearts share Simple's cruder, more realistic appraisal of a given situation For example, Simple, who blames everything bad that has happened to him on race, says: "I have been caught in some kind of riffle since I been black." When Hughes remonstrates with him for always bringing up the race question, Simple's answer is that a Negro does not have to *bring up* the question, it is always there. "I look in the mirror in the morning to shave—and what do I see? Me." Pushing aside all fancy explanations, Simple brings the issue home to himself. A black face in color-conscious America *is* the problem. Simple and every other sensible Negro know that.

There is, of course, a plot running through the six volumes and the many episodes of the series. In the earlier books Simple is trying to save enough money to pay his share for the divorce from his worthless down-home wife so that he can marry the lovely and charming Joyce. In later volumes Simple has married Joyce, and much of the humor (and the satire on middle-class pretensions) comes from her efforts to make Simple "cultured." There are, naturally, other recurring characters: Simple's nephew, his hard-boiled landlady, and the fun-loving bar-fly Zarita. The plot, however, is not the attraction in these episodes; it is but a rack on which to hang Simple's comments on Harlem, on the war, on women, on current events, and, above all else, on *race*. Simple's honest and unsophisticated eye sees through the shallowness, hypocrisy, and phoniness of white and black America alike. Simple is a racist, but he is not blind to black shortcomings. The Negro reader laughs *with* Simple rather than *at* him. As one reads the whole series, one is surprised to discover through Simple's observation how little conditions in America *basically* changed between 1943 and 1965, the year in which *Simple's Uncle Sam,* the last volume, appeared.

In Simple we find all the mixed-up thinking, all the dual loyalties, all the laughable inconsistencies which segregation and discrimination have produced in the darker American brother. So uniform is the pressure on the Negro, even though Simple is an uneducated worker, his responses to this pressure ring true for all classes. In this sense Simple *is* the American Negro.

Not Without Laughter (1930) describes the childhood and growing-up experiences of Sandy in a small Kansas town, which was probably based on the small town in which Hughes was born. The novel is not autobiographical, but the author drew on many of his own experiences to give the work flesh and blood. The work has a certain individuality because it shows Negro life in a small Midwestern town; it also shows that Negroes in such towns were probably not as well off with their partial segregation as Negroes in the South, who were totally segregated.

The titular passage of the novel comes near the end. After describing a typical small-town Negro poolroom session of arguments, near-fights, and tall tales, the author sums up:

> But underneath, all was good-natured and friendly—and through and above everything went laughter . . . That must be the reason, thought Sandy, why poverty-stricken old Negroes like Uncle Dan Givens lived so long—because to them, no matter how hard life might be, it was not without laughter.

If this is the theme of the work the author fails in bringing it out. Aunt Hagar, the grand old matriarch and one of the better characters in the novel, certainly does not find her strength in laughter but rather in the bedrock of Christianity and Christian love. There is also not much laughter in the life of Anjee and in the staid middle-class existence of Tempy and her stuffy husband. For Harriett and Jimboy it is not through laughter that they find release, it is through new sights and new chances to express themselves artistically. It is the way of the troubadour.

If the novel is concerned with a way out for Sandy, the growing boy, it poses certain questions. Sandy's way will obviously not be the religious route of Grandmother Hager who was an ex-slave. It will also not be the route—the hard but fascinating vagabond route—of Harriett and Jimboy. And the author shows his as well as Sandy's contempt for the correct, middle-class way of Tempy and her postal clerk husband. Where then will Sandy go? Which partial escape from the paralyzing limitations of Jim Crow living will he find? The author leaves the answer to the reader.

Langston Hughes did not possess at the time the insight and the maturity necessary to give an in-depth analysis of Negro life in a small early-twentieth-century Kansas town. As a consequence, he "padded" the novel with such worn-out material as the "Stud Negro" story and a scene from Aunt Hager's slave life that could easily have been written by Thomas Nelson Page. The novel has a few authentic and moving scenes, such as Aunt Hager's funeral, but these are not enough to save the work. *Not Without Laughter* is a surface novel. We leave it un- moved.

In 1955 Hughes, in collaboration with Roy de Carava, a brilliant young Negro photographer, published *The Sweet Flypaper of Life,* one of his most charming works. It is a 98-page novella of pictures and printed word. Most of each page is given to superb photographs of Harlemites, young and old. Although the written story on many pages consists of only one or two lines of print, it with the help of the pictures holds the reader captive to the end. There is here a very skillful and impressive fusing of pictorial and written art so that the two become one in the reader's awareness. The little Harlem vignette opens on an appealing note:

> When the bicycle of the Lord bearing His messenger with a telegram for Sister Mary Bradley saying "Come home" arrived at 113 West 134th Street, New York City, Sister Bradley said, "Boy, take that wire right on back to St. Peter because I am not prepared to go. I might be a little sick, but as yet I ain't no ways tired." And she would not even sign for the message—since she had read it first, while claiming she could not find her glasses to sign the slip.

The rest of the novella consists of Mary's talking-to-herself-thoughts about her Harlem family, particularly her favorite grandson, Rodney. As she mentions each, we meet the persona through the photographs. By the end of the work we know Sister Mary's children, grandchildren, and their wives, girl and boy friends, and in-laws. They are a normal ghetto family. This is not a protest novella; there is no sensationalism here. It is a quiet, revealing, and at times poetic delineation of ordinary life *within* the Negro group as seen through the eyes and love and understanding of Sister Mary Bradley. A grand creation herself, with a deeprooted zest for living, we find her at the end of the work, in spite of her age, eyeing a potential husband. "I done caught my feet," she tells us, "in the sweet flypaper of life—and I'll be dogged if I want to get loose."

Countee Cullen

Countee Cullen had a mild case of the dual-allegiance malaise which plagued many of the New Negro writers. In answer to a French critic who questioned his love for Keats and the classics, and who insisted that "the Negro alone has life and action and material unplumbed out of which the new literature is to come," Cullen replied with some warmth:

> Must we, willy-nilly, be forced into writing of nothing but the old atavistic urges, the more savage and none too beautiful aspects of our lives? May we not chant a hymn to the sun-god if we will, create a bit of phantasy in which not a spiritual or a blues appears . . .?[5]

Earlier in the foreword to *Caroling Dusk* (1927), an anthology which he edited, Cullen made the following admission:

> As heretical as it may sound, there is the probability that Negro poets, dependent as they are on the English language, may have more to gain from the rich background of English and American poetry than from any nebulous atavistic yearnings towards an African inheritance.

But in an interview given the same year Cullen confessed that he had often stated his unwillingness to be known as a Negro poet, but added. "Somehow or other . . . I find my poetry of itself treating of the Negro—of his joys and sorrows—mostly of the latter—and of the heights and depths of emotion which I feel as a Negro."[6]

This divided allegiance runs through Cullen's career. A scholar and a lover of traditional literature, he resented the urgings from within *and* without that tried to make him a Negro poet. And yet he realized that some of his best poetry, perhaps most of his best—was racially inspired.

---

5. *The Crisis* (November, 1929), p. 373.
6. Ralph W. Bullock, *In Spite of Handicaps*. New York: Association Press, 1927, p. 31.

This was, evidently, a real dilemma for Countee Cullen, and he expressed in one of his most popular sonnets, "Yet Do I Marvel," his resentment against this peculiar affliction:

> I doubt not God is good, well-meaning, kind,
> And did He stoop to quibble could tell why
> The little buried mole continues blind,
> Why flesh that mirrors Him must some day die,
> Make plain the reason tortured Tantalus
> Is baited by the fickle fruit, declare
> If merely brute caprice dooms Sisyphus
> To struggle up a never-ending stair.
> Inscrutable His ways are, and immune
> To catechism by a mind too strewn
> With petty cares to slightly understand
> What awful brain compels His awful hand.
> Yet do I marvel at this curious thing:
> To make a poet black, and bid him sing!

Countee Cullen was born as Countee Porter in New York City in May, 1903. He lived with his maternal grandmother until he was eleven or perhaps thirteen. She died, and Countee was adopted by the Reverend Frederick A. Cullen, a minister in Harlem. Countee led a sheltered childhood. The Reverend Mr. Cullen, however, was a political activist, and made his adopted son aware of the problems of the day.

Cullen's first poem, "To the Swimmer," was published in the *Modern School Magazine* in 1918 while he was in New York City's public schools. Countee attended DeWitt Clinton High School, where he had a successful career, excelling in oratory, debate, journalism, and poetry. He was editor of the weekly newspaper, vice president of the senior class, and a recipent of top honors at graduation. He attended New York University, where he earned a Phi Beta Kappa key. His first book of verse, *Color* (1925), was published while he was a senior at New York University. Cullen had already published several of his poems by this time in such magazines as *Harper's, Century, The American Mercury,* and the *Nation.* In 1926 he received his M.A. from Harvard. After a short trip abroad with his fosterfather, he worked as assistant editor on *Opportunity: Journal of Negro Life.*

Color received the first award in literature from the William Harmon Foundation in 1927. That year he published *Copper Sun* and *The Ballad of the Brown Girl,* and edited *Caroling Dusk,* an anthology. In 1928 he won a Guggenheim Fellowship and, before going to Paris to study, became engaged to Nina Yolande Du Bois, daughter of W. E. B. Du Bois. The couple married in 1928 and divorced a year later. Cullen stayed in France for two years, finishing "The Black Christ," which he published with other poems in 1929. He taught in the New York public schools from 1929 to 1946. In 1940 he remarried and settled in Tuckahoe, New York. Cullen collaborated with Arna Bontemps in the writing of the play *St. Louis Woman* (based on Bontemps's *God Sends Sunday*), which became a successful Broadway musical in 1946.

Cullen won the Witter Bynner poetry prize three times. He also received (among other awards) the John Reed Memorial Award and the Spingarn Medal.

The work of Cullen is found in nine major publications (see bibliography): one novel, two children's books, a version of *Medea* which also contains poems, and five volumes of verse. Though he wrote effectively in other genres, Cullen is pre-eminently a lyrical poet. As a poet, he admits to being "a rank conservative, loving the measured line and the skillful rhyme." Though he rebelled against being labeled a "Negro poet," he is, if not the finest, certainly one of the best poets of the New Negro Renaissance.

In each of his publications Cullen grouped his racial poems under the heading "Color." Many of the pieces in these sections fall into the alien-and-exile category. Most of the early New Negro poets used this theme, but Cullen used it more persistently and effectively than any of the others.

In poem after poem he states or implies that the American Negro is and can never be other than an alien here, an exile from his African homeland. As such he suffers from the insults and discriminations that unassimilated foreigners of all kinds endure, as well as a few additional ones because of his color. The Negro has not only lost an idyllic mother country, he has also lost his pagan gods, gods which, unlike the pale Christian deities, would be sympathetic to his peculiar needs. The religious loss is stressed more in Cullen's poems than in those of other Renaissance poets. In all probability he used the theme to express poetically some of his own religious concerns, as we shall see below.

In these poems Africa is not actually a real place. It is a symbol, an idealized land in which the Negro was once happy and free. The Harlem Renaissance poets used it to accentuate the differences between the Negro's harsh American existence and that he once led in this legendary "dusky dream-lit land." This subconscious contrast is never absent from the alien-and-exile's thoughts, and it puts a tremendous pressure on him. The best example of the alien-and-exile theme, Cullen's "Heritage," describes dramatically this atavistic "pull":

> What is Africa to me:
> Copper sun or scarlet sea,

> Jungle star or jungle track,
> Strong bronzed men, or regal black
> Women from whose loins I sprang
> When the birds of Eden sang?
> *One three centuries removed*
> *From the scenes his fathers loved,*
> *Spicy grove, cinnamon tree,*
> *What is Africa to me?*

Neither night or day can the speaker find peace or a release from the pull of *Africa* drumming in his blood. Twisting and writhing like a "baited worm," he wants to strip and dance "in an old remembered way." Though he fights against it, he also longs for "quaint, outlandish heathen gods/Black men fashion out of rods. . . ." And he wishes God were black, believing that if He were, He would suffer as the Negro suffers and therefore be more sympathetic to black misery. The poem ends on a note of doubt concerning his ability to fight the pull of the motherland:

> *All day long and all night through,*
> *One thing only must I do:*
> *Quench my pride and cool my blood,*
> *Lest I perish in the flood.*
> *Lest a hidden ember set*
> *Timber that I thought was wet*
> *Burning like the dryest flax,*
> *Melting like the merest wax,*
> *Lest the grave restore its dead.*
> *Not yet has my heart or head*
> *In the least way realized*
> *They and I are civilized.*

Although, as "Heritage" suggests, there is no way of escape for the black exile, there are means of alleviating the pain. One is to glorify the differences between the two groups, making attractive those which the enemy would deride:

> My love is dark as yours is fair
>   Yet lovelier I hold her
> Than listless maids with pallid hair
>   And blood that's thin and colder.

(This is an early variant of the present-day "black is beautiful" slogan.) Another means of alleviating the condition is to rise superior to it through the wisdom and courage that suffering brings:

How being black and living through the pain
Of it, is courage more than angels have.

Suicide is still another way out for the black sufferer, and in one of Cullen's longer poems, "The Shroud of Color," the speaker considers this means:

"Lord, being dark," I said, "I cannot bear
The further touch of earth, the scented air;
Lord, being dark, forewilled to that despair
My color shrouds me in, I am as dirt
Beneath my brother's heel; there is a hurt
In all the simple joys which to a child
Are sweet; they are contaminate, defiled
By truths of wrongs the childish vision fails
To see; too great a cost this birth entails.
I strangle in this yoke drawn tighter than
The worth of bearing it, just to be man.
I am not brave enough to pay the price
In full; I lack the strength to sacrifice."

A final means of alleviating the exile's agony is to acquire a mystic faith in a new world and a better day for the oppressed. One of Cullen's best sonnets, "From the Dark Tower," considers this hope:

We shall not always plant while others reap
The golden increment of bursting fruit,
Not always countenance abject and mute,
That lesser men should hold their brothers cheap; . . .
We were not made eternally to weep.

As stated, Countee Cullen stressed the religious aspect of the alien-and-exile theme, and the last section of "Heritage" is a brilliant poetic reflection of both the speaker's and the author's divided loyalties. Writing his own biographical sketch in *Caroling Dusk,* Cullen makes the following revealing statement: "Born in New York City . . . and reared in the conservative atmosphere of a Methodist parsonage, Countee Cullen's chief problem has been that of reconciling a Christian upbringing with a pagan inclination. His life so far has not convinced him that the problem is insoluble." This was written in 1927. Several poems in his first volume, *Color* (1925), reflected, as did "Heritage," his "pagan inclination," among them "Pagan Prayer" and "Gods."

In his second volume, however, we find signs of a change in the poet's attitude. Although there is a hint of skepticism in "Epilogue," the poem "In Spite of Death" suggests a faith in the existence of an afterlife, and

"The Litany of the Dark People" is almost a direct repudiation of the earlier pagan stand:

> Yet no assault the old gods make
> Upon our agony
> Shall swerve our footsteps from the wake
> Of Thine toward calvary.

In short, *Copper Sun* (1927) prepares the reader for the complete reversal the poet expresses in *The Black Christ and Other Poems* (1929).

The title poem in the *The Black Christ* not only repudiates Cullen's earlier religious position, it also repudiates the whole alien-and-exile attitude as expressed in "Heritage" and other verses on this theme. *The Black Christ,* modeled on a medieval saints' legend, is actually a strong affirmation of faith in Christianity and in the Negro's place in America ("This ground and I, are we not one?"). It may be approached as a *débat* between the Cullen of *Color,* paganistic yet seeking, and the Cullen of *The Black Christ,* who tells us in "Counter Mood":

> I who am mortal say I shall not die;
> I who am dust of this am positive
> That though my nights tend towards the grave, yet I
> Shall on some brighter day arise and live.

With *The Black Christ* volume, the poet took leave of racial writing, of the type of poems he placed under the heading "Color." (We note that in his first volume there are twenty-three poems in this category; in *Copper Sun,* seven; in *The Black Christ,* four, including, of course, the long title poem. *Medea and Some Poems* contains twenty pieces in all, but only one is related to racial matters, and the relationship is oblique.) In one of these "Color" pieces in *The Black Christ,* pointedly entitled "To Certain Critics," Cullen leaves us in no doubt concerning his position:

> Then call me traitor if you must,
> Shout treason and default!
> Say I betray a sacred trust . . . .
> I'll bear your censure as your praise,
> *For never shall the clan*
> *Confine my singing to its ways*
> *Beyond the ways of man.* [italics inserted]

From now on, he seems to be saying, no "racial option" will confine me; I shall write as a poet, not as a "Negro poet." And he stuck to his decision. As stated above, *Medea and Some Poems* (1935), has only one race poem. In 1940 and 1942, with the "aid" of Christopher Cat, he published first *The Lost Zoo* and later *My Lives and How I Lost Them,* both charming and imaginative children's works.

Why did Cullen stop writing racial poems after *The Black Christ?* One answer the poet has given us. Indirectly, he probably gave us another, found also in *The Black Christ.* In a poem called "Self Criticism" the author writes:

> Shall I go all my bright days singing
> (A little pallid, a trifle wan)
> The failing note still vainly clinging
> To the throat of the stricken swan?

And in another, entitled "A Wish," he says:

> I hope when I have sung my rounds
> Of song, I shall have the strength to slay
> The wish to chirp on any grounds,
> Content that silence hold her sway,
> My tongue not rolling futile sounds
> After my heart has had its say.

Perhaps Cullen felt that he had *written out* on racial themes and elected to be silent. The race problem, to a sensitive person, can be an intolerable bore and a great weariness of the soul.

In addition to the "Color" grouping in each volume (except *Medea and Some Poems*), Cullen used the following divisions: in *Color,* "Epitaphs," "For Love's Sake," and "Varia"; in *Copper Sun,* "The Deep in Love," "At Cambridge," "Varia," and "Juvenilia"; and in *The Black Christ and other Poems,* "Varia" and "Interlude." The poems in these sections, as one deduces from the titles, concern themselves with the subjects that lyric poets from the time of the Greeks have written about: love, the joys of nature, the transitoriness of life, and death.

For some reason Cullen was morbidly concerned with death and death-imagery.[7] He uses funereal allusions oftentimes in poetry in which, when first read, they seem out of place. One expects to meet skull-and-cross-bones references in poems like "A Brown Girl Dead," "Requiescam," and "Two Thoughts on Death," but they appear just as frequently in other poems, "The Love Tree," "Advice to a Beauty," and "The Proud Heart." The poet, for some reason, was also morbidly concerned with suicide. For example, "The Wise," "Suicide Chant," "The Shroud of Color," "Mood," and "Harsh World That Lasheth Me"

---

7. For a discussion of this subject, see Robert Fennell, *The Death Figure in Countee Cullen's Poetry,* unpublished master's thesis, Howard University.

are all suicide poems, and there are others. In the last-named poem the poet catalogues ominously the several ways to go:

> I think an impulse stronger than my mind
> May someday grasp a knife, unloose a vial,
> Or with a leaden ball unbind
> The cords that tie me to the rank and file . . . .

It is always dangerous to confuse the author with the speaker in a poem, whether the subject is suicide or love, but one notes that Cullen's love poems *after* his unfortunate first marriage take on a bitter tone. A good example of the type is "Song in Spite of Myself":

> Never love with all your heart,
> It only ends in aching;
> And bit by bit to the smallest part
> That organ will be breaking.

Cullen is excellent as a writer of "Epitaphs." These short, closely packed verses have a bite and a sting uncommon in Renaissance poetry. One of the best known and most often-quoted of these little poems is "For a Lady I Know":

> She even thinks that up in heaven
> Her class lies late and snores,
> While poor black cherubs rise at seven
> To do celestial chores.

Cullen's protest poetry, as exemplified in the above epitaph, was seldom, if ever, a frontal attack. He preferred the oblique, the hinted, the ironic approach. In one of his late poems, "Scottsboro, Too, Is Worth Its Song, (a poem to American poets)," he points out that the Sacco-Vanzetti case brought forth a flood of poetic protest. Thinking about the precedent set:

> Surely, I said,
> Now will the poets sing.
> But they have raised no cry.
> I wonder why.

One of the most brilliant of Cullen's poems in this vein, a piece that has become a protest classic, is entitled "Incident":

> Once riding in old Baltimore,
> Heart-filled, head-filled with glee,
> I saw a Baltimorean
> Keep looking straight at me.

Now I was eight and very small,
    And he was no whit bigger,
And so I smiled, but he poked out
    His tongue, and called me, "Nigger."

I saw the whole of Baltimore
    From May until December;
Of all the things that happened there
    That's all that I remember.

Cullen had the skill of McKay, but not the intensity. He preferred the suggestion to the blunt statement. He pricked rather than slashed.

The verse forms of Cullen, like those of McKay, are traditional: quatrains, couplets, stanzas of varying lengths, and sonnets. He has been criticized for using too slavishly these tried forms, for never, as did Langston Hughes, venturing out into the forms made popular by the New Poetry Movement or forms derived from folk literature. This brings up a foolish question: Would he have been a better poet if he had abandoned his classic models? The trouble with writing like Keats and other nineteenth-century greats is that they are difficult men to follow. Even though Cullen was by no means an unworthy follower of such poets, their greatness tends in some measure to dwarf by comparison his accomplishment. Cullen, however, had a motivation Keats never had. Cullen unlike Keats knew what it meant to be called a *"nigger."*

As a poet Countee Cullen will probably outlast his century. Measured by any standard, his work, particularly the "Color" pieces, will be read as long as protest poems have meaning in America. There are critics who believe that "Heritage" is the best poem published during the Harlem Renaissance.

Countee Cullen's single novel, *One Way to Heaven* (1932), belongs to that group of Harlem novels—among them *Nigger Heaven,* by Van Vechten, and *Home to Harlem,* by McKay—which sprang up during the Renaissance. The works of McKay and Van Vechten played up the more sensational aspects of the black ghetto and were obviously written to cater to the new taste in America for the exotic and primitive. Cullen's novel is more of an "inside" book than McKay's. It was designed to appeal primarily to a Negro audience. As a result, Cullen's picture of Harlem, covering not just the lower-class but the middle-class "intellectuals" as well, is closer to the *real* Harlem than McKay's, though certainy not as colorful. Some critics have blamed Cullen for his twofold approach, claiming that he wrote *two* novellas rather than *one* novel.

The charge is not wholly warranted because the two plots do touch *naturally*—that is, they are not forced beyond plausibility.

Cullen was trying to tell a story about the religious life of the ordinary Harlemites, a story of their church life and what it meant to them. Knowing that this would be a one-sided account, he used contrapuntally the activities of the class to which he belonged to sharpen the focus on both groups. One must remember that Cullen was a part of both the worlds he delineated. Reared in the parsonage of one of Harlem's largest churches, Cullen, even though he was an intellectual, learned to respect the function of the church in Negro life. On the other hand, he was one of the First Fruits of the Harlem Renaissance, but he was never too close to the movement not to see that it too had its charlatans who were just as phony as Sam Lucas the "religious" hustler. Cullen is satirizing both groups, but it is not a strong attack; it is rather the gentle "ribbing" of one who sees the foibles but appreciates the essential worth of both segments of Harlem life.

The central plot of *One Way to Heaven* concerns the love story of Sam Lucas and Mattie Johnson. Sam, a one-armed confidence man, has a peculiar racket. He follows revival services, and when a service reaches its highest emotional pitch and the minister is asking sinners to "come to Jesus," Sam rushes down to the altar, dramatically throws down a razor and a deck of cards, and tells the world that he has been saved. This act invariably produced invitations to dinner and other amenities from the impressed church members. On occasion it brought a collection to send the young man on the way in his new life. Mattie was present the night that Sam put on his act in a Harlem church. She had not felt the urge to go to the mourners' bench even though her aunt and others had been working on her for months. But Sam's performance that evening "brought her over," and she became a convinced and sincere Christian.

Mattie and Sam, of course, fall in love, marry, and for a while are a model Christian couple. Mattie, however, proves to be too much of a Christian for the unregenerate Sam. Her strait-laced, churchgoing ways begin to bore him, and he drifts back to his former worldly ways. Leaving Mattie, he "shacks up" with a less-demanding girl friend. Eventually Sam becomes seriously ill; the girl friend, Emma May, knowing that Sam is dying, fetches Mattie. She takes Sam home and prays fervently for him, but she, too, realizes that he is dying. This is bad enough, but she is more concerned about Sam's chances for salvation. The latter overhears her when she discusses her problem with Aunt Mandy. He learns that both women are convinced that death-bed visions of the "right" kind are a sign that the dying person has been "saved." Touched by Mattie's devotion to him and her genuine concern for his salvation,

Countee Cullen

Photo by Carl Van Vechten, Collection of American Literature, Beinecke Rare Book and Manuscript Library, Yale University.

Sam resolves to feign one more conversion, one more ecstatic experience, "a sweet trick to set at ease the mind of this good woman who loved him."

The two plots of *One Way to Heaven* are joined through Mattie Johnson, who works for Constancia Brandon, a Radcliffe product, the wife of the richest physician in Harlem, and that area's most brilliant and unpredictable hostess. (Incidentally, several persons in this part of the novel were easily recognizable in 1932.) Finding out that Mattie is to marry Sam, Constancia gets the bright idea of having the wedding at her home, making it a social event. Cullen makes Constancia's parties an occasion to satirize the New Negro Renaissance, that is, the spurious persons and activities that crop up in any movement of the sort: black members of a literary club who do not read Negro books, white friends seeking the unusual, and others.

Although none of his satire is vicious or even strong, his most effective and most humorous attacks deal with the Back-to-Africa Movement, with those middle-class Harlem ladies who by raising money for the President of the Nonce (of the future African Empire) become ladies, duchesses, and marquises of the Africa to which, hopefully, they will "return." Cullen here is poking fun at the Garvey movement which, with its colorful uniforms, its pageantry, its black aristocracy, and its intense black nationalism, greatly amused middle-class Harlem during the twenties.

One Way to Heaven is not a strong novel, but it does two things well: it gives a faithful picture of that very important and comprehensive segment of Harlem life, the religious *and* social activities of the *conventional* church; it points out some of the affectations and shortcomings of the New Negro Renaissance. In both cases Countee Cullen gives an inside view.

Arna Bontemps

For some reason, not until recently has Arna Bontemps received the recognition his talent and productivity deserve. Poet, novelist, children's author, anthologist, and playwright, he is almost as many-sided and prolific as his friend and collaborator Langston Hughes. Two things may have worked against Bontemps earlier: first, he did not publish a volume of poems when his friends Cullen, Hughes, and McKay were doing so; and, second, during the forties and fifties he somehow became classed, erroneously, as primarily a writer for children. Fortunately, he has come into his own, and critics now think of him as a significant Renaissance poet and novelist.

Arna Wendell Bontemps was born in Alexandria, Louisiana, on October 13, 1902. His family moved to Los Angeles when Bontemps was three. He attended high school at San Fernando Academy (1917–1920). In 1923 he graduated from Pacific Union College. Up to this time Bontemps had been carefully sheltered from Negro culture. He planned to become a doctor, but the year after graduation he went to Harlem instead to become a New Negro writer. In the 1920's Bontemps taught in private schools in New York and won several poetry prizes. In 1926 and 1927 his poems "Golgotha Is a Mountain" and "The Return" each won the Alexander Pushkin Award for Poetry (offered by *Opportunity: Journal of Negro Life*). Also in 1927 he won first prize in *The Crisis* poetry contest for his poem "Nocturne at Bethesda."

During the 1930's he wrote the novel *God Sends Sunday,* short stories, two more novels, and two children's books. Continuing to write, he taught school in Alabama and Chicago. In the 1940's he studied at Columbia and at the University of Chicago, and began his twenty-two-year tenure as head librarian at Fisk University (1943–1965). In 1956 his *Story of the Negro* received the Jane Addams Children's Book Award; in 1965 he became director of university relations at Fisk; in 1967 *Anyplace But Here* (written in collaboration with Jack Conroy) won the James L. Dow Award of the Society of Midland Authors. He also worked at the Chicago Circle Campus of the University of Illinois and at Yale University, where he was curator of the James Weldon Johnson Collection. Returning to Fisk as writer-in-residence, he died there June 4, 1973.

The poetry of Arna Bontemps has appeared in every major anthology of Negro writing since the Renaissance, but it was not until 1963 that he brought out a collection of his verse, *Personals,* a thin volume of only twenty-three poems published by Paul Bremen in London. During his early years he seemingly had some misgivings about the writing of verse; and he confesses that when he was about twenty, he

> . . . found out that the writing of poetry is both immoral and vicious and out of my inherent integrity burned all of my earlier efforts. Upon this same scene I determined never to write any more of it but rather to henceforth devote my youth and manhood to prose. However, neither of these resolutions have I kept.[8]

8. "Tree," *The Crisis,* XXXIV (April 27, 1927), p. 48.

This earlier hang-up in all probability limited his productivity as a poet. As a result, he published fewer poems than any of the other members of that tight little group of early Harlem poets (Cullen, Hughes, McKay) to which he belonged.

Bontemps' poems make use of several recurring themes: the alien-and-exile allusions so often found in New Negro poetry; strong racial suggestiveness and applications; religious themes and imagery subtly used; and the theme of return to a former time, a former love, or a remembered place. On occasion he combines in a way common to lyrical writing the personal with the racial or the general. Many of these poems are protest poems; but the protest is oblique and suggestive rather than frontal. Over all of Bontemps' poetry there is a sad, brooding quality, a sombre "Il Penseroso" meditative cast. In *Personals* there are no obviously joyous or humorous pieces.

The most popular theme in these verses is that of return. There are seven poems dealing in some way with this subject. The one entitled "Return" has a double thrust, the coming back to an old love which takes on an atavistic coloring: "Darkness brings the jungle to our room:/ the throb of rain is the throb of muffled drums./ . . . This is a night of love/ retained from those lost nights our fathers slept in huts." There is definitely here the kind of alien-and-exile comparison found in these New Negro poems; the highest joy the lovers (real or imagined) can have is the remembered ancestral love in an idyllic Africa.

In a different way, "Southern Mansion" is also a return poem because for the speaker "The years go back with an iron clank. . . ." Two waves of remembered sound come to him: music from the house and the clank of chains in the cotton field. Because of the latter, only ghosts and the poplars "standing there still as death" and symbolizing death—only they—remain.

"To a Young Girl Leaving the Hill Country" is a return poem with a Wordsworthian slant. The speaker tells the girl that she has ignored the hills of her native place, and she will therefore come back a bent old lady "to seek the girl she was in those familiar stones." He continues: "then perhaps you'll understand/ just how it was you drew from them and they from you." For Bontemps, one seemingly finds his identity in a return to his remembered past.

"Prodigal" speaks of returning to old scenes with more understanding: "I shall come back knowing/ the old unanswered questions on your mouth." "Idolatry" tells of a return to a dead love: "For I will build a chapel in the place/ where our love died and I will journey there. . . ." In the poem "Lancelot" the knight himself comes back after many years: "It is long, so long since I was here, Elaine,/ . . . you did not think that I would come again. . . ."

What is this concern with the past—with old loves, old places, ghosts of yesterday? Is there for Bontemps, as for Boswell, greater joy in the backward glance than in the living experience? Is he simply a late romanticist with a yen "For old unhappy far-off things,/ And battles long ago"? The answer is not evident in these poems. Perhaps the answer is what each reader finds in them.

Most anthologies make use of one or more of the following poems by Bontemps: "Nocturne at Bethesda," "Golgotha Is a Mountain," and "A Black Man Talks of Reaping"—and with good cause, for they are works of insight. In the first, "Nocturne at Bethesda," one finds the contemporary loss-of-faith theme joined with the alien-and-exile theme: "The golden days are gone . . . / And why do our black faces search the empty sky?" There is a suggestion here of a double loss for the black man "wandering in strange lands"—the loss of religion and of a homeland. If there is "a returning after death," the speaker tells us to "search for me/ beneath the palms of Africa." In some respects this poem reminds one of Cullen's "Heritage," but as is characteristic of Bontemps, it is a much quieter poem than Cullen's masterpiece.

"Golgotha Is a Mountain," too, employs an atavistic theme. "Some pile of wreckage," we are told, is buried beneath each mountain. "There are mountains in Africa too./ Treasure is buried there," and black men are digging with their fingers for it. "I am one of them," the speaker admits. One day, however, he seems to say, I will crumble and make a mountain. "I think it will be Golgotha." One notes the joining of the personal religious thought with the racial. The return to one's ancestral roots is suggested, but, as in all of these poems, the black man's return is pointed out as being somehow different. In this particular poem there is a hint of future hope for the Negro: " 'Oh, brothers, it is not long!/ Dust shall yet devour the stones/ but we shall be here when they are gone.' " There is also homage to the black man's strongest virtue: endurance.

In "A Black Man Talks of Reaping" one finds the closest approach to direct protest in these poems from *Personals:* "yet what I sowed and what the orchard yields/ my brothers' sons are gathering stalk and root" whereas my children "feed on bitter fruit. This is the kind of muted protest expected of a controlled poet like Bontemps.

The poems of Arna Bontemps lack the clear, unambiguous statement of those of his contemporaries: McKay, Cullen, Hughes. There is modern obscurity in these verses, and the so-called meaning often eludes the reader. Their craftsmanship, however, is impressive. The reader somehow feels a certain rightness in Bontemps' lines, that what he has said could not be expressed otherwise. There is a quiet authority in these poems.

Arna Bontemps

Photo by Carl Van Vechten, Collection of American Literature, Beinecke Rare Book and Manuscript Library, Yale University.

Bontemps' first novel, *God Sends Sunday,* was published in 1931. It is the story of Little Augie, a pint-sized jockey who gets into the money and, of course, throws it away on high living—fine clothes and yellow girls. The book tells much (though not quite enough) of the sporting life—the brothels, balls, and fancy bars—around the turn of the century, an era in which Negro jockeys were popular. Most of the early action takes place in the "fast" towns of New Orleans and St. Louis, and Bontemps managed to get over a little of the spirit and atmosphere necessary to make the novel plausible. But the work is a young man's work. The touch of the beginner is everywhere apparent. For example, the author evidently did not feel up to the task of rendering Little Augie's decline from affluence and power to poverty-stricken old age, and he simply jumps to the last years. Nor could he bring to life several of the characters in Little Augie's world. But the novel's subject matter is unique. It gives a picture of a segment of Negro life that no other novelist has touched. And though there is not much depth here, it is an entertaining and dramatic work.

Because of these qualities, *God Sends Sunday* did not suffer the fate of many first novels. Sensing that it would make a good play, Bontemps, in collaboration with Countee Cullen, went to work on it, and the result was a play, *St. Louis Woman.*[9] Although this work did not make the boards, it came to the attention of Edward Gross, a Broadway producer. After reading the play *and* the novel, Gross decided to make the story of Little Augie into a musical. Bontemps and Cullen rearranged the play for this purpose; Johnny Mercer and Harold Arlen wrote the music and lyrics. *St. Louis Woman* as a musical was a great success, running for 113 performances.

Bontemps' second novel, *Black Thunder* (1936, reprinted 1968), is a much better book in every way than his first; in fact, it is perhaps the author's outstanding publication. An historical novel, it deals with the famous Black Gabriel (Prosser) slave insurrection which occurred in and around Richmond, Virginia, in 1800. In the introduction to the 1968 reprint, Bontemps tells why he chose Gabriel's insurrection in preference to those of Vesey and Nat Turner:

> Denmark Vesey's effort I dismissed first. It was too elaborately planned for its own good. . . . *Nat Turner's Confession,* . . . bothered me on two counts. I felt uneasy about the amanuensis to whom his account was related and the conditions under which he confessed. Then there was the business of Nat's "visions" and "dreams."
> Gabriel's attempt seemed to reflect more accurately for me what I felt then and feel now might have motivated slaves capable of such

9. The original suggestion for a play came from Lawrence Stallings. See Eric Lincoln, "Review of *God Sends Sunday,*" *Courier Magazine Section* (September 11, 1954).

boldness and inspired daring . . . He had by his own dignity and by the esteem in which he was held inspired and maintained loyalty. He had not depended on trance-like mumbo-jumbo. Freedom was a less complicated affair in his case. . . .

Given Bontemps' personality and his sane, down-to-earth approach in racial matters, the choice was a natural one, and he made the most of it. *Black Thunder* tells the story of the 1800 uprising led by Gabriel Prosser and it gives a convincing account of the actions and thinking of this heroic black. Although the account is fictional, it impresses the reader as being *psychologically* true, and that is *the* important thing in a work of this sort. Bontemps does not make Gabriel too brave or too clever. He describes him as a powerful black man with a gift for organization and leadership. He has no visions, is not unusually superstitious, and is not particularly religious. His driving force is a deep conviction that "anything what's equal to a grey squirrel wants to be free." Stubbornly loyal to his followers, he refuses to inform on them. Even at the last when the authorities try to get information, his simple and heroic response is: "Let the rope talk, suh."

Unfortunately, Gabriel is developed so much better than the other characters in the work that we tend to forget them, especially the whites, both slave masters and sympathetic "Jacobins." But the story of Gabriel and his sexy girlfriend, Juba, of the house servants Ben and Pharoah who "sing" to the white folks, and of the other minor leaders of the insurrection is well told. Bontemps has a gift for storytelling and for making his characters talk convincingly. Moreover, he knew well the Virginia folk speech he utilized, and this gives a certain authority to his narration. Symbolically, the novel speaks for the modern Negro. One wonders why the present-day militants have not made better use of it in this respect. Incidentally, Bontemps' Gabriel impresses the Negro reader as being more *authentic* than William Styron's Nat Turner.

In his third novel, *Drums at Dusk* (1939), Bontemps again tries historical fiction, but the work suffers by comparison with the superior *Black Thunder*. A story of the uprising in Haiti, the one that Toussaint would eventually lead, *Drums at Dusk* is more of a "costume piece" than an historical novel. It is the kind of fiction that Frank Yerby writes: the heavy villains in it like Count de Sacy are too villainous; the good persons like M. and Mme. de Libertas are too good to be real; and the hero, young, handsome, aristocratic and Byronesque Diron Desautels, a member of Les Amis des Noirs, is just not flesh and blood. The book is good light reading. One can hardly say more.

Drums at Dusk of a necessity deals with violence, but Bontemps really has no taste for violence, and he gives as little of it as possible in this work. One wonders what Richard Wright would have done with the same materials. The action in *Black Thunder* was much more congenial to Bontemps' temperament because it concerns threatened rather than actual violence. Both works, *Black Thunder* and *Drums at Dusk,* are freedom statements, but the latter has very little of the impact that the story of Black Gabriel has. One moves, the other entertains.

Arna Bontemps is an excellent and prolific producer of children's works. His first, *Popo and Fifina, Children of Haiti* (1932), was done in collaboration with Langston Hughes. The illustrations for the little book were done by the brilliant Negro cartoonist E. Sims Campbell. The volume was something of a pioneering effort. Few, if any, books by Negro writers produced expressly for children were in existence in 1932. Among his other works for the young (see bibliography) are *Golden Slippers* (1941), an "anthology of Negro poetry for young readers"; *The Fast Sooner Hound* (1942), done in collaboration with Jack Conroy, a delightful story of a long-legged, lop-eared hound, "who'd sooner run than eat" and who could outrun the Cannon-Ball Express (there is no racial tag on the work); *We Have Tomorrow* (1945), a series of twelve biographies of young Negroes who were successful in unusual fields; *Sam Patch* (1951), written in collaboration with Jack Conroy and illustrated by Paul Brown, the charming story of Sam Patch, that "high, wide and handsome jumper" who defeated Hurricane Hank, the Kaskaski Snapping Turtle; and *Chariot in the Sky* (1951), illustrated by Cyrus Leroy Baldridge, a full-length book which retells for young readers the story of the Fisk Jubilee Singers.

Bontemps' several anthologies (see bibliography) need not concern us here. It should be noted, however, that they have contributed greatly in the building of the understanding and appreciation we now have of Negro literature. In these days when everybody is printing or reprinting "black" material, we should remember that Bontemps (along with Hughes, Sterling Brown, and a few other critics and anthologists) kept flowing that trickle of interest in Negro American literature—that trickle which is now a torrent.

Jessie Fauset

Although Jessie Redmon Fauset, Walter White, and Nella Larsen do not form a school, they may be considered as a group because they wrote the same kind of novels—novels that dealt almost exclusively with the life of middle-class Negroes; novels that told white America, in effect, that except for superficial differences of color we upper-class Negroes are just like the better-class whites.

It is now fashionable to laugh at this position. Writers of the present-day Black Aesthetic Movement want to be as *un*like middle-class whites as they possibly can. But whatever side we may take on the issue of black nationalism versus integration, we should not overlook or dismiss writers like Fauset, White, and Larsen because they represented the majority position of the period. Although Fisher, Hughes, Cullen, Schuyler, and Thurman satirized on occasion the black middle class, all of them wrote under the influence of the prevailing integration position. Perhaps the one writer who was most at odds with this position was McKay, who emphasized the primitive in his novels, if not in his poetry or life. In short, though there was much talk of African survival, folk material, and primitivism, the majority of New Negro novelists openly or tacitly subscribed to the critical tenets exemplified in the novels of Fauset, White, and Larsen.

Because of their singleness of commitment, these middle-class New Negro novels tended to use the same themes repeatedly. Among them are the following: passing (the crossing of the color line and oftentimes the return); lynching; color differences within the group and their un-pleasant consequences; race praise; loyalty to America, coupled with sharp criticism of its racial policy; the pressure of American prejudice on the black personality; the uniqueness of Harlem; the call of race; the belief that superior achievement will eventually win equality; faith in the "promise" of America in spite of all signs to the contrary. The most prolific, and in many ways the most representative, of these glorifiers of the Negro middle class was Jessie Fauset.

Jessie Redmon Fauset was born in Philadelphia, Pennsylvania. She came from an old middle-class Philadelphia family, the kind known as O. P.'s (old Philadelphians) in the Negro society of the period, and this background had a definite influence on her novels. Educated in the public schools of her native city, Miss Fauset took her B.A. at Cornell

University in 1905, winning election to Phi Beta Kappa at the time. Her further education included an M.A. from the University of Pennsylvania and study at the Sorbonne.

On October 5, 1906, Miss Fauset was appointed teacher of Latin and French in the well-known "M" Street High School in Washington, D.C. (which became in 1916 the equally well-known Dunbar High School). On June 30, 1919, Jessie Fauset resigned from Washington's public schools and in the same year joined the staff of *The Crisis* as literary editor. After seven active years in that position she gave it up in May, 1926, to assume "the less exacting duties" of contributing editor. During her early years with *The Crisis* Miss Fauset also worked with *The Brownies' Book,* at first as literary editor and subsequently as managing editor.

In 1921 Jessie Fauset attended the second Pan-African Congress and wrote for *The Crisis* (November and December, 1921) two articles covering that historic meeting.

After giving up full-time work with *The Crisis,* Miss Fauset returned to teaching, this time in the New York City public schools. She taught first in a Harlem junior high school, later moving to the prestigious DeWitt Clinton High School.

She died in 1961. The obituary in the *New York Times* (May 3, 1961) gave her age as seventy-six.

Her background as an "old-line" Philadelphia Negro, her education at Cornell, Pennsylvania, and the Sorbonne, her teaching positions in Washington and New York City, and her tenure as literary editor of *The Crisis* under Du Bois all placed her in the dead center of the life about which she wrote. Many of the incidents and characters in her novels are based on actual persons and actual occurrences which Negroes of her background knew and experienced.

Between 1924 and 1933 Miss Fauset wrote four novels: *There Is Confusion* (1924); *Plum Bun* (1929); *The Chinaberry Tree* (1931); and *Comedy, American Style* (1933). In each of these works she is trying to show that the lives of middle-class, respectable Negroes can be just as fascinating as those of the "primitives" McKay wrote about. That she did not vindicate her thesis may be attributed more to *her* shortcomings than to those of her materials. Even though present-day critics find serious faults in her technique, the best Negro critics of her generation extravagantly praised her works. For example, William Stanley Braithwaite felt that *There Is Confusion* was an "outstanding achievement in the entire range of fiction." Not only did he believe that Miss Fauset had created "something entirely new in the treatment of race in fiction," but he also contended that in this novel "race fiction emerges from the color line and is incorporated into that general and universal art which detaches itself from prejudice of propaganda and stands out the objective vision of artistic creation."[10]

Braithwaite obviously overpraises *There Is Confusion;* but it is Miss Fauset's fullest and most representative novel, rendering more of the typical attitudes and shibboleths held by the New Negro middle class of the 1920's than any of her others. The story concerns two Negro families: the Marshalls, well-to-do caterers in New York, and the Byes, an old Philadelphia family. (In all probability the Byes were suggested by the well-known biracial Grimkés of South Carolina and Pennsylvania.) The plot, however, is far too involved and unrealistic to be convincing. It makes use of the long arm of coincidence, is overly sentimental, and, in short, serves primarily as a rack on which to hang many of the practices and beliefs of the middle-class Negroes of the period, which makes it both intriguing and instructive.

The principal female character, Joanna Marshall, is a purposeful young woman, determined to be a success herself and equally determined to make her lover, Peter Bye, a success. Although the novel shows the confusion that American race prejudice can cause in the lives of black people no matter how well-prepared they are, it still possesses a great deal of old-fashioned American optimism. Note, for example, Joanna's answer when a friend advises her "to build up colored art":

> "Why I am," cried Joanna astonished. "You don't think I want to forsake—*us*. Not at all. But I want to show *us* to the world. I am colored, of course, but American first. Why shouldn't I speak to all America?"

Joanna shows here the success-oriented, best-foot-forward attitude held by many Negroes in the Renaissance. They believed that "if there's anything that will break down prejudice it will be equality or superiority on the part of colored people. . . ." Joanna later learns that the success formula in racist America does not always work, but she does not lose her faith entirely. As she tells Peter Bye, who is antiwhite, the prejudice of petty whites should not deter blacks: "Oh, we must fight it where we can, but we mustn't let it hold us back." Another character, Brian, discussing Peter Bye's antiwhite bias, comes to this conclusion, which is the overriding theme of the novel:

> "The time comes when he [a Negro] thinks, 'I might just as well fall back . . . a colored man just can't make any headway in this awful country.' Of course, it's a fallacy. And if a fellow sticks it out he finally gets past it, but not before it has worked considerable confusion in his life."

Reading this novel one would never know that there were millions of low-class-vulgar-loud-and-wrong-ghetto-type Negroes in New York,

10. "The New Negro in Literature," *The Crisis* (September, 1924), p. 210.

Jessie Fauset

JESSIE FAUSET

Courtesy of Moorland-Spingarn Research Center, Howard University.

Washington, Boston, and Philadelphia. Miss Fauset never mentions them, and for that reason her novel is limited. She is really trying to make a very small group of Negroes represent all Negroes. Although she did not intend to be, she was just as dishonest critically as were most of the Southern writers of the era—just as one-sided as McKay was in *Home to Harlem*. Rudolph Fisher in *The Walls of Jericho* tried to give, and did give, a fairer picture of Harlem life than either Fauset or McKay.

Plum Bun (1929) deals almost entirely with the passing theme, which it overplays badly. Angela, the major character, is manipulated to show various situations in which passers find themselves and, as such, is more of a puppet than a personality. The pictures of Greenwich Village and of Harlem are severely limited and fail to do justice to life in either section. Her contrived happy ending shows Miss Fauset to be at heart a romanticist in the pejorative sense of the word, and here, as in her first novel, she overuses coincidence. That two sisters, one living in Harlem, the other passing downtown, that each should become involved with the same man (who also passes) without the knowledge of the other seems pretty far-fetched. Miss Fauset, like too many other Harlem Renaissance novelists, felt that she had to bring in a lynching—in her case not a convincing one. Perhaps the most effective part of the work is her analysis of the white characters who found out that Angela was a Negro. Their feelings of shock and hurt, and, above all else, their feeling that they had been in some manner personally deceived, are well delineated.

The Chinaberry Tree (1931) deals not so much with interracial problems per se as it does with *human* problems within a small New Jersey community, including the prevention in the nick of time of a marriage between a half-brother and a half-sister, both illegitimate offspring. The work gives a picture of Negro life in the kind of background Miss Fauset knows well. As a source of information about the way Northern middle-class Negroes lived and thought in the 1920's, the book is valuable.

Comedy: American Style (1933) returns again to the theme of color and passing and of the tragedy which can happen when there are dark and light children in the same family and particularly when the mother of the family has "white fever." For the plot of this work Miss Fauset may have had in mind an actual "color tragedy" which came to a certain nationally known Negro family of the era.

Jessie Fauset was also a minor poet and critic. Her verses, typical lyrics of love and nature, were light and sophisticated, and neither good enough to become an impressive part of the canon of New Negro poetry or bad enough to be overlooked entirely. She appeared in practically all of the anthologies up to about 1941, but has not been kept in later collections. Her best-known poems are "La Vie C'est la Vie," "Noblesse

Oblige," "Words! Words!", "Christmas Eve in France," and "Rondeau." The critical work that is remembered best is "The Gift of Laughter," which discusses *inter alia* America's insistence on having the Negro mainly as a comic character. This essay was published in *The New Negro* (1925) and is still valuable as a record of the Negro's position in the theatre at the time.

The most cursory of glances at the pages of *The Brownies' Book* and *The Crisis* will show that Jessie Fauset was a prolific and versatile contributor to both periodicals during the twenties. She wrote poems (many poems), short stories, reviews, articles, and translations for both magazines. Her contributions include a biographical sketch on Martin R. Delany (*The Crisis,* November, 1926), an article on Henry O. Tanner (April, 1924), and an essay on the European reaction to the Pan-African Congress (*The Crisis,* December, 1921). One learns from her articles that Jessie Fauset had a clear, keen, no-nonsense type of intellect. An unusual woman in several respects, she made a small but significant contribution to the literature and to the intellectual climate of the New Negro Renaissance.

Nella Larsen

Nella Larsen is usually grouped with Jessie Fauset because both play up the same kind of folk, the Negro middle class; both treat passing as a major phenomenon in upper-stratum Negro life; and both practically ignore the presence of the "other" blacks. There is, however, a difference in the treatment of these themes. Nella Larsen is far more intense and bitter than Fauset in her attitude toward an America which forces upon Negroes the agony and frustrations they must endure simply because of the accident of color. And yet this bitterness is seldom overt in her writings. She expresses it, as a good artist expresses it, through the realistic and believable experiences and attitudes of her creations.

Of all the New Negro authors, Nella Larsen is the most elusive in the matter of biographical details, especially dates. Evidently there were certain things in her background which she felt were private, and she kept them that way. A few facts, however, have come to us, several of them taken from the book jacket of her first novel. She was a child of "mixed" parents, her mother a Dane, her father a Negro from the

Virgin Islands (formerly the Danish West Indies). The place of her birth is not known by the present writer. When she was two years old her father died. Soon afterward her mother married again, this time a Dane, by whom she had a second daughter. At eight Nella and her white half-sister attended a small private school in which most of the children were of Scandinavian or German ancestry. When Nella was sixteen she went to Denmark to visit her mother's relatives, staying there for three years.

Returning to America, she entered the nursing school connected with Lincoln Hospital in New York City. Graduating from Lincoln in 1915 (the course required three years of study), Miss Larsen was appointed assistant superintendent of nurses at the Tuskegee Hospital. After serving two years at Tuskegee, she returned to New York, and in 1918 was appointed to the staff of the city's Department of Health. Resigning in 1922 she enrolled in the New York Public Library Training School. After completing the required course, Nella Larsen became first an assistant and later a children's librarian in the New York Public Library, working for a while at the 135th Street branch. She left the system in 1926.

In 1928 Nella Larsen published *Quicksand,* her first novel. The work received the second prize in literature that year given by the Harmon Foundation for "distinguished achievement among Negroes." In 1929 she published *Passing.* In both works she seemingly used a considerable amount of material from her own life.

In 1930 Nella Larsen was involved in a minor incident of alleged plagiarism. Her short story, "Sanctuary," which appeared in the January issue of *The Forum,* bore a striking resemblance, except for dialect and setting, to a story entitled "Mrs. Adis," written by Sheila Kaye-Smith and published in *The Century* (January, 1922). After an investigation the editors of *The Forum* decided that the similarities were simply a matter of coincidence and told their public so very convincingly.

In her later years Nella Larsen lived in Greenwich Village. Some of her friends reported that though she was swarthy in appearance, she probably passed in downtown New York. She finally left the Village and moved to Brooklyn. According to an informant, she was found dead there "several years ago"—a statement made in 1969.

When was she born? If she returned from her visit to Denmark when nineteen, spent three years in Lincoln Hospital Nursing School, and graduated in 1915, then she was probably born about 1893. When did she die? How far back is "several years ago?" Three, four, five, six years or longer? We simply do not know, and there is no card for her in the morgue of the *New York Times.* There are also no terminal dates for her in the card catalog of the Library of Congress.

Quicksand, her first novel, tells the story of mixed-up, complex Helga Crane, the *"illegitimate"* daughter of a black father and a Danish mother. (The epigraph for the work is taken from Langston Hughes's poem "Cross," which treats the theme of interracial mating.) The work itself unfolds on a background that moves from Chicago, to a Negro school in the Deep South, to New York (Harlem), to Denmark, back to New York, and finally to a small town in the South. After being brutally rejected by her white uncle in Chicago, Helga goes to her rich white relatives in Denmark and is lionized by them. But she can find no peace in the white world. Rejecting marriage to Denmark's most prominent artist, she returns to Harlem. Unable to seduce the one man she really wants, Helga impulsively marries a peasant-type Negro minister and becomes a hopeless, drab, child-bearing wife of a boorish preacher in a small Southern town.

Whatever else she may be, Helga Crane is an individual, a neurotic individual, and the novel is a fascinating case study of an unhappy and unfortunate woman. It is important to emphasize Helga's individuality because there is a temptation to blame everything that happens to her on racial grounds. Robert Bone (*The Negro Novel in America*), Saunders Redding (*To Make a Poet Black*), and Hugh Gloster (*Negro Voices in American Fiction*) all state or imply that Helga is a "tragic mulatto" and that her problems come from this status. Although Helga's mixed ancestry and the race situation in America naturally influence her, Miss Larsen seems to be saying that they are not the sole causes of Helga's tragedy. She is the victim of her own inability to make the right decisions, a hang-up which the author suggests *may* come from frustrated love, or from brooding over a father who deserted his family, or from strong unsatisfied sexual urges, or from all of these causes as well as the racial situation. Helga is a superb creation. With the probable exception of Kabnis in Toomer's *Cane,* she is the most intriguing and complex character in Renaissance fiction.

The quicksand motif is used very skillfully in this work. The quicksand, of course, is Helga's own vacillating inner self, which the author renders with appropriate images of suffocation, sinking, drowning, and enclosure. The author is skillful in other respects. Although her dialogue in *Quicksand* is inclined to be too scanty, even inadequate on occasion, she nevertheless is an excellent narrator. More like a drama than a novel, *Quicksand* moves from crisis to crisis, giving small details only when absolutely necessary. Unlike other Harlem novelists, Miss Larsen never deserts the delineation of her major character in order to bring in sensational matter. Her picture of a Negro college in the South is skeletal (compare Ellison in *Invisible Man* on the same subject); her cabaret scenes compared with those of McKay are mild; her Harlem

Nella Larsen

Photo by Carl Van Vechten, Collection of American Literature, Beinecke Rare Book and Manuscript Library, Yale University.

street scenes lack the fullness and preciseness of those of Fisher; and her Southern small town scene has no lynching, no confrontation between white and black. Her main objective was the analysis of the neurotic Helga Crane, and she allowed nothing to take the reader's attention away from this goal.

Passing, though not as good a novel as *Quicksand,* is a moving story of a "tragic mulatto" who crossed the line and then tried to return. The present-day reader may wonder at this morbid concern of New Negro novelists with the passing theme, and ask why. The answer, of course, is not simple, and it may not be understood at all by young blacks, particularly those who believe in black nationalism. But there are reasons which seemed valid at the time. First of all, there was economic motivation. When almost every job of any consequence in the white world, including those of street-car conductors and street cleaners, were closed to the Negro, it was only natural for those who could pass to take advantage of their color. There was also the matter of simple convenience like a meal in a decent restaurant or a room in a modern hotel when one shopped downtown or took a trip to another city. There was always present the pleasure of fooling "Cap'n Charlie" (the white man) who, having set up the foolish caste laws, was then unable to tell who was or who was not a Negro. And there was on occasion a deeper compulsion on the part of a few Negroes to pass—a certain "call of kind" which transcended the routine motivations for crossing the line. Most passers tended to return to the race. This last kind returned only when forced to by discovery. Whatever the present-day reader may think of passing, the New Negro novelist was aware of its dramatic possibilities in fiction, and most of them treated the theme in their novels. At least four novels make the subject their principal concern: Johnson's *Autobiography of an Ex-Coloured Man,* White's *Flight,* Fauset's *Plum Bun,* and Larsen's *Passing.*

Irene Redfield and Clare Kendry, the two main characters in *Passing,* are childhood friends. Both are pretty and could pass; but of the two, Clare is the prettier and the lighter in color. Irene, coming from a solid, middle-class home, marries a Harlem Negro physician and never thinks of passing except for convenience when shopping in downtown New York. Clare, on the other hand, comes from a broken home, is reared by a drunken failure of a father, and after his death is taken in by white aunts who are ashamed of and could not forgive the "tar-brush" stain in her. When the chance comes, Clare runs away to the white world with its opportunity and glamour, and also its eventual heartache and loneliness. Clare, like Helga in *Quicksand,* is a complex creation; unlike Helga, however, she is hard, amoral, and utterly selfish in her search for happiness or, at least, contentment. She does not hesitate to take (or try to take) whatever she desires, including her friend's husband. She seems to have one overriding urge: to return to the Negro world which she left. In her case, however, the return trip ends in tragedy. Clare Kendry belongs with that group of "tragic mulattos" gracing the works of George Washington Cable, Dion Boucicault, and other earlier writers, but she emerges as an individual, not as a stereotype. One tends to pity, in spite of her ruthlessness, this poor, mixed-up child of a bad background, married ironically to a "nigger-hating" white husband. One finds in her a tragic symbol of the whole irrational concern in America over color and race.

It is unfortunate that Nella Larsen limited herself to two novels. She was a sensitive writer, with great skill in narration. It is reasonable to assume, given her intelligence, that she would have improved her fiction techniques if she had written more. As it is, she produced in *Quicksand,* one of the better novels of the Harlem Renaissance.

Rudolph Fisher

Rudolph Fisher, a Harlem physician and roentgenologist, viewed the black community with an understanding and amused eye. To him, it was a place where all kinds of Negroes—good, bad, and indifferent—from several areas—the South, the West Indies, and Africa—found a haven from the hostile white world. Fisher knew Harlem intimately—its con men, its numbers barons, its church goers, its night-life people, its visitors from the outside white world, and, above all else, the new migrants from the South, who found Harlem a miraculous city of refuge. His short stories and novels belong, with Cullen's *One Way to Heaven* and McKay's *Home to Harlem,* to the literature of the black ghetto; but his picture of Harlem is fuller than that of either McKay or Cullen. A comic realist, he laughed at the foibles of all classes of Harlemites from the "rats" (ordinary Harlem folk) to the "dickties"; but his laughter is healthy and therapeutic. It comes from a deeper-than-surface knowledge of and a fondness for the inhabitants of the black city.

Rudolph Fisher was born May 9, 1897, in Washington, D.C. He was reared in Providence, Rhode Island. In 1915 he graduated with honors from Providence's Classical High School; and in 1919 he received an A.B. from Brown University, with a major in English and in biology. At Brown University he was elected to the Phi Beta Kappa, Sigma Xi, and Delta Sigma Rho honorary fraternities; he won the Caesar Misch Prize in German and the Carpenter Prize in public speaking; and he was a James Manning Scholar and a Francis Wayland Scholar. The undergraduate class chose him as the class-day orator, and the faculty elected him to be the commencement day speaker. In 1920 he received an M.A. from Brown University. On June 6, 1924, he graduated from the Howard University Medical School. After interning at Freedman's Hospital for a year, he became a Fellow of the National Research Council of the College of Physicians and Surgeons of Columbia University, where for two years he specialized in biology. In 1927 he began the practice of medicine. Later, after specializing in roent-genology, he opened an X-ray laboratory which was connected with the X-ray Department of the New York Health Department. He served as superintendent of the International Hospital at Seventh Avenue and 138th Street before it closed. Several of his articles were published in leading medical journals.

An excellent musician, Fisher made several arrangements of Negro spirituals, some especially for Paul Robeson. Rudolph Fisher died in 1934; he was thirty-seven years old.

Fisher's first Harlem short story was written while he was in medical school. Called "City of Refuge," it appeared first in *Atlantic Monthly* (February, 1925), later in Locke's *The New Negro*, and subsequently in Foley's the *Best Short Stories of 1925*. The story deals with a theme expressed in its title—a theme which appears often in Fisher's work—the wonder, pleasure, protection, and pride the black newcomer finds in Harlem.

The central character in "City of Refuge," King Solomon Gillis, having killed a white man in his native South, has to leave the region. Because of all the stories he has heard about Harlem, he makes his way there. When he comes up out of the subway in the black city, the first thing he sees is a big black policeman directing traffic and lecturing white drivers. The heart of Gillis fills to overflowing. Harlem is indeed a black man's heaven. Unfortunately, however, Gillis is a yokel and is made a "fall guy" in the dope set-up that he is too ignorant to under-stand. When two white detectives try to arrest him in a night club, he proves to be too much for them, and they have to call for reinforcements. When a Negro officer comes to help in the arrest, King Solomon Gillis, his eyes alight with pride, goes calmly with the black officer. "Even—got—cullud—policemans—," he keeps murmuring to himself. It seems too fantastic to grasp.

"The South Lingers On," published in *Survey Graphic* (March,

1925), republished in *The New Negro* as "Vestiges," consists of five
sketches or vignettes showing the impact of Harlem on the Southern
Negro. The first of the five deals with a Negro preacher whose flock
has left one by one for Harlem. He finds them again, by accident, and
reclaims them from a charlatan. The second sketch (which does not
appear in *The New Negro*) concerns the faith which an unskilled Negro
worker, in spite of disappointments and rebuffs, still has in the promise
of Harlem. The third vignette deals with that much-used character, the
Negro grandmother, who is the family anchor. Unsuccessfully trying to
keep her granddaughter from the sinful ways of the city, the old lady in
her defeat has only one recourse left—prayer. The next deals with the
ambitions of a Negro girl who wants to go to college but whose
Southern-born father feels that graduation from high school is enough.
"Too much learnin' ain' good f' nobody." Pride causes him to change
his mind when his daughter wins a scholarship to Columbia Teachers'
College. The last story concerns two Harlem men about town who drop
in on a tent revival just for kicks. The preaching and the praying are
too much for one of the young men. He has not lost as much of his
Southern upbringing as he had thought. In these sketches Fisher gives
a nonsensational look at the deep imprint which the South has left on its
sons and daughters who made their way North. In these simple and
uncontrived vignettes he has shown Harlem to be, not the fun city of
downtown white thrill seekers, but, actually, a transplanted Southern
community, bigger and brassier, of course, but still essentially a slice of
the South.

The best of Fisher's transplanted-Southerners stories is "Miss Cynthie," which appeared originally in the *Story Magazine* (June, 1933).
It, too, has one of those strong, colorful grandmothers, in this case a
spry and positive old lady known in her native town by black and white
alike simply as Miss Cynthie. She has given her orphaned grandson,
David, a good Christian upbringing; and before he leaves for New York,
she issues that charge which so many Negro parents and grandparents
gave their offspring: "amount to sump'n." She spells it out in specific
career terms:

> "Son, you the only one o' the chillun what's got a chance to amount to
> sump'm. Don't th'ow it away. Be a preacher or a doctor. Work yo' way
> up and don' stop short. If the Lord don' see fit for you to doctor the
> soul, doctor the body. If you don' get to be a reg'lar doctor, be a tooth-
> doctor. If you jes' can't make that, be a foot-doctor. And if you don' get
> that fur, be a undertaker. That's the least you must be. . . . "

After David becomes a great success as a dancer, he sends for his
grandma, but knowing her attitude toward the theatre, he is afraid to
tell her that he is a song-and-dance man. Instead, he takes her to the

Rudolph Fisher

James Weldon Johnson Memorial Collection of Negro Arts and Letters, Beinecke Rare Book and Manuscript Library, Yale University.

Lafayette one night to see his act. Disappointed at first that her boy has failed by not becoming even an undertaker, Miss Cynthie is won over when David sings an old folk song she had taught him: "Oh, I danced with the gal with the hole in her stockin'." When Miss Cynthie sees what joy David has brought to people's lives, she is reconciled.

In several of Dr. Fisher's stories, color prejudice within the Negro group plays a significant part. Fisher, unlike McKay, does not overplay the issue, but he does not ignore or sidestep it. Moreover, he shows that all of the bias is not on one side. One of the most revealing stories of this type is "High Yaller," which appeared in two issues of *The Crisis* (October and November, 1925). It concerns the hard road a light-colored Negro girl has to travel in a community of dark-skinned persons. Trying to make an adjustment, she dates a black boy and gets into trouble with her dark-skinned Negro "friends" on the one hand and white people on the other. Discouraged and disgusted, she gives up the battle for acceptance and crosses over the line.

In addition to the short stories given here, Fisher published the following excellent ones. "Ring Tail," "The Promised Land," "Blades of Steel," and "Guardian of the Law." Dr. Fisher's works have appeared in *Opportunity, The Crisis, Story,* and *The Atlantic Monthly.* Two of his stories have made best-of-the-year anthologies, one in Foley's, the other in O'Brien's. One of them won the first prize in *The Crisis* short-story contest for 1925. Although both Claude McKay and Langston Hughes have written a larger amount of short fiction than Fisher, their works lack the controlled intensity, the suggestiveness, the subtlety, and the overall artistry that his short stories have.

Fisher's first novel, *Walls of Jericho* (1928), was written to show that one could treat the social extremes of Harlem in a unified work. It is a good-natured book, one in which the author satirizes kindly the "dickties" and their pretenses, laughs with the earthy "rats" and pokes fun at the several kinds of white visitors who frequent the black ghetto. The plot is relatively simple. Merrit, a light-skinned Negro attorney, taking advantage of his ability to pass for white, buys a home in one of the last white blocks in Harlem, one of the last to hold out against the black invasion. Three Negro movers bring in Merrit's furniture. One of them, Shine, a huge but essentially gentle Negro, falls in love with Linda, Merrit's maid. Shine's real name is Joshua, and the title deals with his walls of reserve and shyness tumbling into love. The other two movers, Jinx and Bubber, are a comedy team who made the novel a very funny work in 1928, when it appeared. Unfortunately, styles in humor change, and the patter of Jinx and Bubber is boring to a modern reader. Merrit's house is burned, presumably by the whites, and Fisher takes this opportunity to show that the class antagonism between the world of Jinx and Bubber and the world of Merrit falls down in the face of the common enemy, the white. As Bubber expresses it: "Fays [whites] don' see no difference tween dickty shines [upper-class Negroes] and any other kind of shines. One jig [Negro] in danger is ev'ry jig in danger. They'd lick them and come down on us. Then we'd have to fight anyhow." There was no need to fight because it turns out that the house was burned, not by whites, but by one of Merrit's black enemies —one who took advantage of the situation to blame the whites, but who then gave himself away when he got drunk.

One of the most interesting episodes in the book is the GIA Annual Ball, a major social event in Harlem which was attended by all classes of Negroes and many whites—would-be do-gooders and thrill seekers. This is obviously a good-natured spoofing of the annual NAACP Ball, then a social fixture in Harlem. Fisher, among other things, laughs at the whites who fancy they know the Negro, but who cannot tell a Negro from a white man. A prominent, rich, and interested-in-the-problem white woman talks all evening with Merrit without finding out that he is a Negro.

One contribution that this novel makes to so-called Harlem literature is its use of Negro slang or jive talk, particularly the verbal bouts between Jinx and Bubber. Knowing that slang changes quickly, Fisher supplied a glossary for this work. One notes that in 1932 "hunky" was just one of many pejorative terms for Negro. The phrase "right on" in those days meant simply *nevertheless*. The humor of Jinx and Bubber was expressed almost wholly in the slang of the day. It was typical Negro humor—humor which consisted of "slipping" an opponent in the dozens (talking about his antecedents, particularly his mother); calling your opponent "black" in as many new and insulting ways as possible; and describing his dumbness and worthlessness. This type of humor was as old as the minstrel tradition. With the new emphasis on black self-respect, it has fortunately been somewhat dated.

Fisher's overall purpose in this novel was to look at Harlem steadily, see it whole, and show that Harlemites are like all other people—varied and all too human. He was obviously trying to destroy the kinds of myths about Harlem which McKay and Van Vechten had created. The picture in *Walls of Jericho* is not as well painted as that in the short stories, but it is refreshing in its wholeness. Fisher represents the middle-class attitude of his day. He was still able to look objectively at his own people, to laugh at them when they were comical and to criticize them when they did not measure up. When he made the villain in *The Walls of Jericho* a black rather than a white, he is hinting that Negroes, too, cause a lot of their own troubles. "Whitey" is not always to blame.

Until quite recently, when Chester Himes began a series of detective stories, Rudolph Fisher was the only known Negro to write in this field. His pioneering novel, *The Conjure-Man Dies: A Mystery Tale of Dark Harlem,* came out in 1932. A conventional thriller, it has all of the customary trappings of the type: the red herrings, the false starts, the least likely suspect, and a team of detectives—one amateur, the other official police. But the things that give the work an added appeal are, first, its Harlem background and, second, its main character, a Harlem conjure man or fortuneteller who is also an African king—well-educated, brilliant, and regrettably a paranoiac. Against this background of African mysticism, folk superstition, the numbers racket, and the swinging daily life of Harlem, Fisher contrives a plot of classic suspense. Moreover, like S. S. Van Dine, the author, through his erudite amateur sleuth, gives the reader much medical and scientific knowledge, all of it pertinent to the solving of the crime. The humor of the novel is a continuation of that found in *The Walls of Jericho,* and it is furnished by the actions and arguments of the same two characters found in the earlier novel, Jinx and Bubber. If Fisher had lived longer, he probably would have written other detective stories. In Dr. Archer and Dart (an intelligent and rugged police officer, in some ways an ancestor of Chester Himes's Gravedigger and Coffin), Fisher had two excellent characters who would easily lend themselves to a series of Harlem crime stories.

Fisher's style in these novels is clear and uncomplicated. If there is a weakness, it is a tendency to write like a professor on occasion; but he does not have any trouble in making his characters talk convincingly and naturally. One notes that in both these novels, large segments of each dealing with lower-class life, there is absolutely no use of four-letter words and no sex. Fisher, like Du Bois and other New Negro authors, believed in putting one's best foot forward. There were some things that one just did not parade for the white folks to see. McKay had shown the "debauched Tenth" and was condemned for it—by Negroes. Although Dr. Fisher could easily have played *up* the primitive side of Harlem life, he preferred to play it *down*. It was part of the price one's dual-inheritance demanded.

George S. Schuyler

Journalist and novelist, George S. Schuyler has been for more than a half century one of the most versatile and successful Negro newspaper men in America. He has also been one of the nation's most conservative writers, black or white, and one of the most unrelenting enemies of the so-called Communist conspiracy.

In racial matters Schuyler may be called an assimilationist. Writing for *The Nation* in 1926, he states bluntly: ". . . the Aframerican is merely a lampblacked Anglo-Saxon." Continuing in this vein, he asserts: " . . . it is sheer nonsense to talk about 'racial differences' . . . between the American black man and the American white man. . . . In the homes of the same cultural and economic level one finds similar furniture, literature, and conversation. How, then, can the black American be expected to produce art and literature dissimilar to that of the white American?"

This was Schuyler's position in 1926, when, in the midst of the New Negro Renaissance, his contemporaries were talking about the African heritage, the Negro's peculiar endowments, and black nationalism. This is his stand today in the midst of the so-called New Black Renaissance. Whatever else he has been, George Schuyler has been consistent, and he has defended this position stoutly in hundreds of newspaper columns, editorials, and volumes. The assumption of the Negro's essential American-ness undergirds all of his published works.

George S. Schuyler was born in Providence, Rhode Island, but grew up in Syracuse, New York, where he received his grammar- and high-school education. Schuyler joined the United States Army when he was seventeen and became a member of the famous Twenty-Fifth U.S. Infantry regiment. During World War I he was a first lieutenant. He did not go abroad and was mustered out soon after the November 11, 1918, Armistice.

Before he started his journalistic career, Schuyler worked at all kinds of menial labor in several parts of the nation, gaining a first-hand knowledge of the people lowest down on the American ladder. His journalistic career has been varied. He started first with Randolph and Owen's *The Messenger,* the first Negro Socialist magazine in America. He was connected with *The Messenger* from 1923 to 1928; however, in 1924 he also began working for *The Pittsburgh Courier.* As columnist ("Views and Reviews"), editorial writer, and a contributor in other capacities, Schuyler has been with *The Courier* until quite recently. In addition to his *Courier* assignment, Schuyler was connected for about seven years with the NAACP's *The Crisis.*

It is difficult to put into capsule form George Schuyler's prolific and amazing career as a journalist. He has been on important investigating assignments to the Deep South, Africa, Europe, South America, and the West Indies. His articles and essays (see bibliography) have appeared in *The Crisis,* the *Nation, Opportunity, The Messenger, The New Masses, The American Mercury, Reader's Digest,* and many other American, European, and African journals. Because he has been all of his adult life a strong and articulate anti-Communist, he has been featured at one time or another in practically every American conservative newspaper and periodical.

Schuyler has published three full-length works: *Black No More* (1931; 1971), a novel; *Slaves Today* (1931), a novel; and *Black and Conservative* (1966), an autobiography. It is to these we now turn. Our major concern here is with Schuyler the literary artist, not Schuyler the journalist. We know, of course, that we cannot completely separate the two.

The first novel has the long and intriguing title: *Black No More, Being an Account of the Strange and Wonderful Works of Science in the Land of the Free, A. D. 1933–40.* If one were to characterize the work in classical terms, it would be called Juvenalian satire. It is a harsh, iconoclastic, "galloping" attack that slashes, primarily, at all American color shibboleths, black and white. It also slashes at other national weaknesses, among them greed. Highly audacious and irreverent, the work pokes fun at both the NAACP *and* the KKK. It treats the heads of the Urban League and the NAACP just as roughly as it treats the Grand Kleagle. They are all hustlers, Schuyler suggests, and in no way different except in the superficial difference of color.

Black No More is naturally not a serious attack on men like Du Bois, whom he calls Dr. Agamemnon Shakespeare Beard, and other "race leaders." Satire of this sort exaggerates to grotesque lengths certain characteristics of its victims. There is usually a small bit of truth under the burlesque, however, and for Schuyler that truth was that in their exploitation of America's absurd color-phobia, there was no intrinsic difference between white and black race hustlers. This has always been Schuyler's thesis, and he rides it superlatively in this satire.

The plot of *Black No More* concerns the changes—social, political, and financial—which come to America after a Negro scientist, Dr. Crookman, discovers a process to change Negroes from black to white. As a result of Crookman's discovery, there is utter panic among black and white race leaders, race organization men, businessmen, and all the others who made their livings out of race differences. In the end, when practically all Negroes have become white, it is found that the *changed* Negroes are whiter than the original whites. This starts a new panic in the nation, and everybody starts *darkening up* just as frantically as they had earlier tried to bleach their skin and hair. *Black No More* is a rich and delightful spoof on America's foolish color hang-ups. It should appeal to today's readers almost as much as it did to the 1931 audience. Although most Negroes have no desire to be white, many of them have become just as foolish about *blackness* as their parents and grandparents were about *whiteness* in 1931. Human nature has a depressing habit of remaining the same.

Schuyler's second novel, *Slaves Today,* also came out in 1931. It was really an assigned work—a League of Nations commission (whose secretary, Charles S. Johnson, had found out that slavery still flourished in Liberia). The commission discovered that, with the connivance of the Republic's president and other high officials (all of them from the aristocratic American-Liberian ruling class) slaves were "recruited" among the "bush" Negroes and sold on the Spanish colony of Fernando Po situated off the Nigerian coast. The Spaniards paid the Liberian officials, including the president, $50 a head for these unfortunate recruits. This was such a vicious and ironic example of twentieth-century slavery, George Palmer Putnam, the well-known publisher, thought there was a good book in the situation. In 1930 he commissioned Schuyler to go to Liberia, investigate, and write a report. Out of the project came *Slaves Today.*

In his foreword the author tells us: "The material for this narrative was gathered during a three-month sojourn on the West Coast of Africa in the early part of 1931. All of the characters are taken from real life. . . . The author is personally acquainted with them, as he is with most of the Americo-Liberian characters who appear under fictitious names." Schuyler considered Liberia's slave trade "strikingly ironic" because the black republic was founded by freed American Negroes who established it as "a haven for all oppressed black people."

Slaves Today is not a good novel. Schuyler really does not possess the mind-set necessary to write a good work of fiction, particularly one that deals, as this volume does, with romantic love. Schuyler has a good journalist's mind, a satirist's mind, but his mind is too analytical and logical to do justice to the tragic love story he attempts in *Slaves Today.* As a result, what should be the soul-searching experiences of Zo and Pameta, his principal characters, simply do not move us, for they and the other protagonists do not come fully alive. They are puppets the author manipulates to describe the horrible conditions in Liberia in

George S. Schuyler

1931. Schuyler hoped that *Slaves Today* would "help arouse enlightened world opinion against this brutalizing of the native population in a Negro republic." Perhaps it did. Read today as a work of literary art, *Slaves Today* is disappointing.

The author's last full-length publication, *Black and Conservative* (1966), is an autobiography. As a matter of fact, it is perhaps more of an anti-Communist tract than anything else. If Schuyler had told us more about his *other* interests and activities and less about his life-long, obsessive crusade against Communism, he would, we believe, have produced a great autobiographical study. We say this because Schuyler's life has been a full and fascinating odyssey. With the probable exception of Langston Hughes, he knew more about the Negro lower and working classes than any other major writer of the twenties and thirties. Moreover, he knew and worked and feuded with practically all the leaders—political, social, literary—of the New Negro period.

All of these associations and the experiences connected with them could have been fused into a fine work of self-revelation, and *Black and Conservative* in spots is such a work. His early chapters are fresh and revealing. They tell of a fine boyhood with fine parents and a fine old matriarchal grandmother. Subsequent chapters describe his life in the pre-World War I United States Army; and still later chapters describe his bohemian life in New York after World War I. All this is rich material, and delightfully presented. Like most good columnists, Schuyler writes concisely and clearly; he has packed a wealth of good things in these early chapters. And then, unfortunately, George Schuyler discovered that Communism was the great enemy of the modern world, and he decided that it was his mission in life to destroy that enemy. The rest of *Black and Conservative* tends to become a recital of all of the author's fights with, attacks on, and conquests of the Marxian foe. This theme recurs again and again and again, and the reader who before had no interest in the matter begins to feel a little sympathy for the leftist position.

In spite of what we definitely consider an overemphasis on one theme, *Black and Conservative* is a valuable work. It is good, first of all, to hear the conservative side given without circumlocution or apology. Schuyler is that rare bird, a present-day Negro who proudly flaunts his conservative (and reactionary) position. In these days of overemphasis on militancy, it requires a certain kind of courage to be openly against everything that black militancy has advocated. Mr. Schuyler, however, has never lacked courage to take the unpopular side. However much one may disagree with his stand, one is forced to admire a Negro who not only has castigated marches and sit-ins, but who objected strenuously to the giving of the Nobel Peace Prize to Martin

Luther King. The editorial he wrote on King was so strong that Schuyler's own paper, *The Courier,* refused to print it. It was published in William Loeb's *Manchester Union Leader.*

Black and Conservative is valuable for another reason. It gives new insight into some of the not-too-well-known rivalries and feuds among the leaders of the New Negro Movement. Although Schuyler was a contemporary of and worked with the several black leaders, he was never really a part of any clique. Essentially a loner, Schuyler tended to look at things objectively. His picture, focused from a slightly different angle, supplements the pictures we get from Langston Hughes, James Weldon Johnson, and others who wrote of the period in *their* autobiographies.

Schuyler's greatest literary contribution is *Black No More.* Brash, almost crude on occasion, extremely comical, *Black No More* is the best work of prose satire to come from the New Negro Movement. *Black and Conservative,* though one-sided, as has been pointed out, repays reading for the picture it gives of the Renaissance and afterward. And for the student of American journalism, George Schuyler's thousands of columns and editorials in *The Courier* and his many articles in America's best periodicals are a real bonanza. Faithful to his belief that it is nonsense to talk about racial differences, Schuyler, in his caustic and hard-hitting journalistic style, has needled and provoked and incensed Americans, black and white alike, for over fifty years. At this writing, George Schuyler is very much alive and is an active member of the John Birch Society.

Wallace Thurman

Unlike most of his New Negro contemporaries, Wallace Thurman was not a part-time author, but almost from the day he arrived in Harlem from California, a professional man of letters. Born in Salt Lake City in 1902, Thurman was educated at the University of Southern California. According to Langston Hughes (*The Big Sea*), Thurman's ability to read exceptionally fast and his perceptive critical abilities led to his being hired in 1929 as a reader at Macaulay's, the only Negro holding such a position in a big publishing company. Later on, he became a ghost writer for *True Story,* using such names as Ethel Belle Mandrake and Patrick Casey and writing "confessions" in an Irish or Jewish dialect.

Thurman's first widely acclaimed work was a sensational and successful Broadway play, *Harlem* (1929), written in collaboration with William Jordan Rapp, the editor of *True Story*. It dealt with a subject that Rudolph Fisher also used—the impact of the North, particularly of Harlem, on the Negro recently up from the South. Thurman's third novel, *The Interns* (1932), dealing largely with white characters, was also done in collaboration with a white author, Abraham L. Furman. Also in 1932 Thurman was appointed editor-in-chief at Macaulay's.

Wallace Thurman actually lived in two worlds: the downtown world of Macaulay's publishing house and of McFadden's pulp magazines and the uptown world of the New Negro Renaissance. Although he was later highly critical of the movement, he was very much a part of it. In 1926, again according to Hughes, Thurman served as managing editor of *The Messenger* and associated with A. Phillip Randolph, Chandler Owen, and George S. Schuyler. During the summer of 1926, he, Langston Hughes, Zora Neale Hurston, Aaron Douglas, John P. Davis, Bruce Nugent, and Gwendolyn Bennett founded the short-lived "little magazine," *Fire*. He also helped to establish another little magazine, *Harlem,* which was equally short-lived.

But Thurman was not happy in either world. He wanted to be, Hughes tells us, "a *very* great writer like Gorki or Thomas Mann, and he felt that he was merely a journalistic writer." As a result, he became melancholy, suicide-prone, and generally disillusioned. A great deal of this self-recrimination finds its way into the pages of *Infants of the Spring,* his second novel. Thurman wrote articles for the *Independent, Bookman,* and the *New Republic,* as well as scripts for two "adults only" movies in Hollywood. In December of 1934, soon after returning to New York from Hollywood, he died of tuberculosis in the Bellevue Hospital charity ward.

In his first novel, *The Blacker the Berry* (1929), Thurman launched a frontal attack on a wrong which had been perpetrated on dark-skinned Negro women, not by whites but by Negroes themselves. In much of the folk literature and in a great deal of the street-corner-type joking among black men, the dark-skinned girl was the butt of a great deal of coarse, vulgar, and humiliating humor aimed at her color. Typical of these attacks is the well-known doggerel verse:

> Yaller gal rides in a limousine;
> Brownskin gal rides the train.

Black gal rides in an ol' oxcart,
But she gits there jes' the same.

Thurman, writing in the twenties, was one of a very small number of
Negro writers brave enough to make a dark-skinned girl a central figure
in a novel. (Du Bois and Sutton Griggs were among the number.)
Negro heroines, most black novelists felt, had to approximate white
heroines. Black was not considered beautiful, except by the Garveyites,
until about 1960. And one notes that even Thurman never insisted that
his principal character was beautiful or that blackness was a desirable
physical feature. In the color-conscious atmosphere of the 1920's this
would have been unrealistic.

The title of the work comes from a folk saying, "the blacker the
berry, the sweeter the juice." As used by the man in the street, the saying was a dubious compliment, but the whole import of the phrase
makes an excellent, ironic title for a really moving book. *The Blacker
the Berry* details the cruel experiences suffered by Emma Lou Morgan,
a dark-skinned girl born into a Negro family whose "motto" was lighter
and lighter every generation. Emma Lou's mother was light-skinned and
expected that her child would be even fairer than she was. Mrs. Morgan
and her associates firmly believed that "white was right," and when
Emma Lou arrived, it was a great blow. The mother, of course, rejected
the daughter and made Emma Lou's life miserable through odious
color comparisons. The great tragedy of the child's life was that she,
too, came to believe that "white is right."

In order to get away from her rejection at home, Emma Lou goes to
a college in California, seeking freedom from the burden of blackness;
but she soon discovers that her lighter-skinned schoolmates reject her
as decidedly as her family had done. In order to escape the misery
caused by her color, Emma Lou pathetically tries all kinds of skin
whiteners and cosmetics, some of which accentuate rather than attenu-
ate her blackness. Even more pathetically, she desires only light-skinned
men friends and is, as a consequence, tricked, abused, exploited, and
humiliated by a series of worthless lovers and pimps. After a final and
soul-searing experience with one of her "lovers," she seemingly comes
to her senses, and to some sort of terms with herself as she is.

The trouble with *Blacker the Berry* is that it lacks subtlety in its
delineation of Emma Lou and her problem. Surely, no Negro was ever
as color-struck as Emma is depicted, no one quite so foolish. The whole
matter of color prejudice within the group is far more intricate, complex, and tenuous than Thurman makes it out to be in this novel. He
seems to write almost as though he were an outsider, seeing the situation
only in terms of black and white, whereas, as every Negro knows, the

Wallace Thurman

James Weldon Johnson Memorial Collection of Negro Arts and Letters, Beinecke Rare Book and Manuscript Library, Yale University.

presentation of this problem must be done in many shades of grey. Thurman knew this, but sacrificed nuance for sensationalism. His main thesis, of course, is valid. The dark-skinned Negro girl, until recently, has borne a double brunt of the cruelty inflicted by American color prejudice. Although he used a sledgehammer to do so, Thurman certainly drove home this point. Emma Lou, of course, is more than just a character. In her split allegiance and overemphasis on certain white values, she symbolizes the majority Negro attitude of the Renaissance years.

The title of Thurman's second novel, *Infants of the Spring* (1932), is taken from *Love's Labour's Lost* (Act I, Scene i): "Berowne is like an envious sneaping frost/ That bites the first born infants of the spring." The "infants," one takes it, are the first-born and fledgeling creative artists of the Harlem Renaissance, and Thurman was honest enough to make himself, through his spokesman, Raymond, one of these vulnerable infants.

Infants of the Spring is a biting commentary on the failure (in Thurman's opinion) of the New Negro Movement. The action of the novel takes place largely in a house for artists and writers called Niggerati Manor (*nigger* plus *literati*)—a house that functioned very much like Thurman's own residence. In this bohemian setting the author has placed the following fascinating and "representative" Renaissance characters: Raymond Taylor, a young, sensitive writer and the central figure in the work; Stephen Jorgenson, a white man attracted at first and then repelled by Harlem and Negroes; Paul, a Negro painter of the bizarre and erotic; Eustace, a Negro singer who rebels against singing spirituals; and Pelham Gaylord, a would-be creative artist who is actually the servant for the group. Visitors to Niggerati Manor include two Negro girls who come to seek and fight over the favors of white Stephen; Samuel, a white do-gooder who wants to befriend Negroes but who is congenitally incapable of understanding them; Lucille, a mixed-up Negro girl whom Raymond loves; and Barbara, a Jewish girl from the Village who finds that her whiteness is highly appreciated by Negro men. The author also brings to the Manor, under thinly disguised and appropriate pseudonyms, the following New Negro writers: Langston Hughes, Countee Cullen, Eric Walrond, Rudolph Fisher, Zora Neale Hurston, and Alain Locke.

What little action there is in the novel serves as interlude to the continuing dialogue that goes on among the residents of Niggerati Manor, particularly the colloquy between Raymond (who probably represents the author) and Stephen. Both are honest and intelligent observers, and their appraisal of the Renaissance is not flattering. In the early part of the novel we find the following analysis of the Movement:

There had been throughout the nation an announcement of a Negro renaissance. The American Negro, it seemed, was entering a new phase in his development. He was about to become an important factor in the artistic life of the United States. As the middle westerner and the southerner had found indigenous expression, so was the Negro developing his own literary spokesmen.

Word had been flashed through the nation about this new phenomenon. Novels, plays, and poems by and about Negroes were being deliriously acclaimed and patronized. Blues shouters, tap dancers, high yaller chorus girls, and singers of Negro spirituals were reaping much publicity and no little money from the unexpected harvest. And yet the more discerning were becoming more and more aware that nothing, or at least very little, was being done to substantiate the current fad, to make it the foundation for something truly epochal. For the time being, the Negro was more in evidence in the high places than ever before in his American career, but unless, or so it seemed to Raymond, he, Paul and others of the group who had climbed aboard the bandwagon actually began to do something worth while, there would be little chance of their being permanently established. He wondered what accounted for the fact that most Negroes of talent were wont to make one splurge, then sink into oblivion. Was it all the result, as Stephen had intimated, of some deep-rooted complex? Or was it merely indicative of a lack of talent?[11]

One of the high points in the work is the meeting at the Manor called by Dr. Parkes (Alain Locke). "Let me suggest," Parkes tells the group, "your going back to your racial roots, and cultivating a healthy paganism based on African traditions."[12] DeWitt (Cullen) agrees: "The young Negro artist must go back to his pagan inheritance for inspiration and to the old masters for form."[13] "What old black pagan inheritance?" Paul inquires "inelegantly," and then points out that *he,* along with his African ancestors, has also "German, English and Indian ancestors." From this point on the meeting begins to disintegrate. One writer suggests militancy as the Negro artist's duty, another finds in Marxism an answer. In all probability, the position of Thurman is found in the following speech, which is given by Cedric (Walrond) but seconded by Raymond:

"What does it matter," he inquired diffidently, "what any of you do so long as you remain true to yourselves? There is no necessity for this movement becoming standardized. There is ample room for everyone to follow his own individual track. Dr. Parkes wants us all to go back to Africa and resurrect our pagan heritage. . . . Fenderson here wants us all to be propagandists and yell at the top of our lungs at every conceivable injustice. Madison wants us all to take a cue from Leninism and fight

11. Wallace Thurman, *Infants of the Spring,* New York: The Macaulay Co., 1932, pp. 61–62.
12. *Infants of the Spring,* p. 235.
13. Ibid. p. 236.

the capitalistic bogey. Well . . . why not let each young hopeful choose his own path? Only in that way will anything at all be achieved."[14]

When Cedric finished, Raymond made the following comment: "Individuality is what we strive for. Let each seek his own salvation. To me a wholesale flight back to Africa or a wholesale allegiance to Communism or a wholesale adherence to an antiquated and for the most part ridiculous propagandistic program are all equally futile and unintelligent."[15]

Several critics have said that Thurman tried to tear down the beliefs held by other New Negro writers, yet offered nothing constructive in their stead. Others have said that he was hopelessly confused in his own mind on the issues raised by *Infants of the Spring*. It seems to the present writer, however, that Thurman is saying *inter alia* two very definite things. One is that there was too much phoniness in many aspects of the New Negro Movement, especially the "African survival" gambit; and, second, that the artist should resist with Emersonian firmness any capitulation to "badges and names, to large societies and dead institutions," that he must be first, last, and always a free and individual spirit. Thurman, in all probability, would be appalled by the present-day Black Esthetes who insist that all art become a weapon in the fight for liberation.

Infants of the Spring is more criticism than fiction. It therefore fails as a novel. It is, however, a valuable work for those who are interested in the New Negro years. It will serve as a good control for those who tend to find certain origins in the Renaissance that were not there.

Wallace Thurman was only thirty-two when he died. Though it is futile to speculate, one wonders how far his intelligence, his cynical wit, and his flair for satire would have carried him had he lived longer.

Zora Neale Hurston

Always a colorful figure, Zora Neale Hurston was a popular Harlem personality during the early years of the Renaissance, one about whom many amusing anecdotes were told. Calling her Sweetie May Carr,

14. Ibid. pp. 239–240.
15. Wallace Thurman, *Infants of the Spring*. New York: The Macaulay Co., 1932, p. 240.

Wallace Thurman in *Infants of the Spring* makes the following none-too-flattering comment on Miss Hurston:

> Sweetie May was a short story writer, more noted for her ribald wit and personal effervescence than for any actual literary work. She was a great favorite among those whites who went in for Negro prodigies. Mainly because she lived up to their conception of what a typical Negro should be. . . . Given a paleface audience, Sweetie May would launch forth into a saga of the little all-colored Mississippi town where she claimed to have been born. Her repertoire of tales was earthy, vulgar and funny. Her darkies always smiled through their tears, sang spirituals on the slightest provocation, and performed buck dances . . . Sweetie May was a master of southern dialect, and an able raconteur, . . . But Sweetie May knew her white folks. . . .[16]

In *The Big Sea* Langston Hughes says pretty much the same thing that Thurman had said. In calling her a member of the "niggerati" (Negro literati), he is using a satirical term coined by Thurman:

> Of this "niggerati," Zora Neale Hurston was certainly the most amusing. Only to reach a wider audience, need she ever write books—because she is a perfect book of entertainment in herself. In her youth she was always getting scholarships and things from wealthy white people, some of whom simply paid her just to sit around and represent the Negro race for them, she did it in such a racy fashion. She was full of side-splitting anecdotes, humorous tales, and tragi-comic stories, remembered out of her life in the South as the daughter of a traveling minister of God. . . . To many of her white friends, no doubt, she was a perfect "darkie" in the nice meaning they give the term—that is a naive, childlike, sweet, humorous, and highly colored Negro.
>
> But Miss Hurston was clever too. . . .[17]

Zora Neale Hurston, anthropologist and novelist, was born in 1903 in Eatonville, Florida, an all-Negro town. She worked as a maid and waitress, and attended the preparatory school at Morgan College and then Howard University, before entering Barnard College. In 1927 she received her B.A. from Barnard, where she studied anthropology under Franz Boas and served as personal secretary for Fannie Hurst. Boas recommended her to the Association for the Study of Negro Life and History to do special research on the Negro community at Plateau, Alabama. (The Negro people of that community were the descendants of the last slaves to reach the United States in 1859.) As a result of her study, Miss Hurston wrote "Cudjo's Own Story of the Last African Slaves," published in the *Journal of Negro History* in 1927. She was a prize winner in the short-story and one-act play categories of the first

16. Wallace Thurman, *Infants of the Spring*. New York: The Macaulay Co., 1932, p. 229.
17. Langston Hughes, *The Big Sea*. New York: Alfred A. Knopf, 1940, pp. 238–239.

Opportunity literary contest in 1925. In 1932 some of her dramatized folk sketches had a brief run at the John Golden Theatre. She worked with the Federal Theatre Project. When *Jonah's Gourd Vine* was published in 1934, she gained national prominence. In 1936 Miss Hurston received a Guggenheim Fellowship for the study of folklore in the West Indies, which was renewed in 1937. She also researched voodoo and folklore in Haiti and Louisiana.

The young Zora Neale Hurston showed great promise as a collector of folklore and as a fiction writer. Although she produced four novels, two collections, and an autobiography, she seemed to fold up in mid-career. She lived until 1960, but her last publication was in 1948. During her last years she actually worked for a while as a maid for a white woman. At the time of her death she was working on a novel with a biblical setting. In 1960 Zora Neale Hurston died in semi-obscurity and in utter poverty.

In addition to short stories and plays (see bibliography), Miss Hurston produced the following works: *Jonah's Gourd Vine* (1934); *Mules and Men* (1935); *Their Eyes Were Watching God* (1937); *Tell My Horse* (1938); *Moses Man of the Mountain* (1939); *Dust Tracks on a Road* (1942); and *Seraph on the Suwanee* (1948).

Miss Hurston's first, and perhaps best, novel, *Jonah's Gourd Vine,* is based loosely on the lives of her parents. Her intimate knowledge of the material gives the work an immediacy that the other works lack. Moreover, her skillful use of folk customs, folk superstitions, and, above all else, folk speech helps make *Jonah's Gourd Vine* an unusual and fascinating work. Both Dunbar and Chesnutt had used folk material in their fiction, but neither had the knowledge of folk tales that Miss Hurston had (she was a trained anthropologist); and though both knew folk speech, neither gave it the poetic quality that Zora Neale Hurston gives it in this work; neither fused it as thoroughly as she does.

The novel tells about the trials and tribulations of Big John Pearson, a mulatto, a fine-looking physical specimen, a great preacher, and an even greater ladies' man, with all of the charm and the weakness of his breed. Much of the plot centers upon the ups and downs of his life with his wife, the pert, intelligent, and understanding little brown-skinned Lucy Potts. The novel's scene is the rural Deep South with its laughing-singing-tall-tale-telling folk Negroes, with its sometime stormy church life, and with its "good" white folks in the distant background. There is no protest in this novel; it is an *inside* work dealing mainly with Negroes. There are no gouging white landlords or vicious white lynchers. In short, we see here the kind of good-will attitude which will characterize all of Miss Hurston's fiction dealing with Negroes. She simply ignored most of the unpleasant racial aspects of Southern life—

aspects that have to be recognized if a full picture is to be given. This shutting of the eyes on Miss Hurston's part is a kind of artistic dishonesty that takes away from the work. All Southern whites are certainly not villains and oppressors of blacks, but an artist can hardly ignore the system of oppression and discrimination in which Negroes in the thirties lived daily; and yet Miss Hurston, somehow, manages to do so. Fortunately, for her, she has a good story to tell, she knows how to tell it effectively, and she makes brilliant use of a racy folk speech. All of these tend to make the reader forget that he is not hearing the whole story in *Jonah's Gourd Vine.*

In *Their Eyes Were Watching God,* the second novel, Miss Hurston tells a moving story of Janie and her search for love and understanding —a love and understanding which she finds, after two husbands, in carefree, happy-go-lucky Tea Cake who is considerably younger than she is. The action takes place largely in an all-Negro town, one like the one in which Zora Neale Hurston grew up—with excursions to the Everglades and to other parts of Florida where Negroes could find work.

The novel develops slowly. One gets the impression that Miss Hurston, like a folk preacher, is feeling her way, reaching for the right mood, which she finally captures. Until she does, however, she fills in with too many tall tales, too much folk anecdote. She, of course, is trying to give the reader the feeling of the talk and the horseplay which take place on the porch of a small-town general store. The objective is valid, but she tends to overwrite.

In Janie, Zora Neale Hurston has created an unusual and fascinating character. Janie, like her creator, is "different"—an unconventional person and the child of a broken home. A light-colored woman married to a dark-colored man, she has the added problems that color prejudice within the Negro group forces upon such a marriage.

In this novel Miss Hurston tells us a lot about the work that ordinary Negroes did in Florida; she also tells us about life in an all-Negro town. One of her better characters is Janie's second husband, the mayor, store owner, and prime mover in this community. He is a new type of Negro character—a wheeler dealer and in everything except color like his counterpart in white novels and white life.

There is, of course, no bitterness toward whites in *Their Eyes Were Watching God.* At the end Janie is forced to kill Tea Cake in self-defense; for he had developed rabies as a result of being bitten by a mad dog, and tries to kill her. In the subsequent trial the white judge, the white lawyer, and the all-white jury are all far more understanding than Janie's Negro friends and acquaintances. In short, this is another good-will novel dramatizing the racial philosophy of Zora Neale Hurston—a racial philosophy which present-day black writers would consider incredible.

In all probability Miss Hurston was led to write *Moses Man of the Mountain* through her research in anthropology. In *Tell My Horse,* after commenting on the connection between the Haitian voodoo Damballah Ouedo and Moses, she writes: "This worship of Moses recalls the hard-to-explain fact that wherever the Negro is found, there are traditional tales of Moses and his supernatural powers that are not in the Bible, nor can they be found in any written life of Moses."

And in the introduction to the novel itself she makes the following comment about the worship of Moses by Negro people:

> So all across Africa, America, the West Indies, there are tales of the powers of Moses and great worship of him and his powers. But it does not flow from the Ten Commandments. It is his rod of power, the terror he showed before all Israel and to Pharaoh, and THAT MIGHTY HAND.

For Negroes, for the descendants of Africa, Moses is considered more in terms of magic than in any other way; he is accepted "as the fountain of mystic powers."

On the basis of these beliefs and legends concerning Moses held by many different peoples including Negroes, Zora Neale Hurston has presented the great Jewish leader, not as a Jew, but as an Egyptian prince with a social consciousness and as a seer who went to the mountain and "talked" with God. Moses led the grumbling Hebrews (symbolically all men) from the bondage of Egypt (narrow, selfish, and provincial thinking and living) and piloted them to the borders of the Promised Land.

The telling of the story reminds one a little of *Green Pastures* because it is presented in the speech of a folk narrator, a Negro folk narrator. Miss Hurston weaves into her work, not only black folk tales and idiom, but folk material from other cultures. The black, of course, predominates. Although the satire is not stringent, the Bible story of Moses found in the Old Testament takes quite a beating in the Hurston version. In their pigheadedness, in their squabbling, in their reluctance to follow a leader, and in their eternal gripings and whining, the Jews acted "just like niggers." And, of course, there is suggested throughout the work, though never stated, the parallel between Southern slavery for the Negro and Egyptian slavery for the Jew. This parallel appears often in the spirituals; it also appears in the literary productions of Gustavus Vassa and David Walker. (Vassa suggested that Africans might be the "Lost Tribes" of the Jews.) One notes that the wife of Moses, Zipporah, is black, and though she is sketchily drawn, her depiction allows the author to get in some hard blows aimed at the Jewish color prejudice. Aaron and Miriam act like present-day whites when the first Negro family moves into a middle-class neighborhood.

Moses Man of the Mountain, in spite of its racy folk dialogue, and in spite of its unusual approach, does not quite come through as a novel. Except for Moses, the characters are not fully developed. Joshua, Pharaoh (the younger), Aaron, and Miriam are puppets, and the same may be said about most, if not all, the major characters. One must allow, however, for the viewpoint from which the story is told—that of a folk legend. But even after making such an allowance, the work is still not impressive.

Zora Neale's last work of fiction, *Seraph on the Suwanee* (1948), uses white principal characters. In this work she is doing what Yerby and Motley did exclusively and what Richard Wright, William Gardner Smith, Ann Petry, and others did from time to time, which is to leave the Negro problem and write simply as Americans. There is, of course, absolutely no reason why Negro writers should not do this. Ann Petry, for example, knew her New England background in *Country Place* as well as she learned to know Harlem. And Miss Hurston probably knew Florida whites—all kinds. All other things being equal, however, an author writes best about his own group, and this is true of Zora Neale Hurston. *Seraph on the Suwanee* does not move as freely as her two "Negro" works of fiction; it lacks the racy Negro folk speech and seems more highly contrived. No matter how much Miss Hurston knew about Florida poor whites, she instinctively and naturally knew more about Florida Negroes, and the difference shows in this novel.

The story tells of the pathetic and moving efforts of Arvay Henson, a poor white and a neurotic, to understand her progressive and energetic husband, Jim Meserve, a man from a slightly higher family background than hers. Jim has none of the "cracker" mentality that his wife possesses. Through her love for him, she learns to rise above her background. By the end of the novel, after a series of confrontations between the two, they finally come to understand each other and to find happiness. The route, however, to this happy ending tells the reader a lot about work in the turpentine camps, in orange groves, and in the shrimp-fishing industry. The book, however, seems forced. The author manufactures crises at will; many of the characters are stereotypes; and the principal characters, in their several ways, are too good to be real. Miss Hurston is an incurable sentimentalist in her depiction of romantic love. In short, Miss Hurston in this work lacks the sureness she had in her first two novels. For one thing, she could not make full use of that poetic black folk speech that she handled so well in the Negro works. For another, she did not seem to know her material as

Zora Neale Hurston

Photo by Carl Van Vechten, Collection of American Literature, Beinecke Rare Book and Manuscript Library, Yale University.

intimately as she did, let us say, in *Jonah's Gourd Vine,* and she therefore strains after effect. In one work the story limps along, in the other it flows easily, taking the reader along with it.

Zora Neale Hurston's autobiography, *Dust Tracks on a Road,* in its digressions, in its important omissions, its slighting of persons whom Zora Neale did not like, its slurring over of episodes in her own life, and in its emphasis on white rather than Negro friends, reminds one of Claude McKay's autobiography. The personalities of the two writers are alike in several ways.

Let us take the matter of omissions. Miss Hurston, as we learn from the works of Hughes and Thurman, knew all of the Harlem members of that early Renaissance group: Cullen, Hughes, Fisher, Bontemps, and others. Of these writers, she mentions only Hughes, and in a very brief passage. Concerning the Renaissance itself, all she says is that Charles S. Johnson was the real father of the movement, not the others to whom credit is given. Or to take another type of omission—she plays up her friendship with Fannie Hurst, but she does not tell us, as Darwin Turner points out in his introduction to the 1969 Arno Press reprint of *Dust Tracks on a Road,* that "Fannie Hurst discharged her as a secretary because she typed poorly, filed illogically, wrote an undecipherable shorthand, and was habitually late. But Miss Hurst permitted her to remain as a guest in the apartment for more than a year because she was an amusing companion."

Among the other white friends that Zora Neale tells us about are Franz Boas, the famous professor of anthropology at Barnard, whom she calls Papa Franz; and Mrs. R. Osgood Mason, a wealthy woman interested in writers and artists, whom she calls Godmother, and who gave her $200 a month for two years to do research. Concerning Godmother, Miss Hurston writes: "There was and is a psychic bond between us. She could read my mind, not only when I was in her presence, but thousands of miles away"

In *Dust Tracks on a Road* Zora Neale Hurston describes two of her own love affairs. The vagueness of her account, the lack of details, including the names of the men, and practically everything else about these affairs make the reader suspect them—at least *her* account of them. Here and in other sections of the work we are getting, not actual experiences, but experiences "ordered" for a certain effect by the author. All writers of autobiography do this to some extent, but the liberties Miss Hurston takes come dangerously close to plain dishonesty.

The author's two folklore collections, *Mules and Men* and *Tell My Horse,* are fascinating works. Miss Hurston had a natural flair for collecting material from the folk. She had no difficulty in becoming one with the people from whom she sought songs or stories or customs, whether in the Deep South or in Haiti. She also had a great and natural gift as a raconteur of the stories she collected. Although the two works she published are impressive, one likes to think that with her undoubted ability as a collector and interpreter of folklore she would have made a far richer contribution to the field if she had continued to work in it.

Zora Neale Hurston has probably never received from Negro critics the credit she deserves, whereas white critics have occasionally over-praised her work. The reason for this, or at least part of it, is that she wrote counter to the prevailing attitude of protest and militancy which most Negro writers since 1925 have taken. Repelled by Zora Neale Hurston's unrealistic good-will stance, Negro critics have tended to dismiss her. This is unfortunate because, whatever one may think of her racial attitude, she had a real if uneven talent as a fiction writer and superb gifts as a collector and interpreter of folk materials.

Frank Marshall Davis

In the "Forewarning" to *I Am the American Negro* Frank Marshall Davis cautions us not to look for "fairy words" or "a Pollyanna mind" in his writings, but rather for "coarse victuals" and "companions who seldom smile. . . ." "For being black/ In my America/ Is no rendezvous with Venus. . . ." The last poem in the same work, entitled "Frank Marshall Davis: Writer," continues our introduction to the poet, opening with the following lines:

> "He is bitter
> A bitter bitter
> Cynic"
> They said
> "And his wine
> He brews from wormwood."

These two poems constitute not only a characterization of Davis's writings but are a sort of personal manifesto. He felt that no "sensitive Negro" could live in America without "finding his cup holds vinegar and his meat seasoned with gall." To this bitter brew of vinegar and gall, Frank Marshall Davis added a generous amount of leftist ideology, and the product was a series of hard-hitting poems of social criticism which, though now dated, seemed very impressive at the time they were first published.

Frank Marshall Davis was born in Arkansas City, Kansas, on December 31, 1905. He was educated at Friends University in Wichita and at the journalism school of Kansas State College, where he was the first student to be awarded its Sigma Delta Chi Perpetual Scholarship. He studied there for two years and then went to Chicago to work as a journalist. In 1929 Davis returned to school for a year. Then, in 1931, he helped start the *Atlanta Daily World,* later returning to Chicago to work as feature editor of the Associated Negro Press. He worked as a journalist, not only in Chicago and Atlanta, but in Gary, Indiana, as well. *Black Man's Verse* (1935) and *I Am the American Negro* (1937) were highly praised and won for him a coveted Rosenwald Fellowship in Creative Writing. These two volumes, together with *47th Street Poems* (1948), established his reputation as a "socially minded poet." He at one time served as treasurer of the Chicago chapter of the League of American Writers. In recent years he has lived in Hawaii.

The poetical works of Davis are found in the following volumes: *Black Man's Verse* (1935), *I Am the American Negro* (1937), *Through Sepia Eyes, Four Poems by Frank Marshall Davis* (1938), and *47th Street Poems* (1948). Influenced by such "New Poets" as Masters and Sandburg, Davis wrote largely, though not entirely, in free verse, making generous use of verse paragraphs and of catalogues after the manner of Whitman. He was the most outspoken social critic among the Negro poets of the thirties, and his work had a kind of rough Western quality about it that caught the attention. Unfortunately, when poetry is used as a social weapon, it tends to do two things: fall into repetitious slogans and clichés; and, unless it is really great poetry, lose its appeal when new social conditions emerge. For these reasons and others to be discussed later, Frank Marshall Davis did not wear as well as some of his less sensational contemporaries.

Several themes recur often in the works of Davis. One of the most popular is the city of Chicago itself—both the city as a whole as well as its Negro section. Like the small-town boy that he was, Davis seems to be fascinated by the big, masculine, unruly city; and he tries time and again to put in words the essence that is Chicago. The only drawback, however, is that too much of what he writes reminds one of Carl Sandburg's "Stormy, husky, brawling,/ City of the Big Shoulders." Davis wrote many Chicago poems, among them, in *Black Man's Verse,* "Chicago's Congo," "Five Portraits of Chicago at Night," and "South State Street Profile"; in *Through Sepia Eyes,* "Chicago Skyscrapers"; in *I Am the American Negro,* "Washington Park, Chicago"; and in *47th Street,* the title poem. Later, Langston Hughes was to do for Harlem

(*Montage of a Dream Deferred*) what Davis *tried* to do for black Chicago. One of Davis's early attempts in this vein is "Chicago's Congo," whose theme is "From the Congo/ to Chicago/ is a long trek/—as the Crow flies" (note the play on the word *crow*). Weaving in echoes from an African past, the poem gives vignettes of the Negro's existence and potential in the big Western city. Perhaps his best attempt in this vein is his poem called "47th Street." In this work Davis does exactly, but on a larger canvas, what he had done earlier: a series of portraits and vignettes covering all aspects of black life on 47th Street. There is nothing really new here except the description of World War II reactions, but the poem is more restrained, better controlled, better written than earlier works on the same theme.

Like many of the New Negro poets who preceded him, Davis was deeply interested in jazz (and in cabaret life because of its association with jazz); and he has a number of poems on both themes, one or two of them quie ambitious. Unfortunately, the reader of Davis's jazz poems is invariably reminded of Langston Hughes's poems on the subjects and, invariably, compares the two poets. For example, note the following verses from "Jazz Band" (*Black Man's Verse*):

> Play that thing, you jazz mad fools!
> Boil a skyscraper with a jungle
> Dish it to 'em sweet and hot—
> Ahhhhhhh
> Rip it open then sew it up, jazz band!

Note the contrast between them and the following lines from Hughes's "To Midnight Nan at Leroys":

> Strut and wiggle,
> Shameless gal.
> Wouldn't no good fellow
> Be your pal.
>
> *Hear dat music . . .*
> *Jungle night.*
> *Hear that music . . .*
> *And the moon was white. . . .*

One finds in Hughes a sense of rhythm absent in Davis's lines. To put it in modern terms, Hughes had far more soul than Davis, whose attitude toward jazz tended to be more philosophical than that of Hughes.

Frank Marshall Davis's poems of social criticism, as stated, follow the line of attack current at the time he wrote. A typical example of his work is "To Those Who Sing America" (*Through Sepia Eyes*), a left-ist parody on "America" which brings in all of the heroes and villains

Frank Marshall Davis

Courtesy of Moorland-Spingarn Research Center, Howard University.

of the period: Sacco and Vanzetti, Tom Mooney, the Scottsboro Boys, "Mistermorgan," "Misterdupont," and "Mistermellon." The following section will give some idea of Davis's social attitude:

"My country! 'tis of thee, . . ."
(*On the shores of this, my country, dwell Plenty in a forty-room mansion and Poverty in a one-room hovel . . . cotton growers starving, wheat raisers naked . . . a nation turned prostitute for the fat pimps of Politicians and Captains of Industry . . . Sundays all rise to serve a crippled Nordic God . . . His torn-out eyes replaced by dollar signs . . . His belly bloated with the greasy gravy of the Profit System . . . His spindly paralyzed shanks moulded from the spavined bone of the hungry workers . . . his doddering frame supported by the props of Federal Dole and Government Subsidy . . . this is my country with the star spangled robe snatched away*)

Most of Davis's poems of social criticism naturally concerned the American racial problem, and for him as for all other Negro writers of the age lynching was the prime symbol of the failure of the American dream. The poet has several pieces on the subject, among them "Nicodemus Perry," "Sam Jackson," and "Moses Mitchell," all from *I Am the American Negro*. His longest and most ambitious poem on the subject is "Lynched (Symphonic Interlude for Twenty-One Selected Instruments)," a five-page treatment in *Black Man's Verse*. Suggesting in the margins various instruments to accentuate the several moods of horror evoked, the poem makes a strong effort, but somehow does not quite come through—it leaves us unmoved. There is a spark missing. Compare, for example, the mob's reaction as described by Davis:

> For him no sobs
> no anguished cries
> Naught but the mob's
> insatiable hate
> to speed him on
> to be death's mate.
> And in this way . . .
> and in this way
> did White get its revenge.

Compare it with that of the mob in Claude McKay's "The Lynching":

> The women thronged to look, but never a one
> Showed sorrow in her eyes of steely blue;
> And little lads, lynchers that were to be,
> Danced round the dreadful thing in fiendish glee.

In fourteen lines McKay impresses the real horror of lynching upon us far better than Davis does in his diffuse five-page effort. The difference, of course, lies in the respective talents of each man, but the tightness of the sonnet form helped McKay as much as the looseness of free verse hurt Davis.

The title poem in *I Am the American Negro* is another of Davis's long (nine pages) protest poems. More of a pageant than a poem, it reminds one of Du Bois's work of this kind. Using a "tall temple" as background and a shackled brown Giant as the protagonist—a sort of black Prometheus—the poem weaves in a good deal of Negro history, gives a catalogue of the weaknesses and the strengths of the American Negro, and ends on a militant note when the "Voice of Experience" persuades the Giant to "stand erect." When he does so the "temple falls in a crash," and its stones shower down upon the Giant. The last lines of the poem *presumably* give the meaning of this catastrophe: ". . . these stones that formed the temple of America's Social System end the life and problems of the Negro giant as they collapse." Is Davis saying what the present-day black revolutionists repeatedly assert—that the whole structure of the Establishment must be destroyed if the Negro is to be liberated? The only rub here is that Davis's Giant, like Samson, is also killed in the crash.

Another type of protest poem is found in "What Do You Want America?" (*Black Man's Verse*). In these lines he parades the Negro's contribution to America (a device he uses in many of his poems). In this catalogue of black contributors, he misses nobody from Crispus Attucks and Phillis Wheatley on down to Paul Robeson and Countee Cullen. This sort of listing was a feature of early twentieth-century Negro protest poetry.

Frank Marshall Davis has a unique type of protest poem. It is a humorous vignette or portrait (listed in two of his volumes under the heading "Ebony Under Granite") in which he comments ironically on the shortcomings of a particular character. "Giles Johnson, Ph. D." (*Black Man's Verse*) is a good example of the type:

> Giles Johnson
> had four college degrees
> knew the whyfore of this
> the wherefore of that
> could orate in Latin
> or cuss in Greek
> and, having learned such things
> he died of starvation
> because he wouldn't teach
> and he couldn't porter.

The most sensational of Davis's protest poems, "Snapshots of the Cotton South" (*47th Street*), is a harsh, hard-hitting, and, for the era,

a shocking piece that told unpleasant truths about sex-and-racial relations in Dixie. The following section is typical:

> Of course
> There is no intermingling socially
> Between the races. . . .
> Still
> At regular intervals
> The wife of Mobtown's mayor
> Sees an Atlanta specialist
> For syphilis contracted from her husband
> Who got it from their young mulatto cook
> Who was infected by the chief of police. . . .

As stated above, too much of Frank Marshall Davis's poetry has the
faults of all propaganda verse. In his case there are too many gory lynching scenes (one very much like the other), too many catalogues of the
Negro's unappreciated contributions to America, too many clichés about
Capitalism (with a capital "C") and the plight of the worker, black and
white, and too much about the failure of the American Dream. Davis
tends to be heavy-handed in his handling of social themes, and he tends
to repeat himself too often. We need his poetry, however, if we are to
have a complete picture of the impact of Marxism on Negroes during
the thirties and forties.

Sterling A. Brown

Poet, critic, folklorist, scholar, and teacher, Sterling A. Brown is more
of a transitional figure than a First Fruit of the New Negro Renaissance.
The young writers of today, however, when they honor him, as they
frequently do, have insisted on placing him with Hughes and Cullen. As
a matter of record, he came later. His first publication, *Southern Road,*
appeared in 1932. Moreover, although he knew the Harlem writers, he
did not live there, and he did not make use of the alien-and-exile theme
so popular with them. And yet, if one accepts the timetable this work
sets up for the two phases of the Renaissance, he may be placed in this
catagory.

Sterling Brown has not been a prolific writer, but he made up in excellence what, because of his perfectionist tendencies, he lacked in volume. He also had a great impact in terms of influence. Few works in criticism or in poetry have had more effect on young and not-so-young Negro writers than those of Professor Brown. In his books, articles (most notably his monthly reviews of books about and by the Negro in *Opportunity*), the classroom and lecture platform, and his "vagabond" trips which covered the South from the Potomac to the Mississippi, Brown stressed the importance of the Negro's folk material and literature. Beginning his work of indoctrination in the early thirties, when interest in these subjects was at a low ebb, he has seen the new and spectacular interest in Negro American literature now held by the nation—an interest which he helped to create.

Sterling A. Brown was born in Washington, D.C., where he attended the well-known Dunbar High School. In 1922 he received an A.B. from Williams College (Phi Beta Kappa) and in 1923 an M.A. from Harvard University. Although he pursued further graduate study in English at Harvard (1931–1932), he never worked toward a doctorate degree. The University of Massachusetts and Howard University have given him honorary doctorates.

Brown taught at several colleges and universities, including Virginia Seminary and College, Lincoln University (Missouri), and Fisk University. In 1929 he began teaching at Howard University, where he remained until his retirement in 1969. As a visiting professor he taught at several universities: Atlanta University, New York University, Vassar College, the University of Minnesota, the New School, and the University of Illinois (Chicago Circle).

Professor Brown's poems, like his critical essays, have been anthologized widely. His two famous critical works are *Negro Poetry and Drama* (1937) and *The Negro in American Fiction* (1937). In 1941 he co-edited *The Negro Caravan* (Brown, Davis, and Lee), keeping alive an interest in Negro literature at a time when its popularity had dwindled greatly.

A memorable reader of his own poetry, Brown has read at many colleges and universities throughout the nation. He has been recorded by Folkways Records in *Anthology of Negro Poets* and recently in an album on which he reads his own poems. His poems are recorded on other records, including *A Hand's on the Gate*.

A respected folklorist and authority on Negro culture, Brown served on numerous committees and boards: the Carnegie Myrdal Study, the American Folklore Society, the Institute of Jazz Studies, the editorial board of *The Crisis,* the Federal Writers' Project, and the Committee on Negro Studies of the American Council of Learned Societies. With

Rayford Logan he wrote an article on the American Negro for the *Encyclopaedia Britannica.*

Although he has published other poetry since 1932, the bulk of Professor Brown's verse production is found in *Southern Road*—a first volume that ranks with *The Weary Blues* and *Color.* James Weldon Johnson, who wrote the introduction to the book, was among the first to recognize the genius of the new poet. Placing him with Toomer, McKay, Cullen, and Hughes, Johnson labeled the group the five "most outstanding" younger poets, and then added:

> Mr. Brown's work is not only fine, it is also unique. . . . He infused his poetry with genuine characteristic flavor by adopting as his medium the common, racy, living speech of the Negro in certain places of *real* life. For his raw material he dug down into the deep mine of Negro folk poetry . . . he has made more than mere transcriptions of folk poetry, and he has done more than bring to it mere artistry; he has deepened its meanings and multiplied its implications. He has actually absorbed the spirit of his material; made it his own; and without diluting its primitive frankness and raciness, truly re-expressed it with artistry and magnified power. In a word, he has taken this raw material and worked it into original and authentic poetry.

The poetry of Sterling Brown deals mainly with the following general subjects: the *endurance* of the Negro, the stark tragedy which is too often his lot, death as a means of release from his misery, the open road as another escape, and humor as a safety valve. Most of his work may be classed as protest poetry in the classical sense of that now frowned-on term. Brown has been influenced by Negro folk material, by such poets as Sandburg and Frost, and, of course, by the corpus of English and American traditional poetry. His poetical forms reflect all of these influences.

He uses the sonnet form (though not too often), stanzaic forms, the free-verse patterns of the New Poets, and ballad and blues forms, the last-named both in the conventional pattern and in patterns derived from the conventional form. His language is simple, suggestive, and direct, reflecting strongly his interest in the speech of the folk. Several of his best poems use contrapuntally statements in standard English with statements from the reservoir of folk comment (usually given in italics). There is a quality in Brown's poetry that makes it quite different from that of Langston Hughes, although both tended to use the same folk subjects and forms. Brown has more intensity and a deeper concern for dramatic effect. This is not a value judgment concerning the quality of the works of the two poets; it is merely a comparison of the impressions made on one reader.

Of those verses dealing with the endurance theme, "Strong Men" is probably the best and certainly the best known. A "symphonic" work,

it weaves in the narrator's comments on the Negro's treatment from the
slave ship on down to the tenant farm and the black ghetto—weaves
them in contrapuntally with folk sayings:

> They dragged you from homeland . . .
> They scourged you . . .
> They swelled your numbers with bastards. . . .
> They taught you the religion they disgraced.

> You sang:
>> *Keep a-inchin' along*
>> *Lak a po' inch worm* . . .

> You sang:
>> *Walk togedder, chillen,*
>> *Dontcha git weary.* . . .
>>> The strong men keep a-comin' on
>>> The strong men git stronger.

A very effective poem, its "strong men" refrain beats home the unrelenting tenaciousness of the folk Negro, his determination to "keep
a-inchin' along" toward freedom.

A few of these endurance poems assume a stoic and fatalistic acceptance unusual in works by Negroes. In "Old Man Buzzard," for example,
the speaker takes consolation from the thought that hard times come and
go: "Nothin' las' always/ Farz as I know." In "Memphis Blues" the
persona, having in mind that the present-day Memphis, like the ancient
city, may be destroyed, asks of several types of Negroes: "Whatcha
gonna do" when this happens? The answer of "Mistah Working Man"
is typical of the Negro folk spirit: "Gonna put dem buildings up again,/
Gonna put em up dis time to stan'."

An important factor in this determination to keep going is the solid
courage exemplified in folk heroes, a courage that inspires and lightens
momentarily the weary load. The speaker in "Strange Legacies" thanks
Jack Johnson and John Henry for going down like " 'nachal' men." He
also thanks an old Negro couple in Red River Bottom, nameless but
just as heroic, who, when all their belongings are wiped out by the
flood, simply say: *"Guess we'll give it one mo' try./ Guess we'll give it
one mo' try."*

The stark tragedy which too often bedevils black existence, the
second broad theme, is found in many pieces, including "Dark of the
Moon," "Georgia Grimes," "Johnny Thomas," "Frankie and Johnnie"
(a new twist to the old ballad), "Convict," and the title poem, "Southern
Road." Another group of poems, including "Bessie," "Effie," "Maumee
Ruth," "Chillen Get Shoes," portrays the tragic odds against poor Negro

women. All these poems have a strong naturalistic thrust. The lives of these black folk—fallen women, worthless children, and convicts on the chain gang—are as definitely doomed by American injustice as though placed in the hands of some Calvinistic angry God. The strongest poem in this group is "Southern Road." To the rhythmic and sombre accompaniment of hammer blows and the repeated "hunh," the speaker narrates his life, the saga of a damned soul:

> Chain gang nevah—hunh—
> Let me go;
> Chain gang nevah—hunh—
> Let me go;
> Po' los' boy, bebby,
> Evahmo'. . . .

In addition to being one of the finest poems using the blues form, it is also one of the most effective protest poems in Negro American literature.

In a group of these bitter verses on the tragic experience of Negro life, Sterling Brown uses the river as a symbol of God's or nature's total indifference to the lot of the poor. In "The Children of the Mississippi" we are told that these folk, "for all their singing," know fear, grief, and doubt intimately. As "step-children of the Mississippi" they can only ask:

> *What we done done to you*
> *Makes you do lak you do?*
> *How we done harmed you*
> *Black-hearted river?*

The same Job-like questioning, the same Hardyesque lament over nature's indifference is voiced again in "Foreclosure." In this case it is the mighty Missouri which forecloses on Uncle Dan, who, bewildered at his losses, can only curse and shout "in his hoarse old voice/ *'ain't got no right to act dat way at all!/ No right at all!'* " In the meantime, "the old river rolls on, sleepily to the gulf."

In the face of such overwhelming odds, what keeps the black man going, what makes him stubbornly *endure?* Three things, Professor Brown seems to suggest in answer to that question: the Negro's religion, his song, and his ability to laugh not only at "Cap'n Charlie" but also at himself. Taking religion first—Sister Lou could not have made it without a deep and comforting sense of a world to come. The speaker and adviser in "Sister Lou" gives her friend specific and reassuring instructions: "Honey/ Don't be feared of them pearly gates,/ Don't go 'round to de back,/ No mo, dataway/ Not evah no mo'." In the homey speech of Southern Christian folk, the poet paints a heaven of release, not only from having to go to the back doors, but also a heaven in which Sister Lou can assume a simple dignity no poor black woman can find in this world. It is a place in which she, for once, can be *somebody*. This thought has been a rock in a weary land for countless oppressed blacks.

The Negro's song, whether spirituals or blues, has been a safety valve. A singer like Ma Rainey expressed the sorrow and the misery of the lives of poor black folks, and her singing brings release through catharsis:

> O Ma Rainey,
> Li'l an' low
> Sing us 'bout de hard luck
> Roun' our do';
> Sing us 'bout de lonesome road
> We mus' go. . . .

The Negro's ability to laugh, to laugh to keep from crying, has helped to keep his sanity in a world that has been irrationally against him. After reading the bitter poems of Sterling Brown, one is surprised to find that he also has a rich sense of humor. Poems like "Mister Samuel and Sam," "Checkers," "Scotty Has His Say," and the Slim Greer series show not only Brown's ability to laugh and to protest but also his deep knowledge of the life of ordinary black people and of the ways of white folks. To his comment on the human weakness of black and white, the poet adds a special ingredient from folk humor: the tall tale. In "Slim Greer," "Slim Lands a Job," "Slim in Atlanta," and "Slim in Hell," Brown has created not only a new American folk character, but has elevated the tall story into sophisticated art. The rich exaggeration of finding Slim in "Arkansaw" passing for white, "An' he no lighter/ Than a dark midnight"; or of Slim

> Down in Atlanta
> De whitefolk got laws
> For to keep all de niggers
> From laughin' outdoors. . . .

Atlanta made all niggers laugh in a "telefoam booth." Slim, of course, disrupted things by breaking through the waiting lines; getting into a booth, he "laughed four hours/ By de Georgia clocks." The laughter of Slim Greer is often a two-edged laughter. It is a kind that present-day believers in the black revolution seldom use. This is unfortunate. There is therapy in the humor of Slim Greer and Sterling Brown.

There are several poems of Brown which do not fall into the cate-

gories listed. One of them is "Odyssey of Big Boy," a magnificent delineation of the thoughts and experiences of that type of Negro worker
who, always seeking the distant horizon, takes all kinds of jobs in all
kinds of places so long as he keeps moving. The things he asks of life
are simple and fundamental—a job, a good woman; in death he wants
to be with his heroes:

> An' all dat Big Boy axes
>   When time comes fo' to go,
> Lemme be wid John Henry, steel drivin' man,
>   Lemme be wid old Jazzbo,
>   Lemme be wid ole Jazzbo. . . .

Based on a well-known character often seen on the corner of 14th
and You Streets in the nation's capital, "Sporting Beasley" delineates
and immortalizes the "peacock syndrome" often found among oppressed
groups—an effort to find escape from the drabness and ugliness of ghetto
living through the splendor of dress. The Sporting Beasleys of the world
are black Rolands, defiantly and flamboyantly approaching the Dark
Towers of Jim Crow existence. With their tophats jauntily placed, their
red carnations in button holes, their Prince Albert coats and grey morning trousers, and, above all else, with their white spats and canes, they
transcend the littleness of a hostile barnyard world. "Step it, Mr. Beasley,
oh step it till the sun goes down."

One of the best poems that Professor Brown has published since
Southern Road is a perceptive, deeply moving piece entitled "Remembering Nat Turner." Another of his symphonic works, it gives the "feel"
of the sophisticated narrator visiting the scene of the rebellion, the
"faintest recollections" of the Negroes, and the garbled and ignorant
recital of the event by "an old white woman." These three viewpoints
are fused into a brooding impression of the transience of all things
human. The symbol of Nat's forgotten heroic exploits was "a signpost
here with printing on it,/ But it rotted in the hold and thar it lays;/ And
the nigger tenants split the marker for kindling."

The criticism of Sterling Brown has a refreshing common-sense
quality. Belonging to no one school, he brings to his evaluation of literary works a keen and well-stocked mind, excellent academic training,
and a deep sensitivity. Never a black nationalist in his approach, he
assumes that writings by Negroes are American writings, first of all, and
tend to reflect contemporary trends in the national literature far more
than they reflect racial trends. In practically all of Mr. Brown's critical
summaries he includes not only works by Negroes but also works by

white authors *on* the Negro. He does not believe that the Negro has a "peculiar endowment" because he knows how easily such a belief can be stressed "at the expense of the Negro's basic humanity." He would, therefore, not agree with some extreme Black Aesthetics critics who say that whites cannot give a truthful interpretation of the Negro experience. On the other hand, he is convinced that, all other things equal, the black writers would know more intimately the black experience and must, therefore, "accept the responsibility of being the ultimate portrayers of their own":

> As we go to the Russians, the Scandinavians, and the French for the truth about their people; as we go to the workers and not to the stockholders, to the tenants and croppers and not to the landlords, for the truth about the lives of tenants and croppers, so it seems we should expect the truth of Negro life from Negroes. The Negro artist has a fine task ahead of him to render this truth in enduring fiction.

Throughout his critical career, Brown has been concerned with the American tendency to think of the Negro in stereotypes. One of his first works on this subject is a long article which appeared in *The Journal of Negro Education,* vol. II, no. 2 (April, 1933) entitled "Negro Characters as Seen by White Authors." The theme of this study is stated in the following paragraph:

> The Negro has met with as great injustice in American literature as he has in American life. The majority of books about Negroes merely stereotype Negro character. It is the purpose of this paper to point out the prevalence and history of these stereotypes. Those considered important enough for separate classification, although overlappings *do* occur, are seven in number: (1) The Contented Slave, (2) The Wretched Freeman, (3) The Comic Negro, (4) The Brute Negro, (5) The Tragic Mulatto, (6) The Local Color Negro, (7) The Exotic Primitive.

Giving many examples of each stereotype, Professor Brown documents thoroughly and brilliantly his thesis. He concludes: "Authors are too anxious to have it said, 'Here is *the* Negro,' rather than here are a few Negroes whom I have seen."

Brown is at his best when he presents panoramic reviews of large segments of American writing which treats the Negro. If one follows his not-too-frequent surveys, he gets an excellent overall view of the Negro in American literature. Two such volumes—*The Negro in American Fiction* and *Negro Poetry and Drama*—appeared in 1937 as Bronze Booklets, published by the Associates in Negro Folk Education under the general editorship of Alain Locke. The most valuable sections of the first work—valuable not only because of the critical insight they contain but also because they deal with material difficult to find elsewhere—are Chapters I, II, and III. In Chapter I he traces the Negro

Sterling A. Brown

Photo by Roy Lewis.

character from his earliest appearance in such novels as William Hill Brown's *The Power of Sympathy* (1789) and Mrs. Susannah Rowson's *The Inquisition* (1794) down through better known writers, for example, Royal Tyler, and such well-known classic authors as Irving, Cooper, and Melville. Seen through the eyes of a Negro critic, particularly one ever on the lookout for stereotypes, these characters assume new critical dimensions. In Chapter II Brown deals with "The Plantation Tradition," tracing it from *Swallow Barn* (1832) down to such works as Mrs. Mary Schoolcraft's *The Black Gauntlet* (1860). As in Chapter I, he documents his contentions with proslavery writers the average American literature scholar has never heard of. Chapter III deals in the same manner and with the same thoroughness with "Antislavery Fiction," including such Negro writers as William Wells Brown. *The Negro in American Fiction* covers the subject down to 1937, the year of its publication. In later chapters Professor Brown naturally discusses many works treated by other scholars. His insight into controversial figures, Faulkner, for example, is valuable because he is looking steadily at his material and seeing it whole—not through the perspective of some stereotype.

The second volume, *Negro Poetry and Drama,* unlike other well-known works covering the field, examines both black and white authors. It shows, therefore, the reflection in Negro authors of current American literary trends. In addition, it has an excellent section called "Negro Folk Poetry," a subject which the author knows thoroughly. Beginning with the poetry of Jupiter Hammon and Phillis Wheatley, the volume discusses the Negro in poetry down to writers like Vachel Lindsay and Richard Wright. No other work up to this time had treated as a group the poets covered in this volume.

The drama section, again, is something of a pioneering effort in that it traces the Negro in American drama from its beginnings down to 1937. *Plays of Negro Life,* by Locke and Gregory, which came before this work, is an anthology. Johnson's *Black Manhattan* touches on some of the material in Brown's volume, but by no means on all of it. Moreover, Johnson's work tends to be journalistic rather than scholarly. Thus, although *Negro Poetry and Drama* is a modest volume, it holds a secure place in the critical history of Negro American literature. The same, of course, holds for *The Negro in American Fiction.*

In 1941 Sterling Brown (along with Arthur P. Davis and Ulysses Lee) brought out *The Negro Caravan,* an anthology of Negro American writings from 1760 down to 1941. Arranged by types, with full introductions for each type, the work also included a very rich folk section. *The Negro Caravan,* reprinted often since 1941, has become something of a landmark in the study of Negro American literature. In all probability, its popularity helped to keep alive an interest in that literature in the years between the New Negro Renaissance and the Black Arts Revolution of the sixties and seventies. One recent critic, Julius Lester, in the introduction to the 1969 reprint of the work, states: "It [*The Caravan*] comes as close today as it did in 1941 to being the most important single volume of black writing ever published."

In 1951 Professor Brown contributed another of his long summarizing articles, "Athletics and Arts," to *The Integration of the Negro into American Society,* the papers of the Fourteenth Annual Conference of the Division of the Social Sciences, Howard University. One of the outstanding sections of this essay is the one called "Jazz Music," one in which Brown in a very short compass gives a brief but impressive history of jazz from its beginnings down to 1951. A student of the subject since his college days, Professor Brown brings to comments on jazz a deep interest in and a thorough knowledge of the subject. One notes again Brown's integrationist approach to jazz as well as to other fields: "Despite the Negro's undoubted formative influence, jazz does not belong to the Negro. It is not an African music, though some analysts like Rudi Blesh stress the African survivals. It was never completely the American Negro's, or if so only briefly. Music rises over even the high walls of separation."

In his section on "Literature" in the same essay Professor Brown, after a long and searching discussion on the meaning of integration as applied to Negro American writing, takes this position:

> When Negro authors emerge worthy to tell the story, the stories, of the Negro in America, they will write with authenticity and power, not because of any racial *mystique,* but because they have lived the story so fully, brooded upon it so deeply. . . . And that will mean not only that the Negro author is integrated into American literature, but even more that he will be given passport to enter the Republic of Letters of the world.

In 1955 he wrote an essay on "The New Negro in Literature (1925–1955)" for *The New Negro Thirty Years Afterwards (Papers Contributed to the Sixteenth Annual Spring Conference of the Division of Social Sciences, Howard University).* In this article he gives a chronological survey and, therefore, treats many of the writers already touched in earlier papers. His comments on the New Negro Renaissance are intriguing:

> I have hesitated to use the term Negro Renaissance for several reasons: one is that the five or eight years generally allotted are short for the life-span of any "renaissance." The New Negro is not to me a group of writers centered in Harlem during the second half of the twenties. Most of the writers were not Harlemites; much of the best writing was not

about Harlem, which was the show-window, the cashier's till, but no more Negro America than New York is America. The New Negro Movement had temporal roots in the past and spacial roots elsewhere in America, and the term has validity, it seems to me, only when considered to be a continuing tradition.

Professor Brown's latest (at this writing) summary-evaluation, "A Century of Negro Portraiture in American Literature," appeared in *The Massachusetts Review* (Winter, 1966). Covering a wide range, one hundred years of works on and by Negroes, this essay gives an incisive and revealing look at the development of insight on the part of white authors who treat the Negro and at the remarkable growth on the part of the Negro artist. In this study the author once more returns to the theme of stereotypes, the theme he treated fully thirty years earlier. Although he feels that "stereotyping is on the way out," he has to admit that "clichés and stereotypes linger, and even burgeon." He is just as convinced as he was thirty years earlier that the writer, whether black or white, must see "Negro life steadily and whole." He sums up his position with a quote from his 1933 essay, "Negro Character as Seen by White Authors."

> One manifest truth, however, is this: the sincere, sensitive artist, willing to go beneath the clichés of popular belief to get at an underlying reality, will be wary of confining a race's entire character to a half-dozen narrow grooves. He will hardly have the temerity to say that his necessarily limited observation of a few Negroes in a restricted environment can be taken as the last word about some mythical *the* Negro. He will hesitate to do this, even though he had a Negro mammy, or spent a night in Harlem, or has been a Negro all his life. The writer submits that such an artist is the only one worth listening to, although the rest are legion.

Toward the Mainstream
(1940-1960)

Introduction

The course of Negro American literature has been highlighted by a series of social and political crises over the Negro's position in America. The Abolition Movement, the Civil War, Reconstruction, and the riot-and-lynching periods both before and after World War I have all radically influenced Negro writing. Each crisis has brought in new themes, new motivations, new character types, new viewpoints; and as each crisis has passed, the Negro writer tended to drop most of the special attitudes the crisis produced and to move toward the so-called mainstream of American literature.

Between, roughly, 1940 and 1960 two new crises occurred: the integration movement (which was climaxed by the 1954 Supreme Court decision) and the civil rights revolution (which is still with us and which began to take on its present-day characteristics around 1960). Each of these movements has affected Negro writing. Twenty years is obviously a short time in which to show literary changes resulting from *one* movement, to say nothing of two; but we live in stirring and fast-moving times. For example, within a single decade a supposedly well-established program of nonviolence and passive resistance gave way to a new and militant movement that makes the work of Martin Luther King seem almost gradualistic. Riots have taken the place of marches, and the objectives of many Negroes have shifted from integration to goals entirely alien to anything most blacks had envisioned. These changes have been incredibly swift and phenomenal, and Negro literature during the period in question has reflected them to a greater extent than is commonly realized.

Let us examine the integration movement first. Forces of integration had been at work long before 1954, but it is convenient to date the movement from that year. And, of course, the official stamp given it by the Supreme Court accelerated the social changes already in progress. After 1954 the ferment of integration seemed to go to work immediately, not only in the public schools, but in the armed forces, in Southern state universities, and in several other areas as well. A few institutions and localities and segments of the nation naturally held out—and are still holding out—but even the harshest critics of American democracy had to admit that substantial progress toward integration had been made, that the nation had committed itself officially to that ideal. And though the commitment was largely theoretical or, at best, token, it changed to a small degree the racial climate of America.

This change of climate, however, inadvertently dealt the Negro writer of the fifties a crushing blow. Up to that decade Negro literature had been predominantly a protest literature. Ironical though it may seem, the Negro had capitalized on oppression (in a literary sense, of course). Although one may deplore and condem the cause, there is a great creative motivation in a movement, which brings all members of a group together and cements them in a common bond. And that is just what segregation did for the Negro, especially during the twenties and thirties, when full segregation was not only practiced in the South but tacitly condoned by the whole nation. As long as there was this common enemy, there was a common purpose and a strong urge to transform into artistic terms the deep-rooted feelings of bitterness and scorn. When the enemy weakened, he shattered a most fruitful literary tradition. The mere suggestion that integration was possible in the not-too-distant-future tended to destroy during the fifties the protest element in Negro writing.

And one must always keep in mind the paradox involved. There was no actual integration anywhere. There was surface and token integration in many areas, but the everyday pattern of life for the overwhelming majority remained unchanged. But there was—and this is of the utmost importance—the spiritual commitment and climate out of which full integration could develop. The Negro literary artist recognized and acknowledged that climate; he accepted it in good faith; and he resolved to work with it at all costs. In the meantime, he had to live between two worlds, and that for any artist is a disturbing experience. For the Negro writers of the fifties, especially those in their middle years, it became almost a tragic experience because it meant giving up a tradition in which they had done their apprentice and journeyman work, giving it up when they were prepared to make use of that tradition as master craftsmen.

Another disturbing factor which must be considered here is that this change of climate came about rather suddenly. Perhaps it would be more exact to say that the *full awareness* came suddenly because there were signs of its approach all during the forties, and Negro writers from time to time showed that they recognized these signs. But the full awareness did not come until the fifties, and it came with some degree of abruptness. For example, all through World War II, all through the forties, most Negro writers were still grinding out protest and problem novels, many of them influenced by Richard Wright's *Native Son* (1940). The list of these works is impressive. William Attaway's *Blood on the Forge* (1941), Carl Ruthven Offord's *The White Face* (1943), Chester Himes's *If He Hollers* (1945), Ann Petry's *The Street* (1946), Philip Kaye's *Taffy* (1950), and others—practically all of them naturalistic novels with the same message of protest against America's treatment of its black minority.

The poets wrote in a similar view. Margaret Walker's *For My People* (1942), Langston Hughes's *Freedom's Plow* (1943), Gwendolyn Brooks's *A Street in Bronzeville* (1945), and Owen Dodson's *Powerful Long Ladder* (1946) all had strong protest elements; all dealt in part with the Negro's fight against segregation and discrimination at home and in the armed services.

Noting the dates of these works—both fiction and poetry—one realizes that, roughly speaking, up to 1950 the protest tradition was in full bloom, and that most of the best Negro writers were still using it. Then came this awareness of a change in the nation's climate and with it the realization that the old protest themes had to be abandoned. The new climate tended to date the problem works of the forties as definitely as time had dated the New Negro lynching-passing literature of the twenties and thirties. In other words, protest writing had become the first casualty of the new racial climate.

Faced with the loss of his oldest and most cherished tradition, the Negro writer was forced to seek fresh ways to use his material. First of all, he attempted to find new themes within the racial framework. Retaining the Negro character and background, he shifted his emphasis from the protest aspect of Negro living and placed it on the problems and conflicts within the group itself. For example, Chester Himes, pursuing this course in *Third Generation,* does not belabor the white-black problem. His main conflict in this work is that within a Negro family caused by color differences and other problems. The whole racial tone of this novel is quite different from that of *If He Hollers,* a typical protest work. One came out in 1945, the other in 1953. The two books are a good index to the changes that took place in the years separating them.

In like manner Owen Dodson and Gwendolyn Brooks in their respective novels, *Boy at the Window* (1951) and *Maud Martha* (1953), show this tendency to find new themes within the racial framework. Both publications are "little novels," giving intimate and subtle vignettes of middle-class living. Their main stress is on life within the group, not on conflict with outside forces. Taking a different approach, William Demby in *Beetlecreek* (1950) completely reversed the protest pattern by showing the black man's inhumanity to his white brother. In *The Outsider* (1953) Richard Wright took an even more subtle approach. He used a Negro main character, but by adroitly and persistently minimizing that character's racial importance, he succeeded in divorcing him from any real association with the traditional protest alignment. And Langston Hughes in *Sweet Flypaper of Life* (1955), though using all Negro characters, does not touch on the matter of interracial protest. All these authors, it seems to me, show their awareness of the new climate by either playing down or avoiding entirely the traditional protest approach.

Another group of writers (and there is some overlapping here) showed their awareness by avoiding the Negro character. Among them are William Gardner Smith (*Anger at Innocence*), Ann Petry (*Country Place*), Richard Wright (*Savage Holiday*), and Willard Motley (*Knock on Any Door*). None of these works has Negro main characters. With the exception of *Knock on Any Door,* each was a second novel, following a work written in the forties which had Negro characters and background, and which was written in the protest vein. In each case the first work was popular, and yet each of these novelists elected to avoid the theme which gave him his initial success.

So far only the novelists have been mentioned, but Negro poets also sensed the change of climate in America and reacted to it. Incidentally, several of the outstanding protest poets of the thirties dropped out of the picture as poets. It cannot be said, of course, that the new climate alone silenced them, but it was perhaps a contributing cause. It is hard for a mature writer to slough off tradition in which he has worked during all of his formative years. Acquiring a new approach in any field of art is a very serious and trying experience. One must also remember that the protest tradition was no mere surface fad with the Negro writer. It was part of his self-respect, part of his philosophy of life, part of his inner being. It was almost a religious experience with those of us who came up through the dark days of the twenties and thirties. When a tradition so deeply ingrained is abandoned, it tends to leave a spiritual numbness—a kind of void not easily filled with new interests or motivations. Several of the ablest poets—and novelists, too, for that matter—did not try to fill that void.

A few of the poets, however, met the challenge of the new climate, among them the late M. B. Tolson and Gwendolyn Brooks. A comparison of the early and later works of these poets shows a tendency in later works either to avoid protest themes entirely or to approach them more subtly and obliquely. Compare, for example, Tolson's *Rendezvous with America* (1944) with *A Libretto for the Republic of Liberia* (1953). The thumping rhythms of the protest verse in the former work gave way in the latter to a new technique, one that was influenced largely by Hart Crane. With this new work, Tolson successfully turned his back on the tradition in which he came to maturity.

Two works of Gwendolyn Brooks also show a change in attitude. There is far more racial protest in *A Street in Bronzeville* (1945) than in her Pulitzer Prize-winning *Annie Allen* (1949). Moreover, the few pieces in the latter work which concern the "problem" are different in approach and technique from those in her first work. It should be added here that Gwendolyn Brooks since 1960 has moved over into a new position (discussed below).

Summing up then, the integration movement influenced Negro writing in the following ways: it forced the black creative artist to play down his most cherished tradition; it sent him in search of new themes; it made him abandon, at least on occasion, the Negro character and background; and it possibly helped to silence a few of the older writers then living. But before the integration movement could come to full fruition, it was cut off by the civil rights revolution, particularly the black nationalist elements in the revolution. One speaks here, of course, of the literary tendencies of both movements. The main thrust, the principal tenets of black nationalism, in their very essence, negate the paramount aim of the integrationist writer, which is to lose himself in the American literary mainstream.

At this point it should be noted that some of the material discussed here will concern tendencies and themes which came into prominence after 1960. This is unavoidable because several of the authors who during the fifties wrote as integrationists tended to move during the sixties to a black nationalist position. Gwendolyn Brooks and Margaret Walker show this change. One must also bear in mind, as already stated, that twenty years is too short a period to show clear-cut critical changes.

During the 1925 New Negro Renaissance, there was an embryonic black nationalist movement, founded and led by Marcus Garvey. Though short-lived and abortive, it nevertheless influenced to some degree the works of Hughes, Cullen, McKay, and other New Negro poets. But Garveyism never achieved the popularity or possessed the civil and "spiritual" strength that the present-day black nationalist program has. The influence of this movement goes far beyond the obvious and sensational evidences of it seen in the press or on the TV. For better or

of black nationalism have affected the thinking of far
an one would expect, and this influence has brought to
ting new themes and a new attitude on the part of the

ost important of these new attitudes is the repudiation
of American middle-class culture and all of the things—the good, on
occasion, along with the bad—for which that culture stands. This repudiation may take various forms, and it appears in poetry (that of LeRoi
Jones, for example) as well as in novels. One form of this attack concerns the Negro woman. She is accused of emasculating her husbands
and lovers by insisting that they conform to middle-class standards.
This theme is found in Chester Himes's *Third Generation* (also in other
recent works by him), and there is a strain of it in William Melvin
Kelley's *A Drop of Patience* (1965). In Ronald Fair's *Hog Butcher*
(1965) the author not only attacks the Negro middle class in his story,
but in the prologue to Part II he steps into the work, after the manner
of Henry Fielding, and delivers a scathing lecture on the subject.

The most striking statement of the repudiation of America's white
middle class comes from James Baldwin's "Letter to My Nephew" in
The Fire Next Time (1963). "There is no reason for you to try to become like white people and there is no basis whatever for their imper-
tinent assumption that *they* must accept *you*. The really terrible thing,
old buddy, is that *you* must accept *them*. And I mean that very seriously. You must accept them and accept them with love. For these
innocent people have no other hope."

The influence of the Black Revolt is also seen in the revival of the
moribund protest theme in Negro writing. In some cases the protest
novel has returned practically unchanged in the matter of technique and
point of view. Frank London Brown's *Trumbull Park* (1958) and
Richard Wright's *A Long Dream* (1958) are very similar in spirit to the
protest works of the forties. It is curious to note that Wright, after taking a sort of vacation from the protest tradition in *The Outsider* and
Savage Holiday, comes back to it in *A Long Dream;* and though Killens
deals with discrimination in the army and moves his scene finally from
America to Australia in *And Then We Heard the Thunder* (1963)
he is still using the old protest tradition. (This, of course, is no reflection on the quality of the novel.) And William Gardner Smith is doing
the same thing, although in *Stone Face* (1963) he deals primarily with
French prejudice against Algerians. There are, however, two recent
works in this new protest tradition which show freshness and originality.
One of them is Kelley's *A Different Drummer* (1962). Making use of
fantasy, symbol, and other modern devices and techniques, Kelley gives
us not only a new, bitter, and effective type of protest novel, but also a

new type of Negro character as well. Ronald Fair's *Many Thousand Gone* (1966) is equally as fresh in its approach and equally as effective. Through a morbidly exaggerated description of life in a mythical Southern locality, Fair tells us symbolically many things about the race situation in America today. He calls his work "An American Fable."

From the twenties on down to the present the jazz musician has been popular with black writers, but he has never before received the kind and amount of attention now given him. In these days of black nationalism and negritude, the jazz musician has acquired a new significance. He has become for many Negro writers a symbol of the spontaneous creative impulses of the race; he represents black "original genius," something that is not indebted in any way to middle-class culture. As depicted in recent works, the Negro jazz musician is often crude, sexy, uninhibited, uneducated, yet wise with a folk wisdom far superior to that which comes from schools and books. We find variants of this character in John A. Williams' *Night Song* (1961), in Kelley's *A Drop of Patience* (1965), and though the character is not fully developed, in Rufus in Baldwin's *Another Country*. On occasion these characters are based on the actual lives of famous jazz musicians.

Black Revolt literature takes an interesting and by no means simple attitude toward whites—an attitude that ranges from pity and contempt to the kind of sadistic love-hatred found in *Another Country*. In several of these novels the black-man-white-woman love affair is portrayed. We find this not only in Baldwin's work, but also in *A Drop of Patience,* in *And Then We Heard the Thunder,* and in *Night Song* (a very complex analysis of guilt-laden frustration on the part of the man). LeRoi Jones's *Dutchman,* whatever else it may be saying, also comments on this theme. To see the new type of white woman and the new role she is playing in these affairs, one should compare a novel like Himes's *If He Hollers* with, let us say, *Night Song*. It is ironic that the white woman should figure as largely as she does in the literature of the black revolution.

A minor theme of Black Revolt literature deals with the Negro slum boy, usually depicted as the victim of our indifferent middle-class society. Three excellent and intriguing studies of the ghetto kid are found in the following works: Mark Kennedy's *The Pecking Order* (1953), Julian Mayfield's *The Long Night* (1958), and Ronald Fair's *Hog Butcher* (1966). In delineating the "culturally deprived" boy, the authors naturally give a lot of space and attention to police brutality, welfare, bad housing for Negroes, corrupt and prejudiced city officials, and all of the other evils that the present-day militant protest groups attack.

Of the authors not to be considered fully here who began their careers during the period from 1940 to 1960 ("Toward the Mainstream" period), the following concern us: William Attaway, William Demby, William Gardener Smith, Owen Dodson, and Nathan A. Scott, Jr.

The author of *Let Me Breathe Thunder* (1939) and *Blood on the Forge* (1941), William Attaway, in the latter novel, according to the critic Bone, wrote: "By far the most perceptive novel of the Great Migration, it describes the transplanting of the folk from the familiar violence of Southern feudalism to the strange and savage violence of industrial capitalism."[1] As we have seen above, the migration was one of the most important social and historical events that helped to bring about the New Negro Movement. Very few novelists have explored this all-important theme, and none, of course, as sympathetically and artistically as William Attaway. Like too many other Negro artists, he stopped writing far too soon.

Poet, dramatist, fiction writer, Owen Dodson is the author of *Powerful Long Ladder* (1946), a book of verse, *Boy at the Window* (1951), a work of fiction which was reissued in 1967 as *When Trees Were Green,* and many plays, among them *The Divine Comedy,* a poetic drama on the Father Divine movement that was published in part in *The Negro Caravan* (1941). As playwright, director, and head of the drama department at Howard University, Dodson helped to keep flowing the thin trickle of black drama which had come to the forties from the Little Theatre movement of the Renaissance, and which was destined to reach flood stage in the sixties with the advent of LeRoi Jones (Baraka) and others.

A journalist and a creative writer, William Demby is the author of two "different" novels. He is now working on a third, to be called *The Long Bearded Journey. Beetlecreek* (1950), his first work, states in effect the often-overlooked fact that black racism is just as ugly as white racism. The second novel, *Catacombs* (1965), is an experimental work which fuses autobiography, journalistic comment, and an international-interracial love story. It is a sophisticated and complex book.

William Gardner Smith is the author of four novels: *Last of the Conquerors* (1948), which deals with the transplanted race prejudice in the American Army of Occupation in Germany; *Anger at Innocence* (1950), which shows the effect of ghetto life on sensitive minority souls, in this case a Mexican; *South Street* (1954), which is another ghetto novel and a mild precursor of present day treatments of the harsh side of ghetto life; and *The Stone Face* (1963), set in France, which shows that Algerians and other darker peoples as well as Negroes

1. Robert A. Bone, *The Negro Novel in America,* rev. ed. New Haven: Yale University Press, 1965, p. 133.

suffer from racial prejudice. It is therapeutic for black Americans to learn that they are not the only victims of the "stone face."

A brilliant and prolific writer, Nathan A. Scott, Jr., is a classical critic (using the term *critic* in its broadest sense). Trained in three disciplines—theology, philosophy, literature—Dr. Scott brings to his appraisals and judgments a comprehensive and impressive knowledge of the writings of the Western tradition. A universalist in his attitude toward literature, Scott is opposed to the position taken by the Black Arts aesthetes of the 1960's.

Nathan Scott has turned out an incredible amount of scholarly work. At this writing he has published twenty books, contributed articles to twenty-four collections and/or anthologies (six of them Negro collections), and contributed an impressively large number of scholarly essays to at least twenty-five different periodicals here and in England.

Nathan Scott's critical position is basically *religious,* using the term broadly. William V. Spanos states it thus:

> The function of criticism, according to Scott, is thus not only a matter of formal analysis or explication—though he insists on respecting the integrity of literary texts—but also the articulation of the ontological or theological vision that *inheres* in the formal construct, the definition of its relationship to the prevailing world view, and, finally, the evaluation of its religious import (in the broadest sense of the word) from the critic's own ontological standpoint, which in Scott's case is the Christian existential perspective on man and being. . . .
>
> If, as he assumes, literature is by definition an imitation, or better, an imaging forth of human life, its function must ultimately be to deepen the quality of life of man in the world.[2]

In the essays in which he treats Negro authors, Scott tries to put these writers into the larger category of American (and Western) literature rather than into that of black literature. Like Ralph Ellison, he is opposed to any *special* criticism of Negro writing which would ascribe to it some mystique. Scott would never think of an author as being first black and then a writer. Under no circumstances would he entertain the belief that all black writing should be designed to bring about liberation.

There is during this period a decided increase in the writing of autobiography, unfortunately most of it in collaboration with some professional white author. Among the many works of this type one finds the life stories of Joe Louis, Lena Horne, Ethel Waters, Jackie Robinson, Marian Anderson, and several other nationally (and internationally) known Negro athletes and artists. In their way all of these celeb-

2. "The Critical Imperatives of Alienation: The Theological Perspectives of Nathan Scott's Literary Criticism." *The Journal of Religion* (University of Chicago), XLVIII, no. 1 (January, 1968), pp. 91, 93.

rities "made" the mainstream in their respective fields, just as Wright and Ellison made it in literature. Their autobiographies are typical American success stories and in essence are like those written by white artists and athletes who traveled the same road. After about 1960, however, there appears another brand of Negro autobiography, one that is written by a new breed of militant blacks, describing a new world of poverty, dope, prison life, and racial hate.

In summation, one can say that in the years between 1940 and 1960 the Negro writer set out toward the mainstream and, motivated by the new climate which came into existence after the 1954 Supreme Court decision, made outstanding progress. And then about 1960 a new attitude took over for many writers, especially the young blacks. Swayed by the rhetoric and the militant actions of the black revolution, these writers lost all interest in the mainstream and began to produce a new kind of literature, one supposedly written by blacks for blacks, one that sought to repudiate the whole Western tradition and build in its place a new black tradition.

Integrationists and

Transitional Writers

Richard Wright

It has become a critical commonplace to say that with the publication of *Native Son* Negro American literature attained its majority. Although the statement need not be taken literally, it tells us much about the impact this sensational (in the best sense of the word) novel had on the nation. America knew that a major writer, not just an outstanding black writer, but a major American creative artist had arrived on the literary scene.

A modern novel in the fullest sense of the phrase, *Native Son,* making use of contemporary techniques, showed the country the bitterness, the frustration, the violence, and the revolutionary potential which American treatment of the Negro masses had created. And Richard Wright was an ideal person to show these tragic shortcomings, for he was a product of the Deep South, of the Depression, of poverty, of a broken home, and of other handicaps which the black poor have with them always. He was a sensitive, brooding, and intelligent child, youth, and young man—one who was capable of translating into artistic terms two things: what it meant to be a Negro in America and what it meant to America to have created this alien-native son.

Richard Wright was born on a farm near Natchez, Mississippi, in 1908. His family moved to Memphis, Tennessee, when he was a young child. When Richard was six his father deserted the family. Soon afterward his mother suffered partial paralysis and was forced to send Wright and his brother to an orphanage for a short time, and later to the homes of several relatives in Elaine, Arkansas, West Helena, Arkansas, Jackson, Mississippi, and Greenwood, Mississippi. Richard finally settled with his grandmother and his aunt in Jackson, Mississippi. The aunt taught in the Seventh Day Adventist school he attended, and the grandmother was a religious fanatic. Their imposition upon him of the Seventh Day Adventist creed caused him to rebel against formal religion.

When Wright completed junior high school in 1925, he moved to Memphis to work. In 1927 he went to Chicago, where he held such jobs as postal clerk, insurance salesman, and medical research orderly, and was often hungry and on relief. In 1932 he joined the Communist Party through membership in the John Reed Club. After a job in a Southside boys' club and positions as publicity agent for the Federal Negro Theatre and later a white experimental theatre, he was appointed to the Federal Writers' Project in 1937. He went to New York in 1937 to take a position as the Harlem editor of the *Daily Worker*. Wright also edited a Communist Party literary journal called the *New Challenge*.

In a contest sponsored by *Story Magazine* Richard Wright won the first prize of $500 for "Fire and Cloud," a short story, which appeared in his book of novellas *Uncle Tom's Children*. Later he received employment for several months on the WPA *American Guide,* assisting in the writing of a comprehensive essay on Negroes in Manhattan. He wrote critical essays and short stories for several publications, including *The New Republic, New Masses, New Challenge, Left Front,* and *Partisan Review*. In 1939 he received a Guggenheim Fellowship, and the next year published *Native Son*. The same year he married Ellen Poplar, a Jewish girl from Brooklyn, who bore him two daughters, Julia and Rachel. (He had previously had a brief marriage with a ballet dancer, Dhima Meadman.) In 1941 Wright wrote the photo essay *Twelve Million Black Voices,* and in that year also received the Spingarn Medal.

Wright broke with the Communist Party in 1942 because of a long-standing disagreement about the role of the artist. In 1945 *Black Boy* was published, and after World War II the author visited France at the invitation of the French government, later expatriating himself there. He lived a short time in England (where he was unable to obtain permission for permanent residence), and settled in Paris and in Ailly, Normandy. He went to Argentina in 1949 to play the role of Bigger Thomas in the film version of *Native Son*. In 1953 Wright published *The Outsider* and visited the Gold Coast of Africa (Ghana). The published account of his trip, *Black Power,* appeared in 1954. In 1956 *The Color Curtain* and in 1957 *Pagan Spain* were published (both accounts of his experiences on trips). *White Man, Listen!* appeared in 1957. An adaptation of *The Long Dream* was produced in New York, but was unsuccessful. Wright died in a Paris clinic on November 28, 1960. In 1961 *Eight*

Richard Wright

Photo by Carl Van Vechten, Collection of American Literature, Beinecke Rare Book and Manuscript Library, Yale University.

Men, a collection of short stories, was published posthumously, and in 1963 *Lawd Today* was published, also posthumously.

The works of Richard Wright have received their quota of critical interpretation, some of it excellent, some of it far-fetched. Critics have pointed out in detail the major influences on Wright's fiction: naturalism, Marxism, existentialism, and the Negro folk background, among other elements. And in one way or another these commentators have stated Wright's basic objective: to express the great social crime that America perpetrated upon the black masses and the effects of that crime on the life and personality of the Negro.

In *Black Boy,* his autobiography published in 1945, Wright, *inter alia,* has this to say:

(Whenever I thought of the essential bleakness of black life in America, I knew that Negroes had never been allowed to catch the full spirit of Western civilization, that they somehow lived in it, but not of it. . . .)

It is this bleakness, this barrenness in Negro life that Wright depicts. He did not believe that black is beautiful. He felt that black life was ugly, brutal, violent, devoid of kindness and love. And he places much of the blame for this bleakness on that great fog of racial oppression that hung over the Negro like a tremendous, compelling natural force, expelling him from the finer things of Western civilization, dehumanizing and brutalizing him physically and spiritually. In one sense this is Wright's only theme.

Richard Wright was a prolific and many-talented writer (see bibliography). Because of space limitations, the emphasis here is not on his poetry, his drama, and his numerous non-fictional volumes and articles. Rather, it is only with the following major works: *Uncle Tom's Children* (1938, 1940), *Native Son* (1940), *Black Boy* (1945), *The Outsider* (1953), *The Long Dream* (1958), *Eight Men* (1961), and *Lawd Today* (1963).

Uncle Tom's Children ("four novellas" in 1938; "five long stories" in 1940) establishes solidly the theme mentioned above and lays the groundwork for subsequent longer works of fiction.

In "Big Boy Leaves Home" we see the fatalistic and non-rational way in which white hatred worked in the Deep South. At the beginning of the story we find several Negro boys going swimming in the nude in a place not ordinarily used by them. They are seen by a white woman, and by the end of the story two of the boys have been killed by a white man, and Big Boy has been forced to kill the man and leave home. How can such tragedy come from such a trivial incident? It is that tremendous and explosive pressure which hangs over the Negro. Big Boy was fortunate because he fought back and escaped through flight.

His companions, on the other hand, followed the route usually taken by blacks in such a situation.

"Down by the Riverside" (note the suggestive Christian title) gives another example of this second route. Mann (note again the significance of the name) needs to get his wife Lula to the hospital because she is in labor. As the floods have come, there are no boats available and he is compelled to make use of a boat that has been stolen by his friend Bob. Elder Murray leads Mann and his family in prayer before they leave, but Mann carries his gun, knowing how "Christian" white folks are. Because of the difficulties of rowing against the current, Mann stops by a white man's house to use the telephone to seek assistance in getting his wife to the hospital. It so happens that this is the man from whom the boat was stolen. In spite of Mann's emergency, the owner demands that the boat be turned over immediately, and in defense of his family Mann kills the white boat-owner. At the end of the story Mann has lost his wife, and in spite of performing rescue acts beyond the call of duty, in spite of knowing that because of his acts he will be recognized and killed, Mann still continues his rescue work. As a result of his last act of defiance, not to be "shot down like a dog," he brings about his own death at the hands of the soldiers. The story plays ironically on the Christian virtues of prayer, pacifism ("study war no more"), and service to one's fellow man. The only trouble, the story suggests, is that these Christian virtues apply only to whites.

In "Long Black Song," Sarah, a lonely, sensitive young Negro wife, allows herself to be seduced by a white salesman. When her husband Silas finds out, he horsewhips her and then kills the white man. Refusing to run, he fights the mob and, of course, is lynched. At one time Silas bemoans the lot of a black man:

> "The white folks ain never gimme a chance! They ain never give no black man a chance! There ain nothin in yo whole life yuh kin keep from em! They take yo lan! They take yo freedom! They take yo women! N then they take yo life! . . . Yuh die ef you fight! Yuh die ef yuh don fight! Either way yuh die n it don mean nothing. . . ."[1]

Note the last line—the *nothingness* of black living which that great white force produces. Wright, in spite of what Silas says, suggests that an act of defiance though it brings death also brings a portion of dignity. The search for death rather than the ignominy of flight or acceptance is a constant theme in these stories. Some of Uncle Tom's *new* children are defiant, maybe futilely so, but still defiant.

In the next two stories Uncle Tom's *new* children have found a new weapon in the arsenal of liberation: the Communist promise of brother-

---

1. *Uncle Tom's Children*. New York: Harper and Bros., 1938, pp. 211–212.

hood of all of the oppressed. "Fire and Cloud" tells the story of Dan Taylor, a Negro minister who at the beginning of the narrative is a typical Uncle Tom minister trying to please the insurgent element in his own flock *and* the white folks. After a brutal beating by poor whites, he is converted to the Marxist position. He learns that poor whites and poor blacks can and should protest together, and above all else, he learns that "Freedom belongs to the strong!"

This optimistic ending is somewhat out of character for Wright. His treatment of Communists in "Bright and Morning Star" is more realistic and perhaps a better reflection of Wright's ambivalent feelings toward what Communism *could* do for the American Negro. In "Fire and Cloud" Hadley, the white organizer, looks forward to Jan and Max in *Native Son,* but in "Bright and Morning Star" it is Booker, a white infiltrator, who betrays the group to the police. Moreover, Aunt Sue, one of Wright's strongest women characters, is really not converted to Marxism. More of a black individualist than anything else, she goes along with the movement because her Johnny-Boy is in it. And when the mob kills Johnny-Boy, she gets her sheet and gun and starts shooting. She kills Booker first and thereby prevents him from informing on the rest of the members of their group. Like the principal characters in most of these stories, she knows that death can be an affirmation of one's dignity and selfhood, perhaps the only affirmation then possible for the black masses. And Wright infers that out of these defiant acts of affirmation a new breed will arise from the lowliest, the most oppressed. In this he was a prophet.

In "Bright and Morning Star" Wright seems to be ambivalent concerning the role that Communism can play in freeing the Negro masses; that is, he offers it here almost half-heartedly. His attitude toward Communism will again show this ambivalence in *Native Son* in spite of Jan and Max. In *The Outsider* he will turn from Communism in a very dramatic fashion.

Although it was not published until Wright's death in 1963, *Lawd Today,* in all probability, was written between 1935 and 1937. It is considered here after *Uncle Tom's Children* because it deals with a nontypical Wright character. Jake does not belong with Big Boy, Silas, Dan Taylor, Mann, and Aunt Sue. He is not heroic in any sense; he is everything that the white man thinks of as a Negro—as a matter of fact, that is his major trouble. He accepts what whites have told him about himself. Jake is anti-Jewish, anti-Catholic, anti-Communist, and, above all else, anti-Negro. Wright makes Jake ugly physically and spiritually. He is a despicable human being, with no feelings of sympathy and compassion for his brothers in the South or for poor whites or for anything other than what middle-class white thinking tells him to believe.

In his delineation of Jake, Wright is obviously making use of the black tradition of self-abasement so popular among Negroes. But he probably has a purpose in using this tradition. In the earlier part of the novel Jake has a dream in which he finds himself running up endless stairs getting nowhere, and he finds himself saying: "Jeeesus, all that running for nothing. . . . Yeah, there's a trick in this." The American white fog of oppression produces in the heroic black defiance or flight and often death. But it smothers the Jakes of the Negro world, leaving them spiritual ciphers. Although Jake does not realize it, and that is the trick in it, he not only is not going anywhere, he really does not exist.

Native Son represents the culmination of Richard Wright's powers as a novelist. In it he has brought together all of the strands running through earlier works: the flight pattern, the use of naturalism and Marxism, Negro folk materials, the loss of religious faith, the emphasis on violence, defiant death as affirmation and deliverance. The earlier works in which these themes and techniques appeared were experiments in preparation for the big effort. Wright's fictional power moves steadily and surely to the heights of *Native Son* and declines just as surely thereafter.

In *How Bigger Was Born* Wright tells us that after seeing the reviews of *Uncle Tom's Children,* he realized that he had made a naive, a very naive mistake:

> I found that I had written a book which even bankers' daughters could read and weep over and feel good about. I swore to myself that if ever I wrote another book, no one would weep over it; that it would be so hard and deep that they would have to face it without the consolation of tears.

He lived up to his promise. *Native Son* jolted the nation. For the first time a creative writer had effectively and artistically pointed out the brutalizing and dehumanizing results of American racism; for the first time a novelist had dramatized effectively the latent violence and the revolutionary potential in the oppressed Negro masses. Bigger Thomas became a tragic symbol of all that had gone wrong in America's treatment of its largest minority. Bigger Thomas, in short, warned us that there would be Black Panthers, Black Muslims, and other militant separatist groups among America's oppressed and alienated masses.

In the opening chapter of *Native Son* Wright uses the symbol of the cornered rat to characterize Bigger. Bigger is cornered by his ugly family life, with a mother nagging at him to *be a man,* something that patently he is not allowed to be. He is cornered by the fear of whites—a fear he takes out on his Negro buddy. He is cornered by fear of his own "outsideness," which he feels when Mary and Jan try to be friendly. And the great tragedy of all this is that Bigger is absolutely powerless to do anything about it or even to be aware of it until he commits violence. A victim of the great white force which bears relentlessly down upon him, Bigger gets his first glimmering of self-importance after he has killed:

> The thought of what he had done, the awful horror of it, the daring associated with such actions, formed for him for the first time in his fear-ridden life a barrier of protection between him and a world he feared. He had murdered and had created a new life for himself. It was something that was all his own, and it was the first time he had anything that others could not take from him.

This was Bigger's tragedy as a black man. The white tragedy was that in America not even liberals like the Daltons or even radicals like the Communist Jan had any way of understanding Bigger and a million blacks like him. The long, Marxist defense of Bigger at the end of the work tries to explain Bigger, but it, too, has its shortcomings; it too, has some of the blindness of the Daltons and of white America in general.

The critical response to *Native Son* (see bibliography) was greater than to any other prior publication by a Negro. Commentators, black and white, attacked the violence of the work, its structure, its Communist sermon at the end, its crude writing, its creation of a so-called new black stereotype in Bigger, and its picture of Negro life; but no critic has denied the power of the novel and its importance as a twentieth-century American statement.

In *The Outsider* Richard Wright makes use of his new-found interest in existentialism. He also makes use of an attitude toward Communism that is poles apart from the attitude he held earlier. "You are a fact to them, not a person," seems to be his conclusion in this work. Of all the works of Wright, *The Outsider* is perhaps the most repulsive to the squeamish reader, and Cross Damon (note the symbolism in the name) is perhaps the character with whom the readers sympathize least. Even though Bigger was a monster, we feel *with* him because we know that society has made him what he is. Cross Damon, on the other hand, is a self-made would-be god who lives beyond good and evil, as ordinary men see morality. Incidentally, Cross Damon is the least "Negro" of all Wright's black characters. One wonders why Wright bothered to make him a Negro at all. Except for a few good scenes like the one in which Cross secures an illegal birth certificate by putting on an Uncle Tom act, the novel is not racial in the old-fashioned, protest-novel sense of the term. As a matter of fact, the author looked upon Cross Damon as a representative of modern man rather than as black.

The Outsider may be read on more than one level. It is, first of all, a thriller of the most sensational type. When one realizes that Cross Damon kills four persons—three of them for no plausible reason—he wonders about the author's purpose. Wright has always featured violence in his works, but the killing in this novel is almost as arbitrary as that found in comic books and popular detective stories. Is he saying, in effect, that this is really how twentieth-century man acts, with his foolish racism, his atomic bombs, and his senseless wars? Or is he writing a travesty of the violence, sex, and inhumaneness of the literature of the age?

On the second level *The Outsider* is an anti-Communist volume in which he shows both the power of the movement and its great understanding of human nature, as well as its impersonal ruthlessness (note its treatment of Bob and Eva). Wright felt that Communism saw through the hypocrisies and untruths of modern man. It was the inevitable result of Western man's loss of faith in God and in spiritual values; it was the answer to the basic fear that characterized man in a godless industrialized world, but it was utterly impersonal.

The Outsider is, finally, an existentialist novel, perhaps the first novel by a black writer that may be classed as such. At the beginning of the work Wright seems to look upon existentialism as one way out of the wretched position into which modern man, alone and despairing, has allowed himself to fall. In such a world he has freedom to choose, to make himself what he wills without obligation, dependency, or justification. And that is what Cross Damon does. He becomes a god ruthlessly ordering his life and his world through violence. At the end of the work his anguish and forlornness give him doubts concerning the way out through existentialism. When asked as he was dying what his life had been, Damon replies: "It . . . it was . . . horrible . . ."

The Long Dream is not the work that one expected from Richard Wright in 1958. In many respects an old-fashioned protest novel, it seems almost anachronistic after *Native Son* and *The Outsider*. By 1958 Wright was living in Paris and had been away from the South a long time. By 1958 the South also had changed, not dramatically, of course, but it had changed. One wonders if Richard Wright was aware of these changes. In any case, he seems to fall back on recollections of a former day and former conditions—not the South of 1958. At the end of *Black Boy* there is a passage that may explain the tone and the subject matter of *The Long Dream*. "I fled the South so that the numbness of my defensive living might thaw out and let me feel the pain—years later and far away—of what living in the South had meant." In *The Long Dream* Wright resurrects the pain of a Southern childhood and early youth.

The story concerns Fishbelly (Rex Tucker), the son of Tyree, a Mississippi Negro undertaker, racketeer, and businessman. In order to stay in power, Tyree has to play ball with the brutal and degraded white police of the town. Playing ball means not only paying off but also living a fawning, cringing Uncle Tom role—a role incidentally, which Tyree plays masterfully and profitably until a fire-trap dance hall in which he is a silent partner burns with a great loss of life. When Tyree, threatened with exposure, tries to tie in the whites involved, he is killed, but he leaves behind a document that would prove the guilt of the white officials.

After Tyree's death the police try to entrap Fishbelly, a true son of his father in most respects, but in spite of beatings and imprisonment he divulges nothing and is finally freed. He leaves for Paris and from there mails back the incriminating evidence that would destroy the men who had killed his father.

The plot of *The Long Dream* is really tinsel; it is one that appears on television nightly in countless versions. The appeal of the novel (and it has appeal) lies in the delineation of the depths to which Tyree and Fishbelly had to sink before they finally rebelled—one through defiance and death, the other through flight. The book renders fictionally what *Black Boy* had spelled out: that life in the South for the Negro is utterly impossible if the Negro wishes to cling to even one shred of dignity and self-respect. As Fishbelly mused on the plane going to Paris, he knew that he was leaving a life that had "emotionally crucified him." He wondered if there could be any resurrection for him. Wright, too, had been emotionally crucified, and *The Long Dream* reactivates the old hurt.

Of the eight stories which are found in *Eight Men* (1961), six had appeared earlier in other publications, sometimes under slightly different titles, ranging in dates of publication from 1937 to 1957. Five of the six fall in the 1937 to 1949 span (see bibliography for original sources of publication). Taken together, they show Wright's persistent experimentation in finding means to put over his one major message: the varied ways in which the white world has alienated or emasculated the Negro.

"The Man Who Lived Underground" is probably the best—at least it is the most provocative of these stories. With existential overtones, it looks back to Dostoevsky and forward to Ralph Ellison. Its symbolism is rich, and the story parades several themes popular with Wright: flight, brutality and violence, the absurdity of the modern world, the futility of Christianity, and the Negro's loss of identity. Illustrating the last theme, Wright makes use of the protagonist's name only once; and the protagonist, driven into his underground world, forgets his own name. Even though reduced by the white world to the most elemental level—eating and sleeping—the Underground Man learns too much about the sickness of modern life and, of course, is killed by the cops.

"The Man Who Killed a Shadow" tells the tragic story of Saul Saunders, who works in a Washington cathedral. A forty-year-old white woman librarian also employed there tries to seduce him and provoke a rape. When Saul Saunders fails to respond, she slaps him. Saul strikes back, and then, motivated by all of his pent-up confusions and his ignorance of the shadowy white world, he compulsively kills her because he did not know what else to do when she started screaming. Saul, like most black men, lived all of his life in a black world separated from the "unreal" (to him) white world "by a million psychological miles."

The story called "Man of All Work" treats symbolically the alleged emasculation of the black male by American society, although the story is supposedly humorous. It deals with a Negro who because of his wife's illness tries to hold down her job by dressing as a female domestic.

"The Man Who Saw the Flood" concerns the entrapment of the Negro by the Southern share-cropping system. In this story both nature and the system oppress the black man.

Although they are amenable to the overall theme which runs through all of the stories in *Eight Men,* two of them seem slightly out of character for Wright. The first, "Man, God Ain't Like That" is a rather far-fetched account of an African in Paris who comes to believe his master is God and as a consequence kills him to bring about his resurrection. The second, "Big Black Good Man," probably tries to suggest how little the white world understands the Negro. Olaf Jenson, the night clerk in a Copenhagen hotel, is just as ignorant of the intentions of a giant-sized Negro as Saul Saunders was of the white woman's intentions in "The Man Who Killed a Shadow."

"The Man Who Went to Chicago" is an autobiographical account in which the author explores various examples of racism found in the North—examples which, though they lack the violence of the Southern kind, are just as well-defined and just as degrading and dehumanizing as those of the South.

Black Boy (A Record of Childhood and Youth) is a great American autobiography. Unlike the race-praising, name-dropping autobiographies produced by James Weldon Johnson and others, *Black Boy* is written in the passionately militant spirit of Frederick Douglass's slave narrative, which was published one hundred years earlier. With even greater intensity than Douglass, Wright delineates the frustrations and incredible humiliations which came to a sensitive and intelligent Negro boy in the

Deep South trying against unbelievable odds to find out who he was. A depressing book, it reads like a Greek tragedy in its unremitting emphasis on the ugliness, the futility, and the degrading experiences heaped upon a Negro. The book, however, ends on a note of triumph. Near the close of the work Wright describes his moment of truth. In spite of all that the system had tried to do, he tells us, it had failed:

> I was building up in me a dream which the entire educational system of the South had been rigged to stifle. I was feeling the very thing that the state of Mississippi had spent millions of dollars to make sure I would never feel . . . I was beginning to dream the dreams that the state had said were wrong, that the schools had said were taboo.

Saunders Redding

Urbane, moderate, scholarly, Saunders Redding, as both writer and person, exemplifies the best of that middle-class background from which he comes and of the classical education which he received. For three decades his voice has been the voice of protest, yes, of criticism of America, yes—but always the cultured voice of a well-educated and wise observer of the American racial scene.

Now the Ernest I. White Professor of American Studies and Humane Letters at Cornell University, Saunders Redding has had a long, varied, and fruitful career as scholar, educator, and man of letters. Born Jay Saunders Redding in Wilmington, Delaware, in 1906, he attended Lincoln University for one year, then went to Brown, receiving there his A.B. in 1928 and his M.A. in 1932. Since then, he has been awarded six honorary degrees for his literary work. Both as an educator and as a writer, Redding has been an integral part of the two American worlds —the black and the white. He taught at Morehouse, Louisville Municipal College, Southern, Elizabeth City, and Hampton Institute. Redding also taught, either as professor or visiting professor, at Brown University, Duke, the University of North Carolina, Grinnell, George Washington, and, of course, Cornell. He has been on the editorial board of *The American Scholar* and has been published in *The Atlantic Monthly, Harper's, The American Mercury, Transition,* the *Nation, Saturday Review, New Republic, Survey Graphic,* and other periodicals. But for many years he also wrote a book column for the *Afro-American* news-papers and his articles have appeared in *Negro Digest* (now *Black World*) and other black magazines. Professor Redding has received a number of outstanding awards, among them the Rockefeller Foundation Fellowship, the Guggenheim Fellowship, and the Mayflower Award. He has traveled to India for the State Department and lectured in Africa for the American Society of African Culture. He has also been a popular speaker for audiences throughout America.

Redding's first publication, *To Make a Poet Black,* came out in 1939. From that date until the present time he has turned out a steady stream of works in fiction, autobiography and biography, history, essays, reviews, textbooks, and reportage. His major publications, in addition to the first, are: *No Day of Triumph* (1942); *Stranger and Alone* (1950); *They Came in Chains* (Lippincott's People of America series, 1950); *On Being Negro in America* (1951); and *The Lonesome Road* (in Doubleday's Mainstream of America series, 1958).

Most critics consider *No Day of Triumph* (1942) Redding's best volume. It won the Mayflower Award from the North Carolina Historical Society for the best work that year by a resident of the state. A combination of autobiography (the first part) and reportage, the work is a brilliant report on the condition of Southern Negroes in the year that it was planned and written. Redding was given a grant to travel and to report on what he saw. The book is written from the viewpoint of an educated and sensitive Negro who has talked to all kinds of Negroes—peasants, lawyers, landowners, radicals, sharecroppers, physicians, ex-slaves, schoolteachers, barber-shop hangers-on, and others. His travels took him to Virginia, Tennessee, Arkansas, the Delta region, and Texas. Through a series of dramatic episodes, Redding gives the reader a montage of Negro life in the 1940's, a cross section of the day-by-day reaction of blacks to living in the white-dominated South (and America).

Redding, seemingly, had no ideological axe to grind, and as a consequence he is usually objective. In the first pages of the work he talks of his own middle-class background and of the latent conflict between the dark members of his father's family and the light-colored members of his mother's. The color problem within the group was very real to Redding, and he shows his constant awareness of it, not only in *No Day of Triumph,* but in practically all his subsequent works. It becomes especially evident in his one work of fiction.

The book is excellently written. The author renders an experience with economy and restraint. He never overtells or overdramatizes an episode; as a matter of fact, he tends to leave the reader hanging after he has told just enough. In this early work Redding exhibits that style which would

Saunders Redding

Photo by Roy Lewis.

become his trademark through the years. Like Gwendolyn Brooks in poetry, Redding in prose handles words—many of them unusual words —skillfully. His sentences are smooth-flowing yet effectively structured. On occasion he turns out memorable phrases.

Although *No Day of Triumph* is understandably dated, it is an excellent book to read in the climate of the seventies because it gives a picture of conditions hard to conceive of today. Many of the young black writers who insist that the place of the Negro has not changed essentially in America would find this work therapeutic. They could also learn much from Redding's classic restraint and from his objectivity in reporting on the Negro in America in the forties. Today everything black is beautiful. Redding did not find it so.

The author's first publication, *To Make a Poet Black* (1939), is really a pioneer work in the field of Negro literature, if one uses the word *pioneer* with latitude. At the time it appeared, very few critics concerned themselves with Negro American literature. Redding's *To Make a Poet Black* joined the slim ranks of works which helped to keep alive the interest in Negro writing which the New Negro Renaissance had fostered—works by Vernon Loggins, Benjamin Brawley, Sterling Brown, and a few others. In this respect, Redding, along with the other scholars mentioned, helped prepare the ground for the black Renaissance of the sixties.

As stated in the preface of *To Make a Poet Black,* the author's aim was "to bring together certain factual material and critical opinion on American Negro literature in a sort of history of Negro thought in America." He emphasized this approach because he felt that "literary expression for the Negro has not been nor is it wholly now an art in the sense that the poetry and prose of . . . the Irish, is art." Almost from the beginning, Redding states, Negro literature "has been literature either of purpose or necessity," and the study of this literature "becomes therefore a practical, as opposed to purely speculative, exercise." With this approach as his guide, the author writes a highly readable commentary on Negro literature from 1760 to 1939.

Redding does not include all the writers, only those that appeal to him and, of course, those whose works substantiate his thesis. His selection, however, is good, and he brings to his comments a keen awareness and poetic insight. Redding has the gift of words, and he is sometimes able to make striking and unusual remarks about well-known incidents and characters. One of the shortcomings of the work, however, is that most of the authors are treated in too small a compass. On most authors he does not give quite enough to make the work as valuable as it could be. It is a small book—only 142 pages—and one realizes that only so much space could be given to each author. Additional space, however, for all of the major writers would have improved the work considerably. In spite of this shortcoming, *To Make a Poet Black* is still useful as a reference work. It has been reprinted in recent years.

Stranger and Alone (1950), Redding's single work of fiction, is perhaps his most glaring mistake in judgment. He does not have that particular gift that enables a man to write a convincing novel. According to the book jacket on the novel: "The way in which the politicians of the South make use of the mulatto to exploit the Negro is a theme that has never before been fully presented." Perhaps this is true because it is a difficult theme to make into a tenable work of fiction.

The specific problem with *Stranger and Alone* is that Redding, because of the nature of his thesis, is forced to ride it too hard. As a result, he makes his main character a cross between a zombie and a puppet. Shelton Howden never becomes real, he never develops as a character, he is always manipulated to substantiate the author's color-conscious thesis. Because of this, Redding's minor characters appear and are dropped at will. As soon as they serve the purpose of the protagonist, they are dismissed. They are not integrated into the fabric of the novel. After performing a mechanical function, they simply disappear.

It is probable that the author wrote in anger and let his personal feelings smother his artistic judgment. All Negroes Redding's age who have taught school in the South have known personally one or more Negro state school presidents who were dictators. Not all these men were mulatto by any means, and none of them was as undeviatingly objectionable as Redding makes Wimbush. As a matter of fact, the author was so eager to attack the Wimbushes of that era, he neglected to give us a full and authentic picture of the college campuses which they ran like little private kingdoms. This would have been a valuable contribution to Negro literature. In no fiction to date has this world been adequately treated, and it was a fascinating world.

In 1950 Redding also published *They Came in Chains* for Lippincott's People of America series. In this work, which is essentially history, and in *The Lonesome Road* (1958), which he did for Doubleday's Mainstream of America series, Redding dramatizes Negro history. He has a real talent for giving life and meaning to historic episodes. Moreover, he has insight into historic characters; he looks at them with the eye of a dramatist, and he brings them alive, emphasizing their peculiarities as well as their outstanding qualities. As a result, these works become a fusion of history and biography. And, above all else, he *selects* very definitively the episodes and characters that appeal to him so that in the long run the work becomes Redding's personal interpretation of Negro history.

For example, *The Lonesome Road,* which is subtitled *The Story of the Negro's Part in America,* starts with an episode describing the performance of Negro soldiers under Colonel Robert Gould Shaw at Fort Wagner, moves from there to treat the career of Bishop Payne, then to Frederick Douglass and Sojourner Truth, and *inter alia* discusses an all-Negro town and its leader, the career of Chicago *Defender* editor Robert S. Abbott, and ends with a brief and oblique dramatization of Thurgood Marshall and the 1954 Supreme Court decision.

In the earlier work, *They Came in Chains* (1950), though written for the general reader rather than the historian or scholar, Redding traces the Negro in America from his origins in Africa down to 1950. In this work the author has made history dramatic and highly readable. Like Macaulay in the nineteenth century, Redding made history read like fiction. When one considers what he has done with the dry bones of historical fact, one is puzzled by his inability to write good "real fiction" in *Stranger and Alone.*

On Being Negro in America (1951) is, as the author warns us at the outset, a very personal work. It is really Redding's apologia, and by extension the apologia of Negro intellectuals in 1951. Even though highly personal as regards illustrative incidents, Redding expresses the attitude of most black intellectuals of the era—their attitude toward integration, toward Communism as a way out, toward the "deep sickness" which they found in America living.

Of course, there is nothing new in what Redding has said, but it is good to have outstanding Negro spokesmen periodically tell America what its black minority thinks. In addition, this work, as are most of Redding's works, is beautifully written. He has included in his comments two or three poignant autobiographical episodes which add a deeper personal dimension to this apologia than is usually found in works of this sort. *On Being Negro in America* lacks the sensationalism and intensity of a *Black Boy,* but it tells much about that unusual and disturbing experience of being both a Negro and an American.

Chester Himes

A prolific writer, Chester Bomar Himes has gone through two distinct phases in his creating and publishing career. The first runs from 1945 to 1955. During this period he brought out five novels influenced by the Richard Wright school of tough, naturalistic writing. The second phase runs roughly from 1957 to the present. During this period, he published, in addition to *Pinktoes* (1965), a hilarious satire on race-and-sex relations, a series of detective stories which became quite popular, especially in France (Himes lived there for some time). One of his detective novels, *Cotton Comes to Harlem* (1965), was made into a very successful movie. The latest major publication of Chester Himes is a revealing autobiography which he entitles *The Quality of Hurt* (1972).

Born in Jefferson City, Missouri, in 1909, Chester Himes is the son of schoolteacher parents. His early life was spent in several states, including Mississippi and Ohio, as his father moved from job to job. Himes attended the University of Ohio for three years, but he probably learned more at another Ohio institution, the state penitentiary, where he served time for robbery. Like O. Henry, Himes began publishing short stories while in prison. His early stories appeared in *Abbott's Monthly* and *Esquire*. After his release in 1936, Himes began a bizarre life, doing many things, living in many places—Chicago, San Francisco, Los Angeles, and New York. Although he followed other pursuits temporarily, he always came back to his writing. His short stories have appeared in *The Crisis, Opportunity, Coronet, Commentary,* and other periodicals. An expatriate now living in Paris, Himes recently returned to America when his autobiography came out.

The novels of Himes's first phase, with the exception of *Cast the First Stone,* all deal with the repressive, distorting, and emasculating effect that the American race situation has on Negroes, particularly on the black male. Himes's thesis says, in effect, that pressure on the Negro male makes him less than a man. This pressure, according to the author, often works through the Negro middle-class woman who fails to understand her mate and therefore rejects him. When the poor male runs to the white woman for solace, as he often does in Himes's works, he is again rejected, but for different reasons. Chester Himes lacks technical skill as a novelist, and he often exaggerates the effect of race prejudice

Chester Himes

Photo by Carl Van Vechten, Collection of American Literature, Beinecke Rare Book and Manuscript Library, Yale University.

on his characters, but what he lacks in finesse as an artist, he tends to offset by his intensity. It is this intensity that makes his works effective.

If He Hollers deals with life in a Los Angeles shipyard during the war effort. The protagonist is Robert Jones, a tense, intelligent Negro worker who had moved up from common laborer to a job somewhat higher than the ones Negroes usually held. In the course of his work Bob runs afoul of Madge, a white Texan who insults him and, when he retaliates in kind, causes him to be downgraded. She later tries to seduce him, and when caught in the attempt yells "rape." The novel shows Jones being consistently emasculated by Madge, by a white worker who beats him, by the police and the authorities, and by his middle-class girl friend who lectures him on *his* shortcomings and, fully believing in the rightness of White America, urges him to conform. So cowed has Jones become that he is psychologically powerless to carry out his desire to kill the white man who had beaten him:

> I wanted to kill him so he'd know I was killing him and in such a way that he'd know he didn't have a chance. I wanted him to feel as *scared* and *powerless* and *unprotected* as I felt every goddamned morning I woke up. (emphasis added)

The one thing that Robert Jones wanted to be was "just a simple Joe, walking down an American street, going my simple way, without any other identifying characteristics but weight, height, and gender." That, of course, was the last thing that America was willing to give. The picture of American oppression is drawn with anger, and, paradoxically, it is this anger that saves the novel from mediocrity.

The second novel, *The Lonely Crusade,* is another version of the first. In this, however, Lee Gordon, the principal character, is a Negro union organizer who honestly tries to remain loyal to his own convictions concerning labor in spite of tempting and corrupting offers from crooked union, management, and Communist officials, especially the last. When the company offers Gordon a higher position and salary, Gordon quixotically refuses the advancement and is criticized by Ruth, his middle-class wife. Later, when Ruth finds out that Gordon is having an affair with Jackie, a white Communist, she refuses to sleep with him anymore. Gordon, though not the murderer, becomes involved in the killing of a representative of the company. He runs to Jackie for comfort, but she calls the police.

In this work Himes does several things: he criticizes the Communists; he attacks white women who use black men to bolster their own feelings of insecurity; he strikes again at the lack of understanding on the part of middle-class Negro women; and he spells out in great detail how hard, if not impossible, it is for the black Lee Gordons to be men. When

Gordon was in high school he was caught "peeping" in the girls' gymnasium. Not only was he expelled, but the community brought about the tragic ruin of his parents. These things preyed on Gordon's mind, and he became a psychological wreck. "He came to feel that the guilt or innocence of anything he might do would be subjected wholly to the whim of white people. It stained his whole existence with a sense of sudden disaster hanging just above his head, and never afterwards could he feel at ease in the company of white people."

There is probably a considerable amount of autobiography in Himes's next novel, *The Third Generation*. More concerned about dissension *within* the Negro group than about confrontation with the white world, the work treats the differences between light-colored Negroes with a genteel house-servant, slavery background and the dark-skinned peasant field-hand type—differences that are all too often exaggerated. The novel is, additionally, Himes's strongest attack on the strangling and frustrating influence a middle-class Negro woman can have on her man or husband.

The story depicts the lives of the members of the Taylor family—father, mother, and three sons. Mr. Taylor is a trade teacher at first in Negro schools, but because of his wife's inability to get along with colleagues and neighbors he has to change positions often and ends up doing lower type work. Mrs. Taylor, neurotic, light-skinned, a member of the Negro genteel class, really does not learn to love her dark-skinned peasant husband until it is too late. She makes life hell for him and showers all of her affection on her son Charles, having for him the kind of oedipal feelings she had for her own father. The story ends in stark tragedy when the wayward and wild Charles gets involved with a prostitute. Mrs. Taylor goes to the woman's house to get her son. In defending her from an attack by the prostitute's "man," Mr. Taylor is killed. Bitter, Freudian, unrelieved by humor, *The Third Generation* is perhaps as important for what it tells us about the personality of its intense author as it does about the lives of the Taylors.

In *The Primitives* Chester Himes brings to a climax his attack on the black-man-white-woman relationship. Himes was the first Negro writer to attack this relationship so intensely, a relationship that has been used often by black writers of the sixties and seventies. Himes comes from a generation which believed that a white woman spelled trouble for a black man and nothing else. Since writing *The Primitive*, he has probably changed that attitude, but Madge (in his first novel), Jackie (in his second), and Kriss (in this work) are cut from the same cloth. The story of *The Primitives* resolves itself into a kind of tragic duel between Jesse Robinson, a Negro male, and Kriss Cummings, his white mistress. Each character is a study in defeat. Life had given Kriss "a drunkard for a father and a wretch for her first love, two abortions and a loss of fertility, a homosexual for a husband and a bevy of men whose lust she had been forced to satisfy because of their importance." The author describes Kriss as a "thirty-seven-year old, six-thousand-dollar-a-year junior executive, brilliant, healthy and highly respectable." But this is all front. Behind, one finds a defeated, neurotic woman who seeks release through pills, liquor, and sex. Because she feels so inferior, so alienated from her society, she is compelled to seek association with Negroes as a panacea. No matter how far down *she* was, she could still look down on and feel superior to "niggers." This gave some measure of relief.

Jesse Robinson's background was equally insecure. He had tried to be a writer, but had failed because he found out that publishers wanted only a certain type of novel from Negro authors, not the kind he wanted to write. He had also made a failure of his marriage. Society had buffeted Jesse so badly he had become mentally affected; he suffered from blackouts, drank too much, and when drunk had homicidal impulses. In his distorted thinking he had decided that having a white woman would somehow restore his manhood. When he ultimately discovered that Kriss was not the answer to his problem, when he understood her real contempt for "niggers," he killed her in a drunken rage.

Cast the First Stone (1952) is considered last because it does not concern Negro experience and is, therefore, not a protest novel in the sense in which the term is used here. Indirectly, it is a protest novel which asks for a deeper understanding of and more tolerance for the homosexual. The scene is a prison, and Jim Monroe, like Himes, is a would-be writer. The story concerns the relationship, never precisely delineated, between Monroe and the homosexual Dido. Because of the intimacy between the two, Jim loses his chance for a commutation of sentence and is sent to a prison farm. Despondent because of the loss of his friend and about the commutation incident, Dido commits suicide. Written long before the present-day gay liberation movement, this novel shows an awareness and a sympathy on the part of Himes not too common in 1952.

The pornographic satire *Pinktoes* (1965) marks a distinct break with Himes's earlier works. In it we see a new Himes, one who has little in common with the author of those deadly-in-earnest protest novels of the forties and fifties. First of all, *Pinktoes* is a humorous, occasionally hilarious work. Prior to this satire, the light moments in Himes's work are rare. Himes, moreover, has seemingly taken a new look at the white woman, and his second look has none of the bitterness found in his delineation of Madge, Jackie, and Kriss. And, perhaps most important, Himes in *Pinktoes* takes a more sophisticated (even if cynical) look at the problem of race in America. He has lost much of his earlier "racism" and is far more objective in his appraisal of both whites and blacks. Perhaps his European sojourn gave him this new and intriguing perspective.

There is not much plot in *Pinktoes;* what little there is deals with the activities of Mamie Mason, a lusty Harlem hostess who feels that race relations could be improved best in bed—through sex relations between white liberals and influential blacks. To this end she gives a series of parties, and, of course, practices what she preaches by entering wholeheartedly into the bed work. The satire here is double edged, sparing neither middle-class blacks who want to be like whites or liberal whites who are either ignorant or hypocritical. Sex in the work, however, tends to become monotonous, and the humor is not always funny. If Himes tried to write social comment, his effort is not wholly successful.

To date, Chester Himes has published the following detective stories: *The Real Cool Killers* (1959),[2] *The Crazy Kill* (1959), *All Shot Up* (1960), *The Big Gold Dream* (1960), *A Rage in Harlem* (1965), *Cotton Comes to Harlem* (1965), *Run Man Run* (1967), and *Blind Man with a Pistol* (1969). Several observations may be made on these works as a group. The first impression the reader gets is that Harlem contains only "characters"—pimps, prostitutes, numbers barons, cult leaders, homesexuals, all larger than life. And the pace of the black city is nightmarish, the violence almost surrealistic. Himes seems to be giving the kind of picture of Harlem that visiting or tourist whites used to have in their minds when they thought of Harlem. Or maybe it is a picture that Himes, long absent from the present-day reality of Harlem, had in *his* mind. This is not to say that his presentation is totally unrealistic. For example, Himes shows through the relationships between the white police officials and his two black detectives a full awareness of the understanding-gap that has come between whites and blacks in America's inner cities. He is also realistic when he shows that black police can be just as brutal as white when the need arises. And, above all else, Himes has a realistic and profound grasp of the thinking and habits of the Harlem man in the street. In spite of the heightened pace in these works, one can glean from them a revealing social picture of the black ghetto.

In several of these detective stories Chester Himes features a pair of intelligent, down-to-earth, and hard-boiled black police detectives, Coffin Ed Johnson and Grave Digger Jones. Appropriately, the author has not made these officers super-subtle. They are practical men with a great deal of guts, a vast knowledge of the ways of Harlem, and the kind of

2. The dates given here are those of the American paperback publication, not the dates of the French originals.

flamboyance that endears them to the black community (and to the reader).

The detective stories of Chester Himes have not been as popular in America as they have been in France, where they are best sellers. In 1958 Himes was awarded the Grand Prix Policier, the Mystery Writers' Award for that year. Perhaps the French find in Himes's sensational and violent Harlem scenes *their* concept of American life.

Melvin B. Tolson

In an interview entitled "A Poet's Odyssey" Melvin Beaunorus Tolson summarizes his life in the following manner.

> Tennyson's protagonist says in "Ulysses," "Much have I seen and known." And again, "I am a part of all that I have met . . . ."—as shoeshine boy, stevedore, soldier, janitor, packinghouse worker, cook on a railroad, waiter in beach-front hotels, boxer, actor, football coach, director of drama, lecturer for the NAACP, organizer of sharecroppers' unions, teacher, father of Ph.D.'s, poet laureate of a foreign country, painter, newspaper columnist, fourtime mayor of a town, facer of mobs. I have made my way in the world since I was twelve years old.[3]

This capsule autobiography accounts in some measure for the bizarre character of Tolson's works—particularly the latter works. A big, expansive, and many-sided personality, M. B. Tolson had a wide-ranging and retentive mind, a huge capacity for enthusiasm, and a certain gift with words. In his last years he was "discovered" by two distinguished American critics, each explaining at some length Tolson's importance as a poet. But the explanations tended to leave the poet as much an enigma as he was before discovery. Frankly, it is difficult to "account for" Tolson. Between his early works and his later ones, there is a greater difference in subject matter and technique, a greater growth in outlook and sophistication than is found in any other American poet. Comparing Tolson's early and late works, one gets the impression that he is reading two different authors. No critic has accounted for this phenomenal poetic transformation.

The son of a minister, Melvin Beaunorus Tolson was born in

3. Herbert Hill, ed., *Anger and Beyond*. New York: Harper and Row, 1966, p. 184.

Moberley, Missouri, on February 6, 1900. His family was relatively poor. He attended Fisk University, but transferred to Lincoln (Pennsylvania), where he received his B.A. He took his M.A. in English at Columbia University. Tolson taught many years at Wiley College in Texas and at Langston University in Oklahoma. During his lifetime he was known for his debating and drama-club work; his political activities (he was elected mayor of Langston for four terms); and his poetry readings. For many years he wrote a column for the *Washington Tribune* called "Caviar and Cabbage." In 1947 he was commissioned poet laureate of Liberia, and in this capacity he wrote *Libretto for the Republic of Liberia* (1953). His poems have been published in *The Atlantic Monthly, Poetry, Prairie Schooner,* and in a majority of the Negro poetry anthologies. He was written four plays: *The Moses of Beale Street* (in collaboration), *Southern Front,* and dramatizations of Walter White's *Fire in the Flint* and George Schuyler's *Black No More.*

Tolson received fellowships in literature from the Omega Psi Phi Fraternity and the Rockefeller Foundation. "Dark Symphony" won the National Poetry Contest conducted by the American Negro Exposition in Chicago. Another poem, "E. & O. E.," won the Bess Hokin Award of the Modern Poetry Association. He also won high praise from such poets and critics as Allen Tate, Karl Shapiro, and Robert Frost. At the time of his death Tolson was Avalon Professor of the Humanities at Tuskegee.

The first publication of Tolson's to attract national attention was, as stated above, "Dark Symphony," a long poem which won the National Poetry Contest. It was subsequently published in the September, 1941, issue of *The Atlantic Monthly.* Very few Negro poems appeared in *The Atlantic Monthly* during this era; so few, in fact, that *Opportunity* considered the achievement worthy of an article.[4]

Divided into six sections, each named with an appropriate musical movement, "Dark Symphony" is fairly representative of the period in which it was written. It has the usual parade of black heroes (Attucks, Douglass, et al.), the expected protest elements, and the loyalty-in-spite-of-oppression theme which many Negro poets of the era emphasized. In addition, Tolson touches on the ugliness of American capitalism and the failure of American democracy and Christianity. The poem ends on an optimistic note: international brotherhood to be brought about by the peoples of the world. "Dark Symphony" was reprinted in Tolson's first collection of verse, *Rendezvous with America* (1944).

This mixture of patriotism, mild protest, and concern for world

4. "Atlantic Monthly Accepts Poem by Wiley College Professor." *Opportunity* (September, 1941).

Melvin B. Tolson

Courtesy of Johnson Publishing Co.

brotherhood will occur again in other poems in *Rendezvous with America*. At this time Tolson shows a casual interest in Marxism, as did several other major Negro writers of the period. But Tolson's interest is surface, and its strongest manifestation seems to be expressed in the theme of world brotherhood—a theme which he emphasizes not only here but also in his second volume of poetry. A poem entitled "Kikes, Bohunks, Crackers, Dagos, Niggers" is an example of Tolson's concern for getting underdog people together. This piece appeared first in *Modern Quarterly* (Winter, 1939). In the same poem Tolson plays up the melting-pot function of America, calling it an "international river with a legion of tributaries!" He appends, in the manner of Walt Whitman, a catalogue of outstanding Americans from various underdog backgrounds—Jewish, Italian, Negro, and other.

In another section of *Rendezvous with America* Tolson presents a section which he calls "Woodcuts for America." This group of poems had appeared earlier in *Common Ground* (Spring, 1943), and the pieces deal with various national types and with down-to-earth folk wisdom. One poem, "The Man Inside," is dedicated "To the Memory of V. F. Calverton," a well-known liberal editor of the era; another poem, "When Great Dogs Fight," presents the kind of cracker-barrel comment on life that one finds in a poet like Edgar Guest.

Rendezvous with America is by no means an outstanding work. It is not to be classed with the first publications of Cullen, Hughes, and Sterling Brown. Tolson's second collection, however, is quite a different matter.

In order to celebrate the centennial and its International Exposition, Liberia commissioned in 1947 M. B. Tolson as poet laureate to write a commemorative work. (Duke Ellington was also commissioned at the time and composed "Liberian Suite," which had a successful premiere in New York.) By 1950 Tolson had completed a considerable amount of a work which was to be known as *Libretto for the Republic of Liberia* (it was published in 1953). It was the "Ti" section of this poem which appeared in *Poetry* Magazine (1950) that attracted the attention of Allen Tate and eventually brought forth Tate's now-famous preface to the 1953 *Libretto*.

Allen Tate's preface is startling in several respects. After stating that Tolson shows "a great gift for language, a profound historical sense, and a first-rate intelligence at work," Tate asserts: "For the first time, it seems to me, a Negro poet has assimilated completely the full poetic language of the Anglo-American poetic tradition." After making derogatory remarks concerning emphasis on folk idiom or on the romantic creation of a new language within the English language as exemplified in Hughes and Gwendolyn Brooks, and other poets, Tate ends the preface with high praise for Tolson.

> In the end I found that I was reading *Libretto for the Republic of Liberia* not because Mr. Tolson is a Negro but because he is a poet, not because the poem has a "Negro subject" but because it is about the world of all men. And this subject is not merely asserted; it is embodied in a rich and complex language, and realized in terms of the poetic imagination.[5]

Negro scholars naturally disagree with Mr. Tate's contemptuous dismissal of the folk idiom as making for "provincial mediocrity," but they find the real difficulty in his phrase, "the language of the Anglo-American poetic tradition." What does he mean by it? What *is* the language of this tradition? How, for example, does the language of Tolson, even with the Pindaric form, the elaborate allusions, and the Hart Crane influence—how does it differ in essence from, let us say, that of Cullen and Robert Hayden? One notes in passing that Tate praises Tolson for not using Negro language, whereas Shapiro, in a preface to Tolson's next work, praises him for writing "in Negro," whatever that may mean.

The Libretto for the Republic of Liberia is a very difficult poem—even with its sixteen pages of erudite notes in several languages, it is still hard to understand. The work marks a complete break with the poet's former style of writing. Divided into eight sections, each bearing the name of a note on the scale ("Do," "Re," "Mi," and so forth), the poem is written largely in one of the most formal of all poetic forms, the Pindaric ode. In "Do" each stanza asks the question, "Liberia?," and then answers it by telling first what Liberia is not: "No pimple on the chin of Africa" but "Black Lazarus risen from the White Man's grave"; "No Cobra Pirate of the Question Mark," but "American genius uncrowned in Europe's charnel-house." From "Do" the poem seems to progress chronologically, ending with a description of "Futurafrique."

Section "Re" is short and seems to give a capsule history of Songhai, the ancient kingdom, and the glories of Timbuktu. But the white man came and raped Africa. In the old days "The Good Gray Bard in Timbuktu chanted," but now "The Good Gray Bard chants no longer in Timbuktu:/ 'The maggots fat on yeas and nays of nut empires!' "

Section "Mi" continues the history of Liberia, telling about Supreme Court Justice Bushrod Washington (a nephew of George Washington), Francis Scott Key, and other distinguished Americans meeting in Washington and forming the American Colonization Society. Their decisions "verved Black Pilgrim Fathers to Cape Mesurado." In the latter part of

5. *Libretto for the Republic of Liberia.* New York: Twayne Publishers, 1953 (Preface).

the section Liberia's future in rubber and her part in World War II are touched on obliquely.

Section "Fa," using a selection of hostile animals and natural phenomena as symbols, describes apparently the troubles for the new colonists "in the interlude of peace," a phrase which is not clear.

Section "Sol" deals with Elijah Johnson, one of the pioneers, who groans metaphorically from a slave ship, "How long?" The ultimate answer seems to be Liberia, which completed the circle started by the slave ship. Then follows a list of striking African proverbs inserted by Tolson as an answer to Gertrude Stein's ignorant and acid comment that "the Negro suffers from nothingness."[6] The section ends with a comment on Elijah Johnson's refusal to be defeated by hardships. Johnson "broods": "The foxes have holes, the birds have nests,/ And I have found a place to lay/ My head, Lord of Farewells!"

Section "La," among other things, pays homage to a white American, Jehudi Ashmun, who brought fifty-five immigrants to Liberia. Though he had planned to return to America, he remained there to help when he discovered the plight the colonists were in. Tolson has Ashmun declaring: "My Negro kinsmen,/ America is my mother,/ Liberia is my wife,/ And Africa is my brother."

Section "Ti," the part that appeared earlier in *Poetry* Magazine, is long and obscure. The poet seems to be talking of an earlier and more significant Africa whose downfall was brought about by the Europeans: "O Africa, Mother of Science/ . . . What dread grasp crushed your biceps and/ back upon the rack/ chaos of chance and change/ fouled in Malebolgean isolation?/ What dread *elboga* shoved your soul into the *tribulum* of retardation?" We are told, however, that "The Höhere [the higher good] of God's children/ is beyond the sabotaged world"; this Höhere, we are led to believe, will not only come to being in Africa but also in a new world of brotherhood.

The final section, "Do," continues this theme of a better future world, but it begins by describing the many horrors associated with the present ("the old she-fox today"). This section (along with the whole poem) moves to a climax in a series of verse paragraphs, which use technological and locomotive metaphors to describe "Futurafrique" and "The Parliament of African Peoples." "The Futurafrique glitters . . . toward Khopirü" (the word means "To Be" and "The concept embraces the Eternity of Thence, which, free from blind necessity contains the good life"). The poem is tied together structurally through the repetition of a metaphor found first in "Re" and repeated in the very last verse-para-

6. Herbert Hill, ed., *Anger and Beyond,* New York: Harper and Row, 1966, p. 184.

graph of the poem: "and the hyenas whine no more among the barren bones. . . ." The whole thrust of this last part is that Africa, finding its Khopirü, will also find that of the world and usher in a new day of world unity, all distinctions among men eliminated. In finding itself Africa will be rediscovering the glories of Songhai, the old kingdom which the poet describes in earlier sections.

In 1952, a year before the publication of *Libretto,* Tolson, as stated above, won the Bess Hokin Award of the Modern Poetry Association for his poem, "E. & O. E.," excerpts of which are reprinted in *Harlem Gallery* (1965), the poet's last major publication. Tolson, however, had been concerned with this work long before. During the Harlem Renaissance days he wrote a sonnet on Harlem and showed it to one of his friends. After several readings, the friend said, "Melvin, Harlem is too big for a sonnet." By 1930 he had written *Harlem Gallery* in free verse. (He was at Columbia University then on a Rockefeller Foundation scholarship.) He wrote, as he tells us, under the influence of Masters, Browning (character psychology), and Whitman, whose bigness and exuberance intrigued Tolson. He finished the work, but nobody would publish it. He put it away for twenty years. In the meantime, he read Pound, Eliot, Yeats, Baudelaire, Pasternak, and the New Critics. Under the influence of these authors and critics, he rewrote *Harlem Gallery.* Designed to be part of an "epic" poem dealing with Harlem, it was published in 1965 with an introduction by Karl Shapiro.

Shapiro opens his introduction with a startling statement: "A poet has been living in our midst for decades and is almost totally unknown, even by the literati, even by the poets." The reason? "Poetry as we know it remains the most lily-white of the arts. A novelist and pamphleteer like Baldwin is world famous; Tolson, easily the literary equal of any number of Baldwins, is less honored in his own country than the most obscure poetaster." The reason for this situation, Shapiro feels, is that Tolson contravenes the ruling "Graeco-Judaic-Christian" culture and is "in effect the enemy of the dominant culture of our time and place." This accounts for the reception of *Libretto,* which "pulls the rug out from under the poetry of the Academy; on the stylistic level, out-Pounding Pound, it shocks the learned into a recognition of their own ignorance. *Harlem Gallery* pulls the house down around their ears."

"Tolson writes in Negro." After making this cryptic and startling and italicized statement, Shapiro describes English as a "dying language" and repeats and embellishes his assertion: "Tolson writes and thinks in Negro, which is to say, a possible American language. He is therefore performing the primary poetic rite for our literature. Instead of purifying the tongue . . . he is complicating it, giving it the gift of tongues." The critic ends his introduction with the following high compliment:

"*The Harlem Gallery* is as if improvised by one of the great architects of modern poetry. It may be that this work, . . . will turn out to be not only an end in itself but the door to poetry that everyone has been looking for."

The one issue that intrigues Negro critics, especially the younger critics,[7] is the statement "Tolson writes in Negro." How does one write in Negro? Certainly Tolson, with his wide-ranging and erudite allusions from the whole corpus of Western literary culture, is not using what young black writers feel is a Negro (black) language. If one compares the language used by Negro poets since about 1960 with that of Tolson, he will find few if any similarities. Of course, the earthy, ungrammatical language of the new black poets may not be "Negro" either, but it certainly comes closer to what most persons who think in such terms would call "Negro." Tolson himself makes an intriguing, double-edged comment on Shapiro's statement: "I hazard that Shapiro has pillaged my three books and discovered that I, as a black poet, have absorbed the Great Ideas of the Great White World, and interpreted them in the melting pot idiom of my people. My roots are in Africa, Europe, and America."[8]

Though not as hard to understand as *Libretto, Harlem Gallery* also has its difficult passages. Perhaps the main stumbling block to interpretation is the poet's intention. How are we to take this strange work whose two main themes are *art* and the *Negro?* Is Tolson writing seriously or with tongue in cheek? Is he parodying, as one critic, Paul Bremen, suggests, the white man's concept of how a Negro-putting-on-airs would talk? Obviously, there are many comic passages and scenes in the book, but where does the comic aspect end, if it does end? How serious are the comments on art, and what is their relationship to the work as a whole? These questions must be answered before one can evaluate *Harlem Gallery.* If the poem is to be taken as a serious attempt to depict Harlem (and, by extension, the Negro world), then it is a failure —a brilliant failure, perhaps, but still a failure.

The subtitle of *Harlem Gallery* is *Book One: The Curator.* This should not be overlooked because the whole poem seems to be narrated by the Curator, who at one time refers to the work as an "autobio-fragment." (How much of Tolson is the Curator is another question which comes to the reader's mind.) The Curator is the unifying element in a work that does not have an easily discerned structure. The poem is divided into twenty-four sections, each named for a letter of the Greek alphabet. In "Alpha" the poet asks the question: "Black Boy, O Black

7. See Sarah Webster Fabio, "Who Speaks Negro?" *Negro Digest* (December, 1966), p. 55.
8. "Interview," in *Anger and Beyond,* New York: Harper and Row, 1966, p. 184.

174 / PART TWO

Boy,/ is the port worth the cruise?" The rest of the poem *may* be an answer because he returns to the "Black Boy" theme in "Psi," perhaps the most effective section in the poem. The scene of the poem moves from place to place, but the ones which are used most often are apparently the gallery itself, and the Zulu Club. The characters, in addition to the Curator, include the Curator's best friend, Doctor Obi Nkomo, an educated Zulu. (Nkomo may be a snide comment on what Tolson thinks of our present overemphasis on Africa.) Mr. and Mrs. Guy Delaporte III represent the Negro middle class; Black Diamond comes from the black underworld of the numbers and other rackets. John Laugart, the half-blind painter of *The Black Bourgeoisie,* probably symbolizes black artistic honesty, something which does not pay off in worldly success. Hideho Heights is the popular Harlem folk poet, and there are others. These characters, in the gallery itself, in the Zulu Club, and in other Harlem establishments, talk at length about art and about being a Negro. There is much rich humor in the work, some of it based on folk material. There are also several attempts at humor and at realism that somehow fall flat. It is evidently not easy, even for Tolson, to present the earthiness and simplicity of folk speech and action in the formal limits of the Pindaric ode. Moreover, the juxtaposition of low-life cabaret scenes with erudite, or supposedly erudite, comments on the origin and meaning of art makes for a strange mélange. The reader of *Harlem Gallery* often asks himself a question: What is the poet trying to do? The Gallery seems to represent Negro life in America. Is Tolson trying to define (using the word in its broadest sense) the American Negro? (Note the comments in "Psi" on "Who is a Negro?") The reader must answer questions of this sort for himself. And even though he may find no real answers to them, he will certainly find his search through *Harlem Gallery* well worth the effort.

Robert Hayden

Robert Hayden, particularly the Hayden of his last three publications, has little in common with present-day Black Arts poets. For one thing, he believes that the poetry of the Negro, in spite of its specialized content, is "essentially American" and does not stand apart from the rest of our national literature. He also believes that "any poet's most clearly defined task is to create with honesty and sincerity poems that will illuminate human experience—not exclusively 'Negro experience.'"[9] Although his first major publication contains a considerable number of conventionally racial poems, Hayden's later verse, even when using black experience, somehow manages to lift that experience above the narrow and parochial limitations of race.

Robert Hayden was born in Detroit, Michigan. He received his B.A. from Wayne State University and in 1936 joined the Federal Writers' Project, where he headed reseach into local Negro history and the collection of folklore. In 1938 he began graduate studies at the University of Michigan, where he received a teaching assistantship and did advanced work in creative writing, English, and play production. After receiving his M.A., he taught English there for two years. In 1938 and 1942 he won the University's Avery Hopwood award for poetry. His first collection of poetry, *Heart-Shape in the Dust*, was published in 1940.

After working as music and drama critic for the *Michigan Chronicle* in 1946, Hayden joined the faculty of Fisk University (where he remained until 1968) as professor of English. He was awarded a Rosenwald Fellowship in 1947. In 1948 *The Lion and the Archer* appeared. He received a Ford Foundation grant in 1954, and the Grand Prize for Poetry at the First World Festival of Negro Arts in Dakar, Senegal, in 1965, for *A Ballad of Remembrance* (1962). His *Selected Poems* appeared in 1966, and in 1967, *Kaleidoscope: Poems by American Negro Poets,* an anthology edited by Hayden. He has also been poetry editor of the Baha'i magazine, *World Order*. Hayden is now a visiting professor of English at the University of Michigan, and in 1970 his latest volume of poetry, *Words in the Mourning Time,* appeared.

Hayden's poetic career spans the years from the period of the late-Harlem Renaissance down to the current Black Arts Revolution. His first publication shows the influence of the Renaissance, but as that influence diminished, Hayden, unlike Gwendolyn Brooks and others of his generation, did not adopt the militant, nationalist, anti-Western-tradition stance of contemporary Black Arts writers. On the contrary, he has tried in every way to make even his so-called Negro poetry conform to and measure up to the best that Western civilization has produced. A superb craftsman, and a perfectionist, Hayden has consistently written for a "fit audience, though few."

Robert Hayden is not a prolific writer. Most of his work may be found in six thin publications: *Heart-Shape in the Dust* (1940), *Figure*

9. Robert Hayden, ed. *Kaleidoscope*. New York: Harcourt, Brace and World, 1967, p. xxiii.

of Time: Poems (1955), *A Ballad of Remembrance* (1962), *Selected Poems* (1966), *Words in the Mourning Time* (1970), *The Lion and the Archer* (written with Myron O'Higgins in 1948). Hayden does not want anthologists to use poems from his first publication, and he has included none of them in his *Selected Poems*. One can understand this reluctance because too many, though not all, of the pieces in *Heart-Shape in the Dust* are simply dated; others are both dated and repetitious, echoing themes already used too often during the Renaissance years. "Speech," for example, a short poem showing Marxist influence, echoes pieces on the same subject by Hughes, Tolson, and Wright. "Poem for a Negro Dancer" reminds one of verses by Hughes, McKay, and other users of the alien-and-exile theme. "Coleman" treats the lynched-Negro-veteran theme, which was popular with Renaissance writers. "Religioso" has the black Christ motif, which Cullen and others used. "These Are My People (A Mass Chant)" is eight pages long and covers many of the social themes, including the Scottsboro Boys story, found in Negro poems of the 1930's. More protest statement than poetry, it no longer pleases modern readers, partly because we are no longer moved by the subjects treated.

All of the racial and protest poems in *Heart-Shape in the Dust,* however, are not to be dismissed on the above grounds. Several have an intrinsic excellence which transcends any racial or topical limitation. Among these is "Gabriel," a concise, moving poem dealing with the last minutes of Black Gabriel (Prosser), who planned a slave insurrection near Richmond, Virginia, in 1800. Making use of a contrapuntal question and response structure, it gives the last words of Gabriel as he prepares to die on the gallows. In less than fifty short lines the poet crystallizes the heroic defiance and the prophetic implications of Black Gabriel's action. More compact than a ballad-type narrative, it captures in an image the whole thrust of the poem: "Gabriel hangs/ Black-gold in the sun,/ Flame-head of/ Rebellion." The gold, the sun, the flame, all characterize Gabriel's brilliant attempt; they also characterize the brilliance of the poem itself.

Another poem from the first volume, "Obituary," has a similar effect on the reader. Running through it is the quiet but deeply religious strain that crops up often in Hayden's poetry. In this particular work he transmits the simple faith of a hard-working father who " . . . died serenely,/ Having found/ God's footprints flowering/ On mortal ground."

The last poem from *Heart-Shape in the Dust* to be considered is "Bacchanale." Writen in the rhythms of a folk song, and with the acceptance-with-defiance spirit of the blues, the piece shows the strong faith of the folk speaker who has lost both job and girl, but who still is "gonna git high" because "There's gotta be joy somewhere/ For a po' colored boy. . . ."

Robert Hayden

Courtesy of Moorland-Spingarn Research Center, Howard University.

In very few poets is the change of tone so pronounced as in the Robert Hayden of *A Ballad of Remembrance* (1962) when compared with the Robert E. Hayden of *Heart-Shape in the Dust* (1940). The latter shows a young novice poet following, perhaps too closely, models from the New Negro Renaissance. The Hayden of *Ballad of Remembrance* shows a mature craftsman making use of the diction, the forms, and, unfortunately, some of the obscurity of contemporary verse making. One of the several differences between the two Haydens is the attitude toward racial poems. He has not given up Negro subject matter, he has elevated it to a higher plane. He no longer writes old-fashioned protest poems. On the contrary, he plays down the parochial and limiting elements in a given racial situation or incident and, by removing the racial emphasis, he raises the human interest involved. There is nothing peculiar about this method. All good poets do it. We mention it here because it is probably a more difficult achievement for a Negro poet than for—let us say—a Jewish or Irish-American poet. The nation has insisted on the peculiar status of the black and hates to accept him as just another human.

One of the finest poems in the volume, "Middle Passage," shows the new Hayden at his best. Weaving symphonically and brilliantly a ship log of a slaver, it tersely states facts of drought, fire, disease-caused blindness, crazed Negroes, and other horrors of the middle passage. In the Amistad story, the Christian versus the commercial values are woven to play one theme against the other until the poem reaches a climax in perhaps its overriding theme, the "Voyage through death/ to life upon these shores," with its suggestion of sin, death, and salvation for man. No special black awareness is necessary to understand this poem. Although it deals with the middle passage, it is more of a protest against man's inhumanity, against the presence of evil in the world, than against the greed-driven slavers—black as well as white—who dealt in "black gold, black ivory, black seed."

The title poem, "A Ballad of Remembrance," has been handled in the same fashion. Ostensibly it is a poem about New Orleans, written as a "souvenir" for Mark Van Doren. Although Hayden never states it, he tells us through his references to "the Zulu King," "quadroon mermaids," and other images associated with the "down-South arcane city" that he has in mind carnival time in New Orleans, with all of the tawdriness and frivolity which that occasion represents. From this tinsel and lightness and unreality, the poet is rescued by the "meditative, ironic,/ richly human" Van Doren, a symbol of sanity in a carnival world. There are overtones of racial meaning in the poem, but they in no wise impinge upon the charming tribute to Van Doren, through whom the poet can escape the spuriousness of carnival living and find his "true voice again."

In the effort to de-emphasize race in his work, Hayden resorts on occasion to ambiguity. In "Tour 5," for example, the speaker describes a trip South on which the group stops for gas in a town "watched over by Confederate sentinels/ buy gas and ask directions of a rawboned man/ whose eyes revile us as the enemy. . . ." Is it an anti-Negro or an anti-Yankee look? It could be interpreted either way and make sense. This same ambiguity occurs in "Incense of the Lucky Virgin." As soon as the reader sees terms like "High John the Conqueror," he begins to "think black." The poem, however, deals with the poor and superstitious of all groups and with the tragedy that abject poverty can bring. The refrains used at the end of each stanza of this narrative could derive from either white ballad or black blues influence. In such poems race becomes unimportant, and can be dismissed. This seems to be Hayden's overall aim.

Several of Hayden's poems leave the reader with a fullness, a sense of completeness, a sense of having witnessed a whole action. "Middle Passage" is such a poem—one in which he seems to suggest all that can be said about that bitter era in our history. "The Witch Doctor" leaves the same impression. After reading it, one somehow knows the character—knows him because he is so like others we have known in real life. He is an abstracted version of all the religious charlatans. Hayden achieves this effect through a series of pertinent, suggestive, and loaded details: "liveried chauffeur," his leopard skin coat, his eye for sailors in the park, his flamboyant showmanship, and his dancing "encorcelled and aloof,/ the fervid juba of God as lover, healer,/ conjurer. And of himself as God." Although a charlatan in the ordinary sense of the word, the man is true to his personality and to his peculiar and distorted vision, and in that respect has a sort of integrity which intrigues us. And in spite of certain allusions, he is basically not a Negro religious charlatan; he is all of the worldly, earthy, yet somehow inspired "holy men" one meets in all places and in all colors. He lives in the ghettos of Harlem and Chicago, but he is also found in Beverly Hills and in white communes.

In "The Ballad of Nat Turner" the poet has taken one crucial and illuminating experience in Nat Turner's life, and with it has suggested or adumbrated the whole history-making event which occurred in Jerusalem, Virginia, in 1831: the violence, the intense religious fervor, and, above all else, the visions of Nat Turner himself—visions which shaped his career. The poem has a simple but effective structure. The action progresses from the worldliness of the "wicked juba" and "curfew joys" through a withdrawal into the swamp (Dante's "wood") for contemplation and reflection; it then moves to a fiery climax in the ecstatic Miltonic vision of warring angels—a vision in which Nat discovers that the conquering angels had faces "like mine." The poem comes to a quiet ending when Nat Turner, after "a sleep as heavy as death," awakes "newborn" and "purified," arises, prays, returns to humble reality, and bides his time.

In "Runagate Runagate," another striking work inspired by Negro experience, the poet demonstrates again his superb craftsmanship, his ability to weave symphonically several disparate themes into one satisfying harmony. Most of the first movement of the piece tumbles along without punctuation or stop of any kind, describing through form *and* word-sound the headlong, breathless flight of a fugitive. Excerpts from spirituals ("No more auction block for me"), a letter from a plantation owner describing runaway slaves, and the well-known Harriet Tubman episode ("You keep on going now or die") are fused with the names of Douglass, Garrison, Thoreau, John Brown, and other freedom fighters —fused into one strong and impressive affirmation of the human desire for liberty.

Among the new pieces in *Selected Poems,* "The Diver" is perhaps the most provocative and certainly one of the most skillful technically. Sinking from "easeful azure" down to a "dead ship" (an image of death), the diver is entranced by the beauty of the underwater world, and experiences a yearning to "have done with self and/ every dinning/ vain complexity"—a yearning to join those "hidden ones." Like the speaker in Keats's "Ode to a Nightingale," the diver finally flees "the humbling/ kisses that I carved." Again, there is here a subtle accommodation of sound to the ideas invoked: "Freefalling, weightless/as in dreams of/wingless fllight." Through the use of weak endings and suggestive words the poet achieves the ethereal and unearthly quality which his theme demands.

Another work in *Selected Poems,* "The Ballad of Sue Ellen Westerfield," makes use of a subject not often touched nowadays by black writers: the story of a deep and undying love between a Negro woman and a white lover, a love thwarted and frustrated by "the circumstance" (presumably by the American racial situation). Several present-day black novelists have used the black-man-white-woman situation, but few, if any, have been willing, like Hayden, to acknowledge that interracial love is not a one-way street.

Always a skillful craftsman in verse, Hayden has grown and improved with the years. When he decided to abandon the kind of racial protest verse that he wrote in his first work, he seemingly decided to give up most of the conventional verse forms used in the early volume. In *Heart-Shape in the Dust* (1940), for example, one finds quatrains (with varying line-lengths and rhyme-schemes), Shakespearian sonnets, mass chants, and other conventional forms. In his *Selected Poems*

(1966), one finds practically no rhyme (even his sonnet, "Frederick Douglass" is not rhymed). In this later volume, he employs a number of varied, unshackled, free-flowing verse forms, and he handles them effectively and on occasion brilliantly. Among these new forms, we find recurring contrapuntal lines of the sort used by the Pre-Raphaelites (see for example "Night, Death, Mississippi"); repeated last lines with variations of the type used in the blues form (see "Incense of the Lucky Virgin"); verse paragraphs (see "The Ballad of Sue Ellen Westerfield"); and special effects such as the dance rhythm in "O Daedalus, Fly Away Home" ("Night is juba, night is conjo/ Pretty Malinda, dance with me"). In the later poems, one finds occasionally half-rhyme and assonance, but seldom exact rhyme. Perhaps Hayden's most impressive poetic techniques are those found in "The Middle Passage." In this long poem, Hayden subtly and musically blends several kinds of writing— prose statement, refrains, excerpts from other poems, and lines from an old hymn—to produce a symphonic whole. To achieve his effects, the poet depends on the well-chosen, suggestive word *and* a cadence that reflects the varying moods of the poem.

One should note here that a considerable number of poems in each of Hayden's major publications, particularly the later ones, have nothing to do with race. Section Two, for example, in *Selected Poems* consists of verses reflecting the poet's stay in Mexico. Several of his nonracial works, like "The Diver," rank among his most brilliant performances. Though Hayden does not want to be thought of as a *Negro* poet, his ultimate critical assessment may be similar to that of Countee Cullen, who admitted that his strongest poems tended to deal with race.

Margaret Walker

The author of two major publications, *For My People* (1942) and *Jubilee* (1966), Margaret Walker is both poet and novelist. For the first work, she won a place in the Yale Series of Younger Poets and for the second a Houghton Mifflin Literary Award. Between the two works there is an hiatus of twenty-four years, and one is puzzled by it. Why do outstanding Negro writers like Toomer, Ellison, and Walker either produce only one good work or take such a long time to bring out the

Margaret Walker

Photo by Jill Krementz.

second? Thurman raised this question when he attacked the New Negro Renaissance in *Infants of the Spring.* It has not been answered yet.

Margaret Abigail Walker was born in Birmingham, Alabama, on July 7, 1915. Her father, a Methodist minister, and her mother, a music teacher, were both university graduates. She has two sisters and one brother. She received her early education in church schools in Meridian, Mississippi, Birmingham, Alabama, and New Orleans, Louisiana. She received her B.A. from Northwestern University in 1935 and worked in Chicago the next four years as a typist, newspaper reporter, editor of a short-lived magazine, and member of the Federal Writers' Project in Chicago. She has also worked as a social worker in Chicago and New Orleans. In 1939 she entered the University of Iowa, receiving her M.A. in 1940. (In place of a thesis she submitted a collection of poems.) She was appointed professor of English at Livingston College in Salisbury, North Carolina, in 1942. In 1942 *For My People,* her first published book, won the Yale University Younger Poets Competition. (According to *Opportunity,* Stephen Vincent Benét selected it; for his comments, see *New York Times,* November 4, 1942.) In 1944 she received a Rosenwald Fellowship for Creative Writing. She has taught English at West Virginia State College, and since 1949 she has been a member of the faculty at Jackson State College in Mississippi. Mrs. Firnish James Alexander in private life, she is the mother of four children. She submitted *Jubilee* (a novel) in lieu of a dissertation at the University of Iowa, where she received a Ph.D. in creative writing in 1965. This same novel received a Houghton Mifflin Literary Award in 1966 (*Jubilee* has been translated into several languages.) She has been a visiting professor at Northwestern University, and she has directed the Institute for the Study of History, Life, and Culture of Black People at Jackson State College (as of 1969).

Miss Walker is a better poet than she is a novelist, and *For My People* is an excellent first publication. In the foreword to the volume, Stephen Vincent Benét has characterized the work of this (then young) poet:

> Straightforwardness, directness, reality are good things to find in a young poet. It is rarer to find them combined with a controlled intensity of emotion and a language that, at times, even when it is most modern, has something of the surge of biblical poetry. And it is obvious that Miss Walker uses that language because it comes naturally to her and is part of her inheritance.

This "inheritance" is very much present in Margaret Walker's poetry. She has transformed into poetic art the surge and roll, the repetition and alliteration, of a tradition of Baptist and Methodist preaching she knew well as a Southern Negro and particularly as a daughter of a

Methodist minister. James Weldon Johnson used the rhythms and imagery and speech patterns of the Negro folk sermons to write sermons of a folklike nature. Miss Walker transformed the same materials into a general poetic language, one which she used most effectively in her best poems: "For My People," "We Have Been Believers," and "Delta."

Several themes are repeated in Margaret Walker's poems. The one used most often concerns the poet's love of the South. What she is saying again and again is that the South is the Negro's home; he belongs there, but prejudice and oppression keep him away from what is rightfully his. We are told, for example, in "Sorrow Home":

> My roots are deep in southern life; deeper than John
> Brown or Nat Turner or Robert Lee. . . .

> I am no hot-house bulb to be reared in steam-heated flats
> with the music of "L" and subway in my ears. . . .

> I want the cotton fields, tobacco and the cane. . . .

> O Southland, sorrow home. . . . How long will the Klan of
> hate, the hounds and the chain gangs keep me from my
> own?

The poet repeats this theme in "Delta": "We with our blood have watered these fields/ and they belong to us." And in "Southern Song" she tells us: "I want my body bathed again by southern suns, my soul/ reclaimed again from southern lands. . . ." And in the same poem she asks for "the fusion of the South, my body's soul and me." For her the Negro in the North is a disinherited and dispossessed soul, and he wants to know when he *can* come back to his native soil. In "Since 1619" the persona asks pitifully: "How many years since 1619 have I been singing spirituals?/ . . . How long have I been hated and hating?"

There is also a subdued strain of militance in *For My People*. Although there is none of the stridency so often found in protest poetry, especially that of the 1960's, there are strong suggestions that the Negro will not always remain duped and quiescent. In the last sentences of her titular poem, the whole of which is a magnificent protest poem, she states: "Let the martial songs be written/ let the dirges disappear. Let a race of men/ now rise and take control." Although she does not italicize *men,* the sense of emphasis is there. Again, in "We Have Been Believers" the last section sounds a distinct warning:

> We have been believers believing in our burdens and our
> demigods too long. Now the needy no longer weep

and pray; the long-suffering arise, and our fists
bleed against the bars with a strange insistency.

And in "Delta" the speaker declares that the Negro's love for the
"valley" (his native Southland) strengthens the blood within, "banding
the iron of our muscle with anger/making us men in the fields we have
tended. . . ."

There also runs through the poetry of Miss Walker a strain of
brotherhood which is nowhere as bluntly stated as in Tolson's verses,
but nevertheless implied throughout. It is not the brotherhood of a
future Marxist utopia, but one that she phrases in "The Struggle Staggers Us": "There is a journey from the me to you./ There is a journey
from the you to me./A union of the two strange worlds must be." In
"Our Need" she touches again this theme: "We need a wholeness born
of inner strength:/ . . . We need the friendly feel of human forms/
and earth beneath our feet against the storms." This is a refreshing
theme in these days of bitter and didactic poetry.

Part II of *For My People* deals with folk material. It has an unusual
version of "Big John Henry," one that compresses many of his exploits
from birth to death in thirty-two lines. Its version of "Bad-Man Stagolee" ends with his ghost still walking "up and down the shore/ Of Old
Man River round New Orleans/ With her gumbo, rice, and good red
beans!" One of her best folk ballads is that of "Molly Means" "Who
was a hag and a witch;/ Chile of the Devil, the dark, and sitch." This
ballad reads like an incantation, particularly its incremental refrain:

Old Molly, Molly, Molly Means
Cold is the ghost of Molly Means.

Several ballads deal with unfamiliar characters. They may be creations of Miss Walker or regional figures. Among them are the fascinating Poppa Chicken (who was a "sugar daddy and a pimp"); Kissie
Lee, "a very, very tough gal"; and Gus the Lineman, who seemingly
could not be killed by live wires and other deadly instrumentalities but
who succumbed to moonshine and "a little crick."

Although not a great or even a prolific writer of folk ballads, Miss
Walker does catch the spirit of this genre because she knows folk speech
and folk superstitions. These pieces are much better when read aloud
because the writer has captured the rhythms found in original ballads—
the rhythms which give added meaning to such works when read aloud
or sung.

Perhaps the outstanding impression that one gets from Margaret
Walker's three longest poems—"For My People," "We Have Been Believers," and "Delta"—is that she has a great compassion for the op-

pressed, mis-led, and groping Negro masses, but with that compassion goes the faith that a new day will come, "a new earth arise."

According to the dedication of the work, *Jubilee* is based on the life of Miss Walker's great-grandmother, Margaret Duggans Ware Brown. It covers the years prior to the Civil War and carries on through the war into the period of Reconstruction, and it shows all too well the tremendous amount of basic research that went into its making. (As stated earlier, the work was accepted in lieu of a conventional doctoral thesis at the University of Iowa.) *Jubilee* tells us a great deal about the history of the period involved and a great deal more about slavery and the plantation system.

The story itself delineates the life of Vyry, a mulatto house servant, and her patient, long-suffering struggle to attain freedom and dignity. The scene of the novel is the cotton belt in Georgia and Alabama. The master's daughter, Vyry as a child was mercilessly persecuted by the resentful mistress, but she survived and grew up to become the cook for the "big house." She meets Randall Ware, an intelligent free Negro who is the town's blacksmith. He tries to buy Vyry's freedom in order to make her his wife, but is unsuccessful and has to "marry" her slave fashion. When the war comes, Ware goes away to join the Union forces. After the war Vyry waits seven years for Ware's return and then marries legally Innis Brown, a hard-working but unambitious Negro. The two leave the plantation to seek a better life, only to be cheated as sharecroppers and to be burned out by the KKK. The novel, however, ends on a good-will note. Because of her skill as a midwife, Vyry and her husband are welcomed by the white folks of the little place to which they finally move; and these "good" white folks build the couple a house.

One of the flaws in *Jubilee* is that Margaret Walker has crowded too much into her novel. She makes use of practically every stock myth, legend, and situation that we have met before in the slave narratives and in the works of earlier novelists like Wiliam Wells Brown. All of the stereotypes are here: the aristocratic planter who can see his own child abused; the vicious poor white overseer; the intelligent and suspected free Negro; thế abolitionists with their secret meetings; and the enduring, patient slave who gets nothing but punishment for his loyalty —all are here.

Miss Walker has not fused this material sufficiently; she often *tells* when she should *render,* and she has not developed many of her characters fully enough. As a result of these shortcomings, one leaves the novel impressed by the tremendous possibilities this material offers but saddened by the novelist's failure to make it come fully alive.

After a lapse of twenty-eight years Margaret Walker has brought out a new volume of verse. Entitled *Prophets for a New Day* (1970), it was printed by the Broadside Press. Though a very thin volume (it contains only 32 pages), the work is impressive. It is the best poetical comment to come from the civil rights movement—the movement which came to a climax with the march on Washington and which began thereafter to change into a more militant type of liberation effort.

In *Prophets for a New Day* Miss Walker, with poems like "Street Demonstration," "Girl Held Without Bail," and "Sit-Ins," catches the spirit of the civil rights age, when young blacks gladly went to jail for the cause of freedom. "The Ballad of the Free," another liberation poem, treats as kindred souls Nat Turner, Gabriel Prosser, Denmark Vesey, Toussaint L'Ouverture, and John Brown. The inclusion of the last name shows that Miss Walker, though much "blacker" now in her thinking than she was in her early works, has not lost her respect for men of good will, whether black or white. Unlike most present-day Negro writers, she is willing to honor not only abolition heroes like John Brown but white martyrs of the civil rights movement as well ("to Andy Goodman—Michael Schwerner—and James Chaney").

Falling back on her own heritage as the daughter of a minister, Margaret Walker in her title poem, "Prophets for a New Day," makes superb use of soul-moving biblical rhythms and Old Testament characters. The most impressive figure in the series is Amos, the prophet of brotherly love. Amos is Martin Luther King, and her two pieces, "Amos-1963" and "Amos (Postscript-1968)" are excellent and moving poems on the assassinated leader.

One finds again in *Prophets for a New Day* a theme which she used in her first volume of verse: the poet's longing for the Southland, her home. In this new work Miss Walker sees the South ("Jackson, Mississippi" and "Birmingham") in all of its harshness, but in spite of the ugliness there she also finds " . . . light drenched streets puddled with the promise/ Of a brand-new tomorrow."

Gwendolyn Brooks

Never a simple poet, Gwendolyn Brooks has grown more difficult with the years. Like Tolson, she changed her style as well as her viewpoint in mid-career. When she first published in 1945, most Negro writers were literary integrationists, and she definitely held this position. In her last two poetical collections, however, she has abandoned that attitude and gone "black." With the new blackness has come an increase in the obscurity of much of her verse.

Gwendolyn Brooks was born in Topeka, Kansas, and reared in Chicago. She began writing poetry when she was seven years old, and had her first poem published when thirteen. In the same year she published a mimeographed community newspaper called the *Champlain Weekly News*. Miss Brooks graduated from Englewood High School (Chicago) in 1934 and Wilson Junior College in 1936. Married in 1939 to Henry Blakely, she has a son, born in 1940, and a daughter, born in 1951. Her poetry has appeared in *Harper's, Poetry, Common Ground, Yale Review, Saturday Review of Literature, Negro Story,* and other magazines. Her first volume of poetry, *A Street in Bronzeville* (1945), won the Merit Award of *Mademoiselle* magazine. She received a $1,000 prize from the Academy of Arts and Letters in 1946 and two Guggenheim fellowships for study, in 1946 and 1947. Her second volume of poetry, *Annie Allen* (1949), won *Poetry*'s Eunice Tietjens Memorial Award, and then the Pulitzer Prize for poetry in 1950. Miss Brooks has won the Poetry Workshop Award, given by the Midwestern Writers' Conference, three times (1943–1945). In 1964 she won the Friends Literature Award for Poetry and the Thormond Monsen Award for Literature. In 1969 she announced through the *Negro Digest* that she would award two prizes of $250 each to the best poem and best short story published by a black writer each year.

She has taught creative writing and poetry at Columbia, Elmhurst, and Northeastern Illinois State College, all in Chicago; and at the University of Wisconsin. She is a member of the advisory boards of the Institute for International Education, the Society for Midland Authors, and the Illinois Art Council.

The bulk of Miss Brooks's work is found in the following publications: *A Street in Bronzeville* (1945); *Annie Allen* (1949), which won her the Pulitzer Prize in poetry for 1950; *The Bean Eaters* (1960); *In the Mecca* (1968); and *Riot* (1969). In addition, she has published one children's book, *Bronzeville Boys and Girls* (1956); a superb collection of poems entitled *Sélected Poems* (1963); and one short work of fiction, *Maud Martha* (1953).

In her first three volumes of poetry, considered here as a unit, Miss Brooks wrote principally about life in the drab Bronzevilles of America (the black ghettos of our Northern cities); and she wrote with a great understanding of and a vast compassion for the unfortunates who lived in these places. Although she saw them as victims of America's vicious racial pattern, there is very little bitterness or hatred in the poems found in these first three works. On the contrary, she seems to imply that prejudice is a terrible but all-too-human weakness. The poem which best typifies this position is "The Chicago Defender Sends a Man to Little Rock." The reporter finds that, in spite of the violence that occurred there, he cannot write a story that his editor will accept. He discovers that the people in Little Rock "are like people everywhere"—small, petty, weak, and to be pitied rather than hated. After all, "The loveliest lynchee was our Lord."

Much of the poetry in Gwendolyn Brooks's first three works, like most Negro verse, falls into the protest category. But, again, one finds that Miss Brooks's protest poems tend to be subtly ironic or quietly humorous rather than strident or rhetorical or bitter. For example, in "Beverly Hills, Chicago" she relates the reaction of a group of Negroes driving through this upper-class white section:

> Nobody is furious. Nobody hates these people.
> At least, nobody driving by in this car.
> It is only natural, however, that it should occur to us
> How much more fortunate they are than we.[10]

In "The Lovers of the Poor" she describes a group of well-meaning but obtuse whites from the Betterment League being confronted with the actual conditions among the Bronzeville poor:

> Keeping their scented bodies in the center
> Of the hall as they walk down the hysterical hall,
> They allow their lovely skirts to graze no wall,
> Are off at what they manage of a canter. . . .[11]

One of Miss Brooks's finest protest poems, "of DeWitt Williams on his way to Lincoln Cemetery," has no word of protest in it. Consisting of simple factual statements, it suggests a strong indictment of all that race means in our land:

> Born in Alabama.
> Bred in Illinois.
> He was nothing but a
> Plain black boy.
>
> Swing low swing low sweet sweet chariot.
> Nothing but a plain black boy.[12]

Note the effective repetition of the phrase "plain black boy."

10. *Annie Allen*. New York: Harper, 1949, p. 49.
11. *The Bean Eaters*. New York: Harper, 1960, p. 38.
12. *A Street in Bronzeville*. New York: Harper, 1945, p. 21.

Although generally restrained and relatively objective in most of her earlier work, Miss Brooks speaks sharply on the theme of color prejudice within the Negro group, particularly as it applies to the dark-skinned woman. This theme occurs often in her works. There are two very strong poems on this subject in *A Street in Bronzeville:* "the ballad of chocolate Mabbie" and "Ballad of Pearl May Lee." The first deals with the heartache a black child encounters. The second, a very bitter poem, deals with a situation often found in earlier Negro protest poetry: the story of a black man who gets involved with a white woman and is lynched. In the earlier poems the Negro is usually an innocent victim of circumstances, but here the victim neglects his dark girl for the white because he has a fatal taste for "pink and white honey."

This theme of the difficulties that arise between a "sweet and chocolate girl" and a "man of tan" occurs in "The Anniad," and plays a crucial part in the lives of the two lovers. There is also an especially bitter poem in *The Bean Eaters* on the theme; entitled "Jessie Mitchell's Mother," it concerns the unnatural hatred between a dark-skinned daughter and her light-skinned mother. In fact, even though her last two publications abandoned many themes found in the first three, Miss Brooks did not abandon the black-and-tan theme. *In the Mecca* (page 23) has "The ballad of Edie Barrow" who "fell in love with a Gentile boy./ All creamy-and-golden fair"; and, of course, it ends with the usual heart-breaking result of such an affair for the "alien" girl.

We note that most of these pieces on color prejudice are written in the ballad form. We also note that in these ballads, whether on the color theme or in a poem like "The Ballad of Rudolph Reed" (based on the Chicago housing riots), the language is simple and strong, and the passion even stronger. Miss Brooks has told us that the ballad form should have the "beat inevitable," should have "blood," should have "a wildness cut up and tied in little bunches."[13] In some of these ballads we get the impression that Gwendolyn Brooks has somehow stepped into the picture and, forgetting her usual restraint, expressed intense personal feeling.

One of Miss Brooks's most unforgettable and most subtly conceived characters is the title figure in "The Sundays of Satin-Legs Smith."[14] A superb creation, with his wonder suits in "yellow and wine," all drapes, his scented lotion, his artificial flower, and his "hysterical ties," Satin-Legs could easily have become another Sporting Beasley (Sterling Brown's character), heroically and defiantly rising above the drab and sordid Bronzeville environment through sheer sartorial splendor. But Miss Brooks does not yield to that temptation. Satin-Legs, like Beasley, has

13. *The Bean Eaters.* New York: Harper, 1960, p. 19.
14. *A Street in Bronzeville.* New York: Harper, 1945, pp. 24–29.

the peacock syndrome, but unlike Beasley he is not heroic
actually dress his way out of the drabness of Bronzeville. For
is still a self-deceived figure of dry hours and emptiness—
both the sterility of ghetto living and of twentieth-ce
general.

With the publication of *In the Mecca* (1968), Gwendolyn Brooks
begins a new period in her literary career. Like many young and middle-
aged writers, she has come under the influence of the Black Aesthetics
Movement, a movement which began about 1960, and her commitment to blackness is very evident in her last two publications. We note
that the dedication for *In the Mecca* is "to the memory of Langston
Hughes; and to James Baldwin, LeRoi Jones, and Mike Alexandroff,
educators extraordinaire"; and the title poem itself is inscribed "In
Tribute—" to, among others, Don Lee. With Don Lee and LeRoi Jones
as "educators," she has had significant teachers for her new commitment.

The title poem of *In the Mecca* relates the search for Mrs. Sallie's
missing Pepita, and the finding of the child's body under the cot of
Jamaican Edward, one of the dwellers in the Mecca. But this pathetic
little story is secondary to the poet's major purpose: the looking into
the lives and thoughts of the several types who live in this decayed
slum apartment house. Through the search for Pepita, Miss Brooks
presents a number of fascinating characters, all of them somehow the
victims of the Mecca. She also brings to the reader some sense of the
vibrancy, the drama, and that peculiar tenseness which seems to stay
with black ghettos. This old Mecca, of course, is more than just a run-
down apartment house for Negroes; it is a microcosm of the ghettos of
all the Northern cities. Its blight, never stated but implied, is the blight
that comes from being black and poor.

In a series of subtle yet striking portraits, portraits done with a few
short but extremely deft and suggestive lines, Gwendolyn Brooks
catches and crystallizes the peculiarity, the misery, the ambition, the
desire, the frustrations, and all of the other dominant weaknesses
and strengths of her many subjects; for example, "Great-great Gram
hobbles, fumbles at the knob,/ mumbles. . . ." From her slave past
she remembers best the earthen floor of the family cabin and "Something creebled in that dirt" that the children could "pop" and "squish"
with their bare heels.

When she describes the teacher, Alfred, however, Miss Brooks could
have been thinking of herself:

> Ah, his God!—
> To create! To create! To bend with the tight intenseness

over the neat detail, come to
a terrified standstill of the heart, then shiver,
then rush—successfully—
at that rebuking thing, that obstinate and
recalcitrant little beast, the phrase![15]

Among the tenants in the Mecca, the poet places Don Lee and tells us that he wants:

> . . . not a various America.
> Don Lee wants
> a new nation
> under nothing; . . .
> wants
> new art and anthem; will
> want a new music screaming in the sun.

Presumably, Miss Brooks now wants the same thing.

Following the "wants" of Don Lee, she has another tenant, Amos, saying a prayer for America:

> "Bathe her in her beautiful blood.
> A long blood bath will wash her pure . . . .
> Slap the false sweetness from that face.
> Great-nailed boots
> Must kick her prostrate, heel-grind that soft breast,
> outrage her saucy pride . . .
> Let her lie there panting and wild, her pain
> red . . .
> with nothing to do but think, think
> of how she was so grand,
> flogging her dark one with her own hand,
> watching in meek amusement while he bled.
> Then shall she rise, recover.
> Never to forget."

Although the thoughts of a character must not be ascribed to its creator, these lines—and those which tell about "Way-out Morgan" who "listens to Blackness stern and blunt and beautiful," collects guns, and "predicts the Day of Debt-pay shall begin," the day of the avenging blood bath, do tell us how far along the revolutionary line the author has traveled. The contrast between these sentiments and those expressed in "The Chicago Defender Sends a Man to Little Rock" is startling.

15. *In the Mecca*. New York: Harper and Row, 1968, pp. 6–7.

Gwendolyn Brooks

Photo by Roy Lewis.

In the Mecca contains in addition to the title poem nine other pieces —among them one on "Medgar Evers," one on "Malcolm X," and one on "The Blackstone Rangers."

In her most recent published collection, *Riot* (1969), Gwendolyn Brooks continues her journey into blackness. The slim volume of 22 pages was published by the Broadside Press, which represents many young, black, revolutionary poets. The volume is a poem in three parts. According to the back cover of the work: "It arises from the disturbances in Chicago after the assassination of Martin Luther King in 1968."

The titular poem compresses into a page and a half the life and death story of John Cabot, a blue blood. In this short compass Gwendolyn Brooks presents with great skill what the black revolution means to an unprepared upper-class white America. The poem is Gwendolyn Brooks at her best. The second poem in *Riot*, "The Third Sermon on the Warpland (Phoenix)," is written in the poet's obscure style. It seems to give vignettes of the riot and to suggest through its phoenix symbol that good will come with the upheaval:

> The Black Philosopher will remember:
> "There they came to life and exulted,
> the hurt mute.
> Then it was over . . ."

A small volume of 23 pages, Gwendolyn Brooks's latest verse publication (at this writing), *Family Pictures,* was published by the Broadside Press in 1970. The initial poem, "The Life of Lincoln West," is a heart-tearing account of the cruelties encountered by an ugly little black boy. He finds some comfort, however, when a man refers to him as "the real thing"; that is, he was "Not like those diluted Negroes you see so much of on/ the streets these days. . . ." The poem seems to be a parable, and one can interpret it in several ways.

In another piece, "Young Africans," Miss Brooks shows once more her new black position. Concerning the young Africans, she says: "And they await, across the Changes and the spiraling dead,/ our black revival, our black vinegar,/ our hands, and our hot blood." The poem is a very strong affirmation of the revolutionary perspective. Advocating the "hard-heroic" and a "fine fury," Gwendolyn Brooks continues her trek into the heart of blackness.

Miss Brooks calls *Maud Martha* (1953) a novel, and it is certainly more of a novel in form than Toomer's *Cane.* The work, however, is a series of vignettes, penetrating vignettes, which delineate moments in the lives of dark-skinned Maud Martha and her light-skinned husband Paul. It also describes the lives of many other characters, all of them poor, who live in her "kitchenette building." The material is similar to that found in Miss Brooks's earlier poems and in her work *In the Mecca. Maud Martha* gives a low-keyed but subtle picture of the experiences and adjustments of an intelligent, sensitive, poor, black girl in a world where "white is right." Although it has few high spots, *Maud Martha* is one of Gwendolyn Brooks's most sensitive and understanding works. The reader leaves the little volume with a deeper-than-surface insight into the lives of poor black folk in the thirties and forties.

As has been said, *Maud Martha* is a series of vignettes or episodes, but they cling together tenaciously to form a unified picture of the joys and sorrows of this young married couple in a Northern ghetto, with their color differences just one of the crosses they have to bear. The problem of color prejudice within the race comes up often in the works of Gwendolyn Brooks.

Gwendolyn Brooks, like Robert Hayden, is a brilliant craftsman in verse; also like Hayden, she has changed her techniques and verse forms as she has matured. Though never slavishly conventional, in her early works, Miss Brooks employed most of the conventional verse forms, a few of them not often used today. For example, in *Annie Allen,* she has a series of skillful tercets ("Sunday chicken," "old relative," and "downtown vaudeville"); and in "The Anniad," she makes use of a variant of Chaucer's rime royal. In recent years, as stated above, Gwendolyn Brooks has abandoned her former integrationist position and moved steadily towards a black nationalist posture. With this ideological change, there has come a parallel shift in verse techniques. Influenced by the young black revolutionary writers of the 1960's, Miss Brooks has given up, not all, but many of the conventional forms used in her early publications. For one thing, like other modern poets, she employs rhyme very sparingly. Perhaps her most popular form now is the kind of flexible, unrhymed verse paragraph found in the volume *In the Mecca.* These verse paragraphs are naturally of varying lengths, and their moods and verse forms change with the subject matter involved. For example, when she writes about Don Lee, her lines reflect some of the techniques of Don Lee; and when she relates "the ballad of Edie Barrow," she uses rhyme and a ballad-type line.

Miss Brooks often writes short, highly chiseled, one-idea lines, some only one word in length; note for example these verses from "The Chicago Picasso":

> We squirm.
> We do not hug the Mona Lisa
> We
> may touch or tolerate . . . .

Note the alliteration in the last line. It is found also in other poems, including "The Second Sermon on the Warpland": "Salve salvage in the spin./ Endorse the splendor splashes; . . ." Perhaps the most effective element in her poetic technique is word-choice. With strong, suggestive, often-times unusual words—words that startle the reader—Gwendolyn Brooks weaves a brilliant poetic tapestry. Never sentimental, never a mouther of clichés, she brings to any subject the freshness and excitement which characterize good poetry—and good poets.

Ann Petry

Ann Lane Petry came to national attention with the publication of *The Street* (1946), a first novel which won the Houghton Mifflin Literary Award. In this work Miss Petry follows the tradition of hard-hitting social commentary which characterized the Richard Wright school of naturalistic protest writing. *The Street* is perhaps the best novel to come from the followers of Wright. Her last full-length adult novel, *The Narrows* (1953), depicts Negro life in a small New England city, a subject not often treated in black writing.

Ann Petry was born in Old Saybrook, Connecticut, a member of a family that for several generations have been pharmacists in that town. After receiving her degree from the College of Pharmacy, University of Connecticut, she continued for a while the family tradition. However, in 1938 she married and left for Harlem to start a new career as a journalist. Miss Petry worked for the *Amsterdam News* at first and later for *The People's Voice*. Her first published short story was printed in *The Crisis* in 1943. Moving from the journalistic field, Ann Petry joined the New York Foundation in 1944 to work on a sociological study of the effect of segregation on ghetto children. This experience naturally helped to prepare her for the writing of *The Street*. In 1946, the year this work appeared, Martha Foley printed Miss Petry's "Like a Winding Sheet" in the *Best American Short Stories of 1946* and dedicated the volume to Ann Petry. Since 1946, she has written two adult novels, *Country Place* (1947) and *The Narrows* (1953); two works for children, *The Drugstore Cat* (1949); and two for young adults, *Harriet Tubman: Conductor on the Underground Railroad* (1955) and *Tituba of Salem Village* (1963). In addition, she has published a number of short stories in *The Crisis, Opportunity, Cross Section,* and other periodicals and collections. In 1971 a collection of her short stories was reprinted under the title, *Miss Muriel and Other Stories*.

A depressing work, *The Street* follows the thesis implied by this type of naturalistic writing: namely, that the black poor in the ghetto do not have much of a chance to live decent and meaningful lives, to say nothing of happy lives. The main character in the work is Lutie Johnson, a hard-working, intelligent, and ambitious young Negro mother who has come to New York to seek a better chance for herself and for her son. Because they are poor and black, they become victims of 116th Street, a symbol for all that is bad in ghetto living. The rest of the novel spells out in bleak detail the specific forces that bring about their undoing.

Since her husband cannot find work, Lutie has to leave home to get a job in order to support their son. In her absence the husband turns to another woman. On 116th Street in Harlem, where Lutie finally secures an apartment within her means, she and her son become the victims of an assorted group of big-city vicious characters: the depraved janitor in the building, a "madam" who lives in one of the apartments, the lustful white landlord, and a musician (a so-called friend) whom she finally kills. As the novel ends, we find Lutie buying a one-way ticket to Chicago, leaving her son, who has been tricked by the janitor into robbing mail boxes, in the hands of the police.

In an article that appeared in *The Crisis* Miss Petry tells us her objectives in this work:

> . . . my aim is to show how simply and easily the environment can change the course of a person's life . . . .
> I try to show why the Negro has a high crime rate, a high death rate, and little or no chance of keeping his family unit intact in large northern cities. . . .[16]

There is a suggestion of inevitability in the above statement *and* in the novel itself. The trouble is that the environment alone does not "easily" change the course of a ghetto person's life. There are other factors involved. The main thrust of her position is valid: ghetto Negroes do have formidable odds against them, but the simple, realistic truth is that many, perhaps the majority, do survive, do rise above the 116th Streets of America.

The second novel, *Country Place* (1947), is set in a small New England town, the kind of place in which Miss Petry was born and reared. The work follows in the tradition of small-town realistic fiction that goes back to *Main Street* (perhaps to George Crabbe in the eighteenth century). In this novel Ann Petry wrote about a life that in all probability she knew better than the life she wrote about in *The*

16. James W. Ivy, "Ann Petry Talks About First Novel." *The Crisis* (February, 1946), pp. 48–49.

Street. The action is narrated by the town druggist. Miss Petry's family, as noted earlier, have been druggists in Old Saybrook for several generations. In short, Ann Petry knew at first hand the background on which she placed her second novel and the characters that appeared in it.

Country Place deals with the class lines between aristocrats and nobodies, the antiforeign, anti-Roman Catholic prejudices, and the sexual looseness and the ugliness and viciousness found behind the innocent-appearing life in a small town like "Lennox, Connecticut." One of the main characters is Mrs. Gramby, a domineering Yankee aristocrat who eventually overcomes some of her inherited prejudices. The two central characters are Johnnie Roane and Gloria, his wife. A returned veteran, Johnnie finds out that his wife has become the mistress of the town "stud." At the end of the work the good are rewarded and the bad are punished or killed off. Johnnie, aided by Mrs. Gramby, is able to free himself from his straying wife and go to New York to study art, an ambition he had long held. The best drawn character in the work is Weasel, who knew all of the town's skeletons and took joy in telling them. *Country Place* is an entertaining work. It is difficult to say more.

In *The Narrows* (1953) Miss Petry has depicted Negro life in a small New England city. As has been suggested above, this is virtually an untried field for the black writer. Miss Petry seems to be saying in many different ways that these ghettos in small New England cities are far more isolated and cut off from the mainstreams of American life and are far more sterile than the black districts of border and Southern communities. The blacks in these Northern cities are rootless. Having severed, for the most part, their connections with the Southland from which many come, they live on the periphery of these Northern towns and cities, far more cut off than even the most recent European immigrants. Miss Petry naturally does not *say* these things in so many words. She does not have to. Her depiction of life in fictional Monmouth, Connecticut, gives us the message.

In *The Narrows* the author incorporates many of the racial myths well known to Northern-born Negroes and to those who have gone North for an education, especially a New England education. Among them are the examples of the anti-Negro high school teacher who subtly discourages and ridicules young blacks; the different versions of the question often asked by deans and presidents: "Wouldn't you be happier in a Negro school?"; and always the sting of being called *nigger* by immigrants who haven't even learned to speak English.

The major plot of *The Narrows* deals with a theme that was to become fairly popular among Negro writers in the 1960's: that of the relationship between the black man and the white mistress/ wife. Through the soul-searching of her principal character, Ann Petry analyzes this relationship in considerable depth. In this novel Link Williams, a handsome, talented black boy meets quite by accident a patrician white girl, the daughter of the town's richest family and the wife of a socialite. The two fall hopelessly and helplessly in love. Link at first does not know that Camilo is married or that she belongs to the famous Treadway family of Monmouth. When he does find out and does halfheartedly try to break off the affair, it is far too late. Link in the end pays for his innocence and indiscretion in what amounts to an Ivy League type of lynching.

The reader gets the impression that Link, though admirable in many respects, is basically a weak, vacillating character. Miss Petry accounts for this, it seems to us, in two ways. Link was an orphan reared by two very different persons: by puritannical Miss Abbie, who had adopted him, but who in her grief over the loss of her husband temporarily forgot the eight-year-old boy, and by Bill Hod, the worldly town racketeer. The divided loyalties which Link held in all probability helped shape his character. But there was another influence, the author implies. Here is a strikingly handsome star athlete and Phi Beta Kappa graduate of Dartmouth College who returns home and takes a job as bartender in Bill Hod's place. This is all that a New England ghetto has to offer to a trained black youth.

Though it certainly holds the reader's interest, *The Narrows* has serious weaknesses as a novel. First, the author leans too heavily on flashbacks to tell her story. There are too many of them, and after the first few they begin to irritate. Second, Miss Petry puts a heavy strain on our "suspension of disbelief" when she asks us to believe that it would take an intelligent boy like Link Williams two or three months to find out who his girl friend actually was. And third, Ann Petry tries too often to create suspense by having her characters in moments of crisis think back, sometimes for as long as three pages, over past incidents in their lives. Although it may have its aesthetic value, this kind of interior monologue as used by Ann Petry somehow fails to impress.

The Narrows is an exciting work, and it does give us a fresh background, which is sorely needed in Afro-American fiction, but it is not a strong novel. Strangely enough, Miss Petry's delineation of white small-town New England life in *Country Place* is more convincing than her depiction of black life in *The Narrows*. *The Street* is Ann Petry's most impressive novel.

With *The Drugstore Cat* (1949) Ann Petry left adult writing and turned to writing for children and young adults. This first work is for six-to-ten-year-olds. The second work, *Harriet Tubman* (1955), and the third, *Tituba of Salem Village* (1963), are for young adults. On

Ann Petry

Photo by Carl Van Vechten, Collection of American Literature, Beinecke Rare
Book and Manuscript Library, Yale University.

the dust jacket of *Harriet Tubman* Mrs. Petry gives her reason for writing on the famous Underground Railroad worker:

> It is my belief that the majority of textbooks used in high schools do not give an adequate or accurate picture of the history of slavery in the United States. . . . It is to answer this need that *Harriet Tubman* . . . was written.

There is nothing unusual about her approach in either type. Both of the young adult works, however, do give sympathetic and idealized portrayals of two historic black women, and both give a lot of entertaining and informative background material, excellent material to fill in "gaps" which white American history tends to leave.

The short stories of Ann Petry show a great sensitivity. They tend to deal with those subtle aspects of racial hurt which are not always understood by nonblacks. For example, in "Like a Winding Sheet" she shows a Negro, confronted downtown by what he thinks is prejudice, coming home and beating his wife when she playfully calls him "nigger." "In Darkness and Confusion" depicts the action of two respectable, hardworking Harlemites who, thinking about the injustice meted out to their son in an army camp in Georgia, express their anger and frustrations in the Harlem Riot of 1943. Miss Petry's voice is low when she speaks of the tragedy of ghetto living in these stories—the broken homes, the deserted children, the faithless wives, the young girls going on the street—and it is more effective than shouting. These stories show a genuine concern for the unfortunate victims of American racism, and the sincerity of her feelings comes through in the stories. They also show an artist's concern for structure and effect.

Ann Petry's best story, however, differs slightly from the type described above. Entitled "The Bones of Louella Jones," it uses a rich blend of humor, satire, and superstition to poke fun at several things— the way the news is manipulated by journals, at racial science (the physician who was an authority on white and black physical differences), and at racial segregation. The story concerns the dilemma a certain town gets into when it wants to separate the bones (white) of Elizabeth Countess of Castro and the bones (black) of Louella Jones, her servant, after both have been long buried in the same cemetery. After the ghost of Louella has exerted a little pressure, an "either-or" slab has to be placed over the graves in Bedford Abbey.

The word *competent* best describes Ann Petry as a writer. She does several things well, but none superlatively. Her short stories will probably stand up best after the critical years have passed judgment.

198 / PART TWO

Julian Mayfield

In his first two works Julian Mayfield joins the ranks of those novelists and poets who have tried to depict Harlem, that fascinating black metropolis. Harlem was a popular theme during the twenties, and the writers of the sixties and seventies have taken up the theme with a renewed and savage vigor. Let us examine briefly the history of this concern with Harlem.

The tradition actually started with Paul Laurence Dunbar. In his *Sport of the Gods,* written in 1902, Dunbar saw the New York black ghetto (it had not yet moved uptown) as an evil and corrupting influence on the lives of Negro migrants from the South, and he spoke out strongly against this Northern Babylon. But for Langston Hughes, in his first publication, *The Weary Blues* (1926), Harlem was predominantly "Jazzonia," a night-life city where "shameless gals" strutted and wiggled under the garish lights of swinging cabarets. For Rudolph Fisher, Harlem was a "City of Refuge" for the migrant from the South. It was also the scene in which fun-loving, strutting, and signifying Negroes from all over the world met to create a fascinating kaleidoscope of movement and color. For Claude McKay, Harlem was a community of sweetmen, pimps, hedonistic gin-head Susies, and not-so-noble primitives for whom life was a series of parties and more parties. For none of these New Negro writers was Harlem *at first* a tragic city.

The first signs of a changed attitude toward the "Dark Metropolis" began to appear in the writings after the 1935 Riot. Ann Petry in *The Street* (1946) gave a depressing, naturalistic picture of the black center, and, of course, *Invisible Man* (1952) treats Harlem on several no-longer-joyous levels. Perhaps the fullest and most comprehensive delineation of the troubled black city is found in Langston Hughes's *Montage of a Dream Deferred* (1951). In 1957 and 1958, respectively, Julian Mayfield took up the Harlem theme. His treatment of the black city lies somewhere between the starkness of Petry's work and the good-natured climate of Fisher's delineation.

Julian Mayfield was born in Greer, South Carolina, in 1928, but was reared in Washington, D.C., his parents having moved there when he was five years old. Mayfield attended the famous Dunbar High School in the capital, and after graduation joined the peacetime army and served in the Pacific. After his stint in the service he attended Lincoln University in Pennsylvania.

Mayfield has worked at many jobs and professions. He has been "dishwasher, hack driver, shipping clerk, house painter, radio announcer, and newspaperman." He has been connected with the theatre as actor, playwright, and director. He created the role of Absalom in *Lost in the Stars;* his "417" was produced off-Broadway; and he has directed Little Theatre groups in Harlem and in off-Broadway theatres. As a newspaper man, he wrote for the Puerto Rico *World Journal.*

Mayfield was in Ghana when Nkrumah was in power, and during his stay he edited the *African Review,* which was published in Accra. In collaboration with Leslie Lacy, he published *Living Ghana* in 1966. Julian Mayfield's articles and essays have appeared in the *Nation, Commentary, Negro Digest* (now *Black World*), and other periodicals. In addition to articles, essays, and plays (see bibliography), Mayfield has published to date the following novels: *The Hit* (1957), *The Long Night* (1958), and *The Grand Parade* (1961). At this writing, Mayfield is working for the Guyana government, editing a newspaper and working in the information arm of that country's administration.

Mayfield's first novel, *The Hit,* deals primarily with the drab lives of the Cooley family—Hubert the father; Gertrude the mother, and James Lee, their twenty-six-year-old son. It spells out the frustrations that the ghetto has brought to this family of essentially decent people, and it shows the importance of the numbers to a people with little else to look forward to. They are not just poor; that is not the all-important thing. They have lost hope; they lack incentive. They do not see any way out; they are trapped. Only Hubert feels that there is an out, and he, too, is duped. As the lives of these little people unfold, we sense their helplessness, not all of it racial.

The plot of *The Hit* is simple, linear. It narrates the efforts of fifty-year-old Hubert Cooley to get out of the rut in which he finds himself. A janitor in a Harlem apartment house, Hubert feels he deserves better, that he deserves another chance. He is not a worthless no-good "nigger"; he despises that type. He feels that he is "worthy." Had he not owned at various times two grocery stores, a dry-cleaning shop, and a poolroom? Though Hubert is really a born loser, and is a failure as a husband, father, and human being, he has a deep faith that the God who has dealt him so many low blows owes him a break. And he knows that that break will come through a good hit. He *knows* that he will have a good hit, he will get away; therefore he plays $5 or $6 every day he can raise the money. "His life was about to change. It was all in the hands of God." It had to change, Hubert reasoned, if life had any meaning and if God was just, which He was. On the day of the hit Hubert steals $7 from the house expenses and puts it on 417. One notes here that in the ghetto the American faith in the inevitable success which comes from hard work and decency has changed to faith in a special Providence distributed through the numbers. The change is understandable, given the handicaps of the ghetto.

Hubert does hit his number, but he is still a loser. The numbers man does not pay off, and Hubert is left a broken old man at fifty.

Into this simple story the author weaves several themes usually found in this kind of writing, one of them the long-suffering wife who is really the bulwark of the family. To Hubert, Gertrude is a drab, nagging wife with none of the appeal of Sister Clarisse whom he has his eye on. Gertrude knows that "a black woman shall see hard times." She is reconciled to this, but all she asks is a little understanding. The son, James Lee, now twenty-six-years old, sees himself on the verge of repeating his parents' failure. He wants to hold on to his girl friend, yet is afraid of marriage because he has seen what it can do. And, as a consequence, we have a trinity of frustration and near-hopelessness represented in the Cooley family—the three of them largely, but not wholly, victims of the ghetto.

The Long Night (1958), another Harlem novel, treats the ghetto from the viewpoint of a ten-year-old. Although Steely is a stronger-than-usual youngster, Mayfield shows through him the blighting influence of the ghetto on the young. Steely comes from a home that is temporarily fatherless. Before the father, Paul, a law school drop-out, left home, he tried to instill into his son some values. He tried to teach Steely pride of race, and he told the boy about historical black heroes. He emphasized the need to stand up under pressure. But these idealistic efforts, the author implies, are not efficacious in the face of the hard facts of ghetto living.

The plot of *The Long Night* is just as simple as that of the first novel. Steely's mother, Mae Brown, who has been deserted by her frustrated and defeated husband, hits the numbers for $27. She sends Steely to collect the money, telling him, half seriously, not to return unless he can bring back the much-needed money. Steely collects the hit, but is hijacked by some of the older boys of his own Harlem gang. Deciding that he has to raise the money somehow, he sets out on what turns out to be a long and revealing night.

After losing the money to the gang boys, Steely tries first to borrow it from Mr. Lichstein, for whom he often did odd jobs, but Lichstein runs him away. He turns next to another "friend," Sugar Boy, who is lounging in his fine "pad." Sugar Boy gives Steely a dollar and also shoves him away. Finding that friends do not work, Steely takes the next best

Julian Mayfield

Photo by Carl Van Vechten, Collection of American Literature, Beinecke Rare Book and Manuscript Library, Yale University.

way: purse-snatching. Unfortunately, the purse he snatches has only $2 in it. He then steals a bicycle which in turn is stolen from him. He is approached by a "queer," but he has sense enough to know that the queer will not pay $27, or anything approaching that amount. As dawn approaches, he decides to roll a drunk whom he sees in a doorway. The drunk turns out to be his father, Paul Brown. After the initial disgust at finding his father in this condition (he had looked up to him in absentia), his joy at finding his parent overcomes all other feelings. Father and son talk, and as the dawn approaches, they turn their steps homeward and seem to face the day and the days to come with at least a modicum of hope.

The implied happy ending to *The Long Night* has worried some critics of the novel. It should not. The ghetto is a man-destroyer, but it does not work with mathematical certainty. Naturalistic fiction becomes unrealistic when it tries to work too precisely. The fact is that many youngsters reared like Steely do escape the ghetto. With a reclaimed father, that all-important figure in a boy's life, Steely has at least some chance to escape the ghetto.

In *The Hit*, Mayfield, unlike McKay, at least gives a glimpse of the middle-class Harlem. Moreover, he avoids the trap into which too many recent black writers have fallen: making all middle-class Negroes either Uncle Toms or snobbish, or worse. Mayfield also does not belabor the most vicious types of Harlem characters: the dope pushers, pimps, and their kind. Harlem, he suggests, is a bad place for the poor black boy to grow up in, but it is by no means totally hopeless. The plight of the black woman is given realistic treatment in *The Hit*. It was written before the period in which the dark-skinned woman came into her own and became a sort of minor deity. Gertrude is a flesh-and-blood character, strong yet pitiable. There is no Black Power politics, no militancy, no black nationalism, no I-hate-honky fanaticism. The Harlem of 1957 had not yet become the torn and savage city of the sixties and seventies. Mayfield even paints Jewish merchants as human and likable! And the cops have not become "pigs," not even the white ones!

In *The Long Night* the ghetto trap that closed in on Hubert, Gertrude, and James Lee Cooley threatens Steely Brown, a ten-year-old Harlemite. One notes that even in one year (that is, between 1957 and 1958), the climate of Harlem has changed for the worse. The Harlem of *The Hit* is a mild mixture of the ugly and not-so-ugly. But now there are gangs. The frustrated black woman is more likely to take it out on the kids than in the first novel, and she is definitely anti-Negro, whereas the man Paul Brown, another loser, is still an idealist. As a matter of fact, Paul Brown voices an attitude that is now very popular with black writers: Negroes must supply to young blacks a positive image to offset the lack of such images in the public schools. He also sets forth the belief, again now very popular among Black Arts writers, that the American dream is all washed up: "All I ever wanted to do," Paul states, "was to become a full-fledged American, but now I am not so sure."

Mayfield has given us some good scenes of Harlem life: Saturday night on 125th Street; the hustle and bustle of Lenox Avenue; the street smells of the Spanish district; the old folks in the windows, "exiles" in a world that has no time for them. Incidentally, there are more scenes of Harlem's decay in the second novel than in the first, but there is still not the bitterness which characterizes post-sixties ghetto writing. These two works, though transitional, belong in large measure to the positive tradition of protest writing of an earlier day.

One finds in *The Hit* and *The Long Night* a certain poetic quality not felt in Mayfield's third novel, *The Grand Parade*. In the first two novels, using a smaller canvas, restricting himself in each case to a single family unit and avoiding largely the white world, Mayfield was able to give a picture of the ghetto that is poetically convincing, that is authoritative. It seems to us that he lost some of this authority when he abandoned the simple vignette of black city life for the ambitious type of delineation found in *The Grand Parade*.

Written in 1961, the novel's viewpoint wavers between integration and that deep drop into black nationalism which came during the sixties. In spite of the author's attitude toward the mainstream (see below), *The Grand Parade* tries very hard to be a successful mainstream effort. Yet it has a few flashes, in Patty Speed and other low-life characters, of the revolutionary attitudes which would come in the decade. Mayfield attempts to give an *integrated* picture of an American city, developing his plot around two major characters, one black, the other white. Whatever else he tried to do, he certainly attempted to show the oneness of American life, the interaction of black and white in the crooked politics of an American community. Whether he succeeded or not is another matter.

Placed in mythical Gainesboro, an Eastern American city bordering the North and South, *The Grand Parade* deals with the ambition and corruption of politicians, the vice and crookedness of city politics, racial antagonism, and the all-important issue of segregation in the public schools. The work is not impressive because we have heard its message too many times before—in other novels, in the movies, and on the TV screen. The plot and characters are almost stereotypes. We find here an aristocratic and idealistic young white reform mayor, Douglas Taylor, who has to repudiate his old but corrupt friend. Mayor Taylor loses his life in an integration confrontation. Leading black children into a public school in the face of a mob, Mayor Taylor is shot by a white supremacist. We also find an ambitious young Negro politician, Randolph Banks, who is clever but not eaten up with principle, and his brother Lonnie, a dedicated Communist who is dropped from the party when he criticizes the party's stand on domestic issues. We have Patty Speed, a sinister and beautiful Negro girl who comes from the wrong side of the tracks, and who ruthlessly wields power as a gang leader. We have, finally, the alleged rape of a white prostitute by blacks, and the poor white racist who rises to power on race hatred. All of these characters and situations are not only dated *now,* but were partially dated when they were presented in 1961. *The Grand Parade,* as has been implied above, simply lacks the depth necessary to make it either a good or impressive novel.

Julian Mayfield has written several critical articles which repay reading. At the First Conference of Negro Writers in March of 1959, he gave a paper (reprinted in *The American Negro Writer and His Roots,* 1960) entitled "Into the Mainstream and Oblivion." In it he urged the Negro writer not to seek the mainstream, because the American mainstream was no longer a viable force; it lacked concern "for the great questions facing the peoples of the world." He felt that "The Negro writer may conclude that his best salvation lies in escaping the narrow national orbit—artistic, cultural, and political—and soaring into the space of more universal experience."

Lorraine Hansberry

The author of two Broadway plays, one of them the winner of the 1958–1959 New York Drama Critics Award, the other a *cause célèbre* in New York theatre history, Lorraine Hansberry had become something of a legend before her death at the early age of thirty-four. In her intensity, in her compassion, and in her ardent defense of and concern with the lowly and oppressed, she embodied and articulated in her works the best spirit of the young of her time. The late Martin Luther King, Jr., said of her: "Her commitment of spirit . . . her creative literary ability and her profound grasp of the deep social issues confronting the world today will remain an inspiration to generations yet unborn."

Born in Chicago in 1930, Lorraine Hansberry was the daughter of successful and highly respected middle-class parents. After graduating from Englewood High School, where she became interested in drama, she studied for two years at the University of Wisconsin. Miss Hansberry subsequently studied painting at the Art Institute of Chicago, Roosevelt College, and in Guadalajara, Mexico. Finding that her interests and talent were not in art, she went to New York in 1950 and began what was to be her life work, her career as a writer.

Before her writing began to pay off, Miss Hansberry worked at various jobs. Among other things, she was a clerk in a department store, aide to a young theatrical producer, waitress, hostess, and cashier in a restaurant run by the family of Robert Nemiroff, song writer and music publisher. She married Nemiroff in 1953. Lorraine Hansberry died of cancer in 1965.

Miss Hansberry's first play, *Raisin in the Sun,* after successful tryouts in Philadelphia, New Haven, and Chicago, opened on Broadway March 11, 1959, and proceeded to win the 1958–1959 New York Drama Critics Award. Significantly, it won over entries by Tennessee Williams, Eugene O'Neill, and Archibald MacLeish. Claudia MacNeill, Diana Sands, and Sidney Poitier (in his first Broadway starring role) played the principal parts in this popular play.

A Raisin in the Sun (the title taken from a Hughes poem), like Ossie Davis's successful play, *Purlie Victorious,* has, among its other virtues, that of humor. We point this out because in recent years this quality has not been found too often in Negro drama. Since 1960, most Negroes writing about the ghetto have forgotten how to laugh. In her doubled-edged attack on blacks and whites alike in *Raisin in the Sun,* Miss Hansberry joins Dunbar, Schuyler, Hughes, Fisher, Sterling Brown, and other Negro writers who dipped into that unique and richly supplied reservoir of race humor which the black author has at his disposal.

A Raisin in the Sun, however, is not just a humorous play. It is far more than that. In this heart-warming drama of urban Negro life in the North, Miss Hansberry has made use—often brilliant use—of several basic themes which if handled with any degree of skill are guaranteed "good theatre." The first of these is black motherhood. Mama in this play is not only a strong and appealing character; she also symbolizes the courage, the unselfishness, the resourcefulness, and the endurance which black mothers had to possess if their families were to survive. Black literature since about 1960 has glorified the black woman in poetry and fiction as well as in drama, but none of the more recent portraits, it seems to us, has been as effective as Hansberry's Mama.

Another appealing and foolproof theme used by the dramatist is that of the generation gap. Mama—with her old-fashioned common sense and in her tried ways of tolerantly listening to the young folk, correcting them when they were wrong, praising and encouraging them when right —dramatizes this relationship between the generations. One of the high points in the play—actually, one of the most effective scenes in Negro drama—is found in Act I, Scene i, when Mama slaps Beneatha for denying the existence of God. This is a powerful scene. The appeal of the generation gap is enhanced by the religious conflict involved.

Another basic theme in *A Raisin in the Sun* is typically American: the mobility pattern, the upward move of family, spiritually in the better education of the children and physically in the change to a better neighborhood. In this case the basic appeal is strengthened by the race issue. In these days when everybody is *supposedly* guaranteed freedom to live where he pleases, one would think that this housing problem is too dated to be dramatically valid. Actually, it is not. The question involved goes beyond mere housing. It is still the fight of the ambitious poor— whether black or white—to make a better world for the next generation, and that conflict is always with us.

In addition to the "basic" appeals, *A Raisin in the Sun* intrigues the reader and theatregoer because though written in 1958, just before the so-called New Black Renaissance, it looks forward to that movement. The identity theme is here, represented in Beneatha's searching for meaning as a young black girl. The African theme, one that is now so popular, is presented here through the portrait of Asagai the Nigerian student. The dignity theme, the kind of dignity that old, proud black families have, is here. This is a kind of old-fashioned race pride which is without excessive militancy, without high-sounding rhetoric. When Walter, after learning his lesson the hard way, finds himself, he falls back on the family tradition. He tells Mr. Lindner, who had come to buy him off: "What I am telling you is that we called you over here to tell you that we are very proud and that this is—this is my son, who makes the sixth generation of our family in this country, and that we have all thought about your offer and we have decided to move into our house because my father—my father—he earned it."

This fusing of the old, solid elements in Negro life with the promise of the new is beautifully and effectively done by Lorraine Hansberry. The spirit of *A Raisin in the Sun* is integrationist and quite unlike that of black nationalist drama of the sixties (that is, most of it); but the work still appeals, it is still "good theatre."

Speaking of black nationalism, Lorraine Hansberry had, as all who knew her attest, a deep and militant interest in her people, but she never wanted to think of Negroes as being apart from the mainstream. A well-meaning critic once told her that *A Raisin in the Sun* was not "really a Negro play; why this could be about anybody! It's a play about people!" Miss Hansberry's answer was: "Well, I hadn't noticed the contradiction because I'd always been under the impression that Negroes *are* people."

Lorraine Hansberry felt that the artist should write specifically about his subject, as specifically as he can. If he does it well, he will create universal literature. As for *Raisin in the Sun,* Miss Hansberry says, in effect, yes, "it is definitely a Negro play before it is anything else," but it is also more than just that.

Lorraine Hansberry's second play, *The Sign in Sidney Brustein's Window,* made theatre history in a unique way. It opened in New York to mixed reviews; it therefore seemed doomed to immediate closing. But the play lasted 101 nights, kept alive by the efforts and the contributions of a large number of New York's most distinguished people of the literary and theatrical world. During the run of the play Miss Hansberry was in the last stages of terminal cancer. On the night she died, January 12, 1965, the theatre was darkened out of respect to Lorraine Hansberry, and *The Sign in Sidney Brustein's Window* "went into the record books." But the unselfish and vigorous activities which kept alive the play attest to the high regard in which these distinguished Americans held Lorraine Hansberry. She was a remarkable young woman. In some intangible way she represented the positive side of the chaotic times in which we live. Although she knew modern living as few know it, she never lost her belief in the possibilities of the human spirit. *The Sign in Sidney Brustein's Window* is an affirmation of this belief.

Through the actions and statements of well-chosen key modern characters, *The Sign in Sidney Brustein's Window* presents the frustrations, the dilemmas, the boredom, the loss of basic faiths, and other hang-ups that make of modern living an exercise in futility and absurdness. The characters representing these differing hang-ups are Brustein, a thinker, a man of ideas, a man of compassion, but one who until the play's end relies too much on the intellect; his wife Iris, who feels frustrated and inferior because of her job and her husband's idealism and intellectual superiority; Iris's sister Mavis, who is on the surface typically middle class; another sister, Gloria, who is a prostitute; Alton Scales, a Negro who is a victim of *his* prejudices; O'Hara, an opportunistic politician; and David, a homosexual. *The Sign in Sidney Brustein's Window* is a play of ideas; most of the action is talk—comic often, often brilliant. The absurdity, the nothingness of modern life, is paraded, but the playwright never loses her belief in the worth of the human spirit. The work is a strong affirmation, a strong protest against capitulation and acceptance. Miss Hansberry's message (to use an old-fashioned term) may be in Brustein's speech which comes almost at the end of the play.

Lorraine Hansberry

Wally the crooked politician calls Brustein "a fool." Yes, the latter admits:

> Always have been. . . . A fool who believes that death is waste and love is sweet and that the earth turns and men change every day . . . and that people wanna be better than they are . . . and that I hurt terribly today, and that hurt is desperation and desperation is—energy and energy can *move* things . . .

The first reading of *The Sign in Sidney Brustein's Window* gives one the impression that the play is a flippant, ultrasophisticated comment on the chaos of modern life. A second or perhaps a third reading changes that impression entirely.

Lorraine Hansberry's third publication was posthumous. Called *To Be Young, Gifted and Black* (1969), it is an adaptation of parts of plays (some unpublished before), letters, speeches, interviews, and comments of Miss Hansberry made by Robert Nemiroff. This work, the editor tells us, "is the portrait of an individual, the workbook of an artist, and a chronicle of a rebel who celebrated the human spirit." Through copious detail and always in her own words, this posthumous autobiographical statement presents the picture of a charming, witty, and dynamic young black woman who was concerned about those who suffered and were "heavy laden." Too tolerant to be a black nationalist, Lorraine Hansberry was keenly aware of the American Negro's special hell, and she brought to that issue a caustic and penetrating insight.[17]

Ralph Ellison

The names of Ralph Ellison and Richard Wright are often joined for critical comparison. Generally recognized as the two best novelists yet produced by American Negroes, both men have become a part of the literary mainstream and have done so by making use of the myths and critical techniques of the Western world. And yet both owe much to

17. In 1972 Random House published Miss Hansberry's last three dramas, *Les Blancs, The Drinking Gourd,* and *What Use Are Flowers?* under the title: *Les Blancs: The Collected Last Plays of Lorraine Hansberry.* The volume was "edited with critical backgrounds" by Robert Nemiroff, Miss Hansberry's literary executor. For an analysis of these works, see "Lorraine Hansberry's Last Dramas," by W. Edward Farrison. *CLA Journal* (December, 1972).

another tradition—that of the folk Negro. Both also owe a great deal to the dual background that every Negro has. Each had to be two things: Negro *and* American. But the two backgrounds differ greatly. Wright, the product of the Depression, of the Deep South, of a lower-class family, and of a broken home, never forgot the misery that was his lot. Every work he wrote related in one way or another to this agonizing experience. On the other hand, Ralph Ellison came from a lower-middle-class background, not in Mississippi but in Oklahoma. Wright felt deeply the hurt of Negro living; Ellison felt and accepted the challenge of a dual background. Ellison could step outside his Negro experience and view it objectively. The differences between the two men attest to the wide range of life for Negroes in America. It is not as Richard Wright and many young black writers would have us believe—uniformly bleak.

Present-day black authors look at Ellison with mixed feelings.[18] Those who are Marxists have not forgiven him for his picture of the Brotherhood in *Invisible Man*. Those who are black nationalists object to Ellison's insistence that he is a part of the Western humanistic tradition as well as of the Negro American tradition, and that he represents both in his writings. Both groups, however, recognize *Invisible Man* as a significant American novel. It is also the finest product of the integration movement in Negro writing—a movement that began really with the first Negro novel.

Born in Oklahoma City, Oklahoma, in 1914, the son of hard-working and highly informed lower-middle-class parents, Ralph Ellison cultivated during his early years an interest in jazz, in reading, and in the local folk literature. Winning a scholarship to Tuskegee, he studied music there for three years, with the intention of ultimately becoming a composer of symphonies.

Ellison left the South in 1936 for New York City, where he met Richard Wright. After 1937 Ellison wrote and published with some regularity articles and short stories for *New Masses, The Negro Quarterly,* and other periodicals. Although he was interested in the politics of the left, he never became a Communist.

Ralph Ellison, to date, has published two major works: *Invisible Man* (1952) and *Shadow and Act* (1964), the latter a volume of critical essays, interviews, and reviews.

Ellison has received an impressive number of honors, fellowships, and awards. For *Invisible Man* he was given the National Book Award, the Russwurm Award, and the National Newspaper Publishers' Award. In 1965 the *New York Herald Tribune* book review poll named the

18. See the Ellison issue of *Black World* (December, 1970).

work the most distinguished novel written between 1945 and 1965. In addition, Ellison has received a Rosenwald Fellowship and from 1955 to 1957 was a Fellow at the American Academy in Rome. In 1964 he was elected to the American Institute of Arts and Letters.

Ellison has taught, lectured, and served as author-in-residence at Bard College, Stony Brook, Columbia, Bennington, Fisk, Antioch, Chicago, Barnard, Rutgers, and Yale. He has delivered the Gertrude Clark Whittall Lecture at the Library of Congress and the Ewing Lectures at the University of California.

A brilliant critic of literature and jazz, Ralph Ellison in recent years has written for *Partisan Review, The Nation, Harper's,* and many other top-rank periodicals.

Among Ellison's earliest publications was a short story which came out in 1944 called "Flying Home." In this short fiction we have an introduction to the techniques Ellison was later to use superbly in his novel. A narrative concerning an incident in the Air Force school for Negro pilots in the Deep South, the work makes use of realistic details, a flashback technique, the Greek myth of Icarus, a Negro folk story, and miscellaneous symbols of the modern world. Ellison makes the whole story an extended metaphor of the Negro's place in American society.

The simple story concerns Todd, a Negro pilot trainee in Alabama who flies upward too precipitously, strikes a buzzard (Jim Crow), and crashes on the property of a white landowner. When Todd regains consciousness, the first persons he sees are Jefferson, an old Negro sharecropper, and a boy, whom Jefferson sends for a physician. In the interim the old man needles the pilot. Why you want to fly, Boy, he asks, in effect, you *could* get shot for a buzzard. Note the emphasis on *buzzard,* a bird symbolizing the past because it eats dead things. Note also the old stay-in-your-place attitude held not only by whites but by Negroes as well. In his way Jefferson is a buzzard, resenting this fancy new-type Negro.

Jefferson then tells Todd a folk story known to most Negroes: the story of his going to Heaven where he was given six-foot angels' wings. Jefferson, however, flew too fast and dangerously and was thrown out of Heaven. The implications of the story are obvious, and the old man's taunting laughter drives Todd into a screaming rage: "Can I help it because they won't actually let us fly? Maybe we are a bunch of buzzards feeding on a dead horse, but we can hope to be eagles, can't we?"

At the end of the story the white landowner brings in orderlies from a mental institution. "You all know you cain't let the Nigguh get up that high without going crazy. The Nigguh brain ain't built right for high altitudes."

Here is a brilliant mélange of realism, folk story, and symbolism, with a touch of surrealism at the end—the kind of fusion found on a grand scale in *Invisible Man*. In "Flying Home" the artist is in firm control of his material. This reaching for artistic perfection is found in everything that Ellison has done.

In *Invisible Man* Ellison, like the composer of a good symphony, adroitly blends together several motifs, several levels of meaning, and several language styles (each appropriate to the subject matter) to present a complex but unified work—a work that moves from realism to surrealism, a work that makes use of myths, dreams, symbolism, and other techniques of the Western literary tradition coupled with Negro folk material. Attacking the ills of capitalism and of Communism en route, Ellison in this episodic and highly comical prose epic manages to work in, among other things, all of the so-called ways out for the Negro: accommodation, fooling "Cap'n Charlie," militancy, Communism, and black nationalism. His unifying theme is the search for identity on the part of an unnamed black protagonist.

There are naturally many interpretations of *Invisible Man*, almost as many as there are critics who have considered the work. Moreover, Ellison designed the novel with multiple readings in mind. Certain obvious themes do run through the book and are noted by most critics. One of these is the journey from darkness (spiritual) into light. Associated with the theme are the many images and incidents concerned with blindness, among them the blindfold used in the battle royal, the blind speaker (*Homer* Barbee) at Bledsoe's College exercises praising the Founder, the play of light on Bledsoe's glasses after he has told the hero to get power through influential people and "then stay in the dark and use it." Incidentally, the glare from Bledsoe's glasses left the hero's eyes out of focus. Other blind-light images and incidents include: the veteran's amusement, as he and the Protagonist traveled North, over the fact that slaves ran away "not in the light of morning but in the dark of night"; Jack's glass eye; the interview with Emerson's son, who tells the Protagonist that "ambition can be blinding" and that he should not "blind himself" to the truth; when the Protagonist addresses the crowd at the eviction, he tells them that the old folk had a dream book called "The Seeing Eye," but its pages went blank; his first speech to the Brotherhood is on blindness, the blindness of Negroes who have lost the sight of one eye; the dark glasses of Rhinehart; and the final ending in the hole with 1369 lights. At the end he is still invisible, but he is no longer blind.

Another important theme which runs through the work concerns the

19. See Eugenia Collier, "The Nightmare Truth of an Invisible Man." *Black World* (December, 1970), 12–19. See also Darwin Turner, "Sight in *Invisible Man,*" *CLA Journal*, XIII, No. 3 (1970), 258–64.

dreams of the Protagonist.[19] Modern novelists realize that dreams and hallucinations and semiconscious states often give a deeper insight into the actions and so-called truths of man than conscious thought. In his epic concerning a young black's search for identity (and, by extension, the race's search), Ellison makes brilliant use of dreams and semiconscious states to drive home and underscore certain important assertions which the novel makes. He uses them in different ways—as adumbrations of future action, as retrospective comment, and as contrapuntal enlargement of certain crucial episodes in the work.

Let us examine several of these crucial dream experiences. Speaking from his Manhattan cave, the Protagonist tells of a pretty girl's terrifying nightmare in which her face (self) expands until it fills the whole room and becomes a shapeless mass of jellylike substance. To be formless, the narrator tells us, is to be without identity, "to be unaware of one's form is to live a death." This observation apropos of the girl's nightmare leads to the Protagonist's comment, "I, myself, after existing some twenty years, did not become alive until I discovered my invisibility." Invisibility is not formlessness; it is, however, a kind of selfhood whose form certain others cannot recognize.

In the Prologue, to show his hero's confused state, Ellison resorts to a marijuana experience. Smoking a reefer that "some joker" had given him and listening to jazz, the Protagonist suffers a three-level type of hallucination, each one presenting an archetype of black experience. On the first level he finds a cave with an old Negro woman in it singing spirituals. On the second there is a slave auction with a beautiful ivory-colored girl (who reminds him of his mother) being sold. And on the third he hears an old-time black revivalist preaching. The Protagonist is disconcerted by these figures, whom he *hears* rather than sees. They are invisible (to him); though desiring to understand, he cannot because he is caught between the poles of alienation and belonging. The Preacher's sermon tells of the universality and antiquity of blackness, but the Protagonist is still too much a part of the white world to understand.

Turning from the Preacher to the Old Woman singing spirituals, he finds that she has a love-hate regard for the master, who is the father of her sons. In order to prevent her sons from killing him, she poisons the master. Her ambivalence is evident, but she knows (unlike the Protagonist) what she wants and what it costs. She, therefore, chooses freedom in spite of her love for the master. The Protagonist does not yet know what the woman knows, and he tries to question her, but his probing makes her cry. The sons then run him away: "Next time you got questions like that," they tell him, "ask yourself." This marijuana-induced dream underscores the Protagonist's dilemma *after* he became invisible and *before* he finds his selfhood.

Early in the novel the Protagonist has a dream describing his presence at a circus with his grandfather. When the clowns came out, the old man refused to laugh. He then told the grandson to open a briefcase he had, take out the letter it contained, and read it. After going through a seemingly endless number of envelopes, one within the other, he came to the final one which contained this message: "To Whom It May Concern: Keep this Nigger-Boy Running." The old man who had refused to laugh at clowns finds this message extremely funny.

Tightly packed with meaning, this dream puts into focus several important themes or leitmotifs which run through the work: the grandfather himself, the briefcase, the "running" image, and the clown. The white world and the Negroes who are white-oriented contain the black man by sending him on foolish and futile errands. The Negroes who fall for this trick are clowns, and they are like the grinning minstreltype dolls which caused Tod Clifton's death in the novel. The grandfather recognized "clowns" for what they were, but he laughed at the keep-this-nigger-running message because he realized that that strategy could backfire. In his running, the black man, like the Protagonist, can eventually stop being a clown and find out who he is.

The episode in which we find the Protagonist semiconscious in a hospital room, after his fight at the paint factory, tells, through an intricate series of symbols and actions, what America does or seeks to do to the Negro. In this glaring white room (probably the white world), the Protagonist, when he regains consciousness halfway, is subjected to a series of electrical shocks, which may be interpreted as the nation's attempt to shape for its own designs the black man's character. One of the physicians present playfully suggests castration; another comments on the "racial" rhythms produced by the shocks. The Protagonist is partly aware of what is happening to him. "Where did my body end and the crystal white world begin?" he asks himself. That, of course, is a question being asked loudly nowadays. Although he feels like a clown (he is not fully conscious), he has sense enough to tell himself: "When I discover who I am, I'll be free."

This episode constitutes an important turning point in the hero's progress. He cannot go back to his old attitude and goals, not even to his old room. He moves first to Mary's house, then to the Brotherhood and a new name, and then through experiences and disillusionments, one after another, until he lands in his dark cellar. After burning his briefcase papers, he achieves a clear-sighted awareness of what his false identities have been.

At this point he falls into a kind of half-dream, half-hallucination, in which he finds himself a prisoner of Bledsoe and Norton, two of the persons who had kept him running. They want him to come back to the

Ralph Ellison

old lies, but he refuses. They threaten; "Refuse and we'll free you of your illusions," they tell him. He is adamant, and they castrate him, and, throwing his testicles upon a bridge, they pronounce him free of illusion. "Painful and empty," he now sees what he could not see before, and he realizes that "There hang not only my generations wasting upon the water . . . but . . . your universe, and that drip-drop upon the water you hear is all the history you've made, all you're going to make." When the bridge moves like an iron man, the Protagonist struggles up, crying out, "No, no. We must stop him!" He wakes up in the blackness.

In this dream and in the writing of this dream the Protagonist touches upon the real essence of the novel, the idea to which the other dreams have served as clues. Let us review the dreams. The pretty girl's recurring nightmare shows the individual's need to have an undistorted awareness of selfhood. The Protagonist's dream about archetypal racial characters points out his alienation from his own culture and his need to identify with it. The Grandfather dream and the semiconscious state in the hospital show the damage white America can do to the black image of selfhood. The castration dream affirms that, in spite of all else, the destinies of black and white America are inextricably woven. Unless the Negro, contributing from his heritage and retaining his own identity, joins the other group, the nation is headed for chaos: "Our fate is to become one, and yet many. . . . Thus one of the greatest jokes in the world is the spectacle of the whites escaping blackness and becoming blacker every day, and the blacks striving towards whiteness, becoming quite dull and gray. None of us seems to know who he is or where he's going."

In 1964 Ellison published *Shadow and Act,* a significant book of criticism. The essays in the work, the author tells us, are autobiographical in their "basic significance" and are concerned with three general themes: "literature and folklore; Negro musical expression—especially jazz and the blues; and the complex relationship between the Negro American subculture and North American culture as a whole."

The work is definitely in part an *apologia pro vita sua* for Ellison, and it states clearly his critical position at the time. The date of publication gives the work added significance because in the mid-sixties the Black Arts Aesthetics Movement was coming into power. Ellison's critical viewpoints clash strongly and frontally with those of the movement.

Ellison's racial attitude is presented first in the 23-page introduction to *Shadow and Act* in which he talks of his lower-middle-class background in Oklahoma, of his mother, and of the attitudes which the frontier character of his state fostered in him. Because of this kind of childhood, his imagination could transcend the "category of race," and he could conceive of himself as a potential "Renaissance man."

Life in his native city was never as structured as it would have been in the Deep South or in the "deceptively free" Harlem. He and his playmates, therefore, could fashion heroes that were neither white nor black. Whatever these heroes did, however, they performed in "Negro American style," the kind of style blacks had come to recognize and appreciate in Negro jazz players, tap dancers, and athletes. Feeling they could do whatever white boys did and do it better, Ellison and his playmates were not defensive and self-hating. They could make "an affirmation of life beyond all question of our difficulties as Negroes."

Ellison is deeply, almost religiously, interested in the art of writing, and throughout *Shadow and Act* he returns time and again to the subject. In these earlier pages he tells us that a writer must be forever searching into the past. In his particular case he has had to relate himself to his "mixed background" as an American *and* as a Negro. He has also had to find himself in relationship to American and European literatures and through them to find his own true voice. The whole business was a slow and by no means simple or easy process because there was always the need constantly "to stare down the deadly and hypnotic temptation to interpret the world and all its devices in terms of race." Ellison came to believe that the greatest difficulty for a Negro writer was the problem of revealing what he truly felt rather than writing what he was *supposed* to believe. Through learning how to write and through a brief flirtation with Marxism, Ellison states that he began to find out how *he* felt inside. In this growth he never accepted, he insists, any "negative definitions" imposed on him by others. The old "Renaissance man" concept had served him well. Much Negro fiction fails, Ellison believes, because many black writers do not "achieve a vision of life and a resourcefulness of craft commensurate with the complexity of their actual vision." Also, many are afraid "to leave the uneasy sanctuary of race to take their chances in the world of art."

The first article in *Shadow and Act*, "That Same Pain, That Same Pleasure: An Interview," spells out in detail several of the things concerning his background that he had commented on briefly in the introduction. This part of the interview is especially refreshing because so much recent autobiography has stressed only the *pain* of being black. Ellison shows here, as many blacks have found out, that being a Negro in America can be a rewarding and fascinating experience. With their closeness, their jokes, their folk stories, their singing, especially their jazz, Negroes often have a warmth and richness in their living not present in other groups.

Too many Negroes write about themselves in sociological terms, and they are not the only terms, Ellison asserts. As for him, he cont "I felt it important to explore the full range of American Negro huma ity and to affirm those qualities which are of value beyond any question of segregation, economics or previous condition of servitude."

Of all of the revealing essays in this work, the one that tells us most about Ellison as a Negro American artist is "The World and the Jug"— a piece in which he combines two essays he wrote in answer to Irving Howe's article, "Black Boys and Native Sons" (*Dissent,* Autumn, 1963), and Howe's reply (*The New Leader,* February 3, 1964) to Ellison's first essay.

Howe, Ellison argues, seems to feel that "unrelieved suffering" is the only "real" Negro experience, and that as a consequence, the Negro writer must be "ferocious." But, Ellison insists, there is also an American Negro tradition "which teaches one to deflect racial provocation and to master certain pain." A Negro, even a product of Mississippi, is, first of all, a human being and not "an abstract embodiment of living hell" as both Wright and Howe would have us believe. Negroes, Ellison continues, are not mere products of their "socio-political predicament." They are actually the products of the reaction of their social predicament with that of their own will and the "broad American cultural freedom" in which they live. In addition to the hate, fear, and vindictiveness that Wright gives his Negro characters, they also have other human qualities that enable them to endure under pressure, as did Wright. Wright and Howe think of novels as weapons in the struggle for freedom. I believe, Ellison says, that "true novels . . . are ritualistic and ceremonial at their core."

Howe's original essay praised Wright at the expense of Baldwin and Ellison. In that essay Howe spoke of Wright as Ellison's "spiritual father." He was not my "spiritual father," Ellison answers, but a friend. I learned more about myself as a Negro, Ellison contends, through works of world art—Marx, Freud, Eliot, Pound, and others—than I did from reading works by any Negro writer. We must remember, Ellison adds, that the slaves re-created themselves "out of the myths and images of the Old Testament Jews." Ellison then asserts that as Negro *and American,* "I am as writer no less a custodian of the American language than is Irving Howe. I believe a writer," he continues, "should be a writer and not a propagandist, and when he stops writing and elects to take to the platform, it should be his own choosing and not from pressure from would-be managers of society."

This article is a scathing and penetrating analysis of attitudes too often taken by well-meaning white critics when they evaluate black writers. To state it crudely, these white critics tend to use criteria for

ey would not use for white. Ellison brilliantly
he felt it is evidenced in Howe's review of

an early jazz buff, Ellison has written brilliantly
mers. One of the most fascinating articles in
Bird, Bird-Watching, and Jazz." In this piece
only into an analysis of Parker's music and per-
attitudes of the black performing artist and, of
course, the forces at work upon him. Ellison describes the phenomenon
of Bird in terms that transcend racial consideration: Bird "captured
something of the discordances, the yearning, romance and cunning of
the age and ordered it into a haunting art."

Shadow and Act, of course, contains many other essays, reviews, and
articles, among them a provocative review of Black Boy ("Richard
Wright's Blues") and an equally impressive analysis of the Negro in
American films ("The Shadow and the Act"). Shadow and Act is not
only an outstanding critical work, it is also the most clear-sighted, the
most highly informed statement of the integrationist position found in
Afro-American literature to date.

James Baldwin

For almost two decades James Baldwin has served as a kind of measur-
ing rod for the nation's social conscience. He looks upon himself as "not
spokesman exactly, but as public witness to the situation of black
people." As public witness he has reported through his many essays the
racial sickness which America has, and which seems to worsen with the
years. Baldwin has the ability to put into brilliant prose the frustrations
of Negroes. He also knows how to appeal to whites, and they read him
in larger numbers, perhaps, than Negroes do. Whites read him because
of his excellence as a writer and because he needles them more subtly
and more effectively than any other Negro writer. In his essays Baldwin
shows, by the changing positions he takes, the growing chasm between
whites and blacks in America. Like all other sensitive Negroes, he has
been touched by the doctrines of the current black revolution, but he
is really a transitional writer. An avowed integrationist in his early

works, we shall see that in his last published volume he leans heavily toward the black nationalist position. His pilgrimage into blackness has been intense and passionate. His analyses of the progressive disintegration of black-white relationships should have been therapeutic. Unfortunately, however, nobody really listens to such warnings. They serve only as a record of I-told-you-so's.

James Baldwin was born in New York City in 1924, the oldest of nine children. As he tells us in his first book of essays, his childhood was bitter. He was the victim not only of poverty, physical ugliness, and blackness, but also of his stepfather's hatred. His stepfather was a store-front preacher with far more "religion" in his make-up than charity. Baldwin was a very bright youngster with a keen appetite for reading. He was editor of his junior high school newspaper and wrote for the school paper when in DeWitt Clinton High School. Baldwin's formal education ended with his graduation from DeWitt Clinton. He became a boy preacher when he was fourteen, but abandoned his calling at the age of seventeen.

After Baldwin left high school, he drifted from one laboring job to another, suffering in each the hurt of segregation and discrimination that a sensitive black youth would naturally experience. During this period he met Richard Wright, who not only encouraged him in his writing efforts but also helped him to get the Eugene F. Saxton Memorial Trust Award to help him complete a novel on which he was then working. At the time Baldwin was also writing reviews for *The Nation, New Leader, Commentary,* and other periodicals. Becoming disgusted with himself and the progress he was making, Baldwin left America in 1948 and went to Paris with the intention of remaining there. By the time he returned to America, he was a highly successful author and has remained so up to the present.

James Baldwin has won more than his share of the awards, honors, and fellowships which America gives to its talented authors. In addition to the Saxton Award mentioned, he has had a Rosenwald Fellowship, a Guggenheim Fellowship, a National Institute of Arts and Letters Fellowship, a Ford Foundation grant-in-aid, and a *Partisan Review* Fellowship.

Up to this writing, Baldwin has published eleven major works: four novels, four collections of essays, one collection of short stories, and two plays (see bibliography).

The author's first major publication, *Go Tell It on the Mountain* (1953), is a realistic and revealing novel about Harlem ghetto life, the forerunner of many works of fiction dealing with ghetto life. The action of the novel centers in the home and store-front church of the protagonist's preacher-stepfather, Gabriel. *Go Tell It on the Mountain* delineates the self-discovery through conversion of John Grimes, a fourteen-year-old boy. John, like his creator, has three strikes against him: he is black, ugly, and illegitimate. He feels, however, that he will find an answer to his problems in becoming converted, in becoming one of the "saints." One of John's main obstacles to "sainthood" is his deep-rooted dislike of his fanatical stepfather Gabriel. John feels that a true conversion would rid him of this sin.

The book is divided into three sections: "The Seventh Day," "The Prayers of the Saints," and "The Threshing Floor"; the first two, consisting mainly of flashbacks, prepare the reader for the third, in which John joins the ranks of the "saints." John's relationships with his already-saved cousin, Elisha, during these experiences are significant because they hint ever so lightly of a homosexual relationship. In Baldwin's subsequent novels homosexuality is a major theme.

Most critics consider *Go Tell It on the Mountain* Baldwin's best novel, and this well may be. For one thing, the work has many autobiographical segments. When Baldwin delineated John's life in a store-front church, John's attitude toward Gabriel, and John's emotional intensity and conflicts, he probably looked in his own heart and wrote. Because Baldwin knew so thoroughly the ghetto and church life, he spoke with an authority that the reader recognizes. Moreover, he was dealing with root material of great significance to Negro writers: the place of the church and its music. The black church, particularly the store-front church, was a "rock in a weary land" which protected the Negro from a hostile world of whiteness. These things Baldwin knew at first hand, and expressed with passion and often with great beauty, particularly in "The Threshing Floor."

Baldwin's second novel, *Giovanni's Room* (1956), treats openly and with a certain measure of dignity the homosexual theme. In order to get away, one imagines, from the kind of autobiographical slant hinted at in his first novel, Baldwin makes the characters in *Giovanni's Room* white, and places the action on a European background. In this work he implies that Americans are hypocritically moralistic about homosexuality, and when they are forced through natural urges to take part in homosexual acts, they become morbidly guilt-ridden and do foolish things which hurt others. In our stress on so-called manliness, Baldwin seems to be saying, we become unmanly in our attitude toward homosexuality.

Giovanni's Room relates the experiences of David, an American who had run away to Europe from an unfortunate childhood in a motherless home. Before leaving America, David had one homosexual experience, and he brought from it deep scars of guilt. In Paris he meets Hella, and he decides that he has found in her an answer to his confused needs.

219 / integrationists and transitional writers

Before Hella makes up her mind to cast in her lot with David, she asks for time to take a trip to Spain to think things over. While she is gone David meets Giovanni, who is a bartender in a gay bar. Although David actually comes to love Giovanni, he cannot face that fact. His American background bedevils him, and feelings of guilt begin to overwhelm him. Giovanni, on the other hand, accepts the relationship as perfectly natural. In the end David loses both Hella (who learns about his sexual dilemma) and Giovanni. Because he cannot rise above his provincial and, actually, hypocritical prejudices, David seriously hurts both his friends. The work is, among other things, a plea for honesty in sexual matters. Although it gives considerable insight into the homosexual mind, the novel is not an impressive work.

Baldwin's third novel, *Another Country* (1962), has been hailed by a considerable number of critics as an outstanding work. The present writer is never quite sure of the "other" country which Baldwin wishes to point out to his readers. Weaving together several plots, *Another Country* deals with black-white relationships, homo- versus heterosexual relationships, and marital versus extra-marital relationships, each of them crossing and recrossing the paths of the other two. The novel seems to be making a plea for a deeper and more unbiased understanding of human failures *and* virtues, as they are influenced by racial, class, and sexual considerations.

There are several key characters in the work, among them two who give most direction to the development of the story. The first is Rufus Scott, a black jazz musician who kills himself early in the work. Although he dies in the opening chapters, his shadow falls across the lives of all the remaining characters throughout the novel. The second figure is Eric, a white homosexual. Eric is thoroughly at ease with his so-called deviation. He has had sexual relationships with several of the other members of their tight little group—male and female—and in each situation he has served as a calming and therapeutic influence, carrying with him the persons whom he touched to another country, to a higher level of tolerance and understanding.

The plot of the novel is too highly involved to give here, but one episode which comes at the beginning of the work should be mentioned. The mistress of Rufus the jazz musician is a Southern white girl, Leona, whom he brutally mistreats. During their love making, which is more like a rape than anything else, Rufus thinks of her as a "milk-white bitch" and curses her as he viciously performs the sexual act. A considerable number of black novels written during the sixties have variants of the Rufus-Leona black-man-white-woman liaison. The position of the white woman in the black literature of the sixties poses several not easily answered questions.

Baldwin's last novel, *Tell Me How Long the Train's Been Gone* (1968), which in the nature of things should have been his finest, is probably the weakest. The author places his characters and action on a theatrical background. In all probability Baldwin did not know the world of the theatre as well as he did the world of the ghetto and the store-front church. In any case, the reader, at least this reader, is not impressed with the picture of the theatre world found in the work.

The central character in the novel is Leo Proudhammer, a famous Negro actor. As the story opens, he is recuperating from a severe heart attack. During the enforced leisure of his recovery he thinks over his life. Leo's faithful mistress is Barbara, an intelligent middle-class white girl. Although Leo does not brutalize her physically, he does mistreat her, and at one time she seriously contemplates suicide. Toward the end of the work Leo takes a boy friend, a young black nationalist named Christopher. The introduction of Christopher gives Baldwin the opportunity to present some of the attitudes of the current black revolution and to show, among other things, that his interest in blackness has increased considerably since his first novel. But the book, even with the unusual triangle of lover, mistress, and male-mistress or boy friend, says very little that is new. *Tell Me How Long the Train's Been Gone* does not add much, if anything, to Baldwin's stature as a novelist.

The essays of Baldwin are found in four collections (to date), the first published in 1955, the last in 1972. Although he is not usually associated with the Black Revolution of the sixties, these essays show Baldwin's continuing pilgrimage into blackness. They also show that, from the first collection down to the most recent, the author has unwittingly been the gadfly of the movement. Like Malcolm X, Baldwin has known how to draw subtly on that reservoir of racial resentment that all Negroes have. Far more sensitive than Malcolm X, Baldwin articulates persuasively and artistically the various nuances of hurt that Negroes endure. He also knows how to make black people feel superior, and in this activity he automatically joins forces with the black nationalists. Though not generally recognized as such, James Baldwin is one of the authentic voices of the black revolution. One should observe, however, that he did not intentionally assume this role in his early works.

In his first collection of essays, *Notes of a Native Son* (1955), Baldwin writes as an avowed integrationist. In the autobiographical notes at the beginning of the book, he sets the tone for this approach: "I love America more than any other country in the world," he writes, "and exactly for this reason, I insist on the right to criticize her perpetually." From this collection on down to his most recent, Baldwin as a native son has faithfully exercised that right. His criticism of America,

James Baldwin

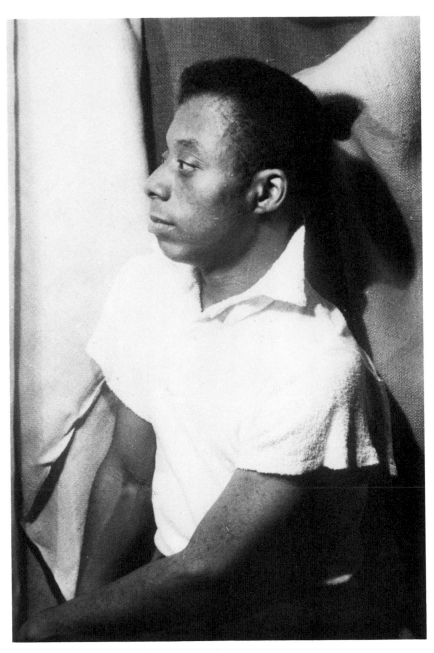

Photo by Carl Van Vechten, Collection of American Literature, Beinecke Rare Book and Manuscript Library, Yale University.

expressed in a thousand-and-one variations, constitutes a substantial portion of practically all his essays.

Two of the best-known and most frequently reprinted essays from the first collection concern Richard Wright. The first of these, "Everybody's Protest Novel," is a brilliant and devastating attack on Harriet Beecher Stowe's *Uncle Tom's Cabin,* and through it, on protest novels as a genre. In her treatment of Uncle Tom, Baldwin is saying, Mrs. Stowe overlooked the fact that her main character, and every other human being, is not merely a member of a society or group or a thing to be explained by science. "He is . . . something more than that, something resolutely indefinable, unpredictable." It is the business of the novelist, Baldwin contends, to show the complexity of the individual man, for in such a delineation we find ourselves.

Although the protest novel, the author continues, is usually considered a good thing in America, a work designed to bring "greater freedom to the oppressed," actually it is not. The protest novel is really a "mirror of our confusion, dishonesty, panic, trapped and immobilized in the sunlit prison of the American Dream." In this respect *Native Son* is *Uncle Tom's Cabin's* descendant. "The failure of the protest novel," Baldwin asserts, "lies in its rejection of life, the human being, the denial of his beauty, dread, power, in its insistence that it is his categorization alone which is real and which cannot be transcended." In this surprising rejection of the long-venerated protest novel, Baldwin served notice that a new, fresh, and keen appraiser had appeared on the literary scene.

In his second essay, "Many Thousands Gone," Baldwin discusses *Native Son* and its main character, Bigger Thomas. After mentioning the rat incident in Wright's novel, Baldwin says: "The premise of the book is . . . clearly conveyed in these first pages; we are confronting a monster created by the American republic and we are, through being made to share his experience, to receive illumination as regards the manner of his life and to feel both pity and horror at his awful and inevitable doom." This is an excellent idea, Baldwin states, and if Wright had been more perceptive we would have a different novel from the one we have; unfortunately, however, Wright "attempted to redeem a symbolical monster in social terms."[20]

The crux of Baldwin's criticism is that Bigger's "force comes, not from his significance as a social (or antisocial) unit, but from his significance as the incarnation of a myth." Although we follow Bigger's career step by step, Baldwin continues, we never get to know him. "What this means for the novel is that a necessary dimension has been cut away;

20. *Notes of a Native Son,* New York: Bantam Books, 1964, pp. 26–27.

this dimension being the relationship that Negroes bear to one another, the depth of involvement and unspoken recognition of shared experience which creates a way of life."[21] *Native Son* reflects, Baldwin asserts, a climate which is common to most Negro protest novels, a climate which says, in effect, that "in Negro life there exists no tradition." This is not true. The fact is that "there has as yet arrived no sensibility sufficiently profound and tough to make this tradition articulate."

The titular essay in *Notes of a Native Son* is a very valuable autobiographical statement. Using his father's life, death, and funeral as a frame, Baldwin tells us a great deal not only about his parent but also about his own life during the forties. The essay ends on an integrationist note. The reader should compare the tone of this ending with the tone of Baldwin's last collection. The contrast is startling.

The second collection of essays, *Nobody Knows My Name* (1961), bears the subtitle *More Notes of a Native Son*. It deals largely with the identity problems most American Negroes have in one way or another. The first essay in the volume, "The Discovery of What It Means to Be an American," concerns the effect of the author's first trip away from his native soil. "I left America," Baldwin tells us, "because I doubted my ability to survive the fury of the color problem here. . . . I wanted to prevent myself from becoming *merely* a Negro; or, even, merely a Negro writer. I wanted to find out in what way the *specialness* of my experience could be made to connect me with other people instead of dividing me from them."

In Paris Baldwin discovered that, like the other Americans there, he had been "divorced from his origins." And this common problem helped to remove the sting of difference he felt at home. "I proved, to my astonishment," he confesses, "to be as American as any Texas G.I."[22] While in Switzerland Baldwin made another discovery about himself. He carried with him two Bessie Smith recordings. Through "her tone and cadence" Bessie helped him to dig back to the way he was as a child. He had never listened to Bessie Smith in America, "but in Europe she helped to reconcile me to being a 'nigger'."[23]

Another revealing and well-known essay found in this volume is a three-part article called "Alas, Poor Richard" which concerns Richard Wright. In the titular section of the three-part essay Baldwin tries to "set the record 'straight,' to 'settle' the account" as regards his well-known relationship with Wright. The essay is sharp on occasion as it describes the course of their friendship and subsequent feud. In the last part of the piece, Baldwin accuses Richard Wright of taking himself too

21. Ibid., p. 27.
22. *Nobody Knows My Name.* New York: Dial, 1961, p. 4.
23. Ibid., p. 5.

seriously, of actually despising his fellow American Negroes, and of not wanting to know his African brothers. Underscoring this accusation, Baldwin make the following general statement apropos of Wright: "Time brought Richard, as it has brought the American Negro, to an extraordinarily baffling and dangerous place. . . . I am suggesting that one of the prices an American Negro pays—or can pay—for what is called his 'acceptance' is a profound, almost ineradicable self-hatred. This corrupts every aspect of his living, he is never at peace again, he is out of touch with himself forever."[24]

Perhaps the best known essay in this collection is "The Black Boy Looks at the White Boy" (it appeared in *Esquire*), a piece which deals with Baldwin's friendship with Norman Mailer. The two men, very much alike in some ways, had a mutual respect for each other, but that did not prevent Baldwin from attacking *The White Negro*. "I could not," Baldwin writes, "with the best will in the world, make any sense out of *The White Negro* and, in fact, it was hard for me to imagine that this essay had been written by the same man who wrote the novels."

Nobody Knows My Name, as do all of Baldwin's collections, goes back home to the author's childhood in Harlem. In this case the "return" essay is called "Fifth Avenue Uptown: a Letter from Harlem." In it he revisits his old blocks and muses about the changes that have come about, the new projects, the Black Muslims, the increase in hatred, the increase in bitterness. He feels a deep sorrow for the children of the slums. In the article he also discusses the differences between Northern and Southern prejudice. The Northerner, he says, "never sees Negroes. Southerners see them all the time. Northerners never think about them whereas Southerners are never really thinking of anything else . . . Neither the Southerner nor the Northerner is able to look at the Negro simply as a man."

Baldwin then restates his deeply held belief, one that recurs again and again in his essays: "It is a terrible, an inexorable, law that one cannot deny the humanity of another without diminishing one's own. . . . Walk through the streets of Harlem and see what we, this nation, have become."[25]

Still exercising his promise to criticize America "perpetually," the author returns to that subject in the essay, "In Search of a Majority." This article reminds one strongly of George Schuyler's essay, "Our Greatest Gift to America," published during the New Negro Renaissance. They both say the same thing, namely, that white Americans measure their status with reference to the Negro. The Negro tells where the bottom is because he is on the bottom. The white man needs this

24. *Nobody Knows My Name,* New York: Dial, 1961, p. 214.
25. *Nobody Knows My Name,* New York: Dial, 1961, p. 71.

kind of buffer, Baldwin implies. If it were not there, white Americans would have to examine themselves too critically for comfort; they would have to deal "with all those vices, all those conundrums, and all those mysteries with which we [the Americans] have invested the Negro race."[26]

As the title suggests, the next collection, *The Fire Next Time* (1962), is a warning to the nation. Unless America comes to its senses, these essays say, in effect, and learns to treat its black minority with decency and fairness—unless the nation finds this kind of understanding (and Baldwin is certain that it will not)—we are in for deep trouble. There are only two articles or letters in this volume: the first, a seven-page section entitled "My Dungeon Shook—Letter to My Nephew on the One Hundredth Anniversary of the Emancipation"; the second, a 91-page essay covering many subjects, entitled "Down at the Cross—Letter from a Region of My Mind."

The "Letter to My Nephew" contains, among other things, the well-known passage on the black man's burden (Baldwin uses the theme often): the duty of Negroes to save America through love. After detailing what America has tried to do to him because he is black, and for no other reason, Baldwin tells his young kinsman:

> The details and symbols of your life have been deliberately constructed to make you believe what white people say about you. Please try to remember that what they believe, as well as what they do and cause you to endure, does not testify to your inferiority but to their inhumanity and fear. . . . There is no reason for you to try to become like white people and there is no basis whatever for their impertinent assumption that *they* must accept *you*. The really terrible thing, old buddy, is that *you* must accept *them*. And I mean this very seriously. You must accept them and accept them with love. For these innocent people have no other hope. . . . And if the word *integration* means anything, this is what it means: that we, with love, shall force our brothers to see themselves as they are, to cease fleeing from reality, and begin to change it. For this is your home, my friend, . . . and we can make America what America must become."[27]

Some critics believe that Baldwin is at his best when he writes about himself—his experiences and convictions. This is probably true, and the second essay in *The Fire Next Time,* the "Letter from a Region of My Mind," bears out brilliantly this contention. A long and diversified article, it begins with the author's analysis of the "prolonged religious crisis" he experienced at the age of fourteen. Baldwin, as we know, became not only a "saint" but also a boy preacher. In describing the decisions he had to make before joining the church, the author spells out in

26. *Nobody Knows My Name.* New York: Dial, 1961, p. 133.
27. *The Fire Next Time.* New York: Delta, 1963, pp. 22–24.

vivid detail the avenues (or rather the lack of t'
black boy from the ghetto had at the time.

When he was seventeen Baldwin gave up the
religion because he had learned that a truly moral hum.
"divorce himself from all the prohibitions, crimes, and hypo.
the Christian church." As a matter of fact, Baldwin, like James Joy
never wholly repudiated his early religious background, and he admits
this:

> The church was very exciting. It took a long time for me to disengage
> myself from this excitement, and on the blindest, most visceral level, I
> never really have and never will. There is no music like that music, no
> drama like the drama of the saints rejoicing, the sinners moaning, the
> tambourines racing, and all those voices coming together and crying
> holy unto the Lord.[28]

Among the other high spots in this exploration of a region of his
mind is Baldwin's long and penetrating account of the visit he paid to
the home of the Honorable Elijah Muhammad, the leader of the Black
Muslims. Baldwin was strangely and strongly impressed by what he
learned from this visit, but not enough to join the sect: "I knew that
Elijah's meaning and mine were not the same."

The essay ends on the theme which he stated in the first of the two
letters: there is nothing to imitate or desire in America's white civilization. It is a burning house and only the Negro can save it.

Baldwin's latest publication, a book of essays entitled *No Name in
the Street,* came out in 1972. In it Baldwin shows signs of weariness;
he is repeating himself. He also shows more deeply than ever before
his disgust at the American racial situation, and because of this disgust,
Baldwin leans strongly in this volume toward the black nationalist position. In one section of the work he highly praises Malcolm X, and by
comparing what happened to St. Joan in Bernard Shaw's play of the
same name, suggests that the same thing could happen to Malcolm X.

> And there is, since his death, a Malcolm, virtually, for every persuasion.
> People who hated him, people who despised him, people who feared him,
> and people who, in their various ways and degrees, according to their
> various lights and darknesses, loved him, all claim him now. It is easy
> to claim him now, just as it was easy for the Church to claim St. Joan.[29]

In this last collection the author also has much to say in appreciation
of the Black Panthers and their several heroes and martyrs. *No Name
in the Street* contains by far the most vitriolic analysis of the racial
situation in America that Baldwin has written. He has come a long way

28. *The Fire Next Time.* New York: Delta, 1963, p. 47.
29. *No Name in the Street.* New York: Dial, 1972, pp. 119–120.

since his first collection in 1955. The bitter and ominous epilogue to *No Name in the Street* shows how far Baldwin has traveled into the region of revolutionary blackness. It also makes use of a theme very popular among contemporary young black writers, the end of Western civilization as we now know it. "People," he writes, "even if they are so thoughtless as to be born black, do not come into this world merely to provide mink coats and diamonds for chattering, trivial, pale matrons, or genocidal opportunities for their unsexed, unloved, and finally despicable men—oh pioneers!

"There will be bloody holding actions all over the world, for years to come: but the Western party is over, and the white man's sun has set. Period."[30]

If there is one theme that runs through practically all of James Baldwin's works, it is this: America's great trouble is that it refuses to look objectively at its history and its essential nature. Blinded by a system of myths, racial and otherwise, which have little or no relationship to reality, the nation stumbles forward, headed for inevitable disaster. In a prose style, ironic, flexible, and at times brilliant, Baldwin drives home this message.

30. Ibid., pp. 196–197.

Postscript

The year, 1960, at which this study ends, was crucial for Negro American literature. The decade of the sixties brought radical changes in the thinking of many black Americans, and these changes were reflected, naturally, in the literature of the period. A quick look at the sixties will show the direction into which this literature moved. Prior to 1960 most Negro writers took it for granted that although they used Negro subject matter, they were *American* writers and their objective was to become a part of the mainstream of the Western literary tradition. During the sixties, however, there came into being a new movement among young black writers (joined by a few of the older), a separatist and black nationalist movement, which insisted that black writing should repudiate the Western tradition and all that it has ever represented. According to these young black nationalists, the Western tradition is intrinsically anti-Negro; moreover, it is a dying tradition, one that has to be replaced through the thinking and creative productions of non-white, non-Western artists.

The writer who spear-headed this new movement, which came to be known as the Black Arts Movement, is LeRoi Jones (Baraka). One of the clearest and strongest statements of the Black Arts position and objectives comes from Baraka's associate, Larry Neal. Writing in *The Drama Review* (Summer, 1968), Neal tells us:

> The Black Arts Movement is radically opposed to any concept of the artist that alienates him from his community. Black Art is the aesthetic and spiritual sister of the Black Power concept. As such, it envisions an art that speaks directly to the needs and aspirations of Black America. In order to perform this task, the Black Arts Movement proposes a radical reordering of the western cultural aesthetic. It proposes a separate symbolism, mythology, critique, and iconology.

In this attempt to bring about a "radical reordering of the western cultural aesthetic," the Black Arts Movement has spawned a new breed of revolutionary young black writers. In their efforts to create a "separate symbolism, mythology, critique, and iconology," they have brought about a New Black Renaissance, one that is similar in many respects to the New Negro Renaissance of the twenties. Many of the important themes and positions used and held by the new writers may be traced to the Renaissance of the twenties. The authors treated in this volume—from Du Bois to Baldwin—have prepared the ground and planted the seed for this bumper harvest of the sixties.

The Black Arts Movement has produced an impressive number of young writers in all of the disciplines, but its major contribution has probably been in the field of poetry. Although young black poets have not broken entirely with the Western tradition, they have introduced poetical techniques and themes which could be called *new*, if one explained the word new. But whether new or not, the works of these young, black revolutionary poets have brought to Afro-American poetry a much-needed freshness and strength. The new poets are legion; among the better known are Don L. Lee, Mari Evans, and Nikki Giovanni.

The novelists of the sixties do not show the cohesiveness of the poets. A few like John Killens and John A. Williams started their careers as integrationists but have moved towards blackness in their later works. Others like Henry Van Dyke, Paula Marshall, William Kelley, Ishmael Reed, and Ernest Gaines show degrees of blackness varying from very little to none at all. And there are still others like Ronald Fair and Sam Greenlee who show definitely and unmistakably the influence of the Black Arts aesthetic. One notes that the best fiction writers of the sixties, unlike the best poets of the decade, have not been drastically touched by the Black Aesthetic.

Prior to the sixties, the outstanding Negro critics—among them Locke, Braithwaite, Brawley, Brown, Redding, Baldwin, Scott, and Ellison—approached a work by a Negro writer as they would any other work written in the Western tradition. They did not feel that a special and different critical apparatus was needed to judge works by Negro artists. The critics of the Black Arts Movement differ strongly with this stand, and they have tried to construct a Black Aesthetic, a special set of critical opinions, rules, and criteria designed to evaluate black writing. Among the outstanding writers in this area are Addison Gayle, George Kent, and Stephen Henderson. Although serious, able, and dedicated scholars, they have not yet succeeded in replacing the critical tenets of the Western literary tradition.

Of the major disciplines, drama during the decade of the sixties gained most in popularity. The gains, of course, are relative because Negro drama during the years prior to 1960 was one of the weaker genres (see Introduction to Part I, above). Influenced by LeRoi Jones, a new revolutionary black drama came into existence after about 1960. A drama of the people, this new development emphasized community theatres—theaters which gave many young writers their first opportunity to be heard. The plays produced by these Black Arts writers tended to deal almost exclusively with the harsh living conditions of the ghetto. Anti-white, anti-Establishment, anti-middle-class Negro, these plays and their authors also tended to glorify ghetto heroes—ex-convicts, hustlers, pimps, and pushers. These playwrights brought a new strength to Negro drama. Unfortunately, however, their emphasis on the ghetto gives a one-sided view of black life. Among the most popular writers of the black drama of the sixties are LeRoi Jones (Baraka), Douglas Turner Ward, Ed Bullins, Lonnie Elder, III, Joseph Walker, and Charles Gordone (the first Negro to win a Pulitzer Prize in drama).

When one looks at the New Black Renaissance and the literature it produced during the 1960's, he finds a strong but unsuccessful effort to establish a viable and convincing black aesthetic; he also finds a new breed of young black writers who, regardless of their failure to reorder the Western cultural aesthetic, have greatly enriched Afro-American literature.

A Selective Bibliography

In this highly selective bibliography I have tried to give, first, a list of anthologies, collections, and critical studies which cover the period from 1900 to 1960; and, second, enough material for each major writer to launch the student into further research. There are problems, however, in all lists of this sort, and a major one is the number of entries allotted each author. Space, naturally, will not allow us to be definitive. Moreover, for all of the "giants" considered here—Du Bois, Hughes, Wright, Ellison, and Baldwin—this is not necessary because there are full bibliographies for each available elsewhere. This writer has, therefore, scanted these authors in order to give more space to those writers not so well covered bibliographically.

Another problem is that of periodicals. How many shall one include? There is no rule of thumb to determine such matters, and in the meanwhile essays, articles, and studies on all Negro writers are pouring from the presses in unprecedented numbers. Under the circumstances, I have taken the only course open: to limit the periodical entries for each writer to those considered most helpful for students.

A writer's work will be divided into primary and secondary categories. In each case books are given first; articles etcetera follow, and each category is arranged chronologically. The organization of entries for an author has been determined by the individual author's variety and number of publication. The authors appear in the bibliography in the order of their appearance in the work.

General Works

Abramson, Doris E. *Negro Playwrights in the American Theatre, 1925–1959*. New York: Columbia University Press, 1969.
Alhamsi, Ahmed and H. K. Wangara. *Black Arts: An Anthology of Black Creations*. Detroit: Broadside, 1969.

The American Negro Writer and His Roots. New York: American Society of African Culture, 1960 (collected essays from the first Conference of Negro Writers).

Baker, Houston A., Jr. *Black Literature in America*. New York: McGraw-Hill, 1971.

Barbour, Floyd B. *The Black Seventies*. Boston: Porter Sargent, 1970.

Bell, Bernard W., ed. *Modern and Contemporary Afro-American Poetry*. Boston: Allyn & Bacon, 1972.

Bone, Robert A. *The Negro Novel in America*. Rev. ed. New Haven, Connecticut: Yale University Press, 1965.

Bontemps, Arna, ed. *American Negro Poetry*. New York: Hill and Wang, 1963 (anthology).

Bontemps, Arna and Langston Hughes, eds. *The Book of Negro Folklore*. New York: Dodd, Mead, 1958.

Brawley, Benjamin. *The Negro Genius*. New York: Dodd, Mead, 1937.

Brawley, Benjamin. *The Negro in Literature and Art*. 3rd ed. New York: Dodd, Mead, 1929.

Brewer, J. Mason. *American Negro Folklore*. Chicago: Quadrangle, 1968.

Bronz, Stephen H. *Roots of Negro Racial Consciousness: The 1920's*. New York: Libra, 1964.

Brooks, Gwendolyn, ed. *A Broadside Treasury, 1965–1970*. Detroit: Broadside, 1971 (anthology).

Brooks, Gwendolyn, ed. *Jump Bad, A New Chicago Anthology*. Detroit: Broadside, 1971.

Brown, Patricia L., Don L. Lee, and Francis Ward, eds. *To Gwen with Love, An Anthology Dedicated to Gwendolyn Brooks*. Chicago: Johnson Publishing Co., 1971.

Brown, Sterling A. *The Negro in American Fiction*. Washington, D.C.: Associates in Negro Folk Education, 1937; New York: Arno, 1969 (also in combination with *Negro Poetry and Drama*. New York: Atheneum, 1968).

Brown, Sterling A. *Negro Poetry and Drama*. Washington, D.C.: Associates in Negro Folk Education, 1937; New York: Arno, 1969 (also in combination with *The Negro in American Fiction*. New York: Atheneum, 1968).

Brown, Sterling A., Arthur P. Davis, and Ulysses Lee, eds. *The Negro Caravan*. New York: Dryden, 1941; New York: Arno, 1969. (anthology).

Bullins, Ed. *New Plays from the Black Theatre*. New York: Bantam, 1969.

Butcher, Margaret J. *The Negro in American Culture*. New York: Knopf, 1956.

Calverton, V. F. *Anthology of American Negro Literature*. New York: Modern Library, 1929.

Chapman, Abraham, ed. *Black Voices*. New York: New American Library, 1968 (anthology).

Clarke, John Henrik, ed. *American Negro Short Stories*. New York: Hill and Wang, 1966 (anthology).

Couch, William, ed. *Black Playwrights; an Anthology*. Baton Rouge, Louisiana: Louisiana State University Press, 1968.

Cullen, Countee, ed. *Caroling Dusk*. New York: Harper's, 1927.

Davis, Charles and Daniel Walden, eds. *On Being Black, Writings by Afro-Americans from Frederick Douglass to the Present*. New York: Fawcett, 1970.

Davis, Arthur P. and Saunders Redding, eds. *Cavalcade: Negro American Writing from 1760 to the Present*. Boston: Houghton Mifflin, 1971.

Dundes, Alan, ed. *Mother Wit from the Laughing Barrel. Readings in the Interpretation of Afro-American Folklore*. Englewood Cliffs, New Jersey: Prentice-Hall, 1973.

Emanuel, James A. and Theodore Gross, eds. *Dark Symphony: Negro Literature in America*. New York: Free Press, 1968.

Ford, Nick Aaron. *The Contemporary Negro Novel, a Study in Race Relations*. Boston: Meador Publishing Co., 1936.

Gayle, Addison, Jr., ed. *The Black Aesthetic*. New York: Doubleday, 1971.

Gayle, Addison, Jr., ed. *Black Expression: Essays by and about Black Americans in the Creative Arts*. New York: Weybright and Talley, 1969.

Gloster, Hugh M. *Negro Voices in American Fiction*. Chapel Hill, North Carolina: University of North Carolina Press, 1948.

Gross, Seymour and John E. Hardy, eds. *Images of the Negro in American Literature: Essays in Criticism*. Chicago: University of Chicago Press, 1966.

Harris, Charles F. and John A. Williams, eds. *Amistad 1*. New York: Random House, 1970.

Harris, Charles F. and John A. Williams, eds. *Amistad 2*. New York: Random House, 1970.

Hayden, Robert, ed. *Kaleidoscope, Poems by American Negro Poets*. New York: Harcourt, Brace, and World, 1967.

Hemenway, Robert, ed. *The Black Novelist*. Columbus, Ohio: Charles E. Merrill, 1970.

Henderson, Stephen E. *Understanding the New Black Poetry, Black Speech and Black Music as Poetic References*. New York: Morrow, 1973.

Hill, Herbert, ed. *Soon, One Morning: New Writings by American Negroes, 1940–1962*. New York: Knopf, 1963.

Hughes, Langston, ed. *The Best Short Stories by Negro Writers: An Anthology from 1899 to the Present*. Boston and Toronto: Little, Brown, 1967.

Hughes, Langston and Arna Bontemps, eds. *The Poetry of the Negro, 1746–1949*. Garden City, New York: Doubleday, 1949; rev. ed. *The Poetry of the Negro, 1746–1970*. Garden City, New York: Doubleday, 1970.

Johnson, Charles S., ed. *Ebony and Topaz: A Collectanea*. New York: National Urban League, 1927.

Johnson, James Weldon, ed. *The Book of American Negro Poetry*. Rev. ed. New York: Harcourt, Brace, 1931.

Jones, LeRoi and Larry Neal, eds. *Black Fire: An Anthology of Afro-American Writing*. New York: Morrow, 1968.

Kerlin, Robert T., ed., Negro Poets and Their Poems. Washington, D.C.: Associated Publishers, 1935.

Kent, George. *Blackness and the Adventure of Western Culture*. Chicago: The Third World Press, 1972 (critical essays).

Lee, Don L. *Dynamite Voices, Black Poets of the 1960's*. Detroit: Broadside, 1971 (criticism).

Locke, Alain. *The New Negro: An Interpretation*. New York: Boni and Liveright, 1925; New York: Atheneum, 1968.

Locke, Alain and Montgomery Gregory. *Plays of Negro Life*. New York: Harper and Bros., 1927.

Loggins, Vernon. *The Negro Author, His Development in America to*

1900. New York: Columbia University Press, 1931; Port Washington, N.Y.: Kennikat Press, 1964.

Lovell, John, Jr. *Black Song: The Forge and the Flame. The Story of How the Afro-American Spiritual was Hammered Out*. New York: Macmillan, 1972.

Major, Clarence. *The New Black Poetry*. New York: International Publishers, 1969.

Margolies, Edward. *Native Sons: A Critical Study of Twentieth Century Negro American Authors*. Philadelphia: Lippincott, 1968.

Mitchell, Loften. *Black Drama: The Story of the American Negro in the Theatre*. New York: Hawthorne Books, 1967.

"The Negro in Literature: The Current Scene." *Phylon* (Negro writers issue) XI (1950), 297–374.

Patterson, Lindsay, ed. *Black Theatre: A Twentieth Century Collection of the Works of Its Best Playwrights*. New York: Dodd, Mead, 1971.

Pool, Rosey E., ed. *Beyond the Blues: New Poems by American Negroes*. Lympne, Kent, England: Hand and Flower, 1962.

Randall, Dudley, ed. *The Black Poets*. New York: Bantam, 1971 (also published by Broadside).

Redding, Saunders. *To Make a Poet Black*. Chapel Hill, North Carolina: University of North Carolina Press, 1939.

Richardson, Willis, ed. *Plays and Pageants from the Life of the Negro*. Washington, D.C.: Associated Publishers, 1930 (anthology).

Shuman, R. Baird, ed. *Nine Black Poets*. Durham, North Carolina: Moore, 1968.

Starke, Catherine Juanita. *Black Portraiture in American Fiction, Stock Characters, Archetypes, and Individuals*. New York: Basic Books, Inc., 1971.

Turner, Darwin T. *Black American Literature*. Columbus, Ohio: Charles E. Merrill, 1969 (formerly three separate publications).

Watkins, Sylvester C. *Anthology of American Negro Literature*. New York: Random House, 1944.

White, Newman I. and Walter C. Jackson. *An Anthology of Verse by American Negroes*. Durham, North Carolina: Trinity College Press, 1924.

Woodson, Carter G. *Negro Orators and Their Orations*. Washington, D.C.: Associated Publishers, 1925.

Authors: Part I

W[illiam] E[dward] B[urghardt] Du Bois (1868–1963)

PRIMARY

BOOKS:

The Suppression of the African Slave Trade to the United States of America, 1638–1870 (Harvard Historical Series, no. 1). New York, London, etc.: Longmans, Green and Co., 1896; New York: Russell and Russell, 1965;

New York: Schocken, 1969; New York: Dover, 1970; Baton Rouge, Louisiana: Louisiana State University Press, 1969.

The Philadelphia Negro: A Social Study (Series in Political Economy and Public Law, XLV). Philadelphia: published for the University of Pennsylvania, 1899 (with a special report on domestic service by Isabel Eaton).

The Souls of Black Folk: Essays and Sketches. Chicago: A. C. McClurg, 1903; A. C. McClurg, 1929, 1931; New York: Blue Heron Press, 1953.

John Brown. Philadelphia: George W. Jacobs, 1909; New York: International Publishers, 1962; Northbrook, Illinois: Metro Books, 1972 (foreword by Blyden Jackson).

The Quest of the Silver Fleece. Chicago: A. C. McClurg, 1911; Miami, Florida: Mnemosyne Publishing Co., 1969; New York: Negro Universities Press, 1969; College Park, Maryland: McGrath, 1969.

Darkwater: Voices from Within the Veil. New York: Harcourt, Brace and Howe, 1920; New York: Schocken Books, 1969; New York: AMS Press, 1969.

The Gift of Black Folk: The Negroes in the Making of America. Boston: Stratford, 1924; New York: Washington Square, 1970; New York: AMS Press, 1971.

Dark Princess: A Romance. New York: Harcourt, Brace, 1928.

Black Reconstruction in America, 1860–1880. New York: Harcourt, Brace, 1935; New York: Meridian Books, 1964.

Black Folk, Then and Now: An Essay in the History and Sociology of the Negro Race. New York: Holt, 1939; New York: Octagon Books, 1970.

Dusk of Dawn: An Essay Toward an Autobiography of a Race Concept. New York: Harcourt, Brace, 1940; New York: Schocken Books, 1968.

With Guy B. Johnson. *Encyclopedia of the Negro: Preparatory Volume with Reference Lists and Reports.* New York: Phelps-Stokes Fund, 1945.

The Ordeal of Mansart. New York: Mainstream, 1957 (volume I of *The Black Flame, A Trilogy;* novel).

Mansart Builds a School. New York: Mainstream, 1959 (volume II of *The Black Flame, A Trilogy;* novel).

Worlds of Color. New York: Mainstream, 1961 (volume III of *The Black Flame, A Trilogy,* novel).

An ABC of Color. Selections from Over a Half Century of the Writings of W. E. B. Du Bois. Berlin, German Democratic Republic: Seven Seas, 1963.

ARTICLES:

"The Crisis." *The Crisis,* I (November, 1910), 10–11.

"The Negro in Literature and Art." *Annals of the American Academy of Political and Social Science,* XLIX (September, 1913), 233–237.

"Returning Soldiers." *The Crisis,* XVII (May, 1919), 14.

"Marcus Garvey." *The Crisis,* XXI (December, 1920), 58–60.

With Alain Locke. "The Younger Literary Movement." *The Crisis,* XXVII (February, 1924), 161–163.

"Race Relations in the United States: 1917–1947." *Phylon,* IX (Third Quarter, 1948), 234–246.

"The Negro and Socialism," in *Toward a Socialist America,* Helen Alfred, ed. New York: Pearce Publications, 1958, pp. 178–191.

"Africa and the French Revolution." *Freedomways,* I (Summer, 1961), 136–151.
"The United States and the Negro." *Freedomways,* I (Spring, 1961), 11–19.
"Conference of Encyclopedia Africana." *Freedomways,* III, no. 1 (Winter, 1963), 28–30.
"Behold the Land." *Freedomways,* IV, no. 1 (Winter, 1964), 8–15.
"The African Roots of War." *Freedomways,* VIII, no. 1 (Winter, 1968), 12–22.
"The American Negro and the Darker World." *Freedomways,* VIII, no. 3 (Summer, 1968), 245–250.

MISCELLANEOUS:

"The American Negro and the Darker World." *Freedomways,* VIII, no. 3 (Summer, 1969), 245–251 (speech delivered on second anniversary of Bandung Conference, April 30, 1957).
"Ghana Calls—a Poem." *Freedomways,* II, no. 1 (Winter, 1962), 71–74.
With Saunders Redding. "Introduction and Preface to *Souls of Black Folk.*" *Freedomways,* II, no. 2 (Spring, 1962), 161–166.
"The Last Message of Dr. W. E. B. Du Bois to the World, Given Verbatim." *Journal of Negro History,* XLIX (April, 1964), 145.
"Selected Poems of W. E. B. Du Bois." *Freedomways,* V, no. 1 (Winter, 1965), 88–102.
"Some Unpublished Writings of W. E. B. Du Bois." *Freedomways* (Special Issue), V, no. 1 (Winter, 1965), 103–128 (Herbert Aptheker, ed.).

SECONDARY

Aptheker, Herbert. "Du Bois as Historian." *Negro History Bulletin,* XXI (April, 1968), 6–16.
Broderick, Frances L. *W. E. B. Du Bois, Negro Leader in a Time of Crisis.* Stanford, California: Stanford University Press, 1959.
Freedomways: W. E. B. Du Bois Memorial Issue. V, no. 1 (Winter, 1965).
Gilbert, Albert C. "Architect of Men's Future—W. E. B. Du Bois." *Freedomways,* II (Winter, 1962), 33–38.
Golden, L. Hanga and Ov. Melikian. "William E. B. Du Bois: Scientist and Public Figure." *Journal of Human Relations,* XIV (First Quarter, 1966), 156–168.
Graham, Shirley. *His Day Is Marching On; a Memoir on W. E. B. Du Bois.* Philadelphia: Lippincott, 1971.
Hansberry, William Leo. "W. E. B. Du Bois' Influence on African History." *Freedomways,* V, no. 1 (Winter, 1965), 73–87.
Harding, Vincent. "W. E. B. Du Bois and the Black Messianic Vision." *Freedomways,* IX (Winter, 1969), 44–58.
Harding, Vincent. "*Our* President's Trip to Peking: Du Bois in China, 1959." *Black World,* XXI, no. 7 (May, 1972), 13–21, 46–47.
Henderson, Lenneal J., Jr. "W. E. B. Du Bois: Black Scholar and Prophet." *Black Scholar,* I (January/February, 1970), 48–57.
Holmes, Eugene C. "W. E. B. Du Bois—Philosopher." *Freedomways,* V, no. 1 (Winter, 1965), 41–46.

Hunton, W. Alphaeus, "W. E. B. Du Bois—The Meaning of His Life." *Freedomways,* III, no. 4 (Fall, 1963), 490–495.

"The Problem of Color in the Twentieth Century: A Memorial to W. E. B. Du Bois." *Journal of Human Relations* (Special Issue), XIV (First Quarter, 1966).

Kaiser, Ernest. "A Selected Bibliography of the Published Writings of W. E. B. Du Bois." *Freedomways,* V, no. 1 (Winter, 1965), 207–213.

King, Martin Luther, Jr. "Honoring Dr. Du Bois." *Freedomways,* VII (Spring, 1968), 104–111 (speech on 100th birthday of Du Bois, International Cultural Evening in New York, February 23, 1968).

Kostelanetz, Richard. "Fictions for Negro Politics: The Neglected Novels of W. E. B. Du Bois." *Xavier University Studies,* VII, no. 2 (1968), 5–39.

Lacey, Leslie. *Cheer the Lonesome Traveler.* New York: Dial, 1970 (biography).

Logan, Rayford Whittingham, ed. *W. E. B. Du Bois: A Profile.* New York: Hill and Wang, 1971.

Meier, A. "From 'Conservative' to 'Radical': the Ideological Development of W. E. B. Du Bois, 1885–1905." *The Crisis,* LXVI (November, 1959), 527–536.

Middleton, William J. "Pan-Africanism: A Historical Analysis and Critique." *Black Scholar,* I (January/February, 1970), 58–64.

Moore, Richard B. "Du Bois and Pan Africa." *Freedomways,* V, no. 1 (Winter, 1965), 166–187.

Ofari, Earl. "W. E. B. Du Bois and Black Power." *Black World,* XIX, no. 10 (August, 1970), 26–28.

Rudwick, Elliott M. "W. E. B. Du Bois and the Universal Races Congress of 1911." *Phylon,* XX, no. 4 (Winter, 1959), 372–378.

Rudwick, Elliott M. *W. E. B. Du Bois, Propagandist of the Negro Protest.* New York: Atheneum, 1968.

Savory, Jerold J. "The Rending of the Veil in W. E. B. Du Bois's *The Souls of Black Folk." CLA Journal,* XV, no. 3 (March, 1972), 334–337.

Sheppard, Wheeler. *Mistakes of Dr. W. E. B. Du Bois; Being the Answer to Dr. W. E. B. Du Bois' Attack Upon the Honorable Marcus Garvey.* Pittsburgh: Goldenwood Print, 1921.

Walden, Daniel, ed. *W. E. B. Du Bois, The Crisis Writings.* Fawcett Premier, p. 567.

Walden, Daniel and Kenneth Wylie. "W. E. B. Du Bois: Pan-Africanism's Intellectual Father." *Journal of Human Relations,* XIV (First Quarter, 1966), 28–41.

James Weldon Johnson (1871–1938)

PRIMARY

BOOKS:

The Autobiography of an Ex-Coloured Man. Boston: Sherman, French, 1912; New York and London: Knopf, 1927; Garden City, New York: Garden City, 1927; New York: Knopf, 1966 (novel).

Fifty Years and Other Poems. Boston: Cornhill, 1917.

Ed., *The Book of American Negro Poetry, with an Essay on the Negro's Creative Genius.* New York: Harcourt, Brace, 1922; Rev. ed., 1931.

Ed., *The Book of American Negro Spirituals.* New York: Viking, 1925 (musical arrangements by J. Rosamond Johnson, additional numbers by Lawrence Brown).

Ed., *The Second Book of Negro Spirituals.* New York: Viking, 1926 (musical arrangements by J. Rosamond Johnson).

God's Trombones: Seven Negro Sermons in Verse. New York: Viking, 1927.

Native African Races and Culture. The Trustees of the John F. Slater Fund. Occasional papers, no. 25. Charlottesville, Virginia, 1927 (pamphlet).

Black Manhattan. New York: Knopf, 1930; New York: Arno, 1968.

Along This Way; the Autobiography of James Weldon Johnson. New York: Viking, 1933, 1968.

Negro Americans, What Now? New York: Viking, 1934, 1938.

Saint Peter Relates an Incident of the Resurrection Day. Selected Poems. New York: Viking, 1930; 1935.

Ed. with J. Rosamond Johnson. *The Books of American Negro Spirituals.* New York: Viking, 1940 (contains *The Book of American Negro Spirituals,* 1925, and *The Second Book of Negro Spirituals,* 1926).

MISCELLANEOUS:

James Weldon Johnson Collection. Yale University, New Haven, Connecticut.

ARTICLES:

"Race Prejudice and the Negro Artist." *Harper's,* CLVII (November, 1928), 769–776.

"The Dilemma of the Negro Author." *American Mercury,* XV (December, 1928), 477–481.

"Negro Authors and Their Publishers." *The Crisis,* XXXVI (July, 1929), 228–229.

SECONDARY

Adelman, Lynn. "A Study of James Weldon Johnson." *Journal of Negro History,* LII (January, 1967), 128–145.

Aptheker, H. "DuBois on James Weldon Johnson." *Journal of Negro History,* LII (July, 1967), 224–227.

Avery, William A. "James Weldon Johnson: American Negro of Distinction." *School and Society,* XVIII (September 3, 1968), 291–294.

Bone, Robert A. *The Negro Novelist in America.* Rev. ed. New Haven, Connecticut: Yale University Press, 1965.

Bronz, Stephen H. *Roots of Negro Racial Consciousness; the 1920's: Three Harlem Renaissance Authors.* New York: Libra, 1964.

Collier, Eugenia W. "James Weldon Johnson: Mirror of Change." *Phylon,* XXI (Winter, 1960), 351–359.

Gloster, Hugh M. *Negro Voices in American Fiction.* Chapel Hill, North Carolina: University of North Carolina Press, 1948.

Claude McKay (1890–1948)

PRIMARY

POETRY COLLECTIONS:

Constab Ballads. London: Watts and Co., 1912.

Songs from Jamaica. London: Augener Ltd., 1912.

Spring in New Hampshire and Other Poems. London: Grant Richard, 1920.

Harlem Shadows. New York: Harcourt, Brace, 1922.

Selected Poems. New York: Bookman, 1953; New York: Harcourt, Brace and Jovanovich, 1969.

Songs of Jamaica. Miami, Florida: Mnemosyne, 1969 (introduction by Walter Jekyll).

The Dialect Poetry of Claude McKay. Freeport, New York: Books for Libraries, 1972.

BOOKS AND NOVELS:

Home to Harlem. New York and London: Harper and Bros., 1928 (novel).

Banjo, a Story Without a Plot. New York and London: Harper and Bros., 1929.

Gingertown. New York and London: Harper and Bros., 1932; Freeport, New York: Books for Libraries, 1972 (short stories).

Banana Bottom. New York and London: Harper and Bros., 1933; Chatham, New Jersey: Chatham Bookseller, 1970; New York: Harcourt, Brace, and Jovanovich, 1970 (novel).

A Long Way from Home. New York: Lee Furman, 1937; New York: Harcourt, Brace, and World, 1970 (introduction by St. Clair Drake); New York: Arno Press, 1969; New York: Harcourt, Brace and Jovanovich, 1970 (autobiography).

Harlem: Negro Metropolis. New York: E. P. Dutton, 1940; New York: Harcourt, Brace and Jovanovich, 1972.

ARTICLES:

"Soviet Russia and the Negro." *The Crisis,* XXVII (December, 1923), 61–65; XXVIII (January, 1924), 114–118.

"Why I Became a Catholic." *Ebony,* I (March, 1946), 32.

"Boyhood in Jamaica." *Phylon,* XIII (Second Quarter, 1953), 134–145.

UNPUBLISHED WRITINGS AND MISCELLANEOUS WORKS:

"Right Turn to Catholicism." Schomburg Collection, New York Public Library (unpublished).

My Green Hills of Jamaica. Schomburg Collection, New York Public Library (written in the mid-1940's) unpublished.

"An Unpublished Letter from Claude McKay, Poet and Littérateur to Margaret Marshall, Editor of *The Nation,* May 23, 1947." *Negro History Bulletin,* XXXI (April, 1968), 10–11.

SECONDARY

Barksdale, Richard K. "Symbolism and Irony in McKay's *Home to Harlem.*" *CLA Journal,* XI, no. 3 (March, 1972), 338–344.

Bone, Robert A. *The Negro Novel in America.* Rev. ed. New Haven, Connecticut: Yale University Press, 1965.

Bronz, Stephen, *Roots of Negro Consciousness; the 1920's: Three Harlem Renaissance Authors.* New York: Libra, 1964.

Cartey, Wilfred. "Four Shadows of Harlem." *Negro Digest,* XVIII (August, 1969), 22–25, 83–91.

Collier, Eugenia W. "The Four-Way Dilemma of Claude McKay." *CLA Journal,* XV, no. 3 (March, 1972), 345–353.

Cooper, Wayne, "Claude McKay and the New Negro of the 1920's." *Phylon,* XXV, no. 3 (Fall, 1964), 297–306.

Emanuel, James A. "The Future of Negro Poetry: A Challenge for Critics," in *Black Expression,* Addison Gayle, Jr., ed. New York: Weybright and Talley, 1969, 100–109 (contains analysis of McKay's "The White House").

Gloster, Hugh M. *Negro Voices in American Fiction.* Chapel Hill, North Carolina: University of North Carolina Press, 1948.

Huggins, Nathan I. *Harlem Renaissance.* New York: Oxford University Press, 1971.

Jackson, Miles M. "Literary History: Documentary Sidelights—James Weldon Johnson and Claude McKay." *Negro Digest,* XVII (June, 1968), 25–29.

Kent, George E. "The Soulful Way of Claude McKay." *Black World,* XX (November, 1970), 37–51.

Margolies, Edward. *Native Sons.* New York: Lippincott, 1968.

Smith, Robert A. "Claude McKay: An Essay in Criticism." *Phylon,* IX (Third Quarter, 1948), 270–273.

Tolson, Melvin B. "Claude McKay's Art." *Poetry,* LXXXIII (February, 1954), 287–290.

Turpin, Waters E. "Four Short Fiction Writers of the Harlem Renaissance —Their Legacy of Achievement." *CLA Journal,* XI, no. 1 (September, 1967), 59–72.

Jean Toomer (1894–1967)

PRIMARY

Cane. New York: Boni and Liveright, 1923; New York: University Place Press, 1967; New York: Harper and Row, 1968.

With Ellsworth Huntington, Whiting Williams and others. *Problems of Civilization.* New York: D. Van Nostrand, 1929 ("Race Problems and Modern Society," by Toomer).

Essentials, by Jean Toomer. Definitions and Aphorisms. Private ed. Chicago: Lakeside Press, 1931.

The Flavor of Man. Philadelphia: Young Friends Movement of the Philadelphia Yearly Meetings, 1949 (William Penn Lecture, 1949).

SECONDARY

Bell, Bernard. "A Key to the Poems in 'Cane'." *CLA Journal,* XIV, no. 3 (March, 1971), 251–258.

Bone, Robert A. *The Negro Novel in America.* Rev. ed. New Haven, Connecticut: Yale University Press, 1965.

Bontemps, Arna. "The Harlem Renaissance." *Saturday Review,* XXX (March 22, 1947), 12–13, 44.

Bontemps, Arna. Introduction, in *Cane.* Third Ed. New York: Harper and Row, 1969.

Bontemps, Arna. "The Negro Renaissance: Jean Toomer and the Harlem Writers of the 1920's" in Hill, Herbert, *Anger and Beyond: The Negro Writer in the United States.* New York: Harper and Row, 1966, 20–36.

Chase, Patricia. "The Women in 'Cane'." *CLA Journal,* XIV, no. 3 (March, 1971), 259–273.

Duncan, Bowie. "Jean Toomer's 'Cane': A Modern Black Oracle." *CLA Journal,* XV, no. 3 (March, 1972), 323–333.

Durham, Frank, comp. *The Merrill Studies in Cane.* Columbus, Ohio: Merrill, 1971.

Farrison, W. Edward. "Jean Toomer's 'Cane' Again." *CLA Journal,* XV, no. 3 (March, 1972), 295–302.

Ford, Nick Aaron. *Black Insights.* Waltham, Massachusetts: Ginn, 1971.

Fullinwider, S. P. "Jean Toomer, Lost Generation, or Negro Renaissance?" *Phylon,* XXVII (Fourth Quarter, 1966), 396–403.

Gloster, Hugh M. *Negro Voices in American Fiction.* Chapel Hill, North Carolina: University of North Carolina Press, 1948.

Huggins, Nathan J. *The Harlem Renaissance.* New York: Oxford, 1971.

Lieber, Todd. "Design and Movement in 'Cane'." *CLA Journal,* XII, no. I (September, 1969), 35–50.

Locke, Alain. *Four Negro Poets.* New York: Simon and Schuster, 1927.

Locke, Alain. "From *Native Son* to *Invisible Man:* A Review of the Literature of the Negro for 1952." *Phylon,* XIV, no. 1 (First Quarter, 1953), 34–44.

Margolies, Edward. *Native Sons.* New York: Lippincott, 1968.

Mason, Clifford, "Jean Toomer's Black Authenticity." *Black World,* XX, no. 1 (November, 1970), 70–76.

Miller, Ruth. *Blackamerican Literature.* Beverly Hills, California: Glencoe, 1971.

Munson, Gorham B. "The Significance of Jean Toomer." *Opportunity,* X, no. 8 (August, 1932), 252.

Redding, Saunders. *To Make a Poet Black.* Chapel Hill, North Carolina: University of North Carolina Press, 1939.

Waldron, Edward E. "The Search for Identity in Jean Toomer's 'Esther'." *CLA Journal,* XIV, no. 3 (March, 1971), 277–280.

Watkins, Patricia. "Is There a Unifying Theme in 'Cane'?" *CLA Journal,* XV, no. 3 (March, 1972), 303–305.

Westerfield, Hargis. "Jean Toomer's 'Fern': A Mythical Dimension." *CLA Journal,* XIV, no. 3 (March, 1971), 303–305.

Alain LeRoy Locke (1886–1954)

BOOKS AND PAMPHLETS:

Syllabus of an Extension Course of Lectures on Race Contacts and Inter-racial Relations: a Study on the Theory and Practice. Washington, D.C.:

Printed by A. S. Pindleton under the auspices of the NAACP of Howard University and the Social Science Club, 1916 (pamphlet).

Ed. *The New Negro; an Interpretation.* New York: Albert and Charles Boni 1925; New York: Johnson Reprint Corp., 1968; New York: Arno, 1968.

Ed. with Montgomery Gregory. *Plays of Negro Life; Source-Book of Native American Drama.* New York and London: Harper and Brothers, 1927; Westport, Connecticut: Negro University Press, 1970.

Four Negro Poets. New York: Simon and Schuster, 1927.

A Decade of Negro Self Expression. Charlottesville, Virginia: Trustees of the John F. Slater Fund, 1928 (pamphlet).

The Negro in America. Chicago: American Library Association, 1933.

The Negro Art: Past and Present. Washington, D.C.: Associates in Negro Folk Education, 1936 (Bronze Booklet No. 3).

The Negro and His Music. Washington, D.C.: Associates in Negro Folk Education, 1936 (Bronze Booklet No. 2).

Ed. *The Negro in Art; A Pictorial Record of the Negro Artist and of the Negro Theme in Art.* Washington, D.C.: Associates in Negro Folk Education, 1940; Chicago; Afro-American Press, 1969.

Ed. with Bernhard J. Stern. *When Peoples Meet; A Study in Race and Culture Contacts.* New York: Committee on Workshops, Progressive Education Association, 1942; rev. ed. New York: Hinds, Hayden and Eldridge, 1946.

Le Rôle du Nègre dans la Culture des Amériques. Port-au-Prince, Haiti. Printed in the United States, 1943.

Diversity Within National Unity. Washington, D.C.: National Council for Social Studies, 1945 (pamphlet).

ARTICLES:

"Oxford Contrasts." *Independent,* LXVII (July 15, 1909), 139–142.

"The American Temperament." *North American Review,* XC (August, 1911), 262–270.

"Negro Poets in the United States," in *Anthology of Magazine Verse for 1913–29 and Yearbook of American Poetry,* by William Stanley Braithwaite. New York: Sully and Co., 1913, 141–151.

"Portrait." *Current History Magazine of the New York Times,* XVIII (June, 1923), 413.

"Roland Hayes: An Appreciation." *Opportunity,* I (December, 1923), 350–351.

"The Colonial Literature of France." *Opportunity,* I (November, 1923), 331–342.

"Apropos of Africa." *Opportunity,* II (February, 1924), 37–40.

"The Negro Speaks for Himself." *Survey,* LII (April, 15, 1924), 71–72.

"A Note on African Art." *Opportunity,* II (May, 1924), 134–140.

"French Colonial Policies (Open Letter to Rene Maran)." *Opportunity,* II (September, 1924), 261–263.

"Enter the New Negro." *Survey,* LIII (March 1, 1925), 631–634.

"Backstage on English Imperialism." *Opportunity,* III (April, 1925), 112–114.

"Command of the Spirit." *Southern Workman,* LIV (July, 1925), 295–296.

"Art of August Mambour." *Opportunity,* III (August, 1925), 240.

"Negro Education Bids for Par." *Survey,* LIV (September 1, 1925), 567–570.

"Technical Study of the Spirituals." *Opportunity,* III (November, 1925), 331–332.

"More of the Negro in Art." *Opportunity,* III (December, 1925), 363–366.

"Nana Amoah: An African Statesman." *Survey,* LV (January, 1926), 434–435.

"The Negro and the American Stage." *Theatre Arts Magazine,* X (February, 1926), 112–120.

"Drama of Negro Life." *Theatre Arts Magazine,* X (February, 1926), 701–706.

"Collection of Congo Art." *Arts,* XI (February, 1927), 60–70.

"The Negro and the American Theatre," in *Theatre,* by Edith Isaacs, ed. Boston: Little Brown and Co., 1927, 290–303.

"Boxed Compass of Our Race Relations." *Southern Workman* (Reprint from *Survey,* January, 1929), LVIII (Feb., 1929), 51–56.

"The Negro Contribution to America." *World Tomorrow,* XII (June, 1929), 255–257.

"Folk Values in a New Medium," in *Folksay: A Regional Miscellany,* with Sterling Brown, Benjamin Botkin, ed. Vol. III. Norman, Oklahoma: University of Oklahoma Press, 1930, 340–345.

"The American Negroes as Artists." *American Magazine of Art,* XXII (September, 1931), 210–220.

"Negro in Art." Association of *American Colleges Bulletin,* XVII (November, 1931), 359–364; also in *Christian Education,* X (November, 1931), 98–103.

"Minorities and the Social Mind." *Progressive Education,* XII (March, 1935), 141–146.

"African Art: Classic Style." *American Magazine of Art,* XXVIII (May, 1935), 270–278.

"Dilemma of Segregation." *Journal of Negro Education,* IV (July, 1935), 406–411.

"Values and Imperatives," in *American Philosophy Today and Tomorrow,* Horace Kallen and Sidney Hook, eds. New York: Furman Co., 1935, 313–333.

"Dark Weather-Vane." *Survey Graphic,* XXV (August, 1936), 457–462.

"Martyrdom to Glad Music: The Irony of Black Patriotism." *Opportunity,* XIV (December, 1936), 38.

"Out of Africa Something New." *Opportunity,* XV (November, 1938), 342.

"Negro's Contribution to America." *Journal of Negro Education,* VIII (January, 1939), 521–529.

Baltimore Museum of Art. *Contemporary Art on Exhibition for February 3–19, 1939* (foreword).

"With Science as His Shield the Educator Must Bridge the Great Divides." *Frontiers of Democracy,* VI (April, 1940), 208–210.

"The Negro in Fiction and Fact," in *Fighting Words,* Donald Ogden Stewart, ed. New York: Harcourt, Brace, 1940, 75–78.

"Of Native Sons: Real and Otherwise." *Opportunity,* XIX (January, 1941), 4–8; XIX (February, 1941), 48–53.

"Chicago's New Southside Art Center." *Magazine of Art,* XXXIV (August, 1941), 370–374.

"Broadway and the Negro Drama." *Theatre Arts.* XXV (October, 1941), 745–752.

Douglass, Frederick. *Life and Times of Frederick Douglass Written for the Frederick Douglass Historical and Cultural League of the First Appearance in the Cause of Emancipation.* New York: Pathway Press, 1941 (foreword).

"Democracy Faces a World Order." *Harvard Educational Review,* XII (March, 1942), 121–128.

"Color: Unfinished Business of Democracy." *Survey Graphic,* XXXI (November, 1942), 454–459.

"Pluralism and Intellectual Democracy," in *Conference on Science, Philosophy, and Religion, Second Symposium.* New York: The Conference, 1942, 196–212.

"Who and What Is a Negro." *Opportunity,* XX (February, 1943), 36–40.

"Understanding World Culture." *Educational Leadership,* I (March, 1944), 381–382.

"The Negro in the Three Americas." *Journal of Negro Education,* XIII (1944), 7–18.

"Whither Race Relations." *Journal of Negro Education,* XIII (1944) 398–406.

SECONDARY

"Bahaism." Columbia Encyclopedia. New York: Columbia University Press, 1950, 136.

Braithwaite, William Stanley. "Alain Locke's Relationship to the Negro in American Literature" (an address delivered in honor of Alain Locke. Unpublished. Howard University Library, Moorland Room).

Brewer, William. "Alain Locke." *Negro History Bulletin,* XVIII (November, 1954), 26–32.

Butcher, Margaret Just. *The Negro in American Culture.* New York: Knopf, 1956.

Current Biography. New York: H. W. Wilson Company, 1944.

Fauset, Arthur Huff. *For Freedom: A Biographical Story of the American Negro.* Philadelphia, Pennsylvania: Franklin Publishing and Supply Company, 1927.

Fennel, Robert. "From Cain's Other Side; An Informal View of Alain Locke." *Recapit,* I (February, 1959), 1–3.

"Goodbye, Messers Chips," *Time,* LXI (June 29, 1953), 68.

Holmes, Eugene Clay. "Alain Locke—Philosopher, Critic, Spokesman." *The Journal of Philosophy,* LIV, no. 5, (February 28, 1957), 113–118.

Holmes, Eugene Clay. "Alain LeRoy Locke: A Sketch." *Phylon* (First Quarter, 1959).

Holmes, Eugene Clay. "The Legacy of Alain Locke." *Freedomways,* III (Summer, 1963), 293–306.

Hughes, Langston. *Pictorial History of Negroes in America.* New York: Crown, 1956.

Midgette, Lillian Avon. "A Bio-bibliography of Alain LeRoy Locke." Atlanta, Georgia: Atlanta University, 1963 (M. A. thesis).

Negro Yearbook. Tuskegee, Alabama: Department of Records and Research, Tuskegee Institute, 1947.

Seifert, Charles C. *The Negro's or Ethiopian's Contributions to Art.* New York: The Ethiopian Historical Publishing Company, 1938.
Twentieth Century Authors: Biographical Dictionary of Modern Literature. New York: H. W. Wilson Company, 1942.
Who's Who in America. Chicago: Marquis, 1954–1955.
Who's Who in Colored America. 6th Ed. New York: Thomas Yenser, 1941–1944.
Work, Monroe Nathan. *A Bibliography of the Negro in Africa and America.* New York: H. W. Wilson Company, 1928.

Langston Hughes (1902–1967)

PRIMARY

POETRY:

The Weary Blues. New York: Knopf, 1926, 1929.
Fine Clothes to the Jew. New York: Knopf, 1927.
The Dream Keeper and Other Poems. New York: Knopf, 1932.
Shakespeare in Harlem. New York: Knopf, 1942.
Fields of Wonder. New York: Knopf, 1947.
One-Way Ticket. New York: Knopf, 1949.
Montage of a Dream Deferred. New York: Henry Holt, 1951.
Selected Poems of Langston Hughes. New York: Knopf, 1959.
Ask Your Mama: 12 Moods for Jazz. New York: Knopf, 1961.
The Panther and the Lash; Poems of Our Times. New York: Knopf, 1967.

NOVELS:

Not Without Laughter. New York and London: Knopf, 1930.
Simple Speaks His Mind. New York: Simon and Schuster, 1950.
Simple Takes a Wife. New York: Simon and Schuster, 1953.
Simple Stakes a Claim. New York: Rinehart, 1957.
Tambourines to Glory. New York: John Day Co., 1958.
Simple's Uncle Sam. New York: Hill and Wang, 1965.

SHORT STORIES:

The Ways of White Folks. New York: Knopf, 1934.
Laughing to Keep from Crying. New York: Henry Holt, 1952.
Something in Common, and Other Stories. New York: Hill and Wang, 1963.

PLAYS:

Five Plays by Langston Hughes. Webster Smalley, ed. Bloomington: Indiana University Press, 1963.

SECONDARY

Allen, Samuel W. "*Negritude* and Its Relevance to the American Negro Writer," in *The American Negro Writer and His Roots.* New York: American Society of African Culture, 1960, 8–20.

Babb, Inez Johnson, "Bibliography of Langston Hughes, Negro Poet." (unpublished Master's thesis, Pratt Institute Library School, 1947).

Barton, Rebecca. *Witnesses for Freedom*. New York: Harper, 1948.

Bone, Robert A. *The Negro Novel in America*. Rev. ed. New Haven, Connecticut: Yale University Press, 1965.

Bontemps, Arna. "The Harlem Renaissance." *Saturday Review of Literature*, XXX (March 22, 1947), 12–13, 44.

Bontemps, Arna. "Negro Poets, Then and Now." *Phylon*, XI (Fourth Quarter, 1950), 355–360.

Bontemps, Arna. "Langston Hughes: He Spoke of Rivers." *Freedomways*, VIII (Spring, 1968), 140–143.

Brawley, Benjamin. *The Negro Genius*. New York: Dodd, Mead, 1937.

Brooks, A. Russell. "The Comic Spirit and the Negro's New Look." *CLA Journal*, VI (September, 1962), 35–43.

Brown, Sterling, Arthur P. Davis, and Ulysses Lee, eds. *The Negro Caravan*. New York: Dryden, 1941.

Burroughs, Margaret. "Langston Hughes Lives!" *Negro Digest*, XVI (September, 1967), 59–60.

Chapman, Abraham. "The Harlem Renaissance in Literary History." *CLA Journal*, XI (September, 1967), 38–58.

Clarke, John Henrik. "Langston Hughes and Jesse B. Semple." *Freedomways*, VIII (Spring, 1968), 167–169.

Cook, Mercer. "President Senghor's Visit: A Tale of Five Cities." *African Forum*, II (Winter, 1967), 74–86.

Davis, Arthur P. "The Harlem of Langston Hughes' Poetry." *Phylon*, XIII (Fourth Quarter, 1952), 276–286.

Davis, Arthur P. "Jesse B. Semple: Negro American." *Phylon*, XV (First Quarter, 1954), 21–28.

Davis, Arthur P. "The Tragic Mulatto Theme in Six Works of Langston Hughes." *Phylon*, XVI (Fourth Quarter, 1955), 195–204.

Davis, Arthur P. "Integration and Race Literature." *Phylon*, XVII (Second Quarter, 1956), 141–146.

Davis, Arthur P. "Langston Hughes: Cool Poet." *CLA Journal*, XI, no. 4 (June, 1968).

Dickinson, Donald C. *A Bio-Bibliography of Langston Hughes, 1902–1967*. Hamden, Connecticut: Archon Books, The Shoe String Press, 1967.

Emanuel, James A. "Langston Hughes' First Short Story: 'Mary Winosky.'" *Phylon*, XXII (Third Quarter, 1961), 267–272.

Emanuel, James A. "The Short Stories of Langston Hughes." (unpublished Ph.D. dissertation, Columbia University, 1962).

Emanuel, James A. *Langston Hughes*. New York: Twayne, 1967.

Emanuel, James A. "'Soul' in the Works of Langston Hughes." *Negro Digest*, XVI (September, 1967), 25–30 (book excerpt).

Emanuel, James A. "'Bodies in the Moonlight': a Critical Analysis." *Readers and Writers*, I (November–January, 1968), 38–39, 42.

Emanuel, James A. "The Short Fiction of Langston Hughes." *Freedomways*, VIII (Spring, 1968), 170–178.

Emanuel, James A. "The Literary Experiments of Langston Hughes." *CLA Journal*, XI (June, 1968).

Embree, Edwin. *Thirteen Against the Odds*. New York: Viking, 1944.

Evans, Mari. "I Remember Langston." *Negro Digest*, XVI (September, 1967), 36.

Farrison, W. Edward. A Review of *Black Misery*, by Langston Hughes. *CLA Journal*, XIII, no. 1 (September, 1969), 87.

Fields, Julia. "The Green of Langston's Ivy." *Negro Digest*, XVI (September, 1967), 58–59.

Gayle, Addison. "Langston Hughes: a Simple Commentary." *Negro Digest*, XVI (September, 1967), 53–57.

Gloster, Hugh M. *Negro Voices in American Fiction*. Chapel Hill, North Carolina: University of North Carolina Press, 1948.

Hentoff, Nat. "Langston Hughes, He Found Poetry in the Blues." *Mayfair* (August, 1958), 26–27.

Holmes, Eugene C. "Langston Hughes: Philosopher-Poet." *Freedomways*, VIII (Spring, 1968), 144–151.

Hudson, Theodore R. "Langston Hughes' Last Volume of Verse." *CLA Journal*, XI (June, 1968).

Isaacs, Harold. "Five Writers and Their African Ancestors." *Phylon*, XXI (Third Quarter, 1960), 247–254.

Jackson, Blyden. "A Word About Simple." *CLA Journal*, XI (June, 1968).

Jackson, Blyden. "The Negro's Image of the Universe as Reflected in His Fiction." *CLA Journal*, IV (September, 1960), 22–31.

Jackson, Blyden. "A Golden Mean for the Negro Novel." *CLA Journal*, III (December, 1959), 81–87.

Johnson, James Weldon, ed. *The Book of American Negro Poetry*. New York: Harcourt, Brace, 1931.

Jones, Harry L. "A Danish Tribute to Langston Hughes." *CLA Journal*, XI (June, 1968).

Kaiser, Ernest. "Selected Bibliography of the Published Writings of Langston Hughes." *Freedomways*, VIII (Spring, 1968), 185–191.

Kemp, Stella. "Langston Hughes Speaks to Young Writers." *Opportunity*, XXIV (April, 1946), 73.

Kinnamon, Keneth. "The Man Who Created Simple." *Nation*, CCV (December 4, 1967), 599–601.

Kramer, Aaron. "Robert Burns and Langston Hughes." *Freedomways*, VIII (Spring, 1968), 659–601.

Loveman, A. "Anisfeld-Wolf Awards." *Saturday Review*, XXX, no. 7 (April 17, 1954), 20.

MacLeod, Norman. "The Poetry and Argument of Langston Hughes." *The Crisis*, XLV (November, 1938), 358–359.

Matheus, John F. "Langston Hughes as Translator." *CLA Journal*, XI (June, 1968).

Mayfield, Julian. "Langston." *Negro Digest*, XVI (September, 1967), 34–35.

Nichols, Lewis. "Langston Hughes Describes the Genesis of His *Tambourines to Glory*." *New York Times*, section 2 (October 27, 1963), 3.

O'Daniel, Therman B. "A Langston Hughes Bibliography." *CLA Bulletin*, VII (Spring, 1951), 12–13.

O'Daniel, Therman B. "Lincoln's Man of Letters." *Lincoln University Bulletin*, LXVII, no. 2 (Langston Hughes Issue, 1964), 9–12.

O'Daniel, Therman B. (ed.) *Langston Hughes, Black Genius*. New York: William Morrow, 1971.

Ovington, Mary White. *Portraits in Color*. New York: Viking, 1927.

Parker, John W. "Tomorrow in the Writing of Langston Hughes." *College English*, X (May, 1949), 438–441.

Patterson, Lindsay. "Langston Hughes—An Inspirer of Young Writers." *Freedomways*, VIII (Spring, 1968), 179–181.

Patterson, Louise Thompson. "With Langston Hughes in the USSR." *Freedomways*, VIII (Spring, 1968), 152–158.

Presley, James. "The American Dream of Langston Hughes." *Southwest Review*, XLVIII (Autumn, 1963), 380–386.

Redding, Saunders. *To Make a Poet Black*. Chapel Hill, North Carolina: University of North Carolina Press, 1939.

Shelton, Robert. "Theatre" ["*Black Nativity* at Philharmonic Hall"]. *Nation*, CXXVI (January 5, 1963), 20.

Spencer, T. J. and Clarence Rivers. "Langston Hughes: His Style and Optimism." *Drama Critique*, VII (Spring, 1964), 99–102.

Turner, Darwin T. "Langston Hughes as Playwright." *CLA Journal*. XI (June, 1968).

Turner, Darwin T. "*The Negro Novel in America:* In Rebuttal." *CLA Journal*, X (December, 1966), 122–134.

Turner, Darwin T. "The Negro Dramatist's Image of the Universe, 1920–1960." *CLA Journal*, V (December, 1961), 106–120.

Turpin, Waters E. "Four Short Fiction Writers of the Harlem Renaissance —Their Legacy of Achievement." *CLA Journal*, XI (September, 1967), 59–72.

Wagner, Jean. "Langston Hughes." *Information and Documents*, No. 135, Paris (January 15, 1961), 30–35.

Wagner, Jean. *Les Poètes Nègres des Etats-Unis*. Paris: Librairie Instra, 1963.

Wertz, I. J. "Langston Hughes: Profile." *Negro History Bulletin* (March, 1964), 146–147.

Countee Cullen (1903–1946)

PRIMARY

COLLECTED POEMS:

Color. New York and London: Harper, 1925; New York: Arno, 1969.

Copper Sun. New York and London: Harper, 1927.

Ed., *Caroling Dusk; an Anthology of Verse by Negro Poets*. New York and London: Harper, 1927.

The Ballad of the Brown Girl: an Old Ballad Retold. New York and London: Harper, 1927.

The Black Christ and Other Poems. New York and London: Harper, 1929.

The Medea and Some Poems. New York and London: Harper, 1935.

The Lost Zoo (A Rhyme for the Young, But Not Too Young), by Christopher Cat and Countee Cullen. New York and London: Harper, 1940; Chicago: Follett, 1969.

On These I Stand: an Anthology of the Best Poems of Countee Cullen. Selected by Himself and Including Six New Poems Never Before Published. New York and London: Harper, 1947.

SHORT FICTION:

"The Frenchman's Bath." *The Magpie*, XXI (November, 1921), 30–32.

"Invictus." *The Magpie*, XXI (October, 1921), 22.

"Modernized Myths." *The Magpie,* XXI (December, 1921), 15–17.
My Lives and How I Lost Them by Christopher Cat in Collaboration with Countee Cullen. New York and London: Harper, 1942.

MISCELLANEOUS PUBLICATIONS:

Introduction to *The House of Vanity,* by Frank Ankenbrand and Benjamin Issac. Philadelphia: Leibman, 1928 (book introduction).
One Way to Heaven. New York and London: Harper, 1932 (novel).
Letter, in *Writers Take Sides: Letters About the War in Spain from 418 American Authors.* New York League of American Writers, 1938, 17 (letter to the editor).
"Invocation." *PM* (October 28, 1943) (featuring the poem "Hillburn the Fair"—letter to the editor).
With Owen Dodson. "The Third Fourth of July: a One-Act Play." *Theatre Arts,* XXX (August, 1946), 488–493 (play).

WORDS TO MUSIC:

"Christus Natus Est." Flushing, New York: D. L. Schroeder, 1945 (a song for mixed voices by Charles Marsh).
"Clinton My Clinton." *The Magpie,* XXI (January, 1922), 14 (music by W. Samuels, arranged by L. F. West).
"The Grim Troubadour, Op. 45." New York: Carl Fisher, 1927 (music by Emerson Whithorne, using three poems by Cullen: "The Love Tree," "Lament," and "Hunger").
"Seven Choruses from *The Medea of Euripides.*" New York: Mercury Music Corp., 1942.
"Tryst." New York: Circle Blue Print Co., n.d. (music by Gene Bone and Howard Fenton from the poem "On Going").
"Saturday's Child." Boston: C. C. Birchard and Co., n.d. (music by Emerson Whithorne from the poems "Saturday's Child," "A Song of Praise," and "To One Who Said Me Nay").

SECONDARY

Allison, Madeline, ed. "The Horizon." *The Crisis,* XXIII (March, 1922), 219 (Cullen's activities at high school).
Allison, Madeline, ed. "The Horizon." *The Crisis,* XXIV (October, 1922), 272 (awards and activities up to Cullen's first year in college).
"Art and the Negro." Springfield, Illinois, *Register,* December 10, 1925.
Baldwin, James. "Rendezvous with Life: an Interview with Countee Cullen." *The Magpie,* XXVI (Winter, 1942), 19–21.
Bland, Edward. "Racial Bias and Negro Poetry." *Poetry,* LXIII (March, 1944), 328–329.
Bone, Robert A. *The Negro Novel in America.* Rev. ed. New Haven, Connecticut: Yale University Press, 1965.
Bontemps, Arna. "Countee Cullen, American Poet." *The People's Voice,* V (January 26, 1946), 52–53.
Bontemps, Arna. "The James Weldon Johnson Memorial Collection of Negro Arts and Letters." *Yale University Library Gazette,* XVIII (October, 1943), 19–26.
Bontemps, Arna. "The Harlem Renaissance." *Saturday Review,* XXX (March 22, 1947), 12–13, 44.

Brawley, Benjamin. "The Negro Literary Renaissance." *Southern Workman,* LVI (April, 1927), 181–182.

Bronz, Stephen A. *Roots of Racial Consciousness; the 1920's: Three Harlem Renaissance Authors.* New York: Libra, 1964.

Brown, Evelyn S. "Distinguished Achievement Recognized." *Southern Workman,* LVI (February, 1927), 85.

Brown, Sterling A. *Negro Poetry and Drama.* Washington, D.C.: Associates in Negro Folk Education, 1937.

Calverton, V. F. "The Negro's New Belligerent Attitude." *Current History,* XXX (September, 1929), 1084.

Calvin, Floyd J. "Countee Cullen Tells How He Writes." *Pittsburgh Courier* section 2, XVIII (June, 1927), 4.

Chamberlain, John. "The Negro as Writer." *The Bookman,* LXX (February, 1930), 609–610.

Clark, Margaret. "Overtones in Negro Poetry." *Interracial Review,* IX (July, 1936), 106.

Clark, Margaret. "The Voice of a Race." *Interracial Review,* IX (April, 1936), 58.

Collier, Eugenia W. "I Do Not Marvel, Countee Cullen." *CLA Journal,* XI (September, 1967), 73–87.

"Conclude Literary Shop Talk Tonight." Massachusetts, *Springfield Union,* VIII (May, 1928), 8.

"Countee Cullen." American Peoples Encyclopedia, 1953 edition, Volume 6, 604.

"Countee Cullen." Encyclopedia Americana, 1957 edition, Volume 8, 295.

Daniel, Walter C. "Countee Cullen as Literary Critic." *CLA Journal,* XIV, no. 3 (March, 1971), 281–290.

Davis, Arthur P. "The Alien-and-Exile Theme in Countee Cullen's Racial Poems." *Phylon,* XIV (Fourth Quarter, 1953), 390–400.

Dinger, Helen Josephine. "A Study of Countee Cullen." (unpublished Master's thesis, Columbia University, 1953).

Dodson, Owen. "Countee Cullen (1903–1946)." *Phylon,* VII (First Quarter, 1946), 19–21.

Dorsey, David F., Jr. "Countee Cullen's Use of Greek Mythology." *CLA Journal,* XIII (September, 1969), 68–77.

Emerson, Dorothy, ed. "The Poetry Corner." *Scholastic,* XXVII (December 7, 1935), 8.

Ferguson, Blanche W. *Countee Cullen and the Negro Renaissance.* New York: Dodd, Mead, 1966.

Gloster, Hugh M. *Negro Voices in American Fiction.* Chapel Hill, North Carolina: University of North Carolina Press, 1948.

Horne, Frank S. "Black Verse." *Opportunity,* II (November, 1924), 330–332.

Huggins, Nathan I. *Harlem Renaissance.* New York: Oxford University Press, 1971.

Jerome, Fred. "Langston Hughes and Countee Cullen: Forces in New Negro Poetry." (unpublished honors thesis, The City College of New York, January, 1960).

Johnson, Charles, ed. "Countee Cullen." *Source Material for Patterns of Negro Segregation.* Volume VIII, New York: Schomburg Collection (unpublished).

Kerlin, Robert T. "Conquest by Poetry." *Southern Workman,* LVI (June, 1927), 283–284.

Kerlin, Robert T. "A Pair of Youthful Negro Poets." *Southern Workman,* LIII (April, 1924), 178–181.

Knox, Winifred. "American Negro Poetry." *The Bookman* (London), LXXXI (October, 1931), 16–17.

Lash, John S. "The Anthologist and the Negro Author." *Phylon,* VIII (First Quarter, 1947), 68–76.

Locke, Alain, ed. *Four Negro Poets.* New York: Simon and Schuster, 1927 (works of Claude McKay, Countee Cullen, Jean Toomer, and Langston Hughes, with critical comments by Locke).

McCormack, Margaret. "Countee Cullen." *Interracial Review,* XII (May, 1939), 74.

Perry, Margaret. *A Bio-Bibliography of Countee P. Cullen (1903–1946)* Westport, Conn.: Greenwood, 1971.

Redding, Saunders, *To Make a Poet Black.* Chapel Hill, North Carolina: University of North Carolina Press, 1939.

Reimherr, Beulah. "Countee Cullen: a Biographical and Critical Study." College Park, Maryland: University of Maryland, (unpublished Master's Thesis, 1960).

Reiss, Winold. "Countee Cullen." *Survey,* LIV (June 1, 1925), 299.

Robb, Izetta W. "From the Darker Side." *Opportunity,* IV (1926), 381–382.

Shillito, Edward. "Poet and the Race Problem." *The Century,* XLVI (July 17, 1929), 915–916.

Smith, Robert A. "The Poetry of Countee Cullen." *Phylon,* XI (Third Quarter, 1950), 216–221.

Taussig, Charlotte E. "The New Negro as Revealed in His Poetry." *Opportunity,* V (April, 1927), 111.

Van Doren, Carl. "The Younger Generation of Negro Writers." *Opportunity,* II (May, 1924), 144–145.

Ward, Edith, ed. "Poetry Corner." *Scholastic,* XXXVI (February 12, 1940), 25.

Webster, Harvey. "A Difficult Career." *Poetry,* LXX (1947), 222–225.

Wells, Henry W. "Old Wine into Old Bottles." *Voices, a Quarterly of Poetry* (Spring, 1947).

Woodruff, Bertram L. "The Poetic Philosophy of Countee Cullen." *Phylon,* I (Third Quarter, 1940), 213–223.

Arna Wendell Bontemps (1902–1973)

PRIMARY

BOOKS:

God Sends Sunday. New York: Harcourt, Brace, 1931; in *Black Theater,* New York: Dodd, Mead, 1971 (dramatized as *St. Louis Woman,* 1946) (novel).

With Langston Hughes. *Popo and Fifina: Children of Haiti.* New York: Macmillan, 1932 (juvenile).

You Can't Pet a Possum. New York: Morrow, 1934 (juvenile).

Black Thunder. New York: Macmillan, 1936; Boston: Beacon, 1968 (novel).

Sad-Faced Boy. Boston: Houghton Mifflin, 1937 (juvenile).

Drums at Dusk. New York: Macmillan, 1939 (novel).

With W. C. Handy. *Father of the Blues, the Autobiography of W. C. Handy,* Arna Bontemps, ed. New York: Macmillan, 1941; reissued 1970.

Ed. *Golden Slippers: An Anthology of Negro Poetry for Young Readers.* New York and London: Harper, 1941.

With Jack Conroy. *The Fast Sooner Hound.* Boston: Houghton Mifflin, 1942 (juvenile).

With Jack Conroy. *They Seek a City.* New York: Doubleday, 1945; revised and expanded into *Anyplace But Here.* New York: Hill and Wang, 1966.

We Have Tomorrow. Boston: Houghton Mifflin, 1945.

With Jack Conroy. *Slappy Hooper, the Wonderful Sign Painter.* Boston: Houghton Mifflin, 1946 (juvenile).

Story of the Negro. New York: Knopf, 1948, 1956 (Jane Addams Award, 1956; juvenile).

With Langston Hughes. *The Poetry of the Negro: 1746 to 1949.* New York: Doubleday, 1949; revised for 1971 publication by Doubleday as *The Poetry of the Negro: 1746 to 1970.*

George Washington Carver, "Supplementary Reader in the Real People Series." Evanston, Illinois: Row Peterson, 1950.

With Jack Conroy. *Sam Patch, The High Wide and Handsome Jumper.* Boston: Houghton Mifflin, 1951; in Grandma Moses Story Book, Random House, 1961 (juvenile).

Chariot in the Sky. Philadelphia: Winston, 1951; New York: Holt, Rinehart and Winston, 1971 (juvenile).

The Story of George Washington Carver. New York: Grosset and Dunlap, 1954.

Lonesome Boy. Boston: Houghton Mifflin, 1955.

With Langston Hughes. *The Book of Negro Folklore.* New York: Dodd, Mead, 1958.

Frederick Douglass: Slave, Fighter, Freeman. New York: Knopf, 1959.

100 Years of Negro Freedom. New York: Dodd, Mead, 1961 (included by American Booksellers Association in collection presented to the White House, 1966, Apollo ed. paperback, A-154).

American Negro Poetry. New York: Hill and Wang, 1963 (selected by American Library Association as one of the 30 adult books recommended for young people, American Century Series paperback, ac-71).

Personals. London: Paul Breman, 1964 (limited ed. poems).

Famous Negro Athletes. New York: Dodd, Mead, 1964 (juvenile).

American Negro Heritage. Arna Bontemps, Historical Editor. San Francisco, California: Century Schoolbook Press, 1965 (adopted by State of California for fifth and eighth grades, 1966).

Ed. *Great Slave Narratives.* Boston: Beacon Press, 1969.

Mr. Kelso's Lion. Philadelphia: Lippincott, 1970.

Free At Last: The Life of Frederick Douglass. New York: Dodd, Mead, 1971 (juvenile).

Ed. *Hold Fast to Dreams; Poems Old and New.* Chicago: Follet, 1969 (anthology).

Young Booker: The Story of Booker T. Washington's Early Days. New
York: Dodd, Mead, 1972.
The Harlem Renaissance. New York: Dodd, Mead, 1972.

SHORT FICTION:
"A Summer Tragedy." *Opportunity,* XI, no. 6 (June, 1933), 174–177, 190;
in Anselment and Gibson, *Black and White,* 206–215; in Chapman,
Black Voices, 88–96; in Clarke, *American Negro Short Stories,* 54–63; in
Davis and Walden, *On Being Black,* 149–158; in Hughes, *The Best Short
Stories by Negro Writers,* 60–69; in James, *From the Roots,* 128–136; in
Singh and Fellows, *Black Literature in America,* 48–56; in Watkins,
Anthology of American Negro Literature, 77–86.
"Barrel Staves." *New Challenge,* I, no. 1 (March, 1934), 16–24.

POEMS PUBLISHED SEPARATELY:
"Spring Music." *The Crisis,* XXX, no. 2 (June, 1925), 93.
"Dirge." *The Crisis,* XXXII, no. 1 (May, 1926), 25.
"Holiday." *The Crisis,* XXXII, no. 3 (July, 1926), 121.
"Nocturne at Bethesda." *The Crisis,* XXXIII, no. 2 (December, 1926), 66.
"Tree." *The Crisis,* XXXIV, no. 2 (April, 1927), 48.
"Reconnaissance, a Poem." *Negro Digest* (September, 1964), 65.

ARTICLES:
"Who Recreates Significant Moments in History." *Opportunity,* XXII
(Summer, 1944), 126–139.
"Special Collections of Negroana." *Library Quarterly,* XVI (July, 1944).
"Pianist with a Mind of Her Own, Hazel Scott." *Scholastic,* LXVI (March
5, 1945), 13–14+.
"Two Harlems." *American Scholar,* XIV, no. 2 (April, 1945), 167–173.
"Langston Hughes." *Ebony* (October, 1946), 19–23.
"Even Money Bet on John Chavis." *Negro Digest* (February, 1950), 63–
67.
"Famous WPA Authors." *Negro Digest* (June, 1950), 43–47.
"White Southern Friends of the Negro." *Negro Digest* (August, 1950),
13–16.
"Buried Treasures of Negro Art." *Negro Digest* (December, 1950), 17–21.
"How I Told My Child About Race." *Negro Digest* (May, 1951), 80–83.
"Chesnutt Papers at Fisk." *Library Journal,* LXXVII (1952), 1288.
"Facing a Dilemma." *Saturday Review* (February 16, 1952), 23+.
"Bud Blooms." *Saturday Review,* XX (September, 1952), 15+.
"Harlem Renaissance." *Saturday Review of Literature,* XXXVI (March
28, 1953), 15–16.
"Three Portraits of the Negro." *Saturday Review of Literature,* XXXVI
(March 28, 1953), 15–16.
"New Black Renaissance." *Negro Digest* (November, 1961), 52–58.
"Evolution of Our Conscience." *Saturday Review,* XLIV (December 9,
1961), 52–53.
"Minority's New Militant Spirit." *Saturday Review,* XLV (July 14, 1962),
30.
"Negro Awakening; What Librarians Can Do." *Library Journal,* LXXXVIII
(September 1, 1963), 2997–2999.
"Negro Poetry—American," in *Encyclopedia of Poetry and Poetics,* Alex

Preminger, ed. Princeton, New Jersey: Princeton University Press, 1965.
"Harlem: the Beautiful Years: A Memoir." *Negro Digest* (January, 1965), 62–65.
"Why I Returned." *Harper's,* CCXXX (April, 1965), 176–182; reprinted in *The South Today,* Willie Morris, ed. New York: Harper and Row, 1965.
"The Negro Contribution to American Letters," in *The American Negro Reference Book,* John P. Davis, ed. New York: Prentice-Hall, 1966.
"A Tribute to Du Bois." *Journal of Human Relations,* XIV (1966), 112–114.
"Harlem in the Twenties." *The Crisis,* LXXIII (October, 1966), 431–434+.
"Lonesome Boy Theme; Address, May 5, 1966." *Horn Book,* XLII (December, 1966), 672–680.
"Langston Hughes: He Spoke of Rivers." *Freedomways,* VIII (Spring, 1968), 140–143.
"The Negro Renaissance: Jean Toomer and the Harlem Writers of the 1920's" in *Anger and Beyond,* Herbert Hill, ed. New York: Harper and Row; introduction to *Cane,* by Toomer, Harper and Row, Perennial Classic, 1969.
"The Black Renaissance of the Twenties." *Black World,* XX, no. 1 (November, 1970).

SECONDARY

Alsterlund, B. *Wilson Library Bulletin,* XX (January, 1946), 332.
Bone, Robert A. *The Negro Novel in America.* Rev. ed. New Haven, Connecticut: Yale University Press, 1965.
Gloster, Hugh M. *Negro Voices in American Fiction.* Chapel Hill, North Carolina: University of North Carolina Press, 1940.
Rider, I. M. "Arna Bontemps." *Horn Book,* XV (January, 1939), 13–19.
"Sad-faced Author." *Horn Book,* XV (January, 1939), 7–12.

Jessie [Redmon] Fauset (1882–1961)

PRIMARY

NOVELS:

There Is Confusion. New York: Boni and Liveright, 1924.
Plum Bun, a Novel Without a Moral. London: Matthews and Marrot, 1928; New York: Stokes, 1929.
The Chinaberry Tree; a Novel of American Life. New York: Stokes, 1931; New York: AMS Press, 1969; New York: Negro Universities Press, 1969; College Park, Maryland: McGrath, 1969.
Comedy: American Style. New York: Stokes, 1933; New York: AMS Press, 1969; College Park, Maryland: McGrath, 1969; New York: Negro Universities Press, 1969.

SHORT FICTION:

"Emmy." *The Crisis,* V, no. 2 (December, 1912), 79–87; V, no. 3 (January, 1913), 134–142.

"My House and a Glimpse of My Life Therein." *The Crisis,* VIII, no. 3 (July, 1914), 143–145.
" 'There Was One Time.' A Story of Spring." *The Crisis,* XIII, no. 6 (April, 1917), 272–277; XIV, no. 1 (May, 1917), 11–15.
"The Treasure of the Poor. From the French of Jean Richepin." *The Crisis,* XV (December, 1917), 63–65 (translation).
"The Sleeper Wakes, a novelette in three installments." *The Crisis,* XX, no. 4 (August, 1920), 168–173; XX, no. 5 (September, 1920), 226–229; (October, 1920), 267–274.
"Joseph and Mary Come to Bethlehem. Translated from an old French *chanson.*" *The Crisis,* XXI, no. 2 (December, 1920), 72–73.
"When Christmas Comes." *The Crisis,* XXV, no. 2 (December, 1922), 61–63.
"Double Trouble." *The Crisis,* XXVI, no. 4 (August, 1923), 155–159; XXVI, no. 5 (September, 1923), 205–209.

POETRY:

"Rondeau." *The Crisis,* III, no. 6 (April, 1912), 252.
"Again It Is September." *The Crisis,* XIV (September, 1917).
"The Return." *The Crisis,* XVII, no. 3 (January, 1919), 118.
"Mary Elizabeth." *The Crisis,* XIX, no. 2 (December, 1919), 51–56.
"Oriflamme." *The Crisis,* XIX, no. 3 (January, 1920), 128.
"The Pool. A Poem. Amédée Brun." *The Crisis,* XXII, no. 5 (September, 1921), 205 (translation).
"La Vie C'est La Vie." *The Crisis,* XXIV, no. 3 (July, 1922), 124.
"Dilworth Road Revisited." *The Crisis,* XXIV, no. 4 (August, 1922), 167.
"Song for a Lost Comrade." *The Crisis,* XXV, no. 1 (November, 1922), 22.
"To a Foreign Maid. A Poem. Translated from the French of Oswalk Durand." *The Crisis,* XV, no. 4 (February, 1923), 158.
"Rencontre." *The Crisis,* XXVII, no. 3 (January, 1924), 122.
"Here's April!" *The Crisis,* XXVII, no. 6 (April, 1924), 277.
"Rain Fugue." *The Crisis,* XXVIII, no. 4 (August, 1924), 155.
"Stars in Alabama." *The Crisis,* XXXV, no. 1 (January, 1928), 14.
" 'Courage!' He Said." *The Crisis,* XXXVI, no. 11 (November, 1929), 378.

ARTICLES AND TRANSLATIONS:

"What To Read." *The Crisis,* III, no. 5 (March, 1912), 211–212.
"The Montessori Method—Its Possibilities." *The Crisis,* IV (July, 1912), 136–138.
"Tracing Shadows." *The Crisis,* X (September, 1915), 247–251.
"Nationalism and Egypt." *The Crisis,* XIX (April, 1920), 310–316.
"New Literature on the Negro." *The Crisis,* XX (June, 1920), 78–83.
"Pastures New." *The Crisis,* XX (September, 1920), 224–226.
With Cezar Pinto, "The Emancipator of Brazil." *The Crisis,* XXI (March, 1921), 208–209.
"Saint George, Chevalier of France." *The Crisis,* XXII (May, 1921), 9–12.
"On the Book Shelf." *The Crisis,* XXII, no. 2 (June, 1921), 60–62.
"Nostalgia." *The Crisis,* XXII (August, 1921), 154–158.
"Impressions of the Second Pan-African Congress." *The Crisis,* XXII (November, 1921), 12–18.
"What Europe Thought of the Pan African Congress." *The Crisis,* II (December, 1921), 60–69.
" 'Looking Backward.' " *The Crisis,* XXIII (January, 1922), 125–126.

"Sunday Afternoon." *The Crisis,* XXIII (February, 1922), 162–164 (essay).

"No End of Books." *The Crisis,* XXIII (March, 1922), 208–210.

"The Symbolism of Bert Williams." *The Crisis,* XXIV (May, 1922), 12–15.

"As to Books." *The Crisis,* XXIV (June, 1922), 66–68.

" 'Batouala' is Translated." *The Crisis,* XXIV (September, 1923), 218–219.

"The Thirteenth Biennial of the N.A.C.W." *The Crisis,* XXIV (October, 1922), 257–260.

With Alain Locke. "Notes on the New Books." *The Crisis,* XXV (February, 1923), 161–165.

"The 'Y' Conference at Talledega." *The Crisis,* XXVI (March, 1923), 123–215.

"Out of the West." *The Crisis,* XXVII (November, 1923), 11–18.

"Henry Ossawa Tanner." *The Crisis,* XXVII (April, 1924), 255–258.

"La Question des Noirs aux Etats-Unis. by Frank L. Schoell." *The Crisis,* XXVIII (June, 1924), 83–86 (translation).

"The Gift of Laughter." *The New Negro* ed. by *Alain Locke.* New York: Albert and Charles Boni, 1925.

" 'Yarrow Revisited.' " *The Crisis,* XIX (January, 1925), 107–109.

" 'This Way to the Flea Market.' " *The Crisis,* XXIX (February, 1925), 161–163.

"The Enigma of the Sorbonne." *The Crisis,* XXIX (March, 1925), 216–219.

"Dark Algiers the White." *The Crisis,* XXIX (April, 1925), 255–258; XXX (May, 1925), 16–22.

"The Eucalyptus Tree." *The Crisis,* XXXI (January, 1926), 116–117.

" 'Rank Imposes Obligation.' A Biographical Essay on Martin Robinson Delany." *The Crisis,* XXXIII (November, 1926), 9–13.

"The Sun of Brittany. Translated from the French." *The Crisis,* XXXIV (November, 1927), 303 (translation).

"In Talladega." *The Crisis,* XXXVI (February, 1928), 47–48.

JUVENILE LITERATURE:

"After School. A Poem." *The Brownies' Book,* I, no. 1 (January, 1920), 30.

"Dedication." *The Brownies' Book,* I, no. 1 (January, 1920), 32.

"That Story of George Washington. A Poem." *The Brownies' Book,* I, no. 2 (February, 1920), 64.

"At the Zoo. Verses." *The Brownies' Book,* I, no. 3 (March, 1920), 85–86.

"The Return of the Bells. A Story." *The Brownies' Book,* I, no. 4 (April, 1920), 99–103.

"The Easter Idyl. A Poem." *The Brownies' Book,* I, no. 4 (April, 1920), 112–113.

"Spring Songs. Verses." *The Brownies' Book,* I, no. 5 (May, 1920), 146–147.

"Turkey Drumsticks. A Thanksgiving Story." *The Brownies' Book,* I, no. 11 (November, 1920), 342–346.

"Merry Christmas To All. A Story." *The Brownies' Book,* I, no. 12 (December, 1920), 355–360.

"Two Christmas Songs. Verses." *The Brownies' Book,* I, no. 12 (December, 1920), 384.

"Ghosts and Kittens. A Story." *The Brownies' Book,* II, no. 2 (February, 1921), 46–51.

"Cordelia Goes on the War Path. A Story." *The Brownies' Book,* II, no. 5 (May, 1921), 148–154.

SECONDARY

Bone, Robert A. *The Negro Novel in America.* Rev. ed. New Haven, Connecticut: Yale University Press, 1965.
Braithwaite, William. "The Novels of Jessie Fauset." *Opportunity,* XII (1934), 24–28.
Brawley, Benjamin. *The Negro Genius.* New York: Biblo and Tannen, 1966 (reprinted from New York: Dodd, Mead, 1937).
Davis, Arthur P. and Saunders Redding. *Cavalcade, Negro American Writing from 1760 to the Present.* Boston: Houghton Mifflin, 1971.
Fauset, Arthur Huff. *For Freedom; a Biographical Story of the American Negro.* Philadelphia: Franklin Publishing and Supply Co., 1929.
Gloster, Hugh M. *Negro Voices in American Fiction.* Chapel Hill, North Carolina: University of North Carolina Press, 1948.
Hemenway, Robert. *The Black Novelist.* Columbus, Ohio: Charles E. Merrill Publishing Co., 1970.
Locke, Alain. *The New Negro.* New York: Arno and the *New York Times,* 1968 (reprinted from the 1925 edition).

Nella Larsen (?1893–1960's?)

PRIMARY

NOVELS:

Quicksand. New York and London: Knopf, 1928; New York: Collier Books, 1971; New York: Negro Universities Press, 1969.
Passing. New York and London: Knopf, 1929; New York: Arno, 1969; New York: Negro Universities Press, 1969; New York: Collier Books, 1971.

MISCELLANEOUS:

"Sanctuary; story." *Forum,* LXXXIII (January, 1930), 15–18.
"Letter Explaining the Circumstances Under Which 'Sanctuary' Was Written." *Forum,* LXXXIII, supplement 41 (April, 1930).

SECONDARY

Bone, Robert A. *The Negro Novel in America.* Rev. ed. New Haven, Connecticut: Yale University Press, 1965.
Brawley, Benjamin. *Negro Builders and Heroes.* Chapel Hill, North Carolina: University of North Carolina Press, 1937.
Brawley, Benjamin. *The Negro in Literature and Art in the United States.* New York: Duffield, 1930.
Gloster, Hugh M. *Negro Voices in American Fiction.* Chapel Hill, North Carolina: University of North Carolina Press, 1948.
Hemenway, Robert. *The Black Novelist.* Columbus, Ohio: Charles E. Merrill Publishing Co., 1970.

Redding, Saunders. *To Make a Poet Black*. Chapel Hill, North Carolina: University of North Carolina Press, 1939.

REVIEWS:

(Of *Quicksand*)
Opportunity, VI (July, 1928), 212–213 (by Eda Lou Walton).
Opportunity, VII (January, 1929), 25.
The Crisis, XXXV (June, 1928), 202.
(Of *Passing*)
Opportunity, VII (August, 1929), 255 (by Mary Fleming Labaree).
The Crisis, XXXVI (July, 1929), 234.

Rudolph Fisher (1897–1934)

NOVELS:

The Walls of Jericho. New York and London: Knopf, 1928; New York: Arno, 1969, 1971.
The Conjure-Man Dies, a Mystery Tale of Dark Harlem. New York: Corvici, Friede, 1932.

SHORT FICTION:

"City of Refuge." *Atlantic Monthly* (February, 1925), 178–187.
"High Yaller." Part I. *The Crisis* (October, 1925), 281–286.
"High Yaller." Part II. *The Crisis* (November, 1925), 33–38.
"Ringtail." *Atlantic Monthly* (May, 1925), 652–660).
"The South Lingers On." *Survey Graphic* (March 1, 1925), 644–647.
"The Backslider." *McClure's* (August, 1927), 16–17, 101–104.
"Blades of Steel." *Atlantic Monthly* (August, 1927), 183–192.
"The Caucasian Storms Harlem." *American Mercury* (August, 1927), 393–399.
"Fire by Night." *McClure's* (December, 1927), 64–67, 98–102.
"The Promised Land." *Atlantic Monthly* (January, 1927), 37–45.
"Common Meter." Part I. *The New York News*, Illustrated Feature Section, February 8, 1930, Schomburg Collection, New York Public Library.
"Common Meter." Part II. *The New York News*, Illustrated Feature Section, February 15, 1930, Schomburg Collection, New York Public Library.
"Dust." *Opportunity* (February, 1931), 46–47.
"Ezekiel." *Junior Red Cross News* (March, 1932), 151–153.
"Ezekiel Learns." *Junior Red Cross News* (February, 1933), 123–125.
"Guardian of the Law." *Opportunity* (March, 1933), 82–85, 90.
"Miss Cynthie." *Story* (June, 1933), 3–15.
"John Archer's Nose." *The Metropolitan, a Monthly Review* (January, 1935), 10–12, 47–50, 53, 67, 69–71, 73–75, 80–81 (posthumous).

UNPUBLISHED WORKS:

"Across the Airshaft." Typed manuscript secured in microfilm form from Brown University Archives, Providence, Rhode Island (short story, n.d.).
"The Lindy Hop." Manuscript secured in microfilm form from Brown University Archives, Providence, Rhode Island (short story, n.d.).

"The Lost Love Blues." Typed manuscript secured in microfilm form from Brown University Archives, Providence, Rhode Island (short story, n.d).

"The Man Who Passed." ("False Face") Typed manuscript secured in microfilm form from Brown University Archives, Providence, Rhode Island (short story, n.d.).

"Miss Cynthie." Typed manuscript secured in microfilm form from Brown University Archives, Providence, Rhode Island (short story, n.d.).

SECONDARY

Bone, Robert A. *The Negro Novel in America.* Rev. ed. New Haven, Connecticut: Yale University Prss, 1965.

Gloster, Hugh M. *Negro Voices in American Fiction.* Chapel Hill, North Carolina: University of North Carolina Press, 1948.

Hemenway, Robert. *The Black Novelist.* Columbus, Ohio: Charles E. Merrill Publishing Co., 1970.

"Rudolph Fisher." *The Crisis* (July, 1925), 132.

"Rudolph Fisher." *McClure's* (August, 1927), 6.

Queen, Eleanor Claudine. "A Study of Rudolph Fisher's Prose Fiction." Unpublished Master's thesis, Howard University, Moorland-Spingarn Collection, 1961.

George Samuel Schuyler (1895–)

BOOKS:

Black No More; Being an Account of the Strange and Wonderful Workings of Science in the Land of the Free, A. D. 1933–1940. New York: Macaulay, 1931.

Slaves Today; a Story of Liberia. New York: Brewer, Warren and Putnam, 1931.

Black and Conservative; the Autobiography of George S. Schuyler. New Rochelle, New York: Arlington House, 1966.

ARTICLES:

"From Job to Job." *The World Tomorrow* (April, 1923).

"The Negro-Art Hokum." *Nation,* CXXII (June 16, 1926), 662–663.

"Blessed Are the Sons of Ham." *Nation,* CXXIV (March 23, 1927), 313–315.

"The Negro's Greatest Gift to America," in *Ebony and Topaz, A Collectanea,* Charles S. Johnson, ed. New York: *Opportunity,* 1927, 122–124.

"Our White Folks." *American Mercury,* XII (December, 1927), 385–392.

"Emancipated Women and the Negro." *The Modern Quarterly,* V (1928–30), 361–363.

"Keeping the Negro in His Place." *American Mercury,* XVII (August, 1929), 469–476.

"The Negro Looks Ahead." *American Mercury,* XIX (February, 1930), 212–220.

"Traveling Jim Crow." *American Mercury,* XX (August, 1930), 423–432.

"Some Unsweet Truths about Race Prejudice," in *Behold America.* New York: Farrar and Rinehart, 1931.

"Memoirs of a Pearl Diver." *American Mercury*, XXII (April, 1931), 487–496.

"The Young Negro Co-operative League." *The Crisis*, XXXIX (January, 1932), 456–472.

"Black America Begins to Doubt." *American Mercury*, XXV (April, 1932), 423–430.

"Mr. Embree Discovers a New Race." *Opportunity*, X (June, 1932), 175–176 (review of Edwin R. Embree, *Brown America*).

"Black Art." *American Mercury*, XXVII (November, 1932), 335–342.

"Uncle Sam's Black Step-Child." *American Mercury*, XXIX (June, 1933), 147–156.

"To Boycott or Not to Boycott? B. A Deadly Boomerang." *The Crisis*, XLI (September, 1934), 259–260, 274.

"Black Paradise Lost." *Opportunity*, XIII (April, 1935), 113–116.

"The Separate State Hokum." *The Crisis*, XLII (May, 1935), 135, 148.

"Freedom of the Press in Mississippi." *The Crisis*, XLIII (October, 1936), 302–303, 306.

"The Job Frontiers for Negro Youth." *The Crisis*, XLIII (November, 1936), 328–329.

"Do We Really Want Equality?" *The Crisis*, XLIV (April, 1937), 102–103.

"Not Gone with the Wind." *The Crisis*, XLIV (July, 1937), 205–206.

"A Treatise on Mulattoes." *The Crisis*, XLIV (October, 1937), 308–309, 318.

"Reflections on Negro Leadership." *The Crisis*, XLIV (November, 1937), 327–328, 347.

"The Rise of the Black Internationale." *The Crisis*, XLV (August, 1938), 255–257, 274–275, 277.

"Negroes Reject Communism." *American Mercury*, XLVII (June, 1939), 176–181.

"Craftsman in the Blue Grass." *The Crisis*, XLVII (May, 1940), 143, 157–158.

"The Negro in the New Order." *Modern Quarterly*, XI (Fall, 1940), 85–87.

"Vacation Daze." *Common Ground*, III (Spring, 1943), 41–44.

"The Negro Press." *The New Leader* (June 26, 1943).

"A Long War Will Aid the Negro." *The Crisis*, L (November, 1943), 328–329, 344.

"Dr. Jekyll and Mr. Hyde and the Negro," in *Anthology of American Negro Literature*, Sylvestre C. Watkins, ed., New York: Random House, 1944.

"More Race Riots Are Coming." *American Mercury*, LIX (December, 1944), 686–691.

"Jim Crow in the North." *American Mercury*, LXVIII (June, 1944), 663–670.

"Haiti Looks Ahead." *Americas*, I (December, 1949), 6–8+.

"What's Wrong with Negro Authors?" *Negro Digest*, VII (May, 1950), 3–7.

"The Van Vechten Revolution." *Phylon*, XI (Fourth Quarter, 1950), 362–368.

"Forty Years of 'The Crisis.' " *The Crisis*, LVIII (March, 1951), 163–164.

"Why I Want to Stay in America." *Negro Digest*, IX (June, 1951), 52–56.

"Are Negroes More Prejudiced Than Whites?" *Negro Digest*, X (November, 1951), 40–43.

"Do Negroes Want to Be White?" *American Mercury,* LXXXII (June, 1956), 55–60.

"Schuyler Calls for Historical Scientists." *Negro History Bulletin,* XVIII (April, 1955), 169–170 (excerpts from address).

"Negro Voter Comes of Age." *American Mercury,* LXXXIV (March, 1957), 99–104.

"Krushchev's African Foothold." *American Mercury,* LXXXVIII (March, 1959), 57–59.

"Freedom Through Finance." *Sepia,* XI (May, 1962), 55–58.

"Blame for the Riots as a Negro Writer Sees It." *U.S. News and World Report,* LXIII (August 14, 1967), 10 (reprint).

"What the Negro Thinks of the South," in *Black American Literature, Essays,* Darwin T. Turner, comp. Columbus, Ohio: Merrill, 1969, 87–90.

MISCELLANEOUS PUBLICATIONS:

Ed. *The National News. The News Magazine of Colored America.* New York: 1912 (magazine).

"Woof." *Harlem,* I (November, 1928), 17–20 (short fiction).

"Black Warriors." *American Mercury,* XXI (November, 1930), 288–297 (short fiction).

The Red Drive in the Colonies. New York: Catholic Information Society, 1947 (15-page pamphlet in series on Communism).

The Communist Conspiracy Against the Negroes. New York: Catholic Information Society, 1947 (16-page pamphlet in series on Communism).

Fifty Years of Progress in Negro Journalism. Pittsburgh, Pennsylvania: Pittsburgh Courier Publishing Co., 1950 (7-page reprint).

"Black No More." *Negro Digest,* VIII (April, 1950), 64–69 (short fiction).

SECONDARY

"George S. Schuyler, Iconoclast." *The Crisis,* LXXII (October, 1965), 484–485 (editorial).

Lee, Carleton L. Review of *Black and Conservative. Negro History Bulletin,* XXX (January, 1967), 22–23.

Mayer, Martin. "Recordings." *Esquire,* LXIII (March, 1965), 52.

"Meet the George Schuylers; America's Strangest Family." *Our World,* VI (April, 1951), 22–26.

Tolson, Melvin B. "George S. Schuyler." *American Mercury,* XXVIII (March, 1933), 373–374.

Winslow, H. F. "George S. Schuyler: Fainting Traveler." *Midwest Journal,* V (Summer, 1953), 24–45.

Wallace Thurman (1902–1934)

PRIMARY

NOVELS:

The Blacker the Berry, a Novel of Negro Life. New York: Macaulay, 1929; New York: Arno, 1969 (introduction by William H. Robinson); New York: Collier Books, 1970 (introduction by Therman B. O'Daniel); New York: Macmillan, 1970.

Infants of the Spring. New York: Macaulay, 1932.
With Abraham L. Furman. *The Interne.* New York: Macaulay, 1932.

MAGAZINE:

Ed. *Fire!!* v. 1, no. 1, November, 1926. Westport, Connecticut: Negro Universities Press, 1970 (reprint of publication issued in New York in 1926).

ARTICLES:

"Negro Artists and the Negro." *New Republic,* LII (August 31, 1927), 37–39.
"Nephews of Uncle Remus." *Independent,* CXIX (September 24, 1927), 296–298.
"Negro Poets and Their Poetry." *Bookman,* LXVII (July 28, 1928), 555–561.

SECONDARY

Bone, Robert A. *The Negro Novel in America.* Rev. ed. New Haven, Connecticut: Yale University Press, 1965.
Brawley, Benjamin. *The Negro Genius.* New York: Biblo and Tannen, 1966.
Brown, Sterling A., Arthur P. Davis, and Ulysses Lee, eds. *The Negro Caravan, Writings by American Negroes.* New York: Dryden, 1941; New York: Arno, 1969, 1970 (introduction by Julius Lester).
Gloster, Hugh M. *Negro Voices in American Fiction.* Chapel Hill, North Carolina: University of North Carolina Press, 1948.
Hughes, Langston. "Black Renaissance," in *The Big Sea.* New York: Knopf, 1940.
Hughes, Langston. "Harlem Literati in the Twenties." *Saturday Review of Literature,* XXII (July 22, 1940), 13–14.
Reviews of *Harlem* by Thurman and William Jourdan Rapp.
Commonweal, IX (March 6, 1929), 514.
Outlook, CLI (March 6, 1929), 381.
Literary Digest, C (March 16, 1929), 21–22.
American Mercury, XVII (May, 1929), 117.
Turner, Darwin, ed. *Black American Literature, Fiction.* Columbus, Ohio: Charles E. Merrill, 1969, 43.

Zora Neale Hurston (1903–1960)

PRIMARY

BOOKS:

Jonah's Gourd Vine. Philadelphia: Lippincott, 1935 (introduction by Fannie Hurst), 1971.
Mules and Men. Philadelphia and London: Lippincott, 1935 (introduction by Franz Boas).
Their Eyes Were Watching God. Philadelphia and London: Lippincott, 1937; New York: Negro Universities Press, 1969 (novel).
Tell My Horse. Philadelphia and New York: Lippincott, 1938; British

version is titled *Voodoo Gods; an Inquiry into Native Myths and Magic in Jamaica and Haiti*. London: Dent and Sons, 1939.

Moses, Man of the Mountain. Philadelphia and New York: Lippincott, 1939 (novel).

Dust Tracks on a Road, an Autobiography. Philadelphia and London: Lippincott, 1942; London and New York: Hutchinson and Co., 1944; New York: Arno, 1969, 1970; Philadelphia: Lippincott, 1971 (introduction by Larry Neal).

Seraph on the Suwanee. New York: Scribner's Sons, 1948 (novel).

SHORT FICTION:

"Drenched in Light." *Opportunity*, II (December, 1924), 371–374.

"Spunk." *Opportunity*, III (May, 1925), 171–173.

"John Redding Goes to Sea." *Opportunity*, IV (January, 1926), 16–21.

"Muttsy." *Opportunity*, IV (August, 1926), 246–250, 267.

"The Gilded Six-Bits," in *Story in America, 1933–1934*, Whit Burnett and Martha Foley, eds. New York: Vanguard, 1934.

"The Conscience of the Court." *Saturday Evening Post*, CCXXII (March 18, 1950), 22–23.

DRAMA:

"The First One," in *Ebony and Topaz*, Charles Spurgeon Johnson, ed. New York: *Opportunity*, National Urban League, 1927.

With Dorothy Waring. *Stephen Kelen-d'Oxylion Presents Polk County, a Comedy of Negro Life on a Sawmill Camp, with Authentic Negro Music, in Three Acts*. New York: 1944 (in the Library of Congress, reproduced from type-written copy; leaves variously numbered; without the music).

ARTICLES:

"The Hue and Cry About Howard University." *The Messenger*, VII (September, 1925), 315–319, 338.

"Fannie Hurst." *Saturday Review of Literature*, XVI (October 9, 1937), 15–16.

"Story in Harlem Slang." *American Mercury*, LV (July, 1942), 84–96.

"Lawrence of the River." *Saturday Evening Post*, CCXV (September 5, 1942), 18+.

"Pet Negro System." *American Mercury*, LVI (May, 1943), 593–600.

"High John de Conqueror; Negro Folklore Offers Solace to Sufferers." *American Mercury*, LVII (October, 1943), 450–458.

"Negroes Without Self-Pity." *American Mercury*, LVII (November, 1943), 601–603.

"Last Slave Ship." *American Mercury*, LVIII (March, 1944), 351–358.

"Rise of the Begging Joints." *American Mercury*, LX (March, 1945), 288–294.

"What White Publishers Won't Print." *Negro Digest*, VII (April, 1950), 85–89.

SECONDARY

Alsterlund, B. Biographical Sketch. *Wilson Bulletin*, XIII (May, 1939), 586.

"Anisfeld Awards to Hurston and Pierson." *Publishers Weekly*, CXLIII (February 27, 1943), 1023.

Bone, Robert A. *The Negro Novel in America,* rev. ed. New Haven, Connecticut: Yale University Press, 1965.

Brawley, Benjamin. *The Negro Genius.* New York: Biblo and Tannen, 1966.

Byrd, James W. "Zora Neale Hurston: a Novel Folklorist." *Tennessee Folklore Society Bulletin,* XXI (1955), 37–41.

Gloster, Hugh M. *Negro Voices in American Fiction.* Chapel Hill, North Carolina: University of North Carolina Press, 1948.

Hughes, Langston. *The Big Sea.* New York: Knopf, 1940.

Hughes, Langston. "Harlem Literati in the Twenties." *Saturday Review of Literature,* XXII (June 22, 1940), 13–14.

Hurst, Fannie. "Zora Hurston: a Personality Sketch." *Yale University Library Gazette,* XXXV (1961), 17–22.

Jackson, Blyden. "Some Negroes in the Land of Goshen." *Tennessee Folklore Society Bulletin,* XIX (1953), 103–107.

Pratt, T. "Zora Neale Hurston: a Memoir." *Negro Digest,* XI (February, 1962), 52–56.

Turner, Darwin T. "The Negro Novelist and the South." *Southern Humanities Review,* I (1967), 21–29.

Turner, Darwin T., ed. *Black American Literature, Fiction.* Columbus, Ohio: Charles E. Merrill, 1969, pp. 49–50.

Turner, Darwin T. In a Minor Chord, *Three Afro-American Writers and Their Search for Identity.* Carbondale: Illinois University Press, 1971. (Toomer, Cullen, Hurston).

Frank Marshall Davis (1905–   )

PRIMARY

COLLECTED POETRY:

Black Man's Verse. Chicago: Black Cat Press, 1935.

I Am the American Negro. Chicago: Black Cat Press, 1937; Freeport, New York: Books for Libraries Press, 1971.

Through Sepia Eyes. Chicago: Black Cat Press, 1938.

47th Street Poems. Prairie City, Illinois: Decker, 1948.

POEMS PUBLISHED SEPARATELY:

"Failure." *Poetry,* XLVIII (August, 1936), 294.

"Chicago Skyscrapers." *Opportunity,* XVII, no. 1 (January, 1939), 5.

"Snapshots of the Cotton South." Sterling A. Brown, Arthur P. Davis and Ulysses Lee. *The Negro Caravan,* New York: Dryden Press, 1941, 392–96.

"Official Answers Chicago Fair Critic." *The Crisis,* XLVIII, no. 2 (February, 1941), 49, 58.

"War Quiz for America." *The Crisis,* LI (April, 1944), 112, 122.

SECONDARY

Brawley, Benjamin. *The Negro Genius.* New York: Dodd, Mead, 1937; New York: Biblo and Tannen, 1966.

Kloder, Helena. "The Film and Canvas of Frank Marshall Davis." *CLA Journal,* XV, no. 1 (September, 1971), 59–63.

Sterling A. Brown (1901–   )

PRIMARY

BOOKS:

Southern Road. New York: Harcourt, Brace, 1932 (poems).

Ed., *American Stuff; an Anthology of Prose and Verse by Members of the Federal Writers' Project, with Sixteen Prints by the Federal Art Project.* New York: Viking, 1937.

The Negro in American Fiction. Washington, D.C.: Associates in Negro Folk Education, 1937; Port Washington, New York: Kennikat, 1968; New York: Argosy-Antiquarian, 1969.

Negro Poetry and Drama. Washington, D.C.: Associates in Negro Folk Education, 1937.

Ed. with Arthur P. Davis and Ulysses Lee. *The Negro Caravan: Writings by American Negroes.* New York: Dryden, 1941; New York: Arno, 1969, 1970 (introduction by Julius Lester).

The Negro in American Fiction. Negro Poetry and Drama. New York: Arno, 1969 (reprint).

Negro Poetry and Drama and The Negro in American Fiction. New York: Atheneum, 1969 (reprint).

With Haynes, George E. *The Negro Newcomers in Detroit. The Negro in Washington.* New York: Arno, 1970 (prepared by the Federal Writers' Project).

POEMS PUBLISHED SEPARATELY:

"When de Saints Go Ma'ching Home." *Opportunity,* V (July, 1927), 198–199.

"After the Storm." *The Crisis,* XXXIV (April, 1927), 48.

"Sporting Beasley." *Theatre Arts,* XVI (February, 1932), 149.

"Master and Man." *New Republic,* LXXXIX (November 18, 1936), 66.

"Break of Day." *New Republic,* XCV (May 11, 1938), 10.

" 'Slim Lands a Job?' 'Old Man Buzzard,' 'Scotty Has His Say.' " *Scholastic,* XXXII (May 21, 1938), 20E+.

"Young Ones." *Poetry,* LII (July, 1938), 189–190.

"Remembering Nat Turner." *The Crisis,* XLVI (February, 1939), 48.

"Bitter Fruit of the Tree." *Nation,* CXLIX (August 26, 1939), 223.

"Break of Day." *Scholastic,* XXXVI (April 29, 1940), 27.

"Glory, Glory." *Scholastic,* XXXVI (April 29, 1940), 25+ (excerpt).

"Out of Their Mouths." *Survey Graphic,* XXXI (November, 1942), 480–483.

"Strong Men." *United Asia,* V, no. 3 (June, 1953), 150.

"Three Poems: 'The Ballad of Joe Meek,' 'An Old Woman Remembers,' 'Southern Cop.' " *Freedomways,* III, no. 3 (Summer, 1963), 405–412.

ARTICLES:

"Roland Hayes." *Opportunity,* III (May, 1925), 173–174 (vignette rev.).

"The Blues as Folk Poetry," in *Folk-Say, A Regional Miscellany,* B. A. Botkin, ed. Norman, University of Oklahoma Press, 1930.

"Our Literary Audience." *Opportunity,* VIII (February, 1930), 42–46, 61.

"Caroling Softly Souls of Slavery." *Opportunity*, IX (August, 1931), 251–252.
"Concerning Negro Drama." *Opportunity*, IX (September, 1931), 284–288.
"Negro Character as Seen by White Authors." *Journal of Negro Education*, II (April, 1933), 179–203; in James A. Emanuel and Theodore L. Gross, *Dark Symphony*, New York: Free Press, 1968, 139–171.
"Signs of Promises." *Opportunity*, X (September, 1932), 287.
"In Memoriam: Charles W. Chesnutt." *Opportunity*, X (December, 1932), 387.
"The Atlanta University Summer Theatre." *Opportunity*, XII (October, 1934), 308–309.
"The Negro in Fiction and Drama." *The Christian Register* (February 14, 1935), 111–112.
"The Negro in American Literature," in *James Weldon Johnson*. Nashville: Department of Publicity, Fisk University, 1941?.
"Words on a Bus." *South Today*, VII (Spring, 1943), 26–28 (sketch).
"Contributions of the American Negro," in F. J. Brown and J. S. Roucek, *One America* (1945), 588–615.
"Count Us In," in *What the Negro Wants*, Rayford W. Logan, ed. Chapel Hill, North Carolina: University of North Carolina Press, 1944, 308–344; in *Primer for White Folks*, Bucklin Moon, ed. Garden City, New York: Doubleday, Doran, 1945, 364–395.
"Georgia Sketches." *Phylon*, VI (Third Quarter, 1945), 225–231.
"The Negro Author and His Publisher." *Negro Quarterly*, I (1945).
"Ralph Bunch—Statesman." *The Reporter*, I (December 6, 1949), 3–6.
"Athletics and the Arts," in *The Integration of the Negro into American Society*. Washington, D.C., Howard University Press, 1951, 117–147.
"The Blues." *Phylon*, XIII (1952), 286–292.
"Negro Folk Expression; Spirituals, Seculars, Ballads, and Work Songs." *Phylon* (First Quarter, 1953), 45–61; in *The Making of Black America*, August Meier, ed. New York: Atheneum, 1969, vol. 2, 209–226.
"A Century of Negro Portraiture in American Literature." *The Massachusetts Review*, VII, no. 1 (Winter, 1966), 73–96; in *Black and White in American Culture*, Jules Chametzky, ed. Amherst: University of Massachusetts Press, 1969, 333–359.

REVIEWS:
"The New Secession—a Review." *Opportunity*, V (May, 1927), 147–148.
"A Romantic Defense." *Opportunity*, IX (April, 1931), 118 (review of *I'll Take My Stand*).
"As to Jungle Ways." *Opportunity*, IX (July, 1931), 219–221 (review of *Jungle Ways*, by William Seabrook).
"Poor Whites." *Opportunity*, IX (October, 1931), 317, 320 (review of *Oklahoma Town*, by George Milburn, *God in the Straw Pen*, by John Fort, *American Earth*, by Erskine Caldwell).
"A Point of View." *Opportunity*, IX (November, 1931), 347, 350 (review of *That Evening Sun Go Down* by William Faulkner).
"Pride and Pathos." *Opportunity*, IX (December, 1931), 381 (review of *The Carolina Low Country*).
"Truth Will Out. Review of *Slave Trading in the Old South* by Frederick Bancroft." *Opportunity*, X (January, 1932), 23–24.

"*Never No More.*" *Opportunity,* X (February, 1932), 55–56 (drama review).

"Joel Chandler Harris." *Opportunity,* X (April, 1932), 119–120 (review of *Joel Chandler Harris: Editor and Essayist,* Julia Collier Harris ed.).

"A New Trend." *Opportunity,* XI (February, 1933), 56 (review of *Inchin' Along, Amber Satyr, Free Born, Georgia Nigger*).

"Alas the Poor Mulatto." *Opportunity,* XI (March, 1933), 91 (review of *Dark Lustre,* by Geoffrey Barnes).

"Banana Bottom." *Opportunity,* XI (July, 1933), 217, 222 (review of *Banana Bottom,* by Claude McKay).

"From the Southwest." *Opportunity,* XI (October, 1933), 313 (review of *Tone the Bell Easy,* by J. Frank Dobie).

"*Imitation of Life;* Once a Pancake. A Review." *Opportunity,* XIII (March, 1935), 87–88.

"The Literary Scene. Chronicle and Comment. Two Negro Poets." *Opportunity,* XIV (July, 1936), 215, 220 (review of *Black Thunder,* by Arna Bontemps and *Black Man's Verse,* by Frank Marshall Davis).

"Book Review of Benjamin Brawley's *Paul Laurence Dunbar.*" *Opportunity,* XV (July, 1937), 216–217.

"Come Day, Go Day." *Opportunity,* XIII (September, 1945), 279–280 (review of *Let the Band Play Dixie,* by Roark Bradford and *Don't You Weep No More,* by Richard Coleman).

MISCELLANEOUS WRITINGS:

Outline for the Study of the Poetry of American Negroes. New York: Harcourt, Brace, 1931 (to be used with *The Book of American Negro Poetry,* by James Weldon Johnson).

The Negro on the Stage, 1937. Materials compiled for the Carnegie-Myrdal Study; available on microfilm from several university libraries including California at Berkeley, Chicago, Fisk, Harvard, North Carolina at Chapel Hill, and Howard University.

SECONDARY

Benét, William Rose. "New Negro Poet." *Saturday Review of Literature,* VII (May 14, 1932), 732.

Bond, F. W. Review of *Negro Poetry and Drama. The Crisis,* XLVI (May, 1939), 154.

Botkin, B. A. Review of *The Negro in American Fiction. Opportunity,* XVII (June, 1939), 184.

Emerson, Dorothy. "Poetry Corner," *Scholastic,* XXXII (May 21, 1938), 20E+.

Gray, James. Review of *The Negro Caravan. Opportunity,* XX (April, 1942), 122–123.

Henderson, Stephen A. "A Strong Man Called Sterling Brown." *Black World,* XIX, no. 11 (September, 1970), 5–12.

Redding, Saunders. *To Make a Poet Black.* Chapel Hill, North Carolina: University of North Carolina Press, 1939.

Strong, M. L. "Poetry Corner," *Scholastic,* XXXVI (April 29, 1940), 25. *Saturday Review of Literature,* XXV (February 21, 1942), 13.

Wagner, Jean. "Sterling Brown," in *Black Poets of the United States, from*

Paul Laurence Dunbar to Langston Hughes. Urbana: University of Illinois Press, 1973. (Translated by Kenneth Douglass from the French, 1962 edition.)

Authors: Part II

Richard Wright (1908–1960)

PRIMARY

BOOKS:

Uncle Tom's Children: Four Novellas. New York and London: Harper and Bros., 1938.

Uncle Tom's Children. New York: Harper, 1947; New York: Harper and Row, 1969.

Native Son. New York and London: Harper and Bros., 1940; New York: Modern Library, 1942; New York: Harper, 1957; New York: Harper and Row, 1966; New York: Harper and Row, 1969 (with introduction: "How Bigger was Born") (novel).

12 Million Black Voices: A Folk History of the Negro in the United States. New York: Viking, 1941; London: L. Drummond, 1947; New York: Arno, 1969.

Black Boy: a Record of Childhood and Youth. New York and London: Harper, 1945; Cleveland and New York: World, 1945; Cleveland: World, 1950; New York: Harper and Row, 1964, 1966.

The Outsider. New York: Harper, 1953; New York: Harper and Row, 1969 (novel).

Black Power: A Record of Reactions in a Land of Pathos. New York: Harper, 1954.

Savage Holiday. New York: Avon, 1954; New York: Universal, 1965.

White Man, Listen! Garden City, New York: Doubleday, 1957; Garden City, New York: Anchor Books, 1964 (introduction by John A. Williams) (essays).

The Long Dream, a novel. Garden City, New York: Doubleday, 1958; Chatham, New Jersey: Chatham Bookseller, 1969.

Lawd Today. New York: Avon, 1963; New York: Walker, 1963.

Eight Men. Cleveland: World, 1969 (short stories).

ARTICLES:

"Blueprint for Negro Writing." *New Challenge,* I (1937), 53–65.

"The Ethics of Living Jim Crow, an Autobiographical Sketch," in *American Stuff, a W. P. A. Writers' Anthology.* New York: 1937, 39–52; in 1940 edition of *Uncle Tom's Children.*

"Early Days in Chicago," in *Cross-section,* Edwin Seaver, ed. New York: Simon and Schuster, 1945, 306–342; in *Eight Men,* 1961.

"Littérature noire américaine." *Temps M,* IV (1948), 193–221.

MISCELLANEOUS PUBLICATIONS:

How "Bigger" Was Born; the Story of Native Son, One of the Most Significant Novels of Our Time, and How It Came to Be Written. New York: Harper and Bros., 1940.

With Paul Green. *Native Son (the Biography of a Young American), a Play in Ten Scenes . . . from the Novel by Richard Wright.* A Mercer Production by Orson Welles, presented by Orson Welles and John Houseman. New York and London: Harper and Bros., 1941.

Ed. Thomas Knipp. *Letters to Joe C. Brown.* Kent, Ohio: Kent State University Libraries, 1968.

SECONDARY

Baker, Houston A. ed. *Twentieth Century Interpretations of Native Son.* Spectrum Books 883.

Baldwin, James. "Alas Poor Richard." *Nobody Knows My Name.* New York: Dial, 1961.

Baldwin, James, "Everybody's Protest Novel." *Partisan Review,* XVI (1949), 578–585; in Baldwin, *Notes of a Native Son.*

Baldwin, James. "Many Thousands Gone." *Notes of a Native Son.* Boston: Beacon, 1955.

Baldwin, James. "Richard Wright." *Encounter,* XVI (1961), 58–60.

Baldwin, James. "Survival of Richard Wright." *Reporter,* XXIV (March 15, 1961), 24.

"Black Boy." *Life,* XVIII (June 3, 1945), 87–93.

Bone, Robert A. *The Negro Novel in America.* Rev. ed. New Haven, Connecticut: Yale University Press, 1965.

Brown, Sterling A. "The Literary Scene, Chronicle and Comment." *Opportunity,* XVI (April, 1938), 120–121.

Burgum, Edwin B. "The Promise of Democracy in Richard Wright's Native Son." *The Novel and the World's Dilemma.* New York: Oxford University Press, 1947.

Charney, Maurice. "James Baldwin's Quarrel with Richard Wright." *American Quarterly,* XV (1963), 65–75.

Cohn, David L. "The Negro Novel: Richard Wright." *Atlantic Monthly,* CLXV (May, 1940), 659–661.

Creekmore, Hubert. "Social Factors in Native Son." *University of Kansas City Review,* VIII (1941), 136–143.

Davis, Arthur P. "*The Outsider* as a Novel of Race." *Midwest Journal,* VII (1955–56), 320–326.

Ellison, Ralph. "Richard Wright's Blues." *Antioch Review,* V (1945), 198–211; in Ellison's *Shadow and Act.*

Embree, Edwin. "Richard Wright, Native Son." *13 Against the Odds,* Port Washington, New York: Kennikat, 1967.

Fontaine, William T. "Toward a Philosophy of the American Negro Literature." *Presence Africaine* (English ed.), Nos. 24–25 (February–May, 1969), 164–176.

Ford, Nick A. "The Ordeal of Richard Wright." *College English,* XV (1953), 87–94.

Ford, Nick A. "Richard Wright, a Profile." *College Jewish Forum,* XXI (1962), 26–30.

Fuller, Hoyt W. "Contemporary Negro Fiction." *Southwest Review,* L (1965), 321–335.

Gerard, Albert. "Humanism and Negritude: Notes on the Contemporary Afro-American Novel." *Diogenes,* XXXVII (1962), 115–133.

Gibson, Donald B. "Richard Wright and the Tyranny of Convention." *CLA Journal,* XII (1968), 344–357.

Gibson, Donald B. "Richard Wright: A Bibliographical Essay." *CLA Journal,* XII (1968), 360–365.

Glicksberg, Charles I. "Existentialism in *The Outsider." Four Quarters,* VII (1958), 17–26.

Gloster, Hugh M. *Negro Voices in American Fiction.* Chapel Hill, North Carolina: University of North Carolina Press, 1948.

Gloster, Hugh M. "Richard Wright: Interpreter of Racial and Economic Maladjustments." *Opportunity,* XIX (1941), 361–365, 383.

Harrington, Ollie. "The Last Days of Richard Wright." *Ebony,* XVI (February, 1961), 83–86.

Hill, Herbert. "Reflections on Richard Wright: A Symposium on an Exiled Native Son," in *Anger and Beyond: The Negro Writer in the United States.* New York: Harper and Row, 1966, 196–212.

Howe, Irving. "Black Boys and Native Sons," in *A World More Attractive, a View of Modern Literature and Politics.* New York: Horizon, 1963.

Howe, Irving. "Richard Wright: A Word of Farewell." *New Republic,* CXLIV (February 13, 1961), 17–18.

Hyman, Stanley Edgar. The Promised End: Essays and Reviews, 1942–1962. Cleveland: World Publishing Co., 1963 ("American Literature and the Folk Tradition," 1958 Brandeis Lecture, debated with Ralph Ellison, *Partisan Review,* Spring, 1958).

Isaacs, Harold R. "Five Writers and Their African Ancestors: Part I." *Phylon,* XXI (1960), 243–265 (Langston Hughes and Richard Wright).

Jackson, Blyden. "Black Boy from America's Black Belt and Urban Ghettos." *CLA Journal,* XII (1968), 287–309.

Jackson, Esther M. "The American Negro and the Image of the Absurd." *Phylon,* XXIII (1962), 359–371.

Jones, Howard M. "Up From Slavery: Richard Wright's Story." *Saturday Review,* XXVIII (March 3, 1945), 9–10.

Kent, George E. "On the Future Study of Richard Wright." *CLA Journal,* XII (1968), 366–370.

Kinnamon, Keneth. "Richard Wright's Use of 'Othello' in 'Native Son.'" *CLA Journal,* XII (1968), 358–359.

Klotman, Phyllis R. and Melville Yancey, "The Gift of Double Vision, Possible Political Implications of Richard Wright's 'Self-Consciousness' Thesis." *CLA Journal,* XVI (September, 1972), 106–116.

Knipp, Thomas, ed. *Richard Wright: Letters to Joe C. Brown.* Kent, Ohio: Kent State University Library, 1968.

Knox, George. "The Negro Novelist's Sensibility and the Outsider Theme." *Western Humanities Review,* XI (1957), 137–148.

Lewis, T. "Saga of Bigger Thomas." *Catholic World,* CLIII (1941), 201–206.

Locke, Alain. "Of Native Sons: Real and Otherwise." *Opportunity,* XIX, (1941) 4–9.

Locke, Alain. "From *Native Son to Invisible Man:* A Review of the

Literature of the Negro: 1936." *Opportunity,* XV (1937), 8–13; Part II, 40–44.

Marcus, Steven. "The American Negro in Search of Identity." *Commentary,* XVI (1953), 456–463 (Baldwin, Ellison, Hughes, Wright).

Margolies, Edward L. *The Art of Richard Wright.* Carbondale, Illinois: Southern Illinois University Press, 1969.

Margolies, Edward L. *Native Sons: A Critical Study of Twentieth Century Negro American Authors.* Philadelphia: Lippincott, 1968.

Maund, Alfred. "The Negro Novelist and the Contemporary American Scene." *Chicago Jewish Forum,* XII (1954), 28–34.

McCall, Dan. *The Example of Richard Wright.* New York: Harcourt, Brace and World, 1969.

Miller, Eugene E. "Voodoo Parallels in 'Native Son.'" *CLA Journal,* XVI (September, 1972), 81–95.

Murray, Albert. "Something Different, Something More." *Anger and Beyond,* Herbert Hill, ed. New York: Harper and Row, 1966, 112–137.

Nutt, Howard. *Special Laughter.* Prairie City, Illinois: James A. Decker, 1940 (introduction by Wright).

Rascoe, Burton. "Negro Novel and White Reviewers." *African Methodist Review,* L (1940), 113–117 (*Native Son*).

Redding, Saunders. "The Alien Land of Richard Wright," in *Soon, One Morning: New Writings by American Negroes, 1940–1962,* Herbert Hill, ed. New York: Knopf, 1963.

Scott, Nathan A. "The Dark and Haunted Tower of Richard Wright." *Graduate Comment,* VII (1964), 92–99.

Scott, Nathan A. "A Search for Beliefs: The Fiction of Richard Wright." *University of Kansas City Review,* XXIII (1956), 19–24, 130–138.

Turner, Darwin T. "The Outsider: Revision of an Idea." *CLA Journal,* XII (June, 1969), 310–321.

Turner, Darwin T. "The Negro Novelist and the South." *Southern Humanities Review,* I (1967), 21–29.

Webb, Constance. *Richard Wright, a Biography.* New York: Putnam, 1968.

Webb, Constance. "What Next for Richard Wright?" *Phylon,* X, no. 2 (Second Quarter, 1949), 161–167.

Saunders Redding (1906–   )

PRIMARY

BOOKS:

To Make a Poet Black. Chapel Hill, North Carolina: University of North Carolina Press, 1939; College Park, Maryland: McGrath Publishing Co., 1968.

No Day of Triumph. New York and London: Harper and Bros., 1942.

They Came in Chains; Americans from Africa. Philadelphia: Lippincott, 1950.

On Being Negro in America. Indianapolis: Bobbs-Merrill, 1951.

An American in India; a Personal Report on the Indian Dilemma and the Nature of Her Conflicts. Indianapolis: Bobbs-Merrill, 1954.

The Lonesome Road: The Story of the Negro's Part in America. Garden City, New York: Doubleday, 1958.

The Negro. Washington, D.C.: Potomac Books, 1967.

Ed. with Arthur P. Davis, *Cavalcade: Negro American Writings from 1760 to the Present.* Boston: Houghton Mifflin, 1971.

ARTICLES:

"Mobbing." *Harper's,* CLXXXV (July, 1942), 189–198.

"A Negro Looks at This War." *American Mercury,* LV (November, 1942), 585–592.

"A Negro Speaks for His People." *Atlantic Monthly,* CLXXI (March, 1943), 58–63.

"Here's a New Thing Altogether." *Survey Graphic,* XXXIII (August, 1944), 358–359+.

"The Negro Author: His Publisher, His Public, and His Purse." *Publishers' Weekly,* CXLVII (1945), 1284–88.

"American Negro Literature." *American Scholar,* XVIII, no. 2 (April, 1949), 137–148.

"Portrait: W. E. Burghardt Du Bois." *American Scholar,* XVIII, no. 1 (January, 1949), 93–96.

"The Negro Writer—Shadow and Substance," in "The Negro in Literature: The Current Scene." *Phylon* (Special Issue), XI (1950), 297–374, 371–373.

"No Envy, No Handicap." *Saturday Review,* XXXVII (February 13, 1954), 23+.

"Up from Reconstruction." *Nation,* CLXXIX (September 4, 1954), 196–197.

"Battle Behind the Lines." *Reporter,* XVIII (January 9, 1958), 29–31.

"Tonight for Freedom." *American Heritage,* IX (June, 1958), 52–55+.

"The Negro Writer and His Relationship to His Roots," in *The American Negro Writer and His Roots,* New York: American Society of African Culture, 1960, 1–8.

"Negro Writing in America." *New Leader,* XLII (May 16, 1960), 8-10.

"In the Vanguard of Civil Rights." *Saturday Review,* XLIV (August 12, 1961), 34.

With W. E. B. Du Bois. "Introduction and Preface to *Souls of Black Folk.*" *Freedomways,* II, no. 2 (Spring, 1962), 161–166.

"Home to Africa: A Journey of the Heart." *The American Scholar,* XXXII, no. 2 (Spring, 1963); reprinted in *Negro Digest,* XII (May, 1963), 80–87.

"Sound of Their Masters' Voices." *Saturday Review,* XLVI (June 29, 1963), 26.

"Modern African Literature." *CLA Journal,* VII (March, 1964), 191–201.

"Man Against Myth and Malice." *Saturday Review,* XLVII (May 9, 1964), 48–49.

"The Problems of the Negro Writer." *Massachusetts Review,* VI (1964), 57–70.

"Since Richard Wright." *American Forum,* I, no. 4 (1966), 21–31.

SECONDARY

Bontemps, Arna. "Facing a Dilemma." *Saturday Review,* XXXV (February 16, 1952), 23+.

Davis, Arthur P. Review of *On Being Negro in America* by J. Saunders Redding. *Phylon,* XII, no. 1 (1952), 64–66.

Turner, Darwin, ed. *Black American Literature, Essays.* Columbus, Ohio: Merrill, 1969, p. 91.

Winslow, Henry F. "Beyond the Seas—an Uneasy World." *The Crisis,* LCII (February, 1955), 77–80.

Chester Himes (1909–   )

PRIMARY

NOVELS:

If He Hollers Let Him Go. Garden City, New York: Doubleday, Doran, 1945.

Lonely Crusade. New York: Knopf, 1947.

Cast the First Stone. New York: Coward-McCann, 1952; New York: New American Library, 1972.

The Third Generation. Cleveland: World Publishing Co., 1954.

The Primitive. New York: New American Library, 1955; New York: Avon, 1965.

For Love of Imabelle. Greenwich, Connecticut: Fawcett, 1957; later titled *A Rage in Harlem,* New York: Avon, 1965.

The Real Cool Killers. New York: Avon, 1959; London: Panther, 1969.

The Crazy Kill. New York: Avon, 1959; London: Panther, 1968.

Run, Man Run. New York: Putnam's Sons, 1966.

The Big Gold Dream. New York: Avon, 1960; London: Panther, 1968.

All Shot Up. New York: Avon, 1960; London: Panther, 1969.

Pinktoes. Paris: Olympia Press, 1961; London: Arthur Baker, 1961; Putnam, 1965 (original title, *Mamie Mason*)

The Heat's On. New York: Putnam's Sons, 1966; London: Muller, 1966 (subsequently changed to *Come Back, Charleston Blue,* Berkeley, 1972).

Cotton Comes to Harlem. New York: Putnam's Sons, 1965.

Blind Man With a Pistol. New York: William Morrow, 1969 (paperback titled *Hot Day, Hot Night,* New York: Dell, 1970).

AUTOBIOGRAPHY:

The Quality of Hurt. New York: Doubleday, 1972.

SHORT FICTION:

"Crazy in the Stir." *Esquire,* II (August, 1934), 23, 114–116.

"To What Red Hell." *Esquire,* II (October, 1934), 100–101, 122, 127.

"The Visiting Hour." *Esquire,* VI (September, 1936), 76, 143–146.

"The Night's for Cryin'." *Esquire,* VII (January, 1937), 64, 146–148.

"Every Opportunity." *Esquire,* VII (May, 1937), 99, 129–130.

"Salute to the Passing." *Opportunity,* XVII (March, 1939), 74–79.

"Marihuana and a Pistol." *Esquire,* XIII (March, 1940), 58.

"Face in the Moon." *Coronet,* February, 1941.

"The Things You Do." *Opportunity,* XIX (May, 1941), 141–143.

"Lunching at the Ritzmore." *The Crisis,* XLIX (October, 1942), 314–315, 331.

"In the Night." *Opportunity,* XX (November, 1942), 334–335, 348–349.

"Two Soldiers." *The Crisis,* L (January, 1943), 13–29.

"Heaven Has Changed." *The Crisis,* L (March, 1943), 78–83.
"So Softly Smiling." *The Crisis,* L (October, 1943), 302, 314–316.
"All He Needs Is Feet." *The Crisis,* L (November, 1943), 332.
"Money Don't Spend in the Stir." *Esquire,* XXI (April, 1944), 75, 174–175.
"All God's Children Got Pride." *The Crisis,* LI (June, 1944), 188–189, 204.
"The Song Says 'Keep on Smiling.' " *The Crisis,* LII (April, 1945), 103–104.
"The Something in a Colored Man." *Esquire,* XXV (January, 1946), 120–158.
"To End All Storms." *The Crisis,* LV (July, 1948), 205, 220.
"Mama's Missionary Money." *The Crisis,* LVI (November, 1949), 303, 307.
"The Snake." *Esquire,* LII (October, 1959), 147–149.

ARTICLES:

"Now Is the Time! Here Is the Place!" *Opportunity,* XX (September, 1942), 271–273.
"Zoot Riots Are Race Riots." *The Crisis,* L (July, 1943), 200–201, 222.
"Negro Martyrs Are Needed." *The Crisis,* L (May, 1944), 159–174.
"Equality for 125,000 Dead." *Chicago Defender,* 1945.
"Second Guesses for First Novelists." *Saturday Review of Literature,* XXIX (February 16, 1946), 13.
"Rejoinder." *Commentary,* L (May, 1948), 473–474.
"Author's Protest." *Commentary,* L (May, 1948), 474.
"Harlem ou le cancer de l'Amérique." *Présence Africaine,* no. 45 (Spring, 1963), 46–81.
"My Favorite Novel." *New York Times* Book Review, June 4, 1967, p. 6 (about *The Primitive*).
"The Dilemma of the Negro Novelist in the United States," in *Beyond the Angry Black,* John A. Williams, ed. New York: Cooper Square, 1966, 52–58.

MISCELLANEOUS PUBLICATIONS:

"This Cleveland," in *Cleveland Daily News,* 1939 (over 40 prose poems).
"Letter to *New Masses* about *Native Son,*" in *"Native Son:* Pros and Cons." *New Masses* (May 21, 1940), 23–24.
"Review of *The Street* by Ann Petry." *New Masses,* 1946.
"A Letter of Protest to His Publishers from Chester Himes in Spain." *Negro Digest,* XVIII (May, 1969), 98.

SECONDARY

Bone, Robert A. *The Negro Novel in America.* Rev. ed. New Haven, Connecticut: Yale University Press, 1965.
Chelminski, Rudolph. "Hard-bitten Old Pro Who Wrote Cotton." *Life,* LXI (August 28, 1970), 60–61.
"Chester Himes." *Encyclopedia International.* 2nd ed. New York: Grolier, 1968.
Fabre, Michel. "A Case of Rape." *Black World,* XXI, no. 5 (March, 1972), 39–48.

Farrison, W. Edward. Review of *The Quality of Hurt. CLA Journal,* XVI (September, 1972), 117–119.

Fuller, Hoyt W. "Traveler on the Long, Rough, Lonely Old Road: An Interview with Chester Himes." *Black World,* XXI, no. 5 (March, 1972), 4–22.

Hairston, Loyle. Review of *The Quality of Hurt. Freedomways,* XII, no. 2 (Second Quarter, 1972), 155–158.

Huggins, Nathan I. "The Quality of Hurt." *New York Times* Book Review, March 12, 1972, pp. 5, 32.

Margolies, Edward. "The Thrillers of Chester Himes," in *Studies in Black Literature* (June, 1970), 1–11.

Margolies, Edward. *Native Sons: a Critical Study of Twentieth Century Negro American Authors.* Philadelphia: Lippincott, 1968.

Margolies, Edward. "Experiences of the Black Expatriate Writer: Chester Himes." *CLA Journal,* XV (June, 1972), 421–427.

Reed, Ishmael. "Chester Himes: Writer." *Black World,* XXI, no. 5 (March, 1972), 23–38.

Sanders, Archie D. "The Image of the Negro in Five Major Novels by Chester Himes." Washington, D.C.: Howard University, 1965. M.A. thesis, department of English.

Williams, John A. "My Man Himes." *Amistad I* (1969), 25–93 (interview).

Melvin B[eaunorous] Tolson (1900–1966)

PRIMARY

POETRY COLLECTIONS:

Rendezvous with America. New York: Dodd, Mead, 1944.
Libretto for the Republic of Liberia. New York: Twayne, 1953.
Harlem Gallery, Book I: The Curator. New York: Twayne, 1965.

POEMS PUBLISHED SEPARATELY:

"Kikes, Bohunks, Crackers, Dagos, Niggers." *The Modern Quarterly,* XI (1938–1941), 18–19.
"The Braggart." *Common Ground,* IV (Summer, 1944), 74.
"Libretto for the Republic of Liberia." *Poetry,* LXXVI, no. 4 (July, 1950), 208–215.
"E. & O. E." *Poetry,* LXXVIII (September, 1951), 330–344, 369–372 (with notes).
"Man from Halicarnassus." *Poetry,* LXXXI (October, 1952), 75–77.

ARTICLES:

"Richard Wright: Native Son." *The Modern Quarterly,* XI, no. 5 (1938–1941), 19–24.
"Claude McKay's Art." *Poetry,* LXXXIII (February, 1954), 287–290.
"A Poet's Odyssey," in *Anger and Beyond: The Negro Writer in the United States,* Herbert Hill, ed. New York: Harper and Row, 1966.
Tolson, Melvin B. "A Poet's Odyssey." *Anger and Beyond: The Negro Writer in the United States,* Herbert Hill, ed. New York: Harper and Row, 1966, 181–203 (an interview).

Fabio, Sarah Webster. "Who Speaks Negro?" *Negro Digest,* XVI (December, 1966), 54–58.
McCall, Dan. "The Quicksilver Sparrow of M. B. Tolson." *American Quarterly,* XVIII (1966), 538–542.
Randall, Dudley. "Melvin B. Tolson: Portrait of a Poet as Raconteur." *Negro Digest,* XV (January, 1966), 54–57.
Shapiro, Karl. "Melvin B. Tolson, Poet." *Book Week, New York Herald Tribune,* January 10, 1965; reprinted in *Negro Digest,* XIV (May, 1965), 75–77.
Tate, Allen. "Preface to Libretto for the Republic of Liberia." *Poetry,* LXXVI (1950), 216–218.
Thompson, Dolphin G. "Tolson's Gallery Brings Poetry Home." *Negro History Bulletin,* XXIX, no. 3 (December, 1965), 69–70.

Robert [Earl] Hayden (1913–   )

PRIMARY

COLLECTED POEMS:

Heart-Shape in the Dust. Detroit: Falcon Press, 1940.
With Myron O'Higgins. *The Lion and the Archer.* New York: Hemphill Press, 1949 (n.p.).
Figure of Time: Poems. Nashville: Hemphill Press, 1955.
A Ballad of Remembrance. London: P. Breman, 1962.
Selected Poems. New York: October House, 1966.
Words in the Mourning Time. New York: October House, 1970.
The Night-Blooming Cereus. London: P. Bremen, distributed by Broadside, Detroit, 1972.

ANTHOLOGIES:

Ed., *Kaleidoscope: Poems by American Negro Poets.* New York: Harcourt, Brace and World, 1967.
Ed., with David J. Burroughs and Frederick R. Lapides. *Afro-American Literature: an Introduction.* New York: Harcourt, Brace and Jovanovich, 1971.

POEMS PUBLISHED SEPARATELY:

"Gabriel (Hanged in 1800 as Leader of a Slave-Revolt)." *Opportunity,* XVII, no. 10 (October, 1939), 300.
"To a Young Negro Poet." *Opportunity,* XVIII, no. 4 (April, 1940), 116.
"We Have not Forgotten." *Opportunity,* XVIII, no. 10 (October, 1940), 304.
"O Daedalus, Fly Away Home." *Poetry,* LXII (July, 1943), 192–193.
"Frederick Douglass." *Atlantic Monthly,* CLXXIX (February, 1947), 124.

SECONDARY

Galler, D. "Three Recent Volumes." *Poetry,* CX (1967), 268.
Negro History Bulletin, XXI (October, 1957), 15.

Pool, Rosey E. "Robert Hayden: Poet Laureate." *Negro Digest,* XV (June, 1966), 39–43.

Margaret Walker (1915–   )

PRIMARY

BOOKS:

For My People. New Haven, Connecticut: Yale University Press, 1942 (foreword by Stephen Vincent Benét); New York: Arno, 1968 (poetry).
Jubilee. Boston: Houghton Mifflin, 1966 (novel).
Prophets for a New Day. Detroit: Broadside, 1970 (poetry).
How I Wrote Jubilee. Chicago: Third World Press, 1972.

POEMS PUBLISHED SEPARATELY:

"Dark Blood." *Opportunity,* XVI, no. 6 (June, 1938), 171.
"Ex-slave." *Opportunity,* XVI, no. 11 (November, 1938), 330.
"Palmettos." *Opportunity,* XVII, no. 1 (January, 1939), 14.

ARTICLES:

"Nausea of Sartre." *Yale Review,* XLII, no. 2 (December, 1952), 251–261.
"Willing To Pay the Price," in *Many Shades of Black,* by Wormley, Stanton L., and Lewis H. Fenderson. New York: Morrow, 1969.
"Soul-Searching in Tennessee." *Saturday Review,* L (January 7, 1967), 35.

MISCELLANEOUS PUBLICATIONS:

Excerpt from *Jubilee* (1966), "Chapter One," in Chambers, *Right On,* 27–40.

SECONDARY

Book reviews located in *Book Review Digest.*
Current Biography (1943).
Davis, Lester. Review of *Jubilee. Freedomways,* VII, no. 3 (Summer, 1967), 258, 260.
Emanuel, James A. and Theodore L. Gross, eds. *Dark Symphony, Negro Literature in America.* New York: Free Press, 1968, 493–494.
Giddings, Paula. " 'A Shoulder Hunched Against a Sharp Concern': Some Themes in the Poetry of Margaret Walker." *Black World,* XXI, no. 2 (December, 1971), 20–25.
Lee, Ulysses. *"For My People." Opportunity,* XX (December, 1942), 379–380 (book review).

Gwendolyn Brooks (1917–   )

PRIMARY

BOOKS:

A Street in Bronzeville. New York: Harper, 1945.
Annie Allen. New York: Harper, 1949; Westport, Connecticut: Green-

wood Press, 1971 (poems).

Maud Martha, a novel. New York: Harper, 1953.

Bronzeville Boys and Girls. New York: Harper, 1956.

The Bean Eaters. New York: Harper, 1960 (poems).

Selected Poems. New York: Harper and Row, 1963.

A Portion of That Field; the Centennial of the Burial of Lincoln. Urbana, Illinois: University of Illinois Press, 1967.

For Illinois, 1968; a Sesquicentennial Poem. Chicago(?) 1968.

In the Mecca. New York: Harper and Row, 1968 (poems).

Riot. Detroit, Michigan: Broadside Press, 1969.

Family Pictures. Detroit, Michigan: Broadside, 1970.

Aloneness. Illustrated by Leroy Foster. Detroit, Michigan: Broadside, 1971

Ed., *A Broadside Treasury.* Detroit, Michigan: Broadside, 1971.

Ed., *Jump Bad; a New Chicago Anthology.* Detroit, Michigan: Broadside, 1971.

The World of Gwendolyn Brooks. New York: Harper and Row, 1971 (*A Street in Bronzeville, Annie Allen, Maud Martha, The Bean Eaters, In the Mecca*).

MISCELLANEOUS:

"They Call It Bronzeville." *Holiday,* X (October, 1951), 60–64.

"We're the Only Colored People Here," in *The Best Short Stories by Negro Writers,* by Langston Hughes, 1967, 202–204 (excerpt from *Maud Martha,* 1953).

"Paul Robeson." *Freedomways,* XI, no. 1 (First Quarter, 1971), 104 (poem).

"Thank You." *Black World,* XXI, no. 1 (November, 1970), 42 (poem).

"Helen," in *Soon, One Morning, New Writings by American Negroes,* Herbert Hill, New York: Knopf, 1963, 320–322; *Black and White, Stories of American Life,* Carol Anselment and Donald Gibson, New York: Washington Square Press, 1971 (excerpt from *Maud Martha,* 1953).

SECONDARY

Benson, Brian J. Review of *In the Mecca* by Gwendolyn Brooks, *CLA Journal,* XIII, no. 2 (December, 1969), 203.

Brown, Frank London. "Chicago's Great Lady of Poetry." *Negro Digest,* XI (December, 1961), 53–57.

Burrow, W. "Five Fabulous Females." *Negro Digest,* XII (July, 1963), 78–83.

Contemporary Authors, Volume I (1962).

Crockett, J. "An Essay on Gwendolyn Brooks." *Negro History Bulletin,* XIX, no. 2 (November, 1955), 37–39.

Current Biography (1950).

Cutler, B. "Long Reach, Strong Speech." *Poetry,* CIII (1964), 388–389.

Davis, Arthur P. "The Black-and-Tan Motif in the Poetry of Gwendolyn Brooks." *CLA Journal,* VI, no. 2 (December, 1962), 90–97.

Davis, Arthur P. "Gwendolyn Brooks: A Poet of the Unheroic." *CLA Journal,* VII (December, 1963), 114–125.

Baker, Houston A. "The Achievement of Gwendolyn Brooks." *CLA Journal,* XVI (September, 1972), 23–31.

Emanuel, James A. "A Note on the Future of Negro Poetry." *Negro American Literature Forum,* I (Fall, 1967), 2–3.

Fuller, James A. "Notes on a Poet." *Negro Digest,* XI (August, 1962), 50+.

Garland, P. "Gwendolyn Brooks: Poet Laureate." *Ebony,* XXIII (July, 1968), 48–50+.

Harriott, F. "Life of a Pulitzer Poet." *Negro Digest,* VIII (August, 1950), 14–16.

Kent, George E. "The Poetry of Gwendolyn Brooks." Part I, *Black World* (September, 1971); Part II, *Black World* (October, 1971).

Kunitz, Stanley. "Bronze by Gold." *Poetry,* LXXVI (1950), 52–56.

Littlejohn, David. *Black on White.* New York: Grossman, 1966.

Miller, Jeanne-Marie A. "Poet Laureate of Bronzeville, U.S.A." *Freedomways,* X (First Quarter, 1970), 63–75.

Rivers, Conrad Kent. "Poetry of Gwendolyn Brooks." *Negro Digest,* XIII (June, 1964), 67–68.

Rollins, Charlemae. *Famous American Negro Poets.* New York: Dodd, Mead, 1965.

Twentieth Century Authors. First Supplement (1955).

Ann [Lane] Petry (1911–   )

PRIMARY

BOOKS:

The Street. Boston: Houghton Mifflin, 1946 (novel).

Country Place. Boston: Houghton Mifflin, 1947; Chatham, New Jersey: Chatham Bookseller, 1971.

The Drugstore Cat. New York: Crowell, 1949 (juvenile).

The Narrows. Boston: Houghton Mifflin, 1953 (novel).

Harriet Tubman, Conductor on the Underground Railroad. New York: Crowell, 1955.

Tituba of Salem Village. New York: Crowell, 1964 (young adults).

Legends of the Saints. New York: Crowell, 1970 (juvenile).

Miss Muriel and Other Stories. Boston: Houghton Mifflin, 1971.

SHORT FICTION:

"On Saturdays the Siren Sounds at Noon." *The Crisis,* L (December, 1943), 368–369.

"Olaf and His Girl Friend." *The Crisis,* LII (May, 1945), 135–137, 147.

"Like a Winding Sheet." *The Crisis,* LII (November, 1945), 317–381, 331; in *Best American Short Stories.* New York: Houghton Mifflin, 1946, 302–315.

"The Bones of Louella Brown." *Opportunity,* XXV (Fall, 1947), 189–192, 226–230.

"In Darkness and Confusion," in *Cross Section.* New York: L. B. Fischer, 1947, 98–128.

"Miss Muriel," in *Stories in Black and White,* by Eva H. Kissin, Philadelphia: Lippincott, 1970, 23–77.

SECONDARY

Bone, Robert A. *The Negro Novel in America.* Rev. ed. New Haven, Connecticut: Yale University Press, 1965.

Dempsey, David. "Uncle Tom's Ghost and the Literary Abolitionist." *Antioch Review,* VI (1946), 442–448.

Green, Marjorie. "Ann Petry Planned to Write." *Opportunity,* XXIV, no. 2 (April–June, 1946), 78–79.

Ivy, James. "Ann Petry Talks About First Novel." *The Crisis,* LIII, no. 1 (January, 1946), 48–49.

Ivy, James. "Mrs. Petry's Harlem." *The Crisis,* LIII, no. 5 (May, 1946), 154–155 (review of Petry's *The Street*).

Maund, Alfred. "The Negro Novelist and the Contemporary American Scene." *Chicago Jewish Forum,* XII (1954), 28–34.

"On an Author." New York *Herald Tribune,* August 16, 1953.

Richardson, Ben. *Great American Negroes.* New York: Crowell, 1956.

Julian Mayfield (1928–   )

PRIMARY

BOOKS:

The Hit. New York: Vanguard, 1957 (novel).

The Long Night. New York: Vanguard, 1958 (novel).

The Grand Parade. New York: Vanguard, 1961 (subsequently changed to *Nowhere Street;* (novel).

Ed. *Ten Times Black.* New York: Bantam Books, 1972 (10 black writers. Evan K. Walker, Hank Gay, Sam Greenlee, Nikki Giovanni, Maya Angelou, Sandra Drake, Rosa Guy, Barbara Woods, Clarence Major, Julian Mayfield).

SHORT STORIES:

"Black on Black: A Political Love Story." *Black World,* XXI (February, 1972), 54–71.

ARTICLES:

"Numbers Writer: a Portrait." *Nation,* CXC (May 14, 1960), 424–425.

"Into the Mainstream and Oblivion." *The American Negro Writer and His Roots,* New York: American Society of African Culture, 1960, 29–34.

"The Cuban Challenge." *Freedomways,* I (Summer, 1961), 185–189.

"Challenge to Negro Leadership." *Commentary,* XXXI (April, 1961), 297–305.

"Love Affair with the United States." *New Republic,* CXLV (August 7, 1961), 25.

"And Then Came Baldwin." *Freedomways,* III (Spring, 1963), 143–155.

"Tale of Two Novelists." *Negro Digest,* XIV (June, 1965), 70–72.

"Black Writer's Views on Literary Lions and Values." *Negro Digest,* XVII (January, 1968), 16.

"Legitimacy of Black Revolution." *Nation,* CCVI (April 22, 1968), 541–543.

"New Mainstream." *Nation,* CCIV (May 13, 1968), 638.
"Crisis or Crusade? An Article-Review of Harold Cruse's *Crisis of the Negro Intellectual.*" *Negro Digest,* XVII (June, 1968), 10–24.

SECONDARY

Graham, Shirley. Review of *The Grand Parade, Freedomways,* I (Summer, 1961), 218–223.
Review of *The Grand Parade. Interracial Review,* XXXV (May, 1962), 127.
"Up Tight." *Ebony,* XXIV (November, 1968), 46–48.

Lorraine Hansberry (1930–1965)

PRIMARY

BOOKS:

A Raisin in the Sun; a Drama in Three Acts. New York: Random House, 1959.
The Movement; Documentary of a Struggle for Equality. New York: Simon and Schuster, 1964.
The Sign in Sidney Brustein's Window, a Drama in Three Acts. New York: Random House, 1965; New York: S. French, 1965.
Les Blancs and the Last Plays of Lorraine Hansberry. New York: Random House, 1972.

ARTICLES:

"Strange Flower." *Liberation,* IV (May, 1959), 14–15.
"Me Tink Me Hear Sounds in de Night." *Theatre Arts,* XLIV (October, 1960), 9–11+.
"This Complex of Womanhood." *Ebony,* XV (August, 1960), 40.
"This Complex of Womanhood." *Ebony,* XVIII (September, 1963), 88.
"American Theatre Needs Desegregating, Too." *Negro Digest,* X (June, 1961), 28–33 (reprinted from *Theatre Arts*).
"A Challenge to Artists (Speech Delivered at Rally to Abolish the House Un-American Activities Committee, Manhattan Center, NYC, October 27, 1962)." *Freedomways,* III (Winter, 1963), 31–35.
"The Nation Needs Your Gifts: Memo to Negro Youth." *Negro Digest,* X (June, 1961), 28–33 (reprinted from *Theatre Arts*).
"The Legacy of W. E. B. Du Bois." *Freedomways,* V (Winter, 1965), 19–20.
"My Name Is Lorraine Hansberry, I Am a Writer." *Esquire,* LXXII (November, 1969), 140–141.

SECONDARY

Baldwin, James. "Sweet Lorraine." *Esquire,* LXXII (November, 1969), 139–140.
Davis, Ossie. "The Significance of Lorraine Hansberry." *Freedomways,* V (Summer, 1965), 396–402.

"Elegy for Lorraine; Presentation of To Be Young, Gifted and Black." *Time*, XXXIX (January 10, 1969), 43.

Farrison, W. Edward. "Lorraine Hansberry's Last Dramas." *CLA Journal* (Dec., 1972), 188–98.

Isaacs, Harold. "Five Writers and Their African Ancestors: Part II." *Phylon*, XXI (Winter, 1960), 329–336.

Nemiroff, Robert. *To Be Young, Gifted, and Black; Lorraine Hansberry in Her Own Words*, adapted by Robert Nemiroff. Englewood Cliffs, New Jersey: Prentice-Hall, 1969 (introduction by James Baldwin).

Ness, David E. Review of *Les Blancs: Freedomways*, XII, no. 3 (Third Quarter, 1972), 245–248.

Oliver, Edith. "Off Broadway; Presentation of *To Be Young, Gifted and Black*." *New Yorker*, XLIV (January 11, 1969), 58.

"People Are Talking About . . ." *Vogue*, CXXXIII (June, 1959), 78–79.

"Playwright." *New Yorker*, XXXV (May 9, 1959), 33–35.

"Surprise." *Newsweek*, LIII (April 20, 1959), 75.

Weales, G. "Losing the Playwright." *Commonweal*, XC (September 5, 1969), 542–543.

Les Blancs. Criticism:

Nation, CCXI (November 30, 1970), 573.

Nation, CCXI (December 7, 1970), 606.

New Yorker, XLVI (November 21, 1970), 104.

Newsweek, LXXVI (November 30, 1970), 98.

Ralph Ellison (1914–   )

PRIMARY

BOOKS:

Invisible Man. New York: Random House, 1952 (novel).

Shadow and Act. New York: Random House, 1964 (essays).

SHORT FICTION:

"Slick Gonna Learn." *Direction* (September, 1939), 10–16.

"Afternoon," in *American Writing*, Hans Otto Storm, et al, eds. Prairie City, Illinois: Decker, 1940, 28–37; *Negro Story Magazine*, I, no. 5 (March–April, 1945), 3–8 (incorporated into *Invisible Man*).

"Mister Toussan." *New Masses*, XLI, no. 5 (November 4, 1941), 19–20; *Negro Story Magazine*, I, no. 2 (August, 1944), 37–41.

"That I Had the Wings." *Common Ground*, III, no. 4 (Summer, 1943), 30–37.

"Flying Home," in *Cross Section*, Edwin Seaver, ed. New York: Fisher, 1944, pp. 469–485; *Best Short Stories of World War II*, 1957; *The Best Short Stories by Negro Writers*, Langston Hughes, ed. Boston: Little, Brown, 1967, 151–170.

"It Is a Strange Country." *Tomorrow*, III, no. 11 (July, 1944), 41–44; *I Have Seen War*, 1960.

"King of the Bingo Game." *Tomorrow*, IV, no. 2 (November, 1944), 29–33.

"The Invisible Man." *Horizon*, XCIII, no. 4 (October, 1947), 104–117; subsequently reprinted as "Battle Royal."

"Battle Royal." *'48, The Magazine of the Year*, II, no. 1 (January, 1948), 14–32; in *A New Southern Harvest*, Robert Penn Warren and Albert Erskine, eds. New York: Dell, 1957, 172–185; *Stories of Modern America*, H. Gold and D. L. Stevenson, eds. New York: St. Martins, 1961.

"Invisible Man: Prologue to a Novel." *Partisan Review*, XIX, no. 1 (January, 1952), 31–40.

"Did You Ever Dream Lucky?" *New World Writing*, No. 5 Mentor Book. New York: The New American Library of World Literature, 1954, 134–145.

"A Coupla Scalped Indians," in *New World Writing*, No. 9, Mentor Book. New York: The New American Library of World Literature, 1956, 225–236.

"And Hickman Arrives." *The Noble Savage*, I (1956).

"It Always Breaks Out." *Partisan Review*, XXX, no. 1 (Spring, 1963), 13–28.

"Out of the Hospital and Under the Bar," in *Soon, One Morning*, Herbert Hill, ed. New York: Knopf, 1963, 242–290.

"Song of Innocence—Excerpt from a Novel in Progress." *The Iowa Review*, I, no. 2 (Spring, 1970), 30–40.

ARTICLES:

"Anti-Semitism among Negroes." *Jewish Peoples Voice*, III, no. 4 (April, 1939), 3, 8.

"Judge Lynch in New York." *New Masses*, XXXII, No. 8 (August 15, 1939), 15–16.

"Camp Lost Colony." *New Masses*, XXXIV, no. 7 (February 6, 1940), 18–19.

"A Congress Jim Crow Didn't Attend." *New Masses*, XXXV, no. 8 (May 14, 1940), 5, 7–8.

"They Found Terror in Harlem." *Negro World Digest*, I, no. 1 (July, 1940), 43–45.

"The Birthmark." *New Masses*, XXXVI, no. 2 (July 2, 1940), 16–17; *Negro World Digest*, I, no. 4 (November, 1940), 61–65; *Negro Story Magazine*, 1945 (can be classified as either a vignette or a short story).

"Richard Wright and Negro Fiction." *Direction*, IV, no. 5 (Summer, 1941), 12–13.

"Philippine Writers Report." *Direction*, IV, no. 5 (Summer, 1941), 13.

"Recent Negro Fiction." *New Masses*, XL, no. 6 (August 5, 1941), 22–26.

"The Way It Is." *New Masses*, XLV, no. 3 (October 20, 1942), 9–11; *Shadow and Act*, 1964, 282–293.

"Eyewitness Story of Riot." New York *Post* (August 2, 1943), 4.

"Beating that Boy." *The New Republic*, CXIII, no. 17 (October 22, 1945), 535–536; *Shadow and Act*, 1964, 95–101.

"Richard Wright's Blues." *Antioch Review*, V, no. 2 (Summer, 1945), 198–211; *The Antioch Review Anthology*, Paul Bixler, ed. Cleveland: World, 1953, 267–275; *Shadow and Act*, 1964, 77–94.

"The Shadow and the Act." *The Reporter*, I, no. 17 (December 6, 1949), 17–19; *Shadow and Act*, 1964, 273–281.

"Invisible Man: Prologue to a Novel." *Partisan Review,* XIX, no. 1 (January, 1952), 31–40.

"Twentieth-Century Fiction and the Black Mask of Humanity." *Confluence,* II, no. 4 (December, 1953), 3–21; *Shadow and Act,* 1964, 24–44.

"Introduction to Flamenco." *Saturday Review,* XXXVII, no. 50 (December 11, 1954), 38–39.

"Living with Music." *High Fidelity,* V, no. 10 (December, 1955), 60–62, 130, 132; *Shadow and Act,* 1964, 187–198.

"Society, Morality, and the Novel." *The Living Novel: a Symposium,* Granville Hicks, ed. New York: Macmillan, 1957.

"Change the Joke and Slip the Yoke." *Partisan Review,* XXV, no. 2 (Spring, 1958), 212–222; in *Shadow and Act.*

"Charlie Christian Story." *Saturday Review,* XLI, no. 20 (May 17, 1958), 42, 43, 46; in *Shadow and Act.*

"Remembering Jimmy." *Saturday Review,* XLI, no. 28 (July 12, 1958), 36, 37; in *Views of America* (1960); in *Shadow and Act.*

"As the Spirit Moves Mahalia." *Saturday Review,* XLI, 39 (September 27, 1958), 41, 43, 69, 70; in *Entrances and Exits* (1962–63); in *Shadow and Act.*

"The Golden Age, Time Past." *Esquire,* LI, no. 1 (January, 1959), 107–110; in *Shadow and Act.*

"Stephen Crane and the Mainstream of American Fiction," in *The Red Badge of Courage and Four Great Stories by Stephen Crane.* New York: Dell, 1960, 7–24 (introduction); in *Shadow and Act.*

"Talks About James Baldwin." *Negro Digest,* XI (September, 1962), 61; reprinted from the *University of Chicago Magazine.*

"A Rejoinder," in "The Critic and the Writer—An Exchange." *The New Leader,* XLVII, no. 3 (February 3, 1964), 15–22; in *Shadow and Act.*

"On Becoming a Writer." *Commentary,* XXXVIII, no. 4 (October, 1964), 57–60; in *Shadow and Act.*

With Karl Shapiro. *The Writer's Experience: Lectures by Ralph Ellison and Karl Shapiro.* Washington: Published for the Library of Congress by the Gertrude Clarke Whittall Poetry and Literature Fund [for sale by the Superintendent of Documents, U.S. Government Printing Off.], 1964.

"The Blues." *The New York Review,* I, no. 12 (February 6, 1964), 5–7; in *Shadow and Act* (review of LeRoi Jones's *Blues People*).

"Harlem is Nowhere." *Harper's,* CCXXIX, VIII (August, 1964), 53–57; in *Shadow and Act* (excerpt from *Shadow and Act*).

SECONDARY

Baumback, Jonathan. "Nightmare of a Native Son," in *The Landscape of Nightmare.* New York: 1965, 68–86.

Bennett, John Z. "The Race and the Runner: Ellison's *Invisible Man*." *Xavier University Studies,* V, 12–16.

Bennett, William. "Black and Blue; Negro Céline." *American Mercury,* LXXIV (June, 1952), 100–104.

Bloch, Alice. "Sight Imagery in *Invisible Man.*" *English Journal,* LV, 1019–1021, 1024.

Bluestein, Gene. "The Blues as a Literary Theme." *Massachusetts Review,* VIII, 593–617.

Bone, Robert A. "Ralph Ellison and the Uses of Imagination." *Tri-Quarterly,* no. 6 (1966), 39–54; in *Anger and Beyond,* 86–111.

Bone, Robert A. *The Negro Novel in America.* Rev. ed. New Haven, Connecticut: Yale University Press, 1965.

Brown, Lloyd W. "Ralph Ellison's Exhorters: The Role of Rhetoric in *Invisible Man.*" *CLA Journal,* XIII, no. 3 (1970), 289–303.

Cambon, Glauco. "Ralph Ellison della invisibla." *Aut. Aut.,* III (March, 1953), 135–144.

Clipper, Lawrence J. "Folkloric and Mythic Elements in *Invisible Man.*" *CLA Journal,* XIII, no. 3 (1970), 229–241.

Corry, John. "An American Novelist Who Sometimes Teaches." *New York Times* Magazine, November 20, 1965, 54.

Covo, Jacqueline. "Ralph Waldo Ellison: Bibliographic Essays and Finding List of American Criticism, 1952–1964." *CLA Journal,* XV, no. 2 (December, 1970), 171–196.

Fass, Barbara. "Rejection of Paternalism: Hawthorne's 'My Kinsman Major Molineux' and Ellison's 'Invisible Man,' " *CLA Journal,* XV, no. 2 (December, 1971), 171–196.

Ford, Nick Aaron. "Four Popular Negro Novelists." *Phylon,* XV (March, 1954), 29–39 (Ellison, Baldwin, Wright, Yerby).

Fraiberg, S. "Two Modern Incest Heroes." *Partisan Review,* XXVIII (1961), 646–661.

Gottesman, Ronald, comp. *The Merrill Studies in Invisible Man.* Columbus, Ohio: Merrill, 1971.

Heermance, J. N. "The Modern Negro Novel." *Negro Digest,* XIII (May, 1964), 66–76.

Horowitz, Floyd R. "Ralph Ellison's Modern Version of Brer Bear and Brer Rabbit in *Invisible Man.*" *Midcontinent American Studies Journal,* IV, no. 2 (1963), 21–27.

Horowitz, Floyd R. "Enigma of Ellison's Intellectual Man." *CLA Journal,* VII (December, 1963), 126–132.

Horowitz, Floyd R. "An Experimental Confession from a Reader of *Invisible Man.*" *CLA Journal,* XIII, no. 3 (1970), 304–314.

Hux, Samuel Holland. "American Myth and Existential Vision: The Indigenous Existentialism of Mailer, Bellow, Styron, and Ellison," *DA,* XXXVI, 5437, University of Connecticut.

Howe, Irving. "Black Boys and Native Sons." *Dissent* (1963), 353–368; in Howe's *World More Attractive,* New York, 1963.

Hyman, Stanley Edgar. "The Negro Writer in America: An Exchange." *Partisan Review,* XXV (1958), 197–211.

Hyman, Stanley Edgar. "Ralph Ellison in Our Time," in *Standards: A Chronicle of Books for Our Time.* New York, 1966, 249–253.

Kent, George E. "Ralph Ellison and Afro-American Folk and Cultural Tradition." *CLA Journal,* XIII, no. 3 (1970), 265–276.

Klein, Marcus. "Ralph Ellison's *Invisible Man,* in *After Alienation,* Cleveland, 1964, 71–146; in *Images of the Negro in American Literature,* Gross and Hardy, eds. Chicago: University of Chicago Press, 1966, pp. 249–264.

Klotman, Phyllis R. "The Running Man as Metaphor in Ellison's *Invisible Man.*" *CLA Journal,* XIII, no. 3 (1970), 277–288.

Kostelanetz, Richard. "Politics of Ellison's Booker: *Invisible Man* as Symbolic History." *Chicago Review*, XIX, no. 2 (1967), 5–26.

Kostelanetz, Richard. "Negro Genius." *Twentieth Century*, CLXXV, no. 1033 (1967), 49–50.

Lee, L. L. "The Proper Self: Ralph Ellison's *Invisible Man.*" *Descant*, X (Spring, 1966), 38–48.

Lehan, Richard. "The Strange Silence of Ralph Ellison." *California English Journal*, I (1965), 63–68.

Lewis, R. W. B. "Ellison's Essays." *New York Review of Books* (January 28, 1964), 19–20.

Lieberman, Marcia R. "Moral Innocents: Ellison's 'Invisible Man' and 'Candide.' " *CLA Journal*, XV, no. 1 (September, 1971), 64–79.

Long, Madeleine J. "Sartrean Themes in Contemporary American Literature." *DA.* 28 (1967), 1439 A (Columbia).

Ludington, Charles T., Jr. "Protest and Anti-Protest: Ralph Ellison." *Southern Humanities Review*, IV, no. 1 (Winter, 1970), 31–40.

Margolies, Edward. "History As Blues: Ralph Ellison's *Invisible Man,*" in *Native Sons: A Critical Study of Twentieth-Century Negro American Authors*, Philadelphia, 1968, 127–148.

Mengeling, Marvin E. "Whitman and Ellison: Older Symbols in a Modern Mainstream." *Walt Whitman Review*, XII, 67–70.

Nash, R. W. "Stereotypes and Social Types in Ellison's *Invisible Man.*" *Sociological Quarterly*, VI (Autumn, 1965), 349–360.

O'Daniel, Therman B. "Image of Man as Portrayed by Ralph Ellison's *Invisible Man.*" *CLA Journal*, X (June, 1967), 277–284.

Olderman, Raymond M. "Ralph Ellison's Blues and *Invisible Man.*" *Wisconsin Studies in Literature*, VII (1966), 142–159.

Randall, John H., III. "Ralph Ellison: *Invisible Man.*" *Revue des Langues Vivantes* (Brussels), XXXI, 24–44.

Reilly, John M., comp. *Twentieth Century Interpretations of Invisible Man; a Collection of Critical Essays.* Englewood Cliffs, New Jersey: Prentice-Hall, 1970.

Rodnon, Stewart. "Ralph Ellison's 'Invisible Man': Six Tentative Approaches." *CLA Journal*, XII, no. 3 (March, 1969), 244–256.

Sanders, Archie D. "Odysseus in Black: An Analysis of the Structure of *Invisible Man.*" *CLA Journal*, XIII, no. 3 (1970), 217–228.

Schafer, W. J. "Ralph Ellison and the Birth of the Anti-hero." *Critique*, X, no. 2, 81–93.

Singelton, M. K. "Leadership Mirages as Antagonists in *Invisible Man.*" *Arizona Quarterly*, XXII, no. 2 (Summer, 1966), 157–171.

Tischler, N. M. "Negro Literature and Classic Form." *Contemporary Literature*, X (Summer, 1969), 352–365, reply with rejoinder, T. A. Vogler (Winter, 1970), 130–135.

Turner, Darwin T. "Sight in *Invisible Man.*" *CLA Journal*, XIII, no. 3 (1970), 258–264.

Vogler, Thomas A. *"Invisible Man:* Somebody's Protest Novel." *The Iowa Review*, I, no. 2 (Spring, 1970), 64–82.

Warren, Robert Penn. "The Unity of Experience." *Commentary*, XXXIX (1965), 91–96.

Wilner, Eleanor R. "The Invisible Black Thread: Identity and Nonentity in *Invisible Man.*" *CLA Journal*, XIII, no. 3 (1970), 242–257.

Zietlow, Edward R. "Wright to Hansberry: The Evolution of Outlook in

Four Negro Writers," (Wright, Ellison, Baldwin, Hansberry), *DA*. XXVIII, 701 A (University of Washington).

James Baldwin (1924–   )

PRIMARY

NOVELS:

Go Tell It on the Mountain. New York: Knopf, 1953; New York: Dial, 1963.
Giovanni's Room. New York: Dial, 1956.
Another Country. New York: Dial, 1962.
Tell Me How Long the Train's Been Gone. London: Joseph, 1968; New York: Dial, 1968.

ESSAY COLLECTIONS:

Notes of a Native Son. Boston: Beacon, 1955. New York: Dial, 1963.
Nobody Knows My Name; More Notes of a Native Son. New York: Dial, 1961.
The Fire Next Time. New York: Dial, 1963; London: Hutchinson, 1967 (introduction by John Wain).
No Name in the Street. New York: Dial, 1972.

MISCELLANEOUS PUBLICATIONS:

Blues for Mister Charlie, New York: Dial, 1964 (play).
With Richard Avedon. *Nothing Personal*. New York: Atheneum, 1964 (photos by Richard Avedon, text by James Baldwin).
Going to Meet the Man. New York: Dial, 1965 (short stories).
The Amen Corner; New York: Dial, 1968 (play).
With others, *Black Anti-Semitism and Jewish Racism*. New York: R. W. Baron, 1969 (introduction by Nat Hentoff).
With Margaret Mead. *A Rap on Race*. Philadelphia: Lippincott, 1971.
With Nikki Giovanni. *A Dialogue*. Philadelphia: Lippincott, 1972.

SECONDARY

Alexander, Charlotte A. *Baldwin's Go Tell It on the Mountain, Another Country*, and Other Works; a Critical Commentary. New York: Distributed by Monarch Press, 1966.
Allen, Walter. *The Modern Novel in Britain and the United States*. New York: Dutton, 1964.
Barksdale, Richard K. " 'Temple of the Fire Baptized.' " *Phylon*, XIV (1953), 326–327.
Bigby, C. W. "The Committed Writer: James Baldwin as Dramatist." *Twentieth-Century Literature*, XIII (1967), 39–48.
Blaisdel, Gus. "James Baldwin, the Writer." *Negro Digest*, XIII (January, 1964), 61–68.
Boyle, Kay. "Introducing James Baldwin," in *Contemporary American*

Novelists, Moore, Harry T., ed. Carbondale, Illinois: Southern Illinois University Press, 1964.

Bone, Robert A. "The Novels of James Baldwin." *Tri-Quarterly*, II (Winter, 1965), 3–20 (reprinted in *The Negro Novel* by Bone).

Bonosky, Phillip. "The Negro Writer and Commitment." *Mainstream*, XV (February, 1962), 16–22.

Cartey, Wilfred. "The Realities of Four Negro Writers." *Columbia University Forum*, IX, no. 3 (1966), 34–42.

Charney, Maurice. "James Baldwin's Quarrel with Richard Wright." *American Quarterly*, XV (1963), 65–75.

Clark, Kenneth B. "A Conversation with James Baldwin." *Freedomways*, III (Summer, 1963), 361–368.

Coles, Robert. "Baldwin's Burden." *Partisan Review*, XXXI (1964), 409–416.

Collier, Eugenia W. "The Phrase Unbearably Repeated." *Phylon*, XXV (1964), 288–296.

Collier, Eugenia W. "Thematic Patterns in Baldwin's Essays." *Black World*, XXI (June, 1972), 28–34.

Cox, C. B. and A. R. Jones. "After the Tranquilized Fifties: Notes on Sylvia Plath and James Baldwin." *Critical Quarterly*, VI (1964), 107–122.

Eckman, Fern M. *The Furious Passage of James Baldwin*. New York: M. Evans, distributed by Lippincott, Philadelphia, 1966; New York: Popular Library, 1967.

Elkoff, Marvin. "Everybody Knows His Name." *Esquire*, LXII, no. 2 (1964), 59–64, 120–123.

Featherstone, J. "Blues for Mr. Baldwin." *New Republic*, CLIII (November 27, 1965), 34–46.

Fisher, Russell G. "James Baldwin: A Bibliography, 1947–1962." *Bulletin of Bibliography*, IV (1965), 127–130.

Foote, Dorothy N. "James Baldwin's 'Holler Books.' " *CEA Critic*, XXV, no. 8 (1963), 8, 11.

Friedenberg, Edgar Z. "Another Country for an Arkansas Traveler." *New Republic*, CXLVII (August 27, 1962), 23–26.

Fuller, Hoyt W. "Contemporary Negro Fiction." *Southwest Review*, L (1965), 321–335.

Gayle, Addison. "In Defense of James Baldwin." *CLA Journal*, X (March, 1967), 201–208.

Golden, Harry. "A Comment on James Baldwin's Letter." *The Crisis*, LXX (March, 1963), 145–146.

Graves, Wallace. "The Question of Moral Energy in James Baldwin's *Go Tell It on the Mountain*." *CLA Journal*, VII (March, 1964), 215–223.

Gross, Theodore. "The World of James Baldwin." *Critique*, VII, no. 2 1965), 139–149.

Hagopian, John V. "James Baldwin: The Black and the Red-White-and-Blue." *CLA Journal*, VII (December, 1963), 133–140.

Hassan, Ihab. "The Novel of Outrage: A Minority Voice in Postwar American Fiction." *American Scholar*, XXXIV (1965), 239–253.

Hassan, Ihab. *Radical Innocence*. Princeton, New Jersey: Princeton University Press, 1961.

Heermance, J. Noel. "The Modern Negro Novel." *Negro Digest*, XIII (May, 1964), 66–76.

Hernton, Calvin C. "Blood of the Lamb," in Calvin C. Hernton, *White Papers for White Americans*. Garden City, New York: Doubleday, 1967, 105–147.

Hoffman, Stanton. "The Cities of Night: John Rechy's *City of Night* and the American Literature of Homosexuality." *The Critical Review,* XVII, nos. 2–3 (1964), 195–206.

Isaacs, Harold. "Five Writers and Their African Ancestors: Part II." *Phylon,* XXI (Winter, 1960), 317–336 (Baldwin, Ellison, Hansberry).

Kazin, Alfred. "The Essays of James Baldwin," in *Contemporaries.* Boston: Little, Brown, 1962, pp. 254–256.

Kent, George E. "Baldwin and the Problem of Being." *CLA Journal,* VII (March, 1964), 202–214.

Killens, John O. "Broadway in Black and White." *American Forum,* I, no. 3 (1965), 66–70.

Kindt, Kathleen A. "James Baldwin, A Checklist: 1947–1962." *Bulletin of Bibliography,* XXIV (1965), 123–126.

Klein, Marcus. "James Baldwin." *After Alienation: American Novels in Mid-Century.* Cleveland: World, 1964.

Lash, John S. "Baldwin Beside Himself: A Study in Modern Phallicism." *CLA Journal,* VIII (December, 1964), 132–140.

Leaks, Sylvester. "I Know His Name." *Freedomways,* III (Winter, 1963), 102–105.

Lee, Robert A. "James Baldwin and Matthew Arnold: Thoughts on 'Relevance,' " *CLA Journal,* XIV (March, 1971), 324–330.

Levin, David. "Baldwin's Autobiographical Essays: The Problem of Negro Identity." *Massachusetts Review,* V (1964), 239–247.

MacInnes, Colin. "Dark Angel: The Writings of James Baldwin." *Encounter,* XXI (August, 1963), 22–33.

Marcus, Steven. "The American Negro in Search of Identity." *Commentary,* XVI (1953), 456–463 (Baldwin, Ellison, Hughes, Wright).

Markholt, Ottilie. "White Critic, Black Playwright: Water and Fire." *Negro Digest,* XVI (April, 1967), 54–60.

Mayfield, Julian. "And Then Came Baldwin." Freedomways, III, no. 2 (Spring, 1963), 143–155.

Meriwether, L. M. " 'The Amen Corner.' " *Negro Digest,* XIV (January, 1965), 40–47.

Meriwether, L. M. "James Baldwin: Fiery Voice of the Negro Revolt." *Negro Digest,* XII (August, 1963), 3–7.

Morrison, Allan. "The Angriest Young Man." *Ebony,* XVI (October, 1961), 23–30.

Murray, Albert. "Something Different, Something More," in *Anger and Beyond: The Negro Writer in the United States,* Herbert Hill, ed. New York: Harper and Row, 1966.

Newman, Charles. "The Lesson of the Master: Henry James and James Baldwin." *Yale Review,* LVI (1966), 45–59.

O'Daniel, Therman B. "James Baldwin: An Interpretive Study." *CLA Journal,* VII (September, 1963), 37–47.

"Ralph Ellison Talks About James Baldwin." *Negro Digest,* XI (September, 1962), 61 (reprinted from *The University of Chicago Magazine*).

Roth, Phillip. "Channel X: Two Plays on the Race Conflict." *New York Review of Books,* II (May 28, 1964), 10–13.

Sayre, Robert F. "James Baldwin's Other Country." *Contemporary Ameri-*

can Novelists, Harry T. Moore, ed. Carbondale, Illinois: Southern Illinois University Press, 1964, pp. 158–169.

Spender, Stephen. "James Baldwin: Voice of a Revolution." *Partisan Review*, XXX (1963), 256–260.

Standley, Fred L. "James Baldwin: The Crucial Situation." *South Atlantic Quarterly*, LXV (1966), 371–381.

Strong, Augusta. "Notes on James Baldwin." *Freedomways*, II (Fall, 1962), 167–171.

Watson, Edward A. "The Novels of James Baldwin: Case-Book of a 'Lover's War' with the United States." *Massachusetts Review* VI (1965), 385–402.

Index